1

MINORU TOYODA

●

TRANSLATED AND ADAPTED BY DAVID AND ERIKO WALSH

LETTERED BY FOLTZ DESIGN

BALLANTINE BOOKS • NEW YORK

Love Roma 1 is a work of fiction. Names, characters, places, and incidents are the products of the author's imagination or are used fictitiously. Any resemblance to actual events, locales, or persons, living or dead, is entirely coincidental.

2005 Del Rey® Trade Paperback Edition

Published in the United States by Del Rey Books, an imprint of The Random House Publishing Group, a division of Random House, Inc., New York.

Del Rey is a registered trademark and the Del Rey colophon is a trademark of Random House, Inc.

Library of Congress Control Number: 2005926810

ISBN 0-345-48262-X

Printed in the United States of America

www.delreymanga.com

1 2 3 4 5 6 7 8 9

First Edition

Lettered by Foltz Design

TABLE OF CONTENTS

Honorifics Explained

Throughout the Del Rey Manga books, you will find Japanese honorifics left intact in the translations. For those not familiar with how the Japanese use honorifics, and, more important, how they differ from American honorifics, we present this brief overview.

Politeness has always been a critical facet of Japanese culture. Ever since the feudal era, when Japan was a highly stratified society, use of honorifics–which can be defined as polite speech that indicates relationship or status–has played an essential role in the Japanese language. When addressing someone in Japanese, an honorific usually takes the form of a suffix attached to one's name (e.g. "Asuna-san"), as a title at the end of one's name, or in place of the name itself (e.g. "Negi-sensei" or simply "Sensei!").

Honorifics can be expressions of respect or endearment. In the context of manga and anime, honorifics give insight into the nature of the relationship between characters. Many translations into English leave out these important honorifics, and therefore distort the feel of the original Japanese. Because Japanese honorifics contain nuances that English honorifics lack, it is our policy at Del Rey not to translate them. Here, instead, is a guide to some of the honorifics you may encounter in Del Rey Manga.

-san: This is the most common honorific and is equivalent to Mr., Miss, Ms., Mrs., etc. It is the all-purpose honorific and can be used in any situation where politeness is required.

-sama: This is one level higher than -san. It is used to confer great respect.

-dono: This comes from the word tono, which means lord. It is an even higher level than -sama and confers utmost respect.

-kun: This suffix is used at the end of boys' names

-chan: This is used to express endearment, mostly toward girls. It is also used for little boys, pets, and between lovers. It gives a sense of childish cuteness.

Bozu: This is an informal way to refer to a boy, similar to the English terms "kid" or "squirt."

Sempai/ Senpai: This title suggests that the addressee is one's senior in a group or organization. It is most often used in a school setting, where underclassmen refer to their upperclassmen as sempai. It can also be used in the workplace, such as when a newer employee addresses an employee who has seniority in the company.

Kohai: This is the opposite of -sempai, and is used toward underclassmen in school or newcomers in the workplace. It connotes that the addressee is of a lower station.

Sensei: Literally meaning "one who has come before," this title is used for teachers, doctors, or masters of any profession or art.

-[blank]: This is usually forgotten on these lists, but it's perhaps the most significant difference between Japanese and English. The lack of honorific means that the speaker has permission to address the person in a very intimate way. Usually, only family, spouses, or very close friends have this kind of license. Known as yobisute, it can be gratifying when someone who has earned the intimacy starts to call one by one's name without an honorific. But when that intimacy hasn't been earned, it can also be insulting.

A Note from the Author

THE PERSON WHO CREATED THIS STORY - MINORU TOYODA

I'M TIRED

Nice to meet you

THIS IS MY FIRST SERIES. I'M VERY HAPPY.

MINORU TOYODA

presents

LOVE ROMA

1

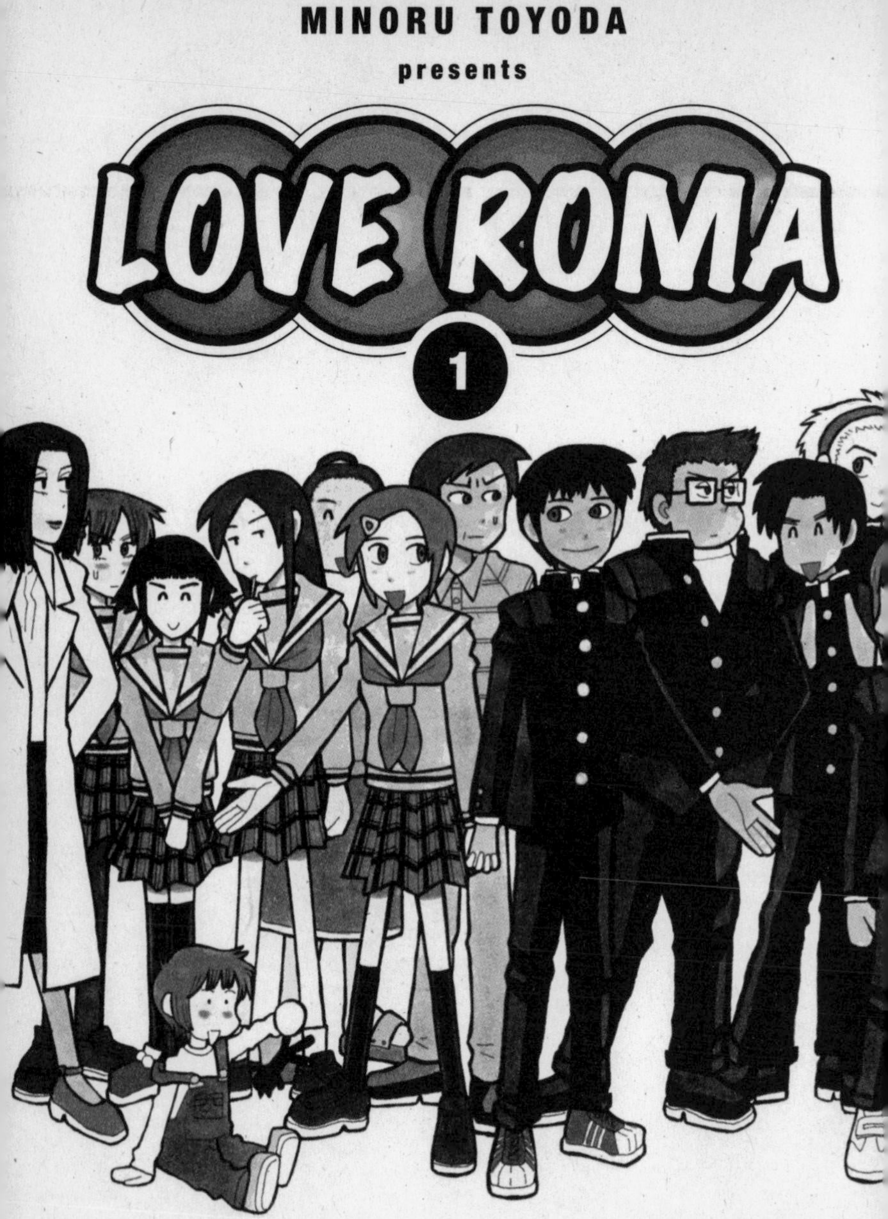

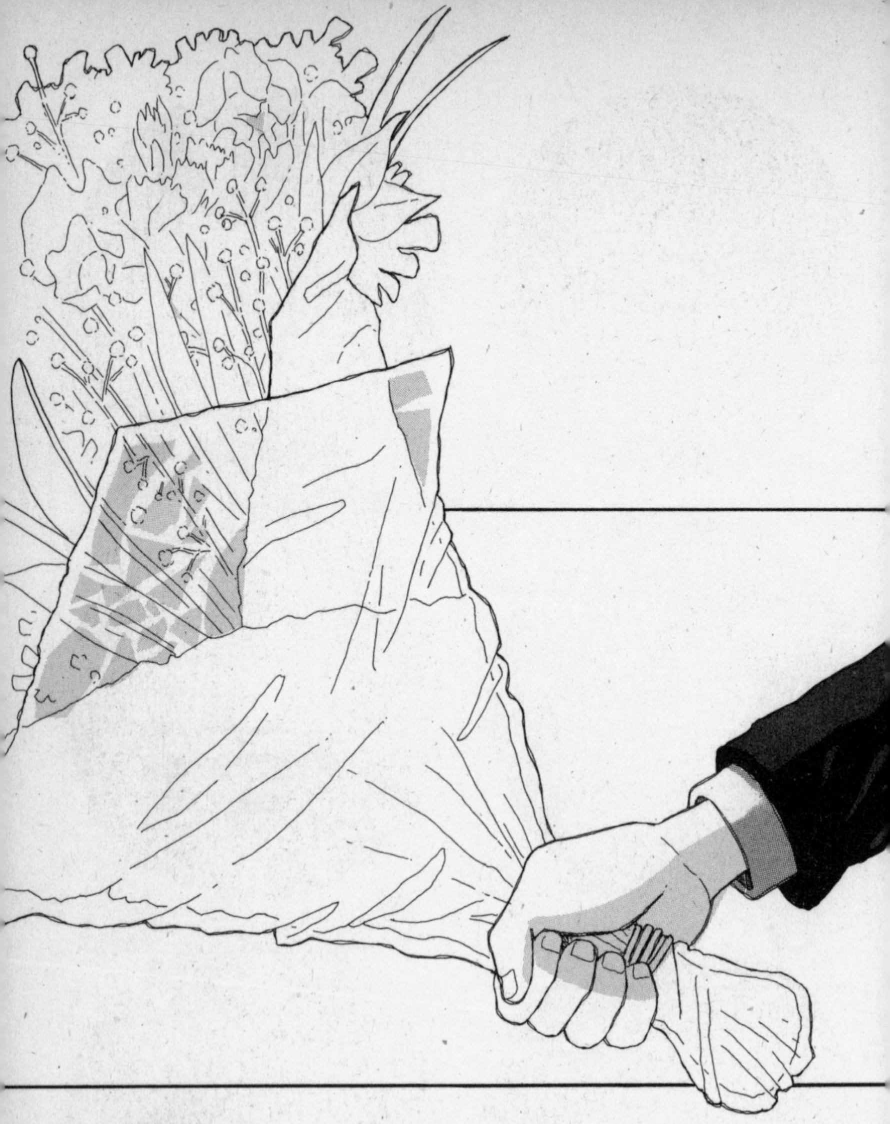

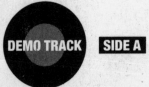

DEMO TRACK **SIDE A** **IT'S NICE TO MEET YOU. I'M HOSHINO**

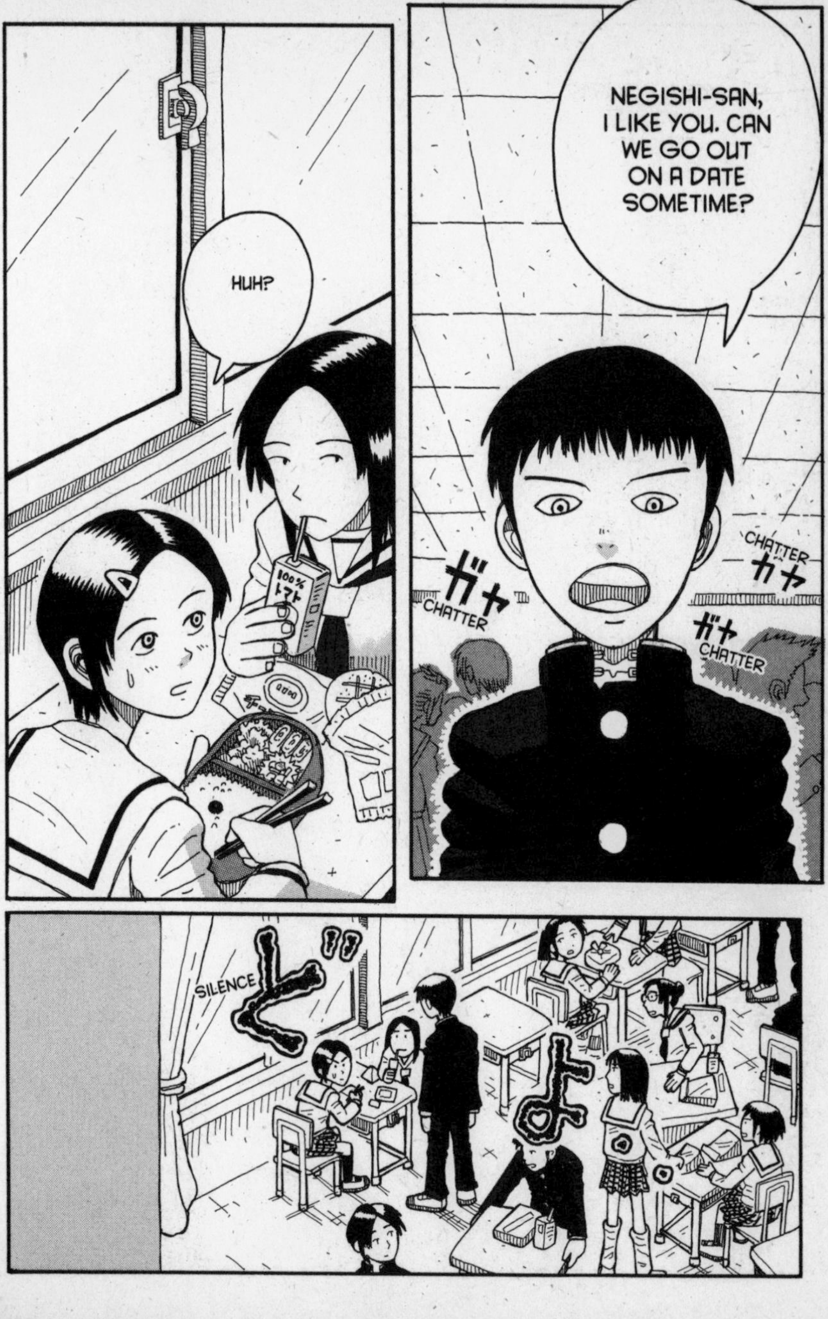
NEGISHI-SAN, I LIKE YOU. CAN WE GO OUT ON A DATE SOMETIME?
ガヤ
CHATTER
ガヤ
CHATTER
ガヤ
CHATTER
HUH?
100% トマト
SILENCE

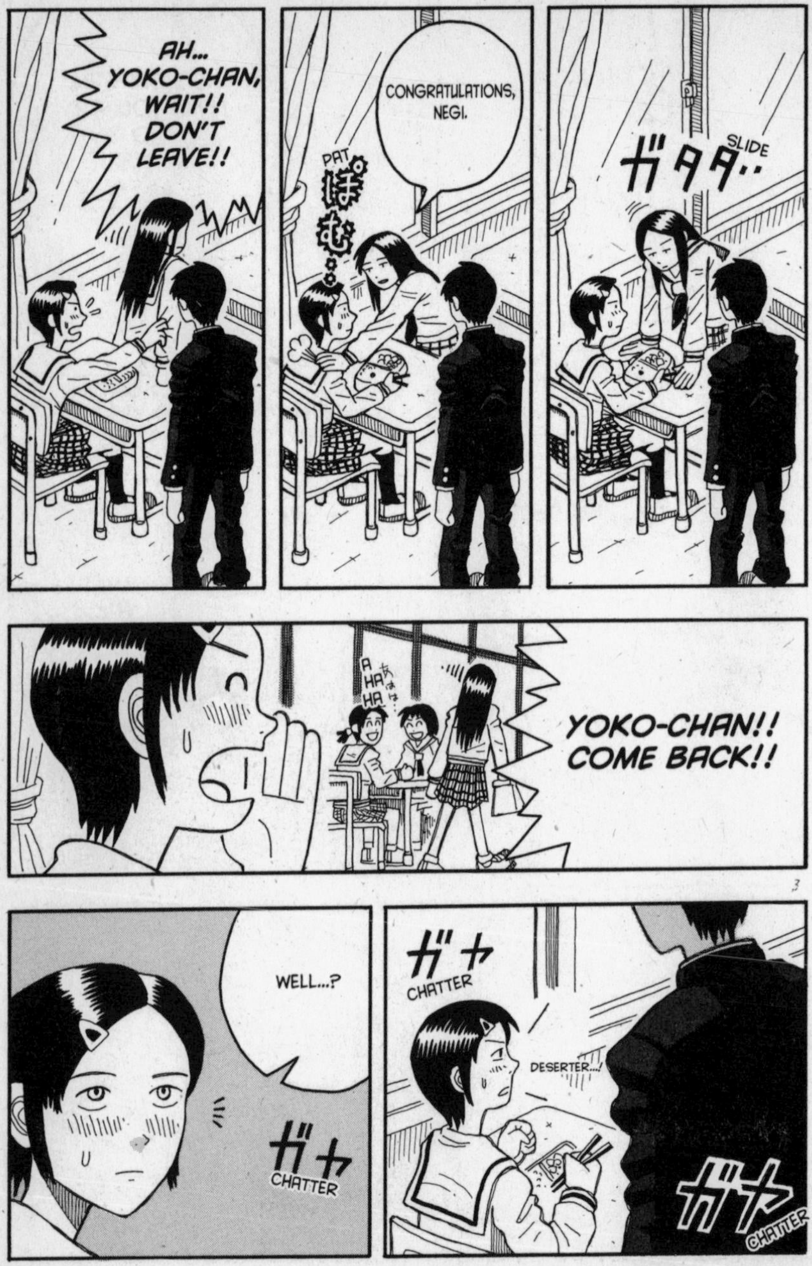
ガタタ‥
SLIDE
PAT
ぽむ
CONGRATULATIONS, NEGI.
AH... YOKO-CHAN, WAIT!! DON'T LEAVE!!
YOKO-CHAN!! COME BACK!!
A HA HA
あはは…
ガヤ
CHATTER
DESERTER...!
ガヤ
CHATTER
WELL...?
ガヤ
CHATTER

3

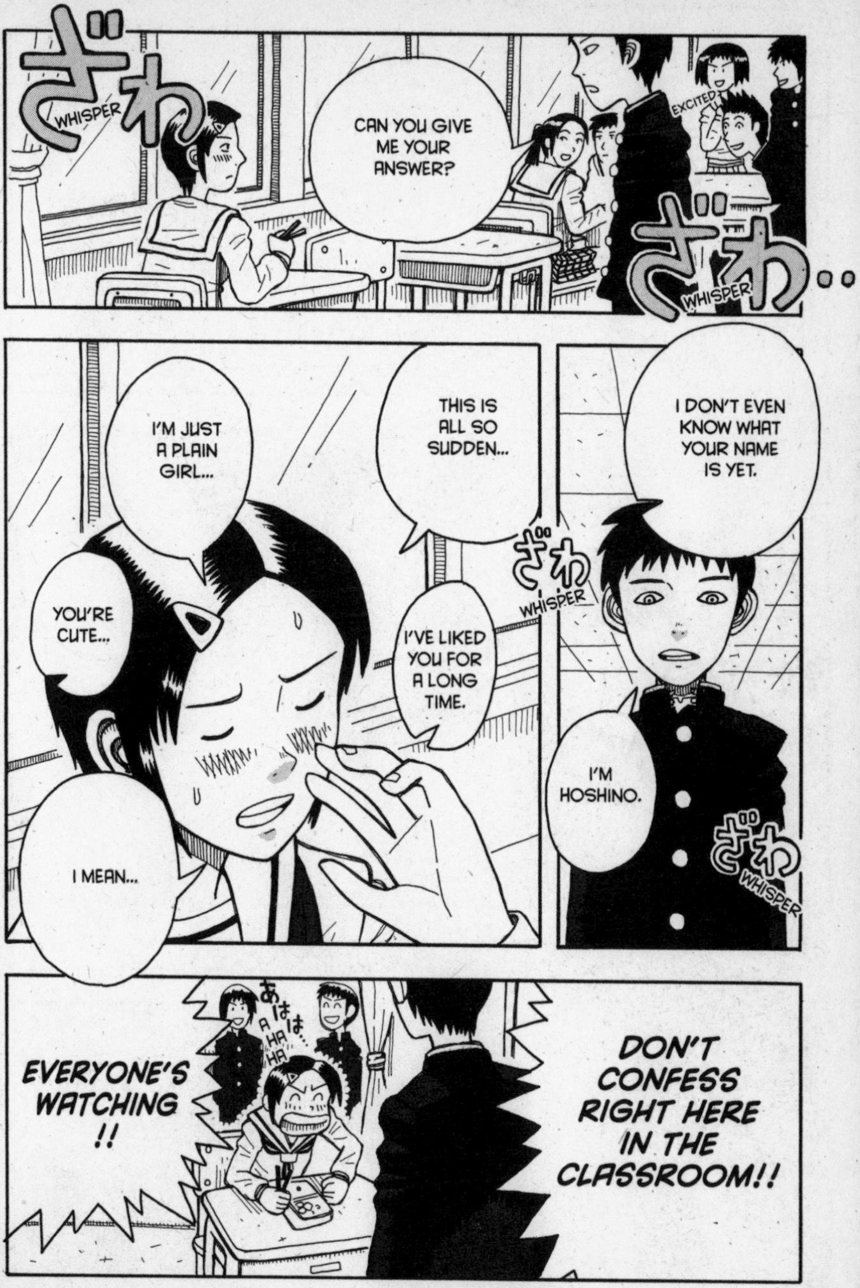
EXCITED
ざわ..
WHISPER
CAN YOU GIVE ME YOUR ANSWER?
ざわ
WHISPER
I DON'T EVEN KNOW WHAT YOUR NAME IS YET.
ざわ
WHISPER
I'M HOSHINO.
ざわ
WHISPER
THIS IS ALL SO SUDDEN...
I'M JUST A PLAIN GIRL...
I'VE LIKED YOU FOR A LONG TIME.
YOU'RE CUTE...
I MEAN...
DON'T CONFESS RIGHT HERE IN THE CLASSROOM!!
あはは…
A HA HA
EVERYONE'S WATCHING !!

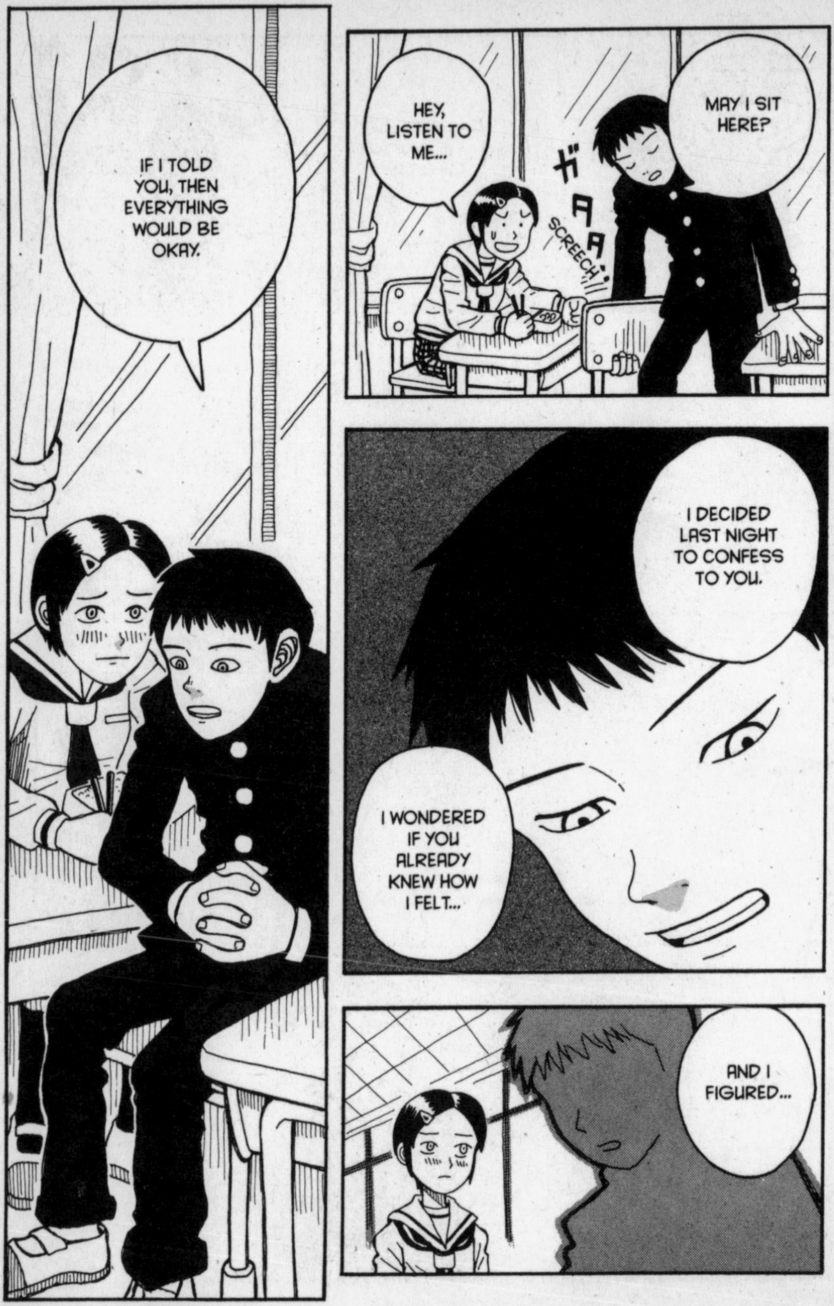
MAY I SIT HERE?
HEY, LISTEN TO ME...
ガタタ
SCREECH
I DECIDED LAST NIGHT TO CONFESS TO YOU.
I WONDERED IF YOU ALREADY KNEW HOW I FELT...
AND I FIGURED...
IF I TOLD YOU, THEN EVERYTHING WOULD BE OKAY.

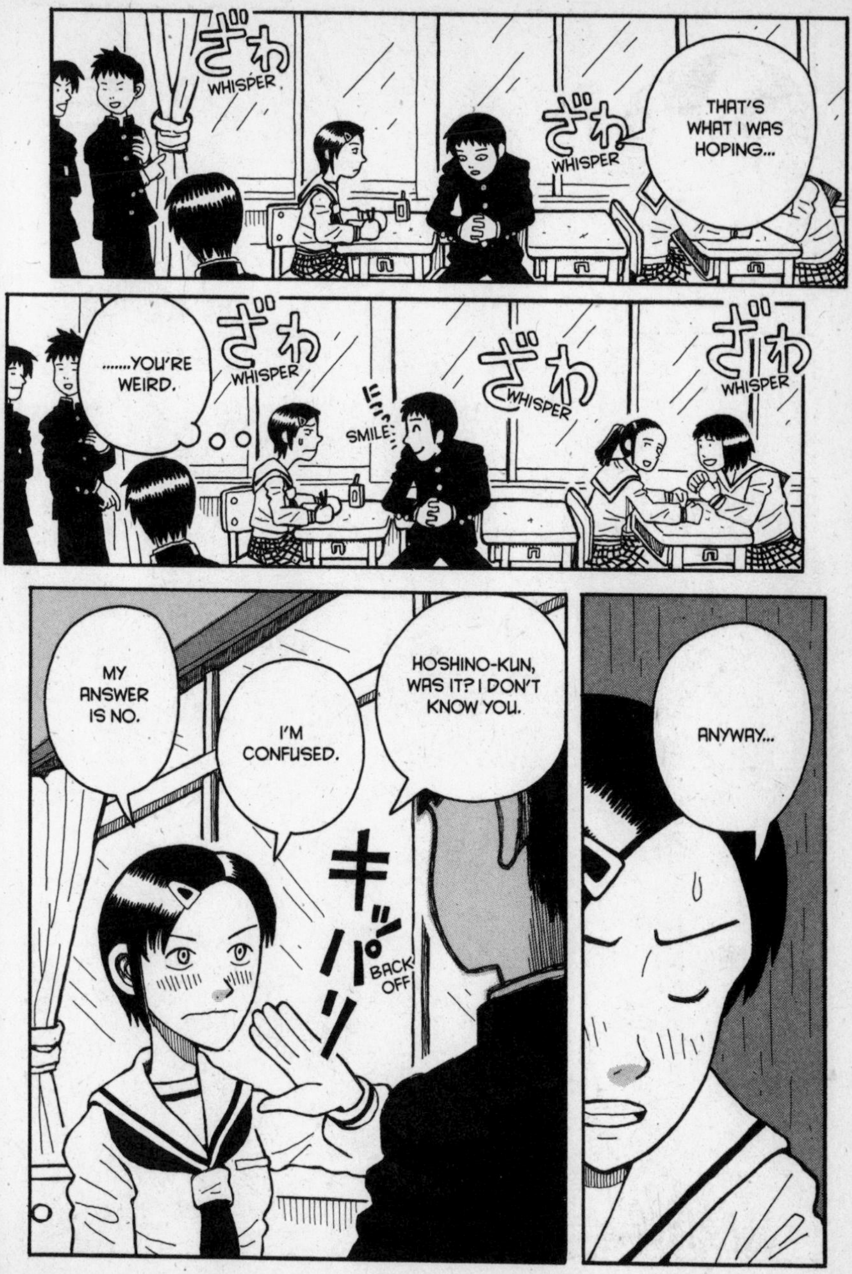
THAT'S WHAT I WAS HOPING...
ざわ WHISPER
ざわ WHISPER
ざわ WHISPER
ざわ WHISPER
ざわ WHISPER
......YOU'RE WEIRD.
SMILE
ANYWAY...
HOSHINO-KUN, WAS IT? I DON'T KNOW YOU.
I'M CONFUSED.
MY ANSWER IS NO.
キッパッ BACK OFF

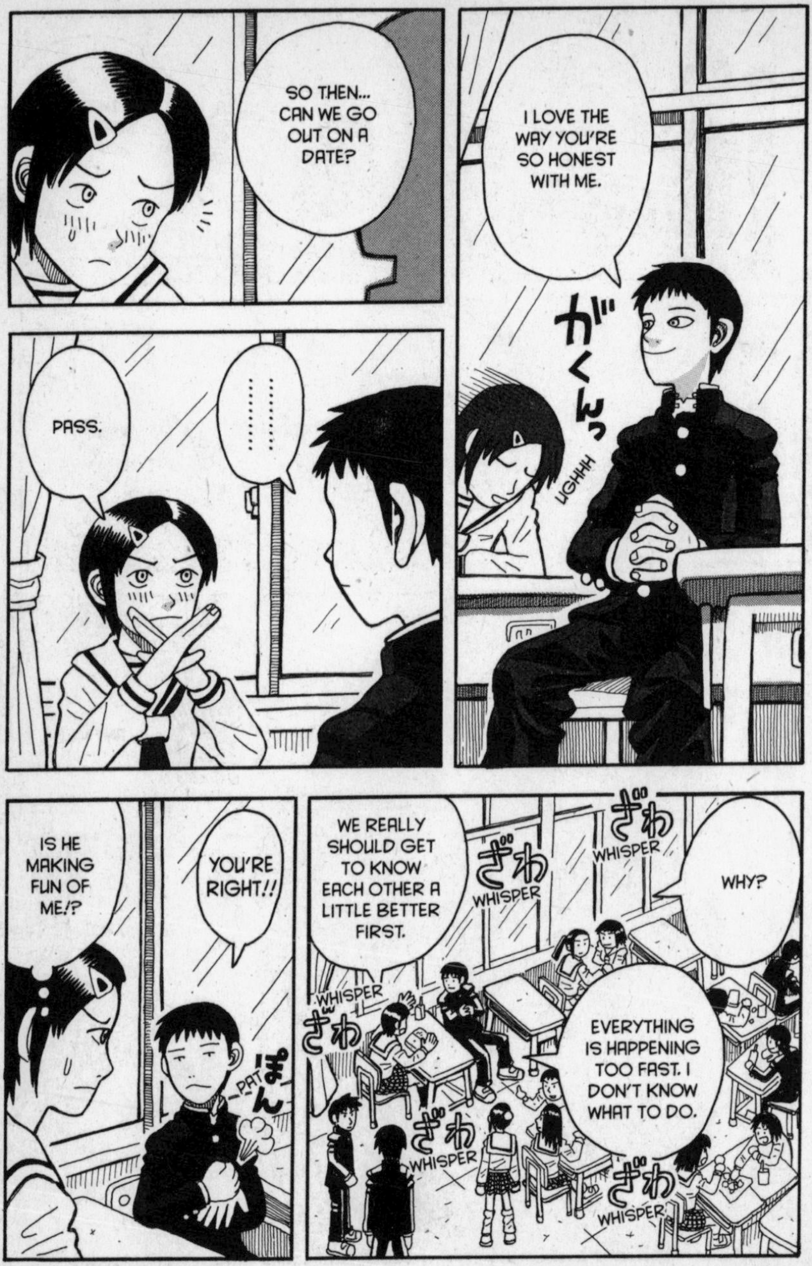
I LOVE THE WAY YOU'RE SO HONEST WITH ME.
がくんっ
UGHHH
SO THEN... CAN WE GO OUT ON A DATE?
......
PASS.
WHY?
ざわ
WHISPER
ざわ
WHISPER
EVERYTHING IS HAPPENING TOO FAST. I DON'T KNOW WHAT TO DO.
WE REALLY SHOULD GET TO KNOW EACH OTHER A LITTLE BETTER FIRST.
WHISPER
ざわ
ざわ
WHISPER
ざわ
WHISPER
YOU'RE RIGHT!!
ぽん
PAT
IS HE MAKING FUN OF ME!?

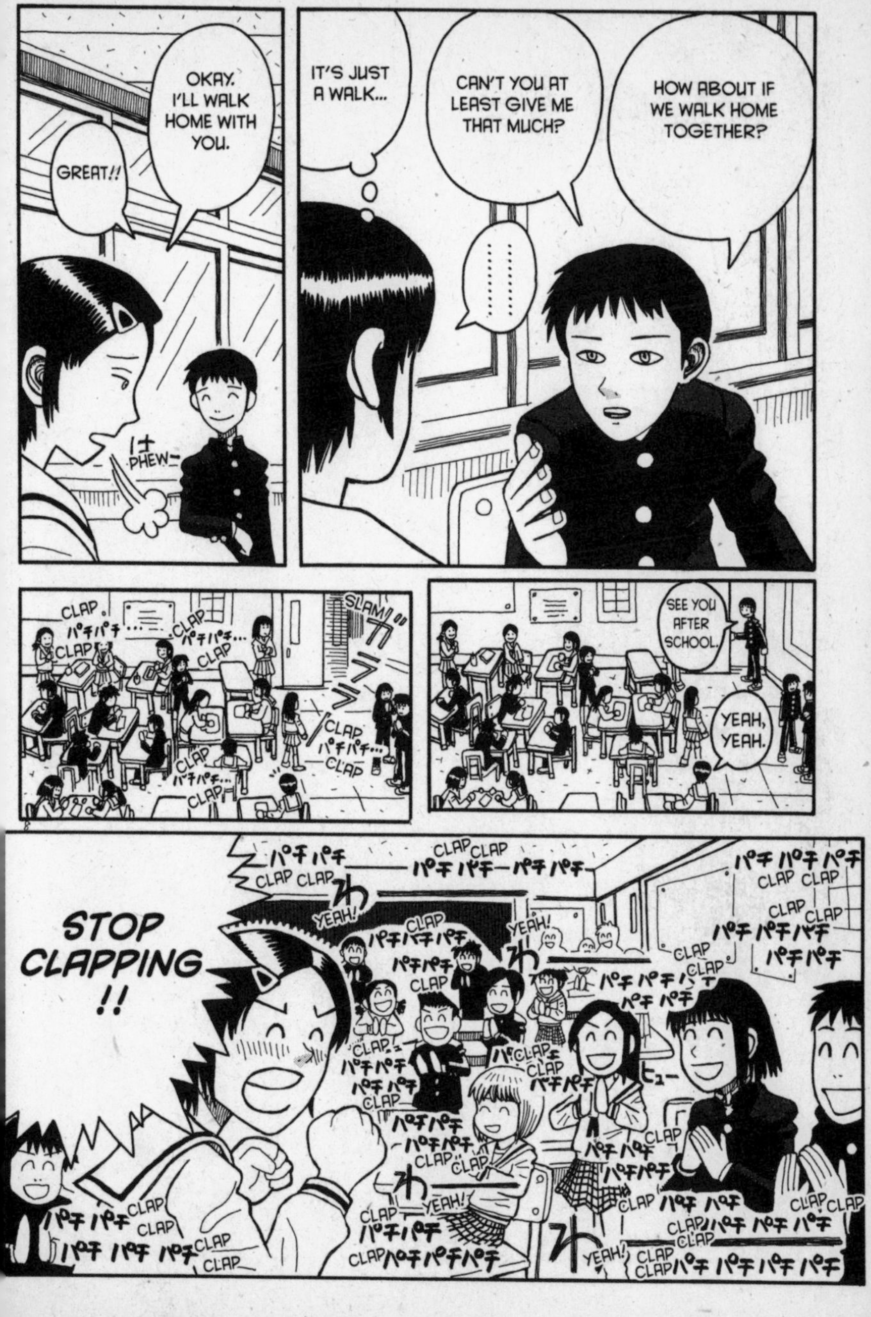
HOW ABOUT IF WE WALK HOME TOGETHER?
CAN'T YOU AT LEAST GIVE ME THAT MUCH?
......
IT'S JUST A WALK...
OKAY. I'LL WALK HOME WITH YOU.
GREAT!!
ハー PHEW–
SEE YOU AFTER SCHOOL.
YEAH, YEAH.
SLAM ガラ
CLAP パチパチ… CLAP
CLAP パチパチ… CLAP
CLAP パチパチ… CLAP
CLAP パチパチ… CLAP
CLAP パチパチ… CLAP
パチパチ CLAP CLAP
CLAP CLAP パチパチーパチパチ
パチパチパチ CLAP CLAP
わ YEAH!
わ YEAH!
CLAP パチパチパチ
パチパチ CLAP
パチパチパチ パチ パチ
CLAP CLAP
CLAP ヒュー パチパチ パチパチ CLAP
パCLAP ヒュー CLAP パチパチ
ヒュー
パチパチ パチパチ CLAP CLAP
パチパチ CLAP パチパチ
わ YEAH!
CLAP パチパチ
CLAP パチ パチ
CLAP CLAP パチ パチ パチ
わ YEAH!
CLAP CLAP パチ パチ パチ パチ
STOP CLAPPING!!
パチパチ CLAP CLAP
パチ パチ パチ CLAP CLAP
CLAP パチパチパチ

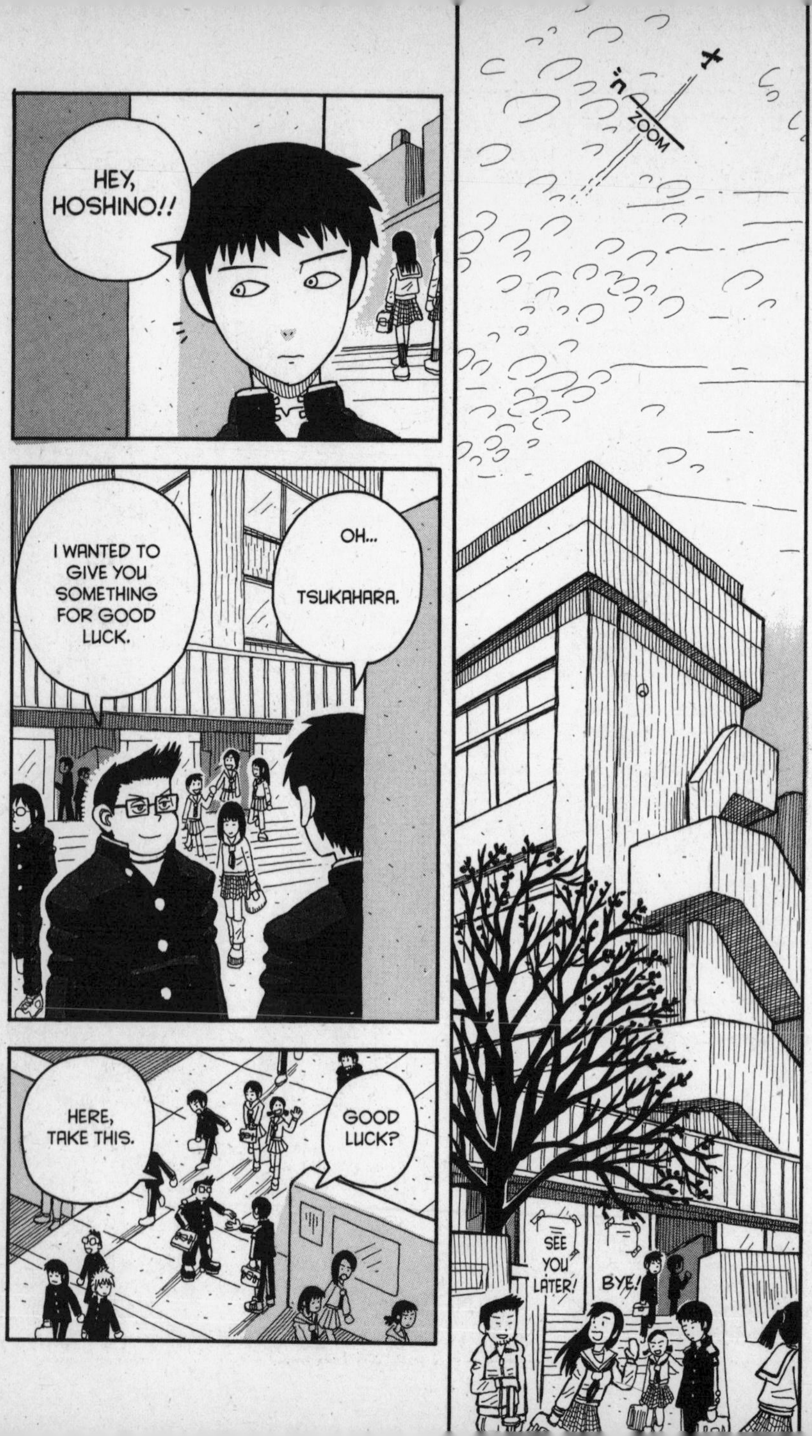
ZOOM
BYE!
SEE YOU LATER!
HEY, HOSHINO!!
OH...
TSUKAHARA.
I WANTED TO GIVE YOU SOMETHING FOR GOOD LUCK.
GOOD LUCK?
HERE, TAKE THIS.

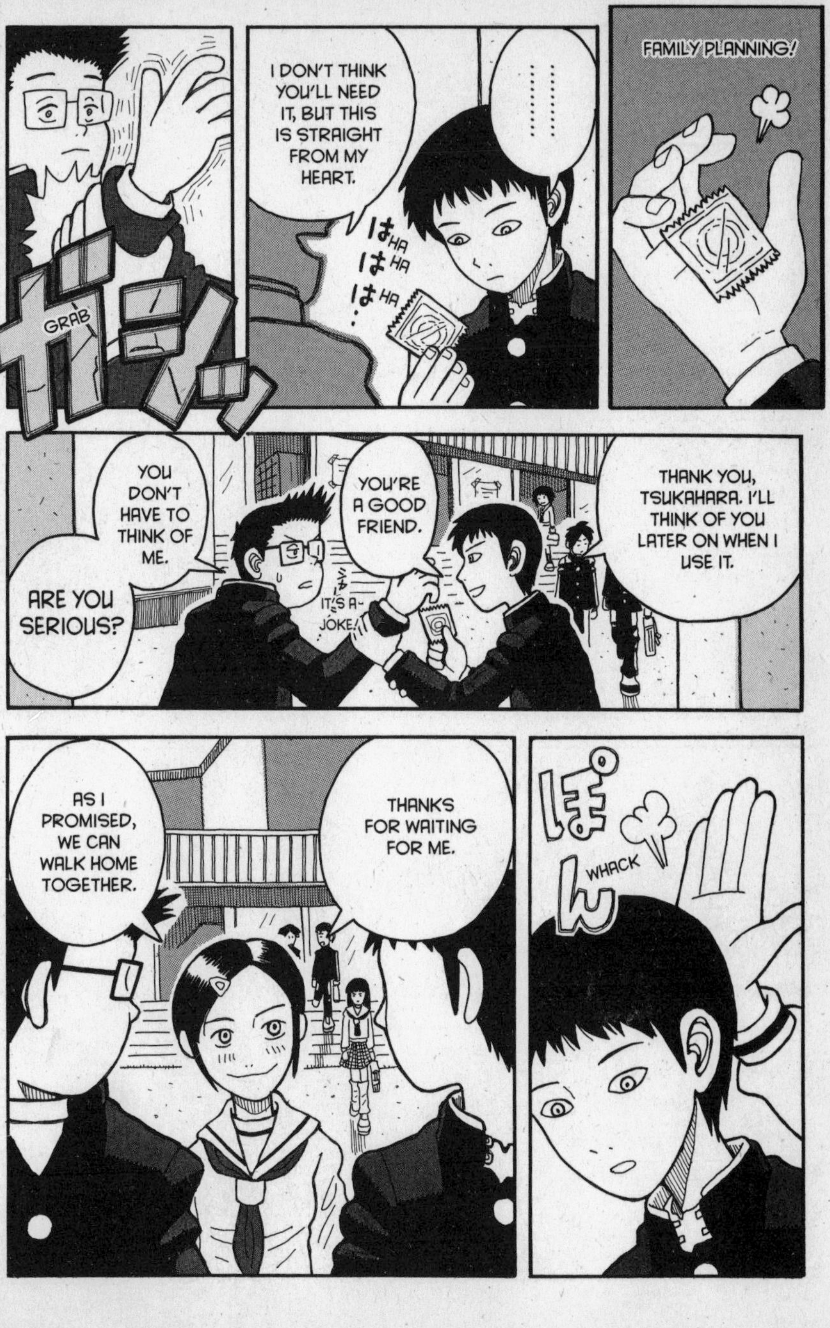
FAMILY PLANNING!
......
I DON'T THINK YOU'LL NEED IT, BUT THIS IS STRAIGHT FROM MY HEART.
は HA
は HA
は HA
ガシッ
GRAB
THANK YOU, TSUKAHARA. I'LL THINK OF YOU LATER ON WHEN I USE IT.
YOU'RE A GOOD FRIEND.
IT'S A JOKE!
YOU DON'T HAVE TO THINK OF ME.
ARE YOU SERIOUS?
ぽん
WHACK
THANKS FOR WAITING FOR ME.
AS I PROMISED, WE CAN WALK HOME TOGETHER.

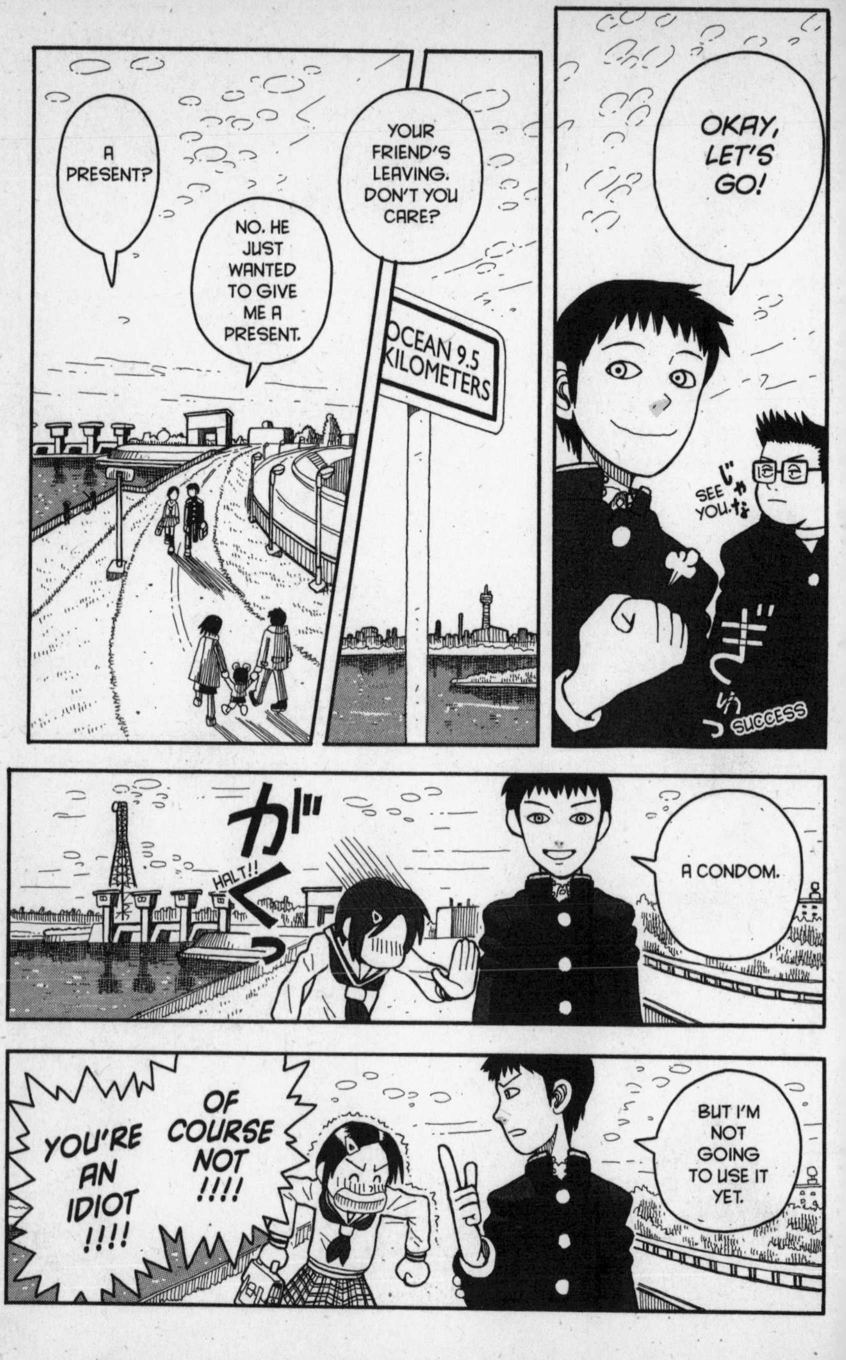
OKAY, LET'S GO!
SEE YOU.
SUCCESS
YOUR FRIEND'S LEAVING. DON'T YOU CARE?
OCEAN 9.5 KILOMETERS
NO. HE JUST WANTED TO GIVE ME A PRESENT.
A PRESENT?
A CONDOM.
HALT!!
BUT I'M NOT GOING TO USE IT YET.
OF COURSE NOT !!!!
YOU'RE AN IDIOT !!!!

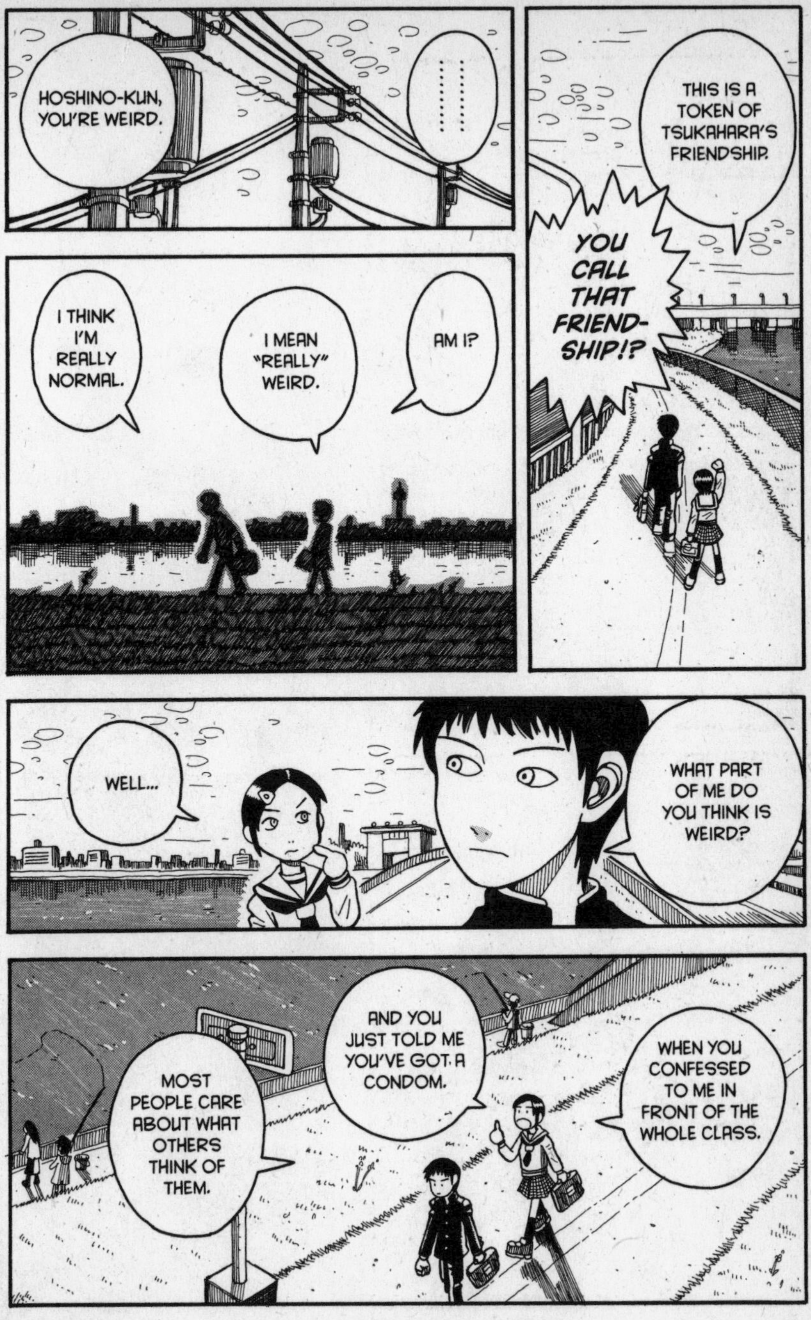
THIS IS A TOKEN OF TSUKAHARA'S FRIENDSHIP.
YOU CALL THAT FRIEND-SHIP!?
......
HOSHINO-KUN, YOU'RE WEIRD.
AM I?
I MEAN "REALLY" WEIRD.
I THINK I'M REALLY NORMAL.
WHAT PART OF ME DO YOU THINK IS WEIRD?
WELL...
WHEN YOU CONFESSED TO ME IN FRONT OF THE WHOLE CLASS.
AND YOU JUST TOLD ME YOU'VE GOT A CONDOM.
MOST PEOPLE CARE ABOUT WHAT OTHERS THINK OF THEM.

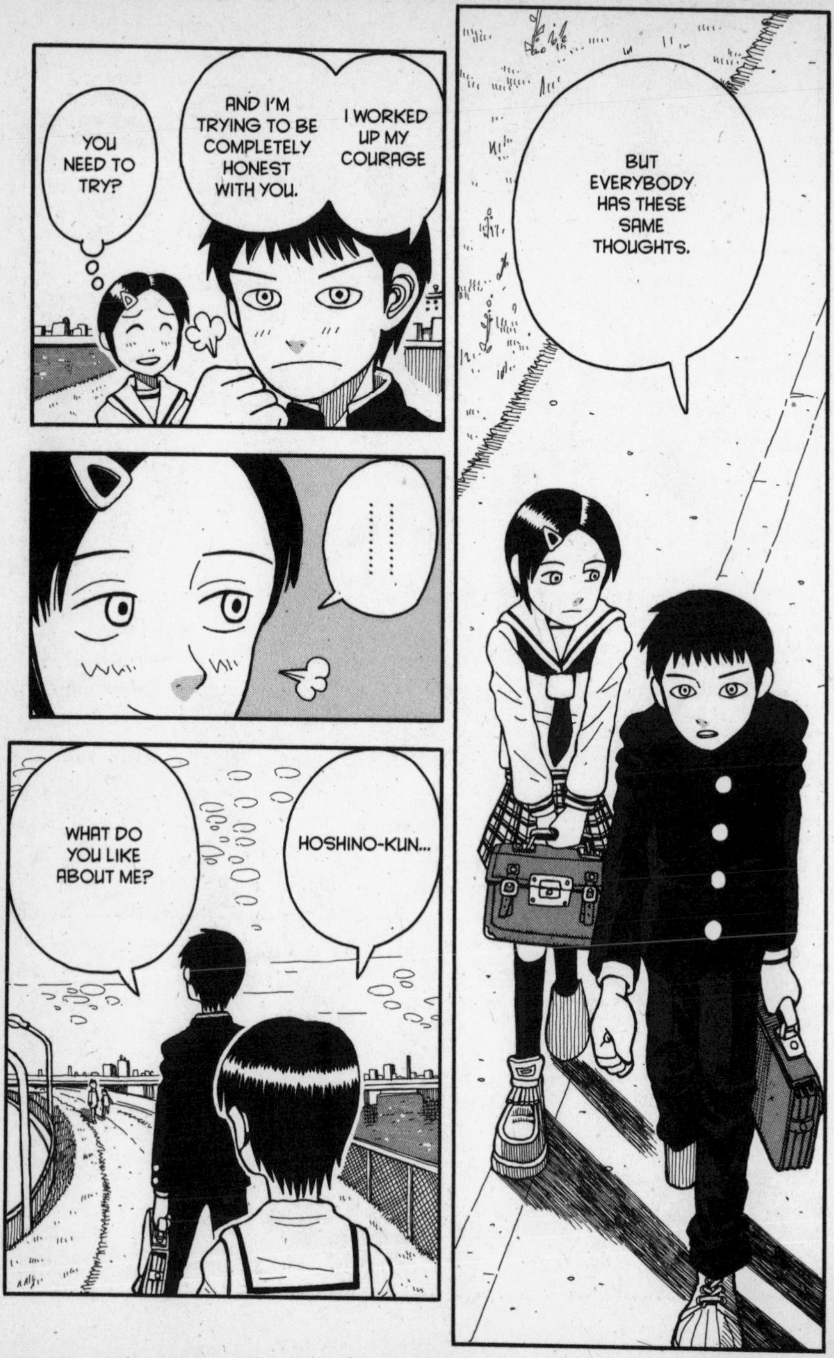
BUT EVERYBODY HAS THESE SAME THOUGHTS.
I WORKED UP MY COURAGE
AND I'M TRYING TO BE COMPLETELY HONEST WITH YOU.
YOU NEED TO TRY?
……
HOSHINO-KUN...
WHAT DO YOU LIKE ABOUT ME?

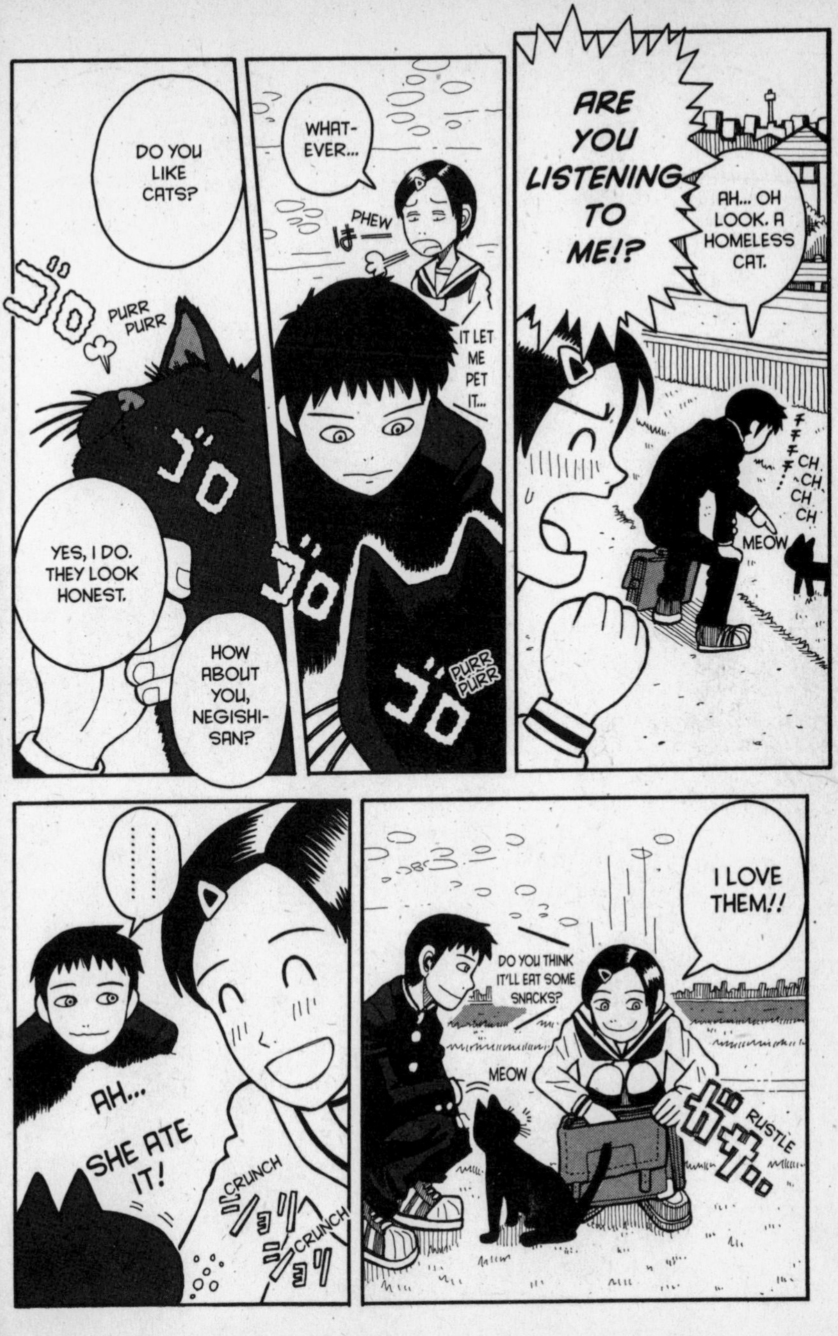
ARE YOU LISTENING TO ME!?
AH... OH LOOK. A HOMELESS CAT.
チチチ...
CH. CH. CH CH
MEOW
WHAT-EVER...
はー
PHEW
IT LET ME PET IT...
ゴロ
PURR PURR
DO YOU LIKE CATS?
ゴロ
PURR PURR
YES, I DO. THEY LOOK HONEST.
HOW ABOUT YOU, NEGISHI-SAN?
I LOVE THEM!!
DO YOU THINK IT'LL EAT SOME SNACKS?
MEOW
ガサ
RUSTLE
......
AH... SHE ATE IT!
CRUNCH
CRUNCH

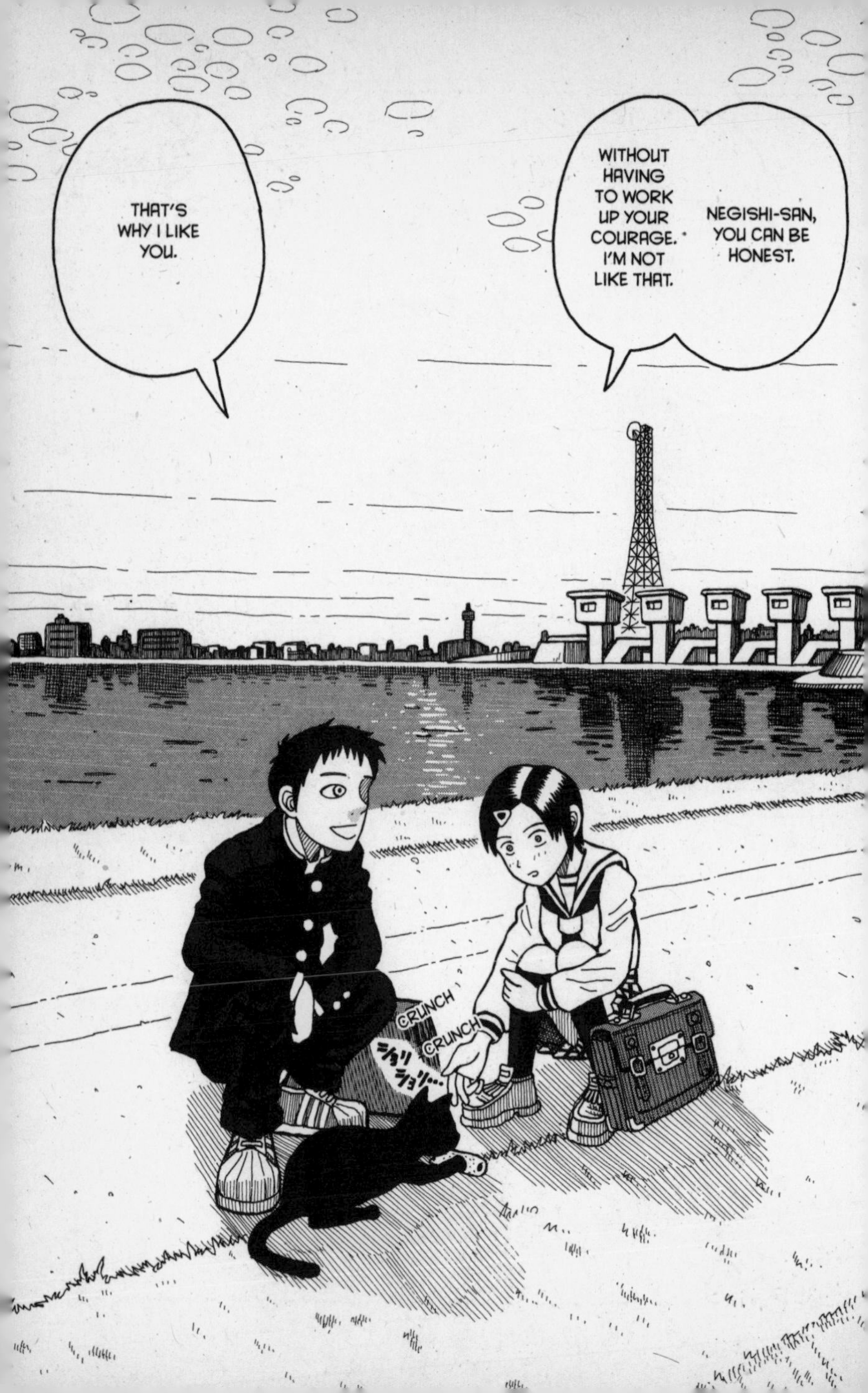
NEGISHI-SAN, YOU CAN BE HONEST.
WITHOUT HAVING TO WORK UP YOUR COURAGE. I'M NOT LIKE THAT.
THAT'S WHY I LIKE YOU.
CRUNCH
CRUNCH
ショリ
ショリ…

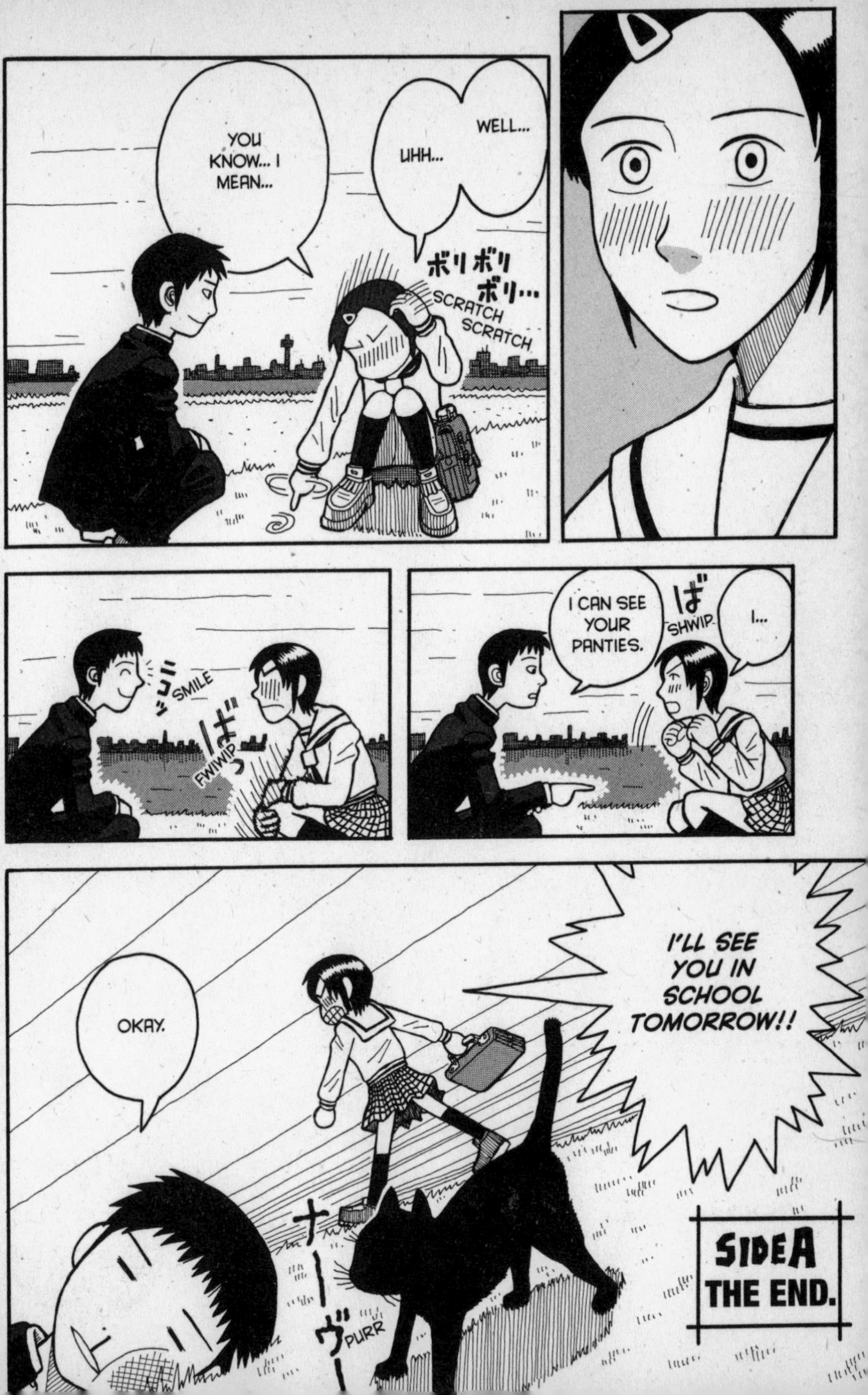
WELL...
UHH...
ボリボリボリ...
SCRATCH SCRATCH
YOU KNOW... I MEAN...
I...
ば
SHWIP
I CAN SEE YOUR PANTIES.
ニコッ
SMILE
ばっ
FWIWIP
I'LL SEE YOU IN SCHOOL TOMORROW!!
OKAY.
SIDE A THE END.
ナ
ヴ
PURR

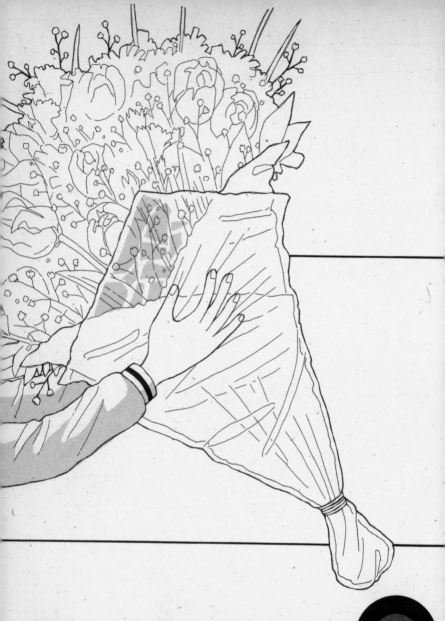

SIDE B   I'M NEGISHI, IT'S NICE TO MEET YOU   **DEMO TRACK**

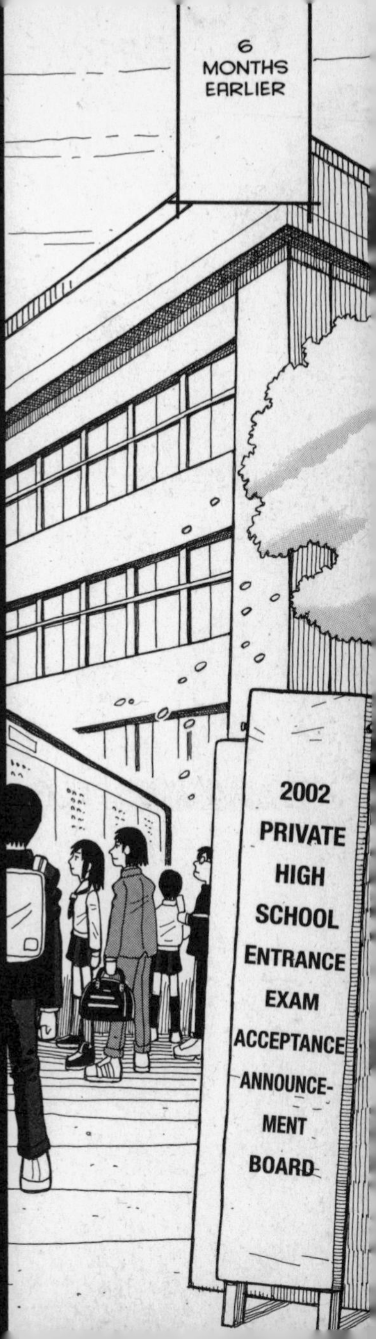
6 MONTHS EARLIER
2002 PRIVATE HIGH SCHOOL ENTRANCE EXAM ACCEPTANCE ANNOUNCEMENT BOARD
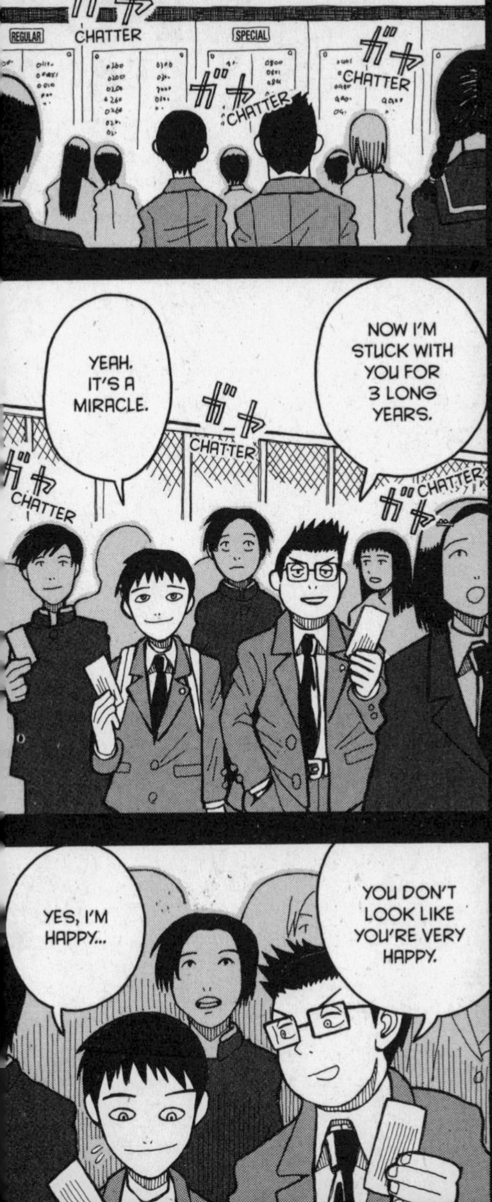
ガヤ CHATTER
SPECIAL
ガヤ CHATTER
ガヤ CHATTER
REGULAR
ガヤ CHATTER
NOW I'M STUCK WITH YOU FOR 3 LONG YEARS.
ガヤ CHATTER
ガヤ CHATTER
YEAH. IT'S A MIRACLE.
ガヤ CHATTER
YOU DON'T LOOK LIKE YOU'RE VERY HAPPY.
YES, I'M HAPPY...

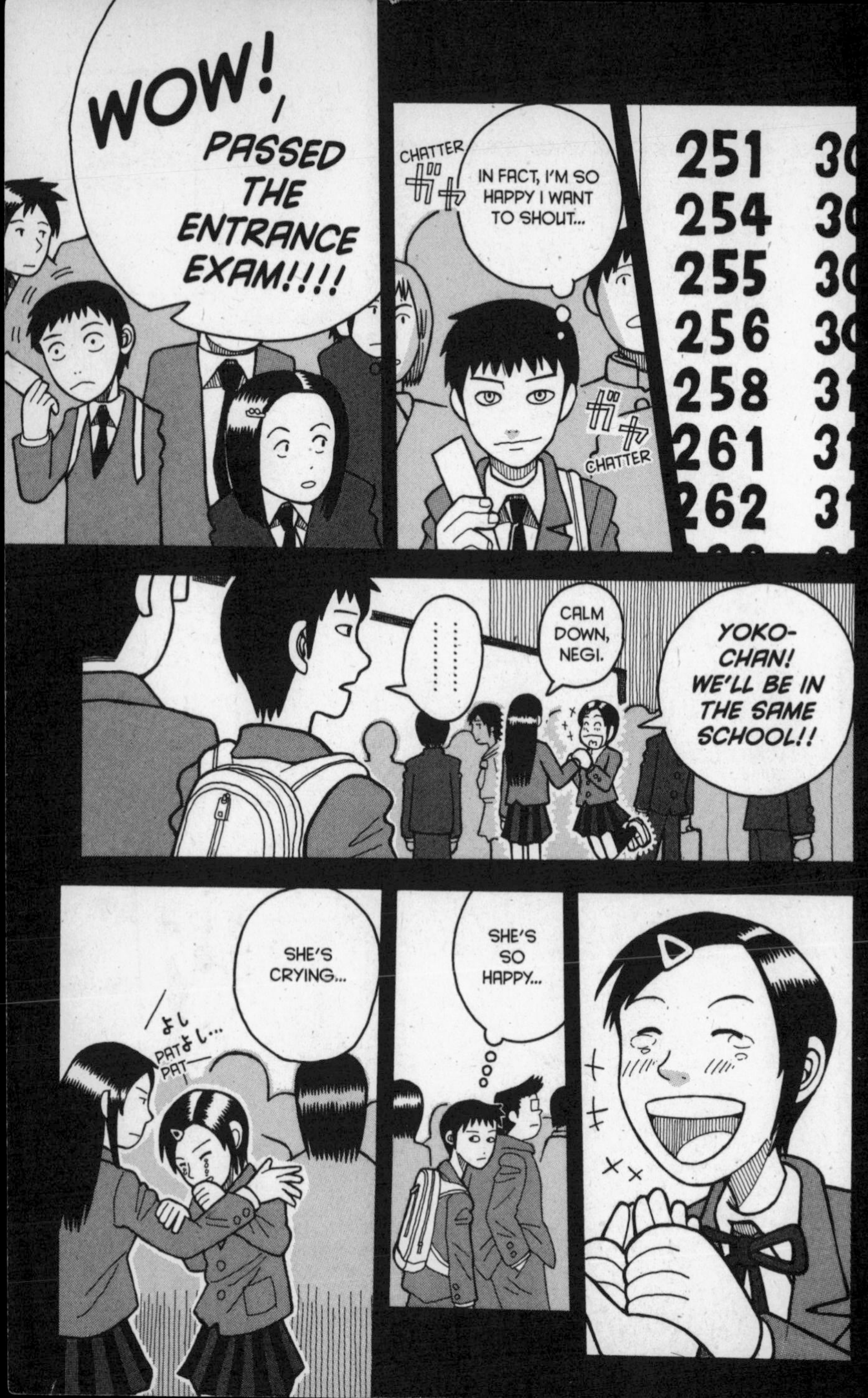
251
254
255
256
258
261
262
CHATTER ガヤ
IN FACT, I'M SO HAPPY I WANT TO SHOUT...
ガヤ CHATTER
WOW! I PASSED THE ENTRANCE EXAM!!!!
YOKO-CHAN! WE'LL BE IN THE SAME SCHOOL!!
CALM DOWN, NEGI.
......
SHE'S SO HAPPY...
SHE'S CRYING...
よし PAT よし... PAT—

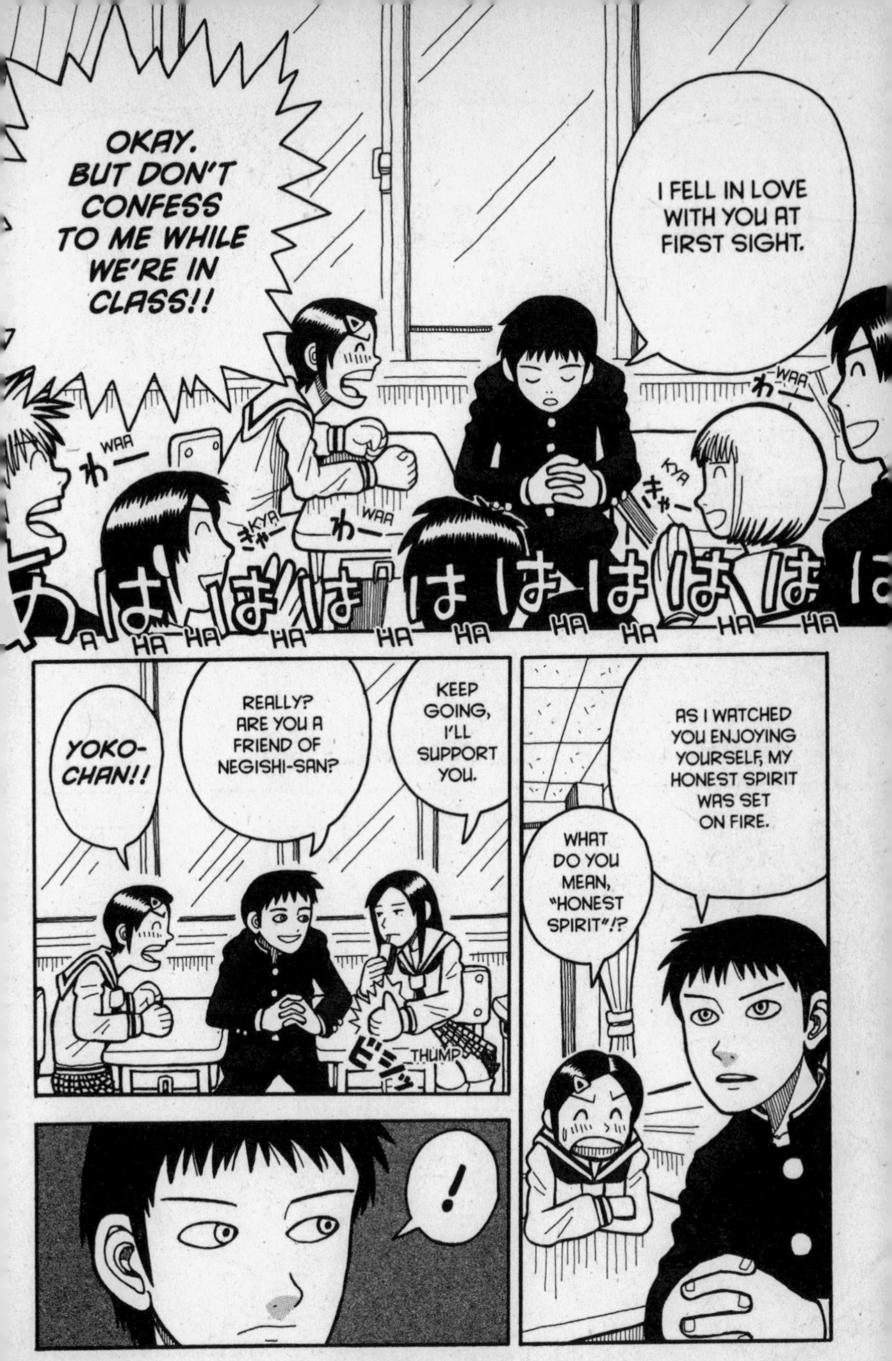
I FELL IN LOVE WITH YOU AT FIRST SIGHT.
OKAY. BUT DON'T CONFESS TO ME WHILE WE'RE IN CLASS!!
わー WAA
きゃー KYA
わー WAA
きゃー KYA
わー WAA
あははははははははは
A HA HA HA HA HA HA HA HA HA
AS I WATCHED YOU ENJOYING YOURSELF, MY HONEST SPIRIT WAS SET ON FIRE.
WHAT DO YOU MEAN, "HONEST SPIRIT"!?
KEEP GOING, I'LL SUPPORT YOU.
REALLY? ARE YOU A FRIEND OF NEGISHI-SAN?
YOKO-CHAN!!
ビシッ THUMP
!

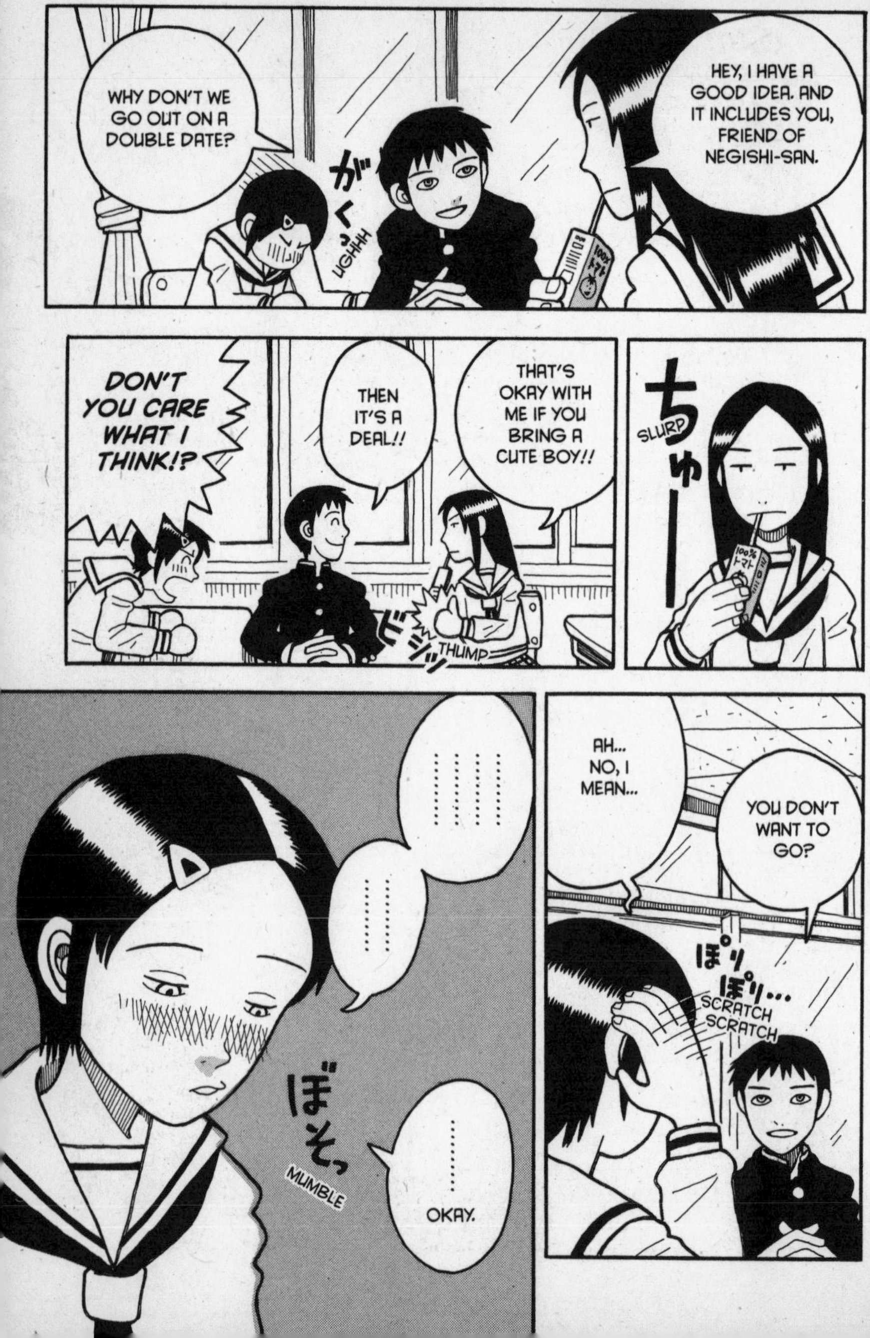
HEY, I HAVE A GOOD IDEA. AND IT INCLUDES YOU, FRIEND OF NEGISHI-SAN.
WHY DON'T WE GO OUT ON A DOUBLE DATE?
がくっ
UGHHH
ちゅー
SLURP
THAT'S OKAY WITH ME IF YOU BRING A CUTE BOY!!
THEN IT'S A DEAL!!
DON'T YOU CARE WHAT I THINK!?
ビシッ
THUMP
YOU DON'T WANT TO GO?
AH... NO, I MEAN...
ぽりぽり...
SCRATCH SCRATCH
ぼそっ
MUMBLE
...... OKAY.

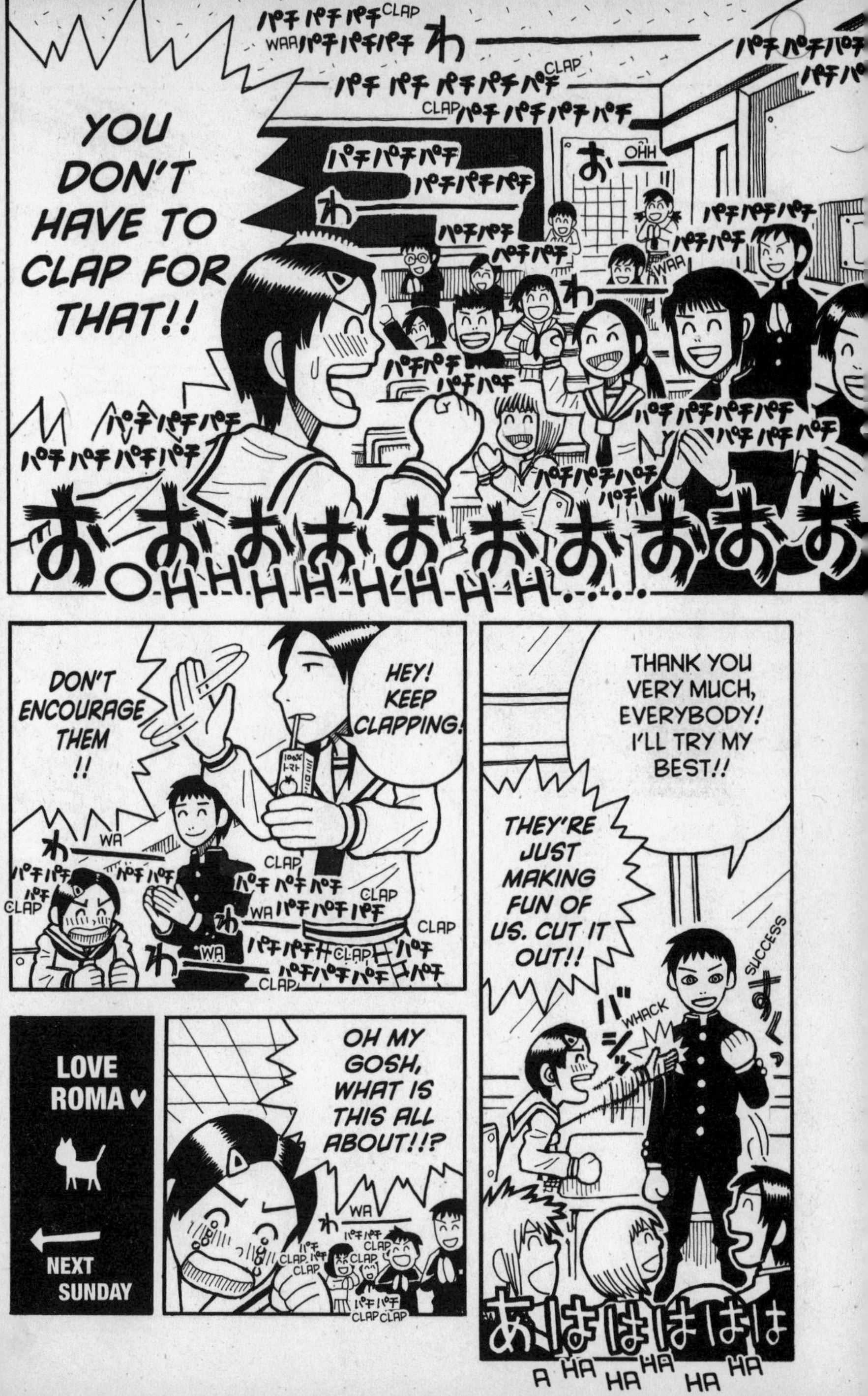
パチパチパチ CLAP
WAA パチパチパチ わ
パチパチパチパチパチ CLAP
CLAP パチパチパチパチ
お OHH
YOU DON'T HAVE TO CLAP FOR THAT!!
おおおおおおおおおお OHHHHHHHHH.....
THANK YOU VERY MUCH, EVERYBODY! I'LL TRY MY BEST!!
THEY'RE JUST MAKING FUN OF US. CUT IT OUT!!
バシッ WHACK
すっ SUCCESS
あはははははは A HA HA HA HA HA
HEY! KEEP CLAPPING!
DON'T ENCOURAGE THEM!!
わ WA
CLAP
わ WA
OH MY GOSH, WHAT IS THIS ALL ABOUT!!?
わ WA
LOVE ROMA ♥
NEXT SUNDAY

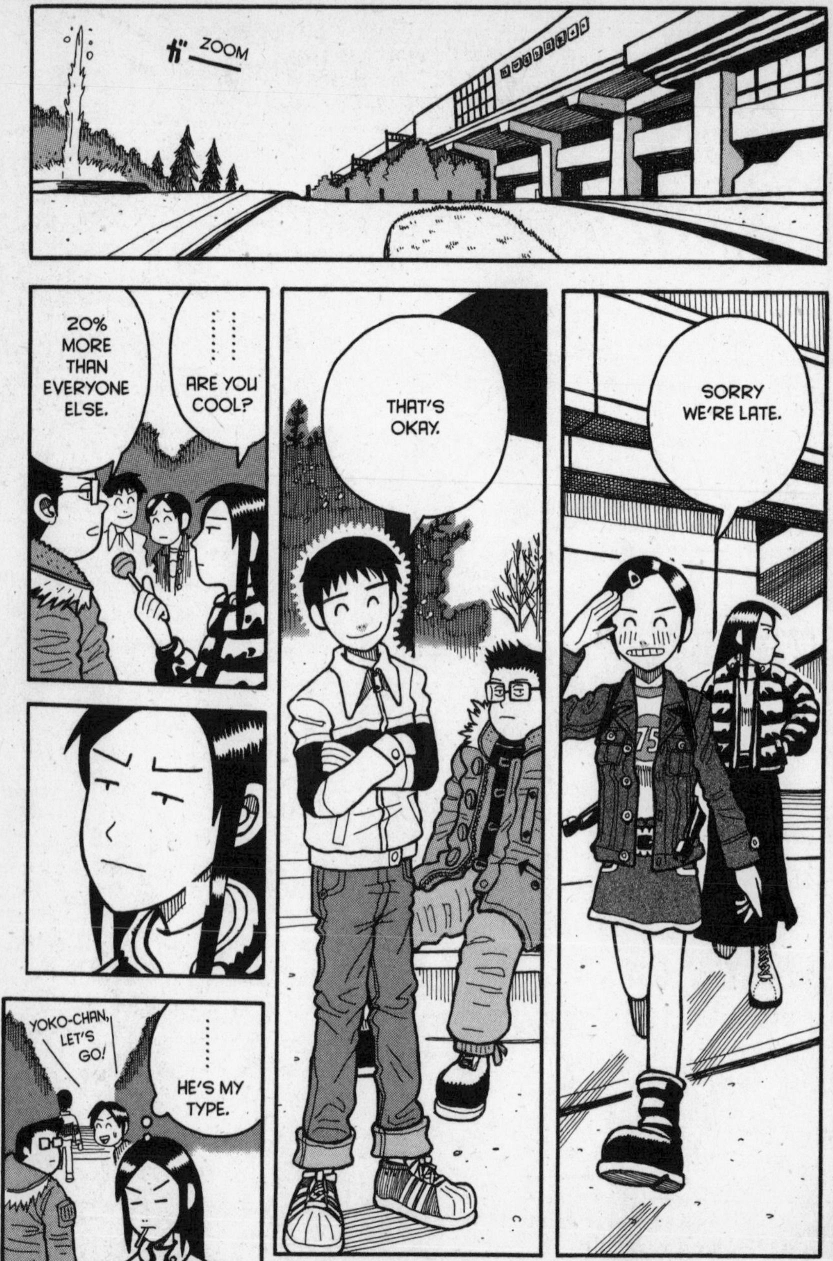
ガ
ZOOM
SORRY WE'RE LATE.
THAT'S OKAY.
...... ARE YOU COOL?
20% MORE THAN EVERYONE ELSE.
...... HE'S MY TYPE.
YOKO-CHAN, LET'S GO!

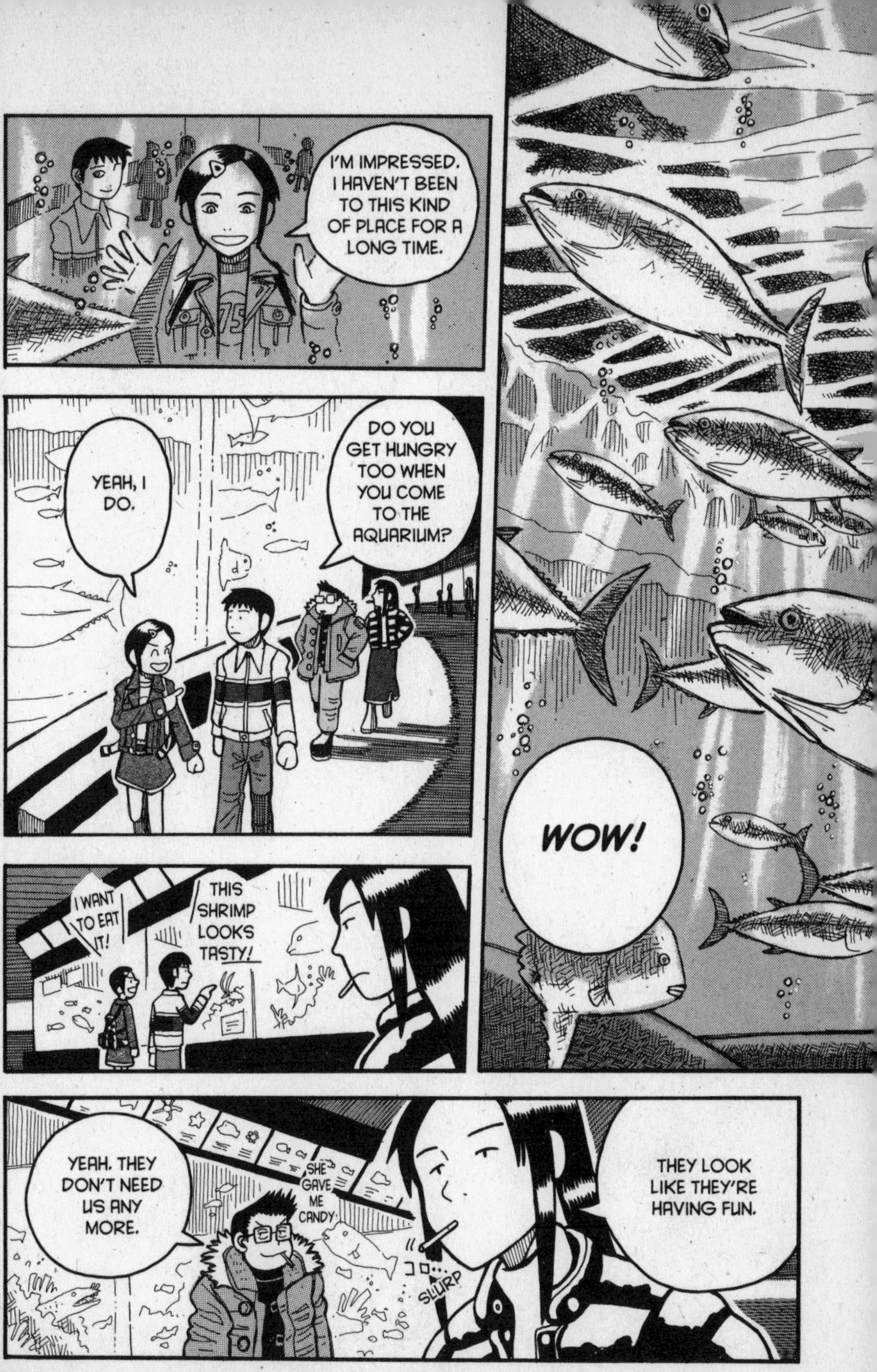
WOW!
I'M IMPRESSED. I HAVEN'T BEEN TO THIS KIND OF PLACE FOR A LONG TIME.
DO YOU GET HUNGRY TOO WHEN YOU COME TO THE AQUARIUM?
YEAH, I DO.
THIS SHRIMP LOOKS TASTY!
I WANT TO EAT IT!
THEY LOOK LIKE THEY'RE HAVING FUN.
コロ…
SLURP
SHE GAVE ME CANDY
YEAH. THEY DON'T NEED US ANY MORE.

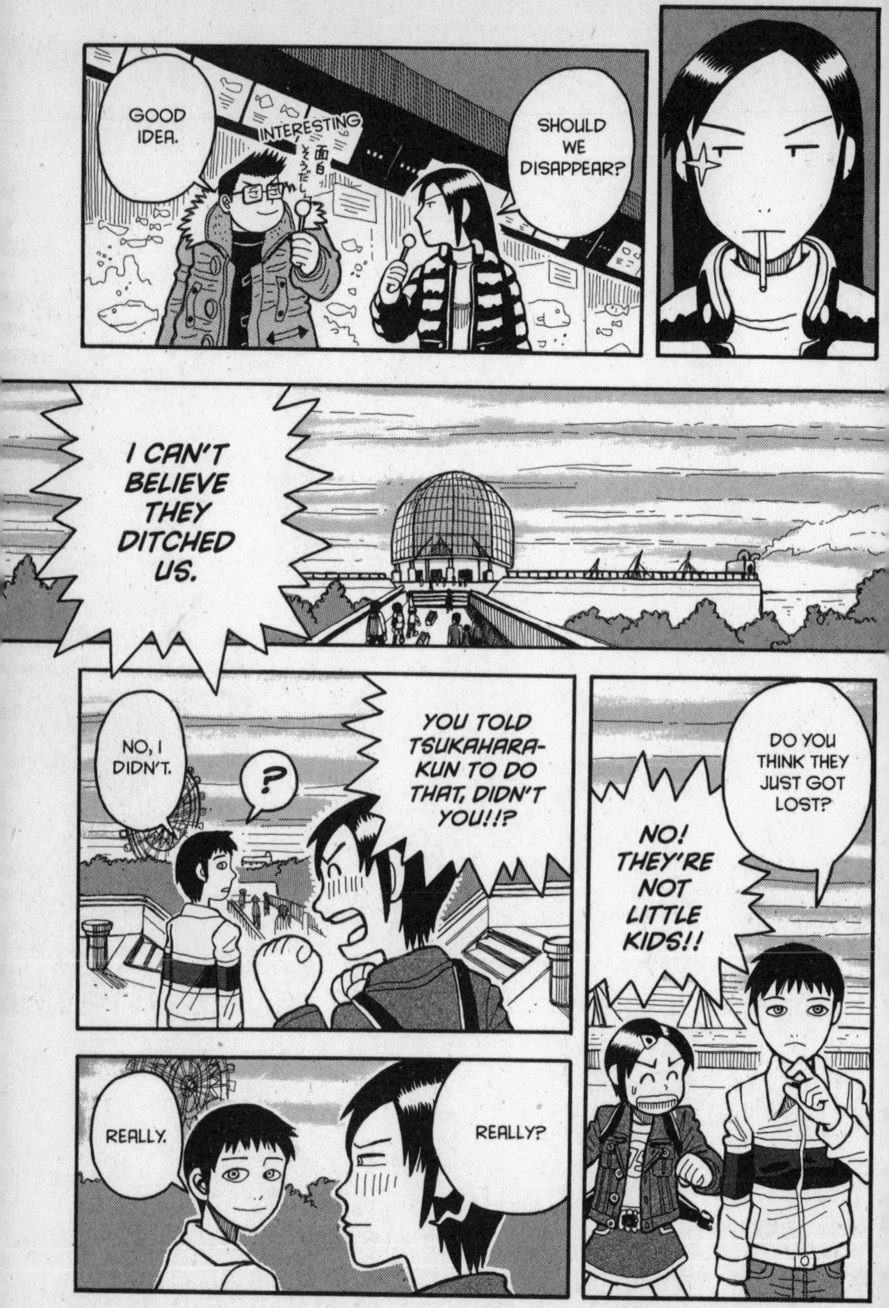
SHOULD WE DISAPPEAR?
INTERESTING
面白そうだし
GOOD IDEA.
I CAN'T BELIEVE THEY DITCHED US.
DO YOU THINK THEY JUST GOT LOST?
NO! THEY'RE NOT LITTLE KIDS!!
YOU TOLD TSUKAHARA-KUN TO DO THAT, DIDN'T YOU!!?
?
NO, I DIDN'T.
REALLY?
REALLY.

......

SMILE

AHH...

THAT'S OKAY.

I'M SORRY I DIDN'T TRUST YOU.

HEY, DO YOU WANT TO GO RIDE THE FERRIS WHEEL?

I WOULD NEVER LIE TO YOU, NEGISHI-SAN.

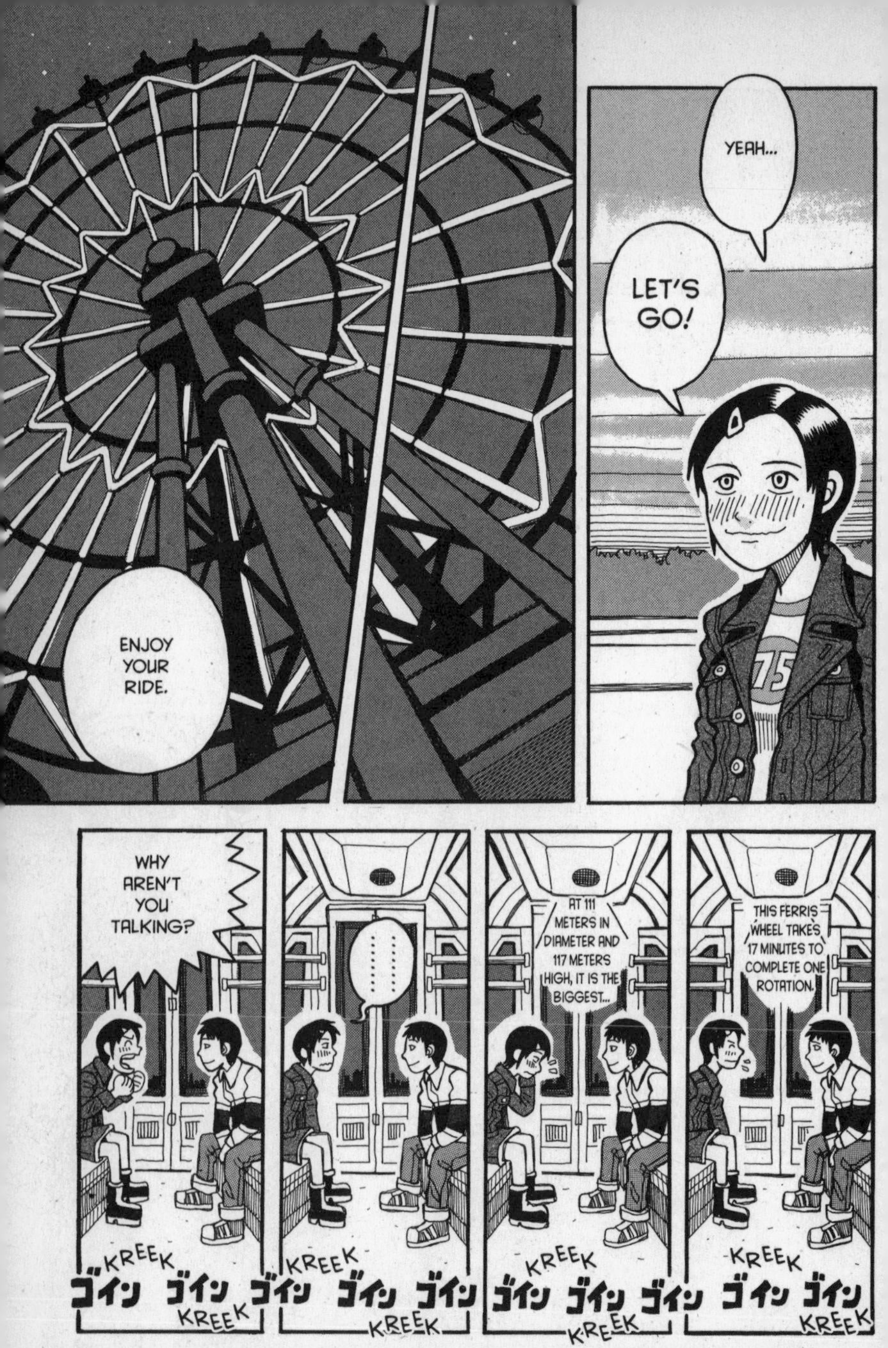
YEAH...
LET'S GO!
ENJOY YOUR RIDE.
THIS FERRIS WHEEL TAKES 17 MINUTES TO COMPLETE ONE ROTATION.
KREEK
ゴイン ゴイン
KREEK
AT 111 METERS IN DIAMETER AND 117 METERS HIGH, IT IS THE BIGGEST...
KREEK
ゴイン ゴイン ゴイン
KREEK
KREEK
ゴイン ゴイン ゴイン
KREEK
WHY AREN'T YOU TALKING?
KREEK
ゴイン ゴイン ゴイン
KREEK

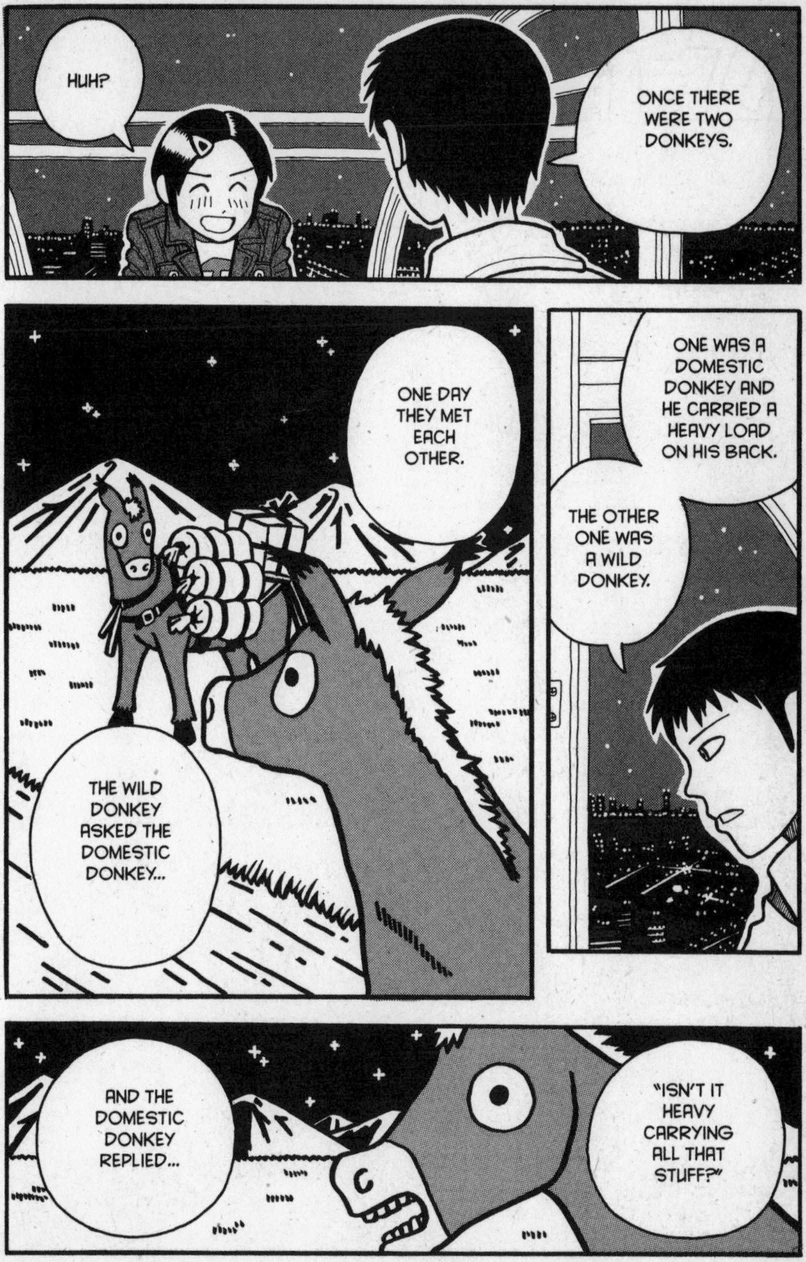
ONCE THERE WERE TWO DONKEYS.
HUH?
ONE WAS A DOMESTIC DONKEY AND HE CARRIED A HEAVY LOAD ON HIS BACK.
THE OTHER ONE WAS A WILD DONKEY.
ONE DAY THEY MET EACH OTHER.
THE WILD DONKEY ASKED THE DOMESTIC DONKEY...
"ISN'T IT HEAVY CARRYING ALL THAT STUFF?"
AND THE DOMESTIC DONKEY REPLIED...

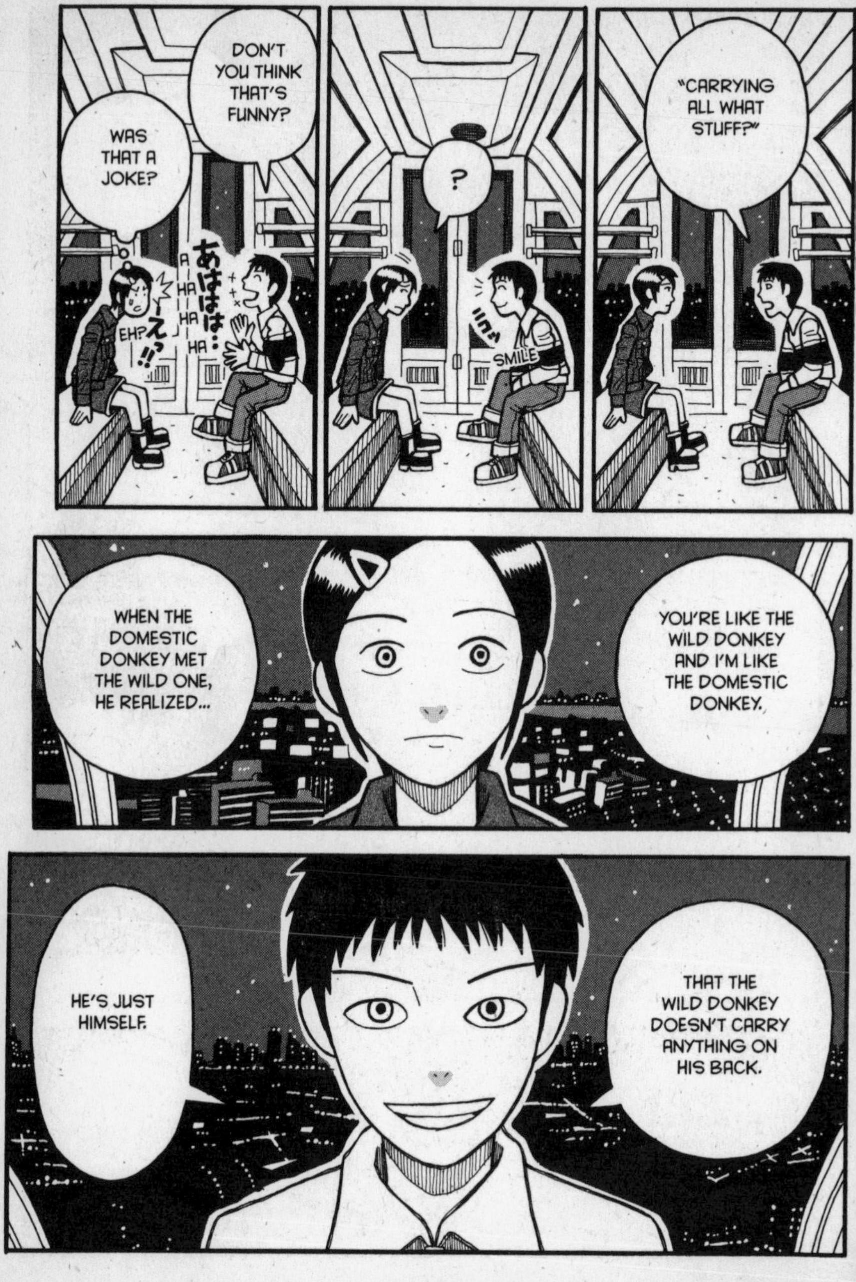
"CARRYING ALL WHAT STUFF?"
?
ニコッ
SMILE
DON'T YOU THINK THAT'S FUNNY?
WAS THAT A JOKE?
あははは…
A HA HA HA
えっ!!
EH?
YOU'RE LIKE THE WILD DONKEY AND I'M LIKE THE DOMESTIC DONKEY.
WHEN THE DOMESTIC DONKEY MET THE WILD ONE, HE REALIZED...
THAT THE WILD DONKEY DOESN'T CARRY ANYTHING ON HIS BACK.
HE'S JUST HIMSELF.

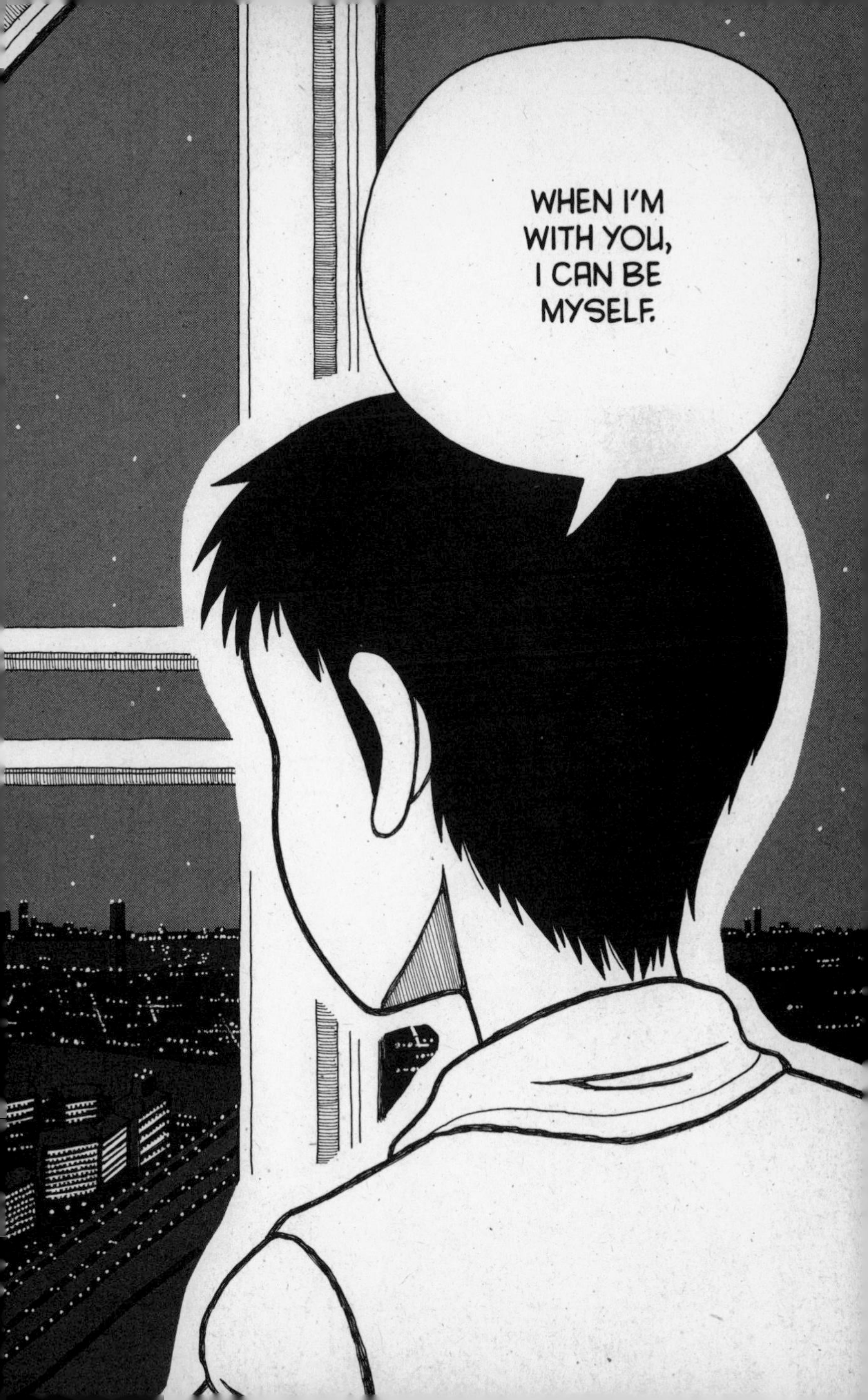
WHEN I'M WITH YOU, I CAN BE MYSELF.

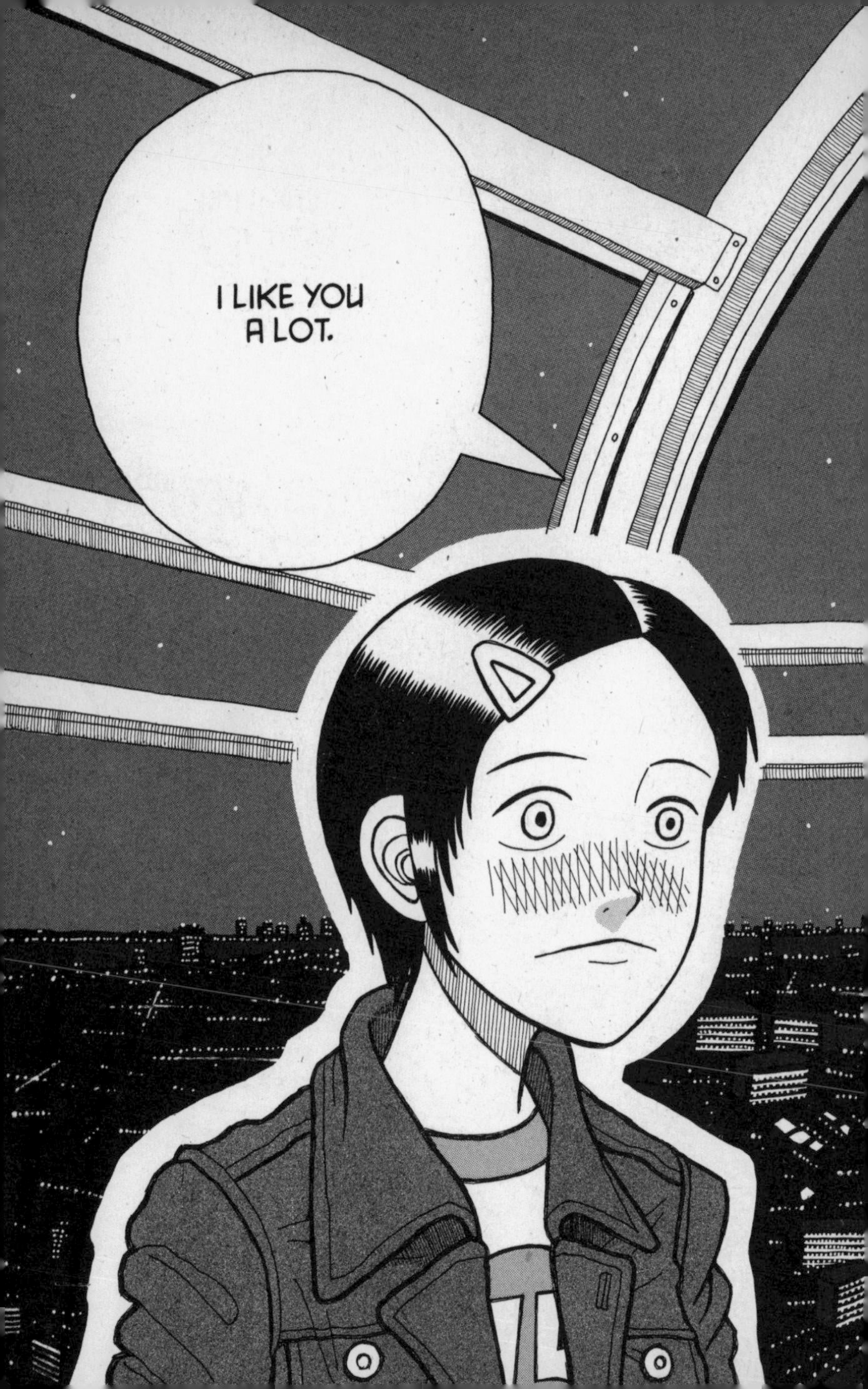
I LIKE YOU A LOT.

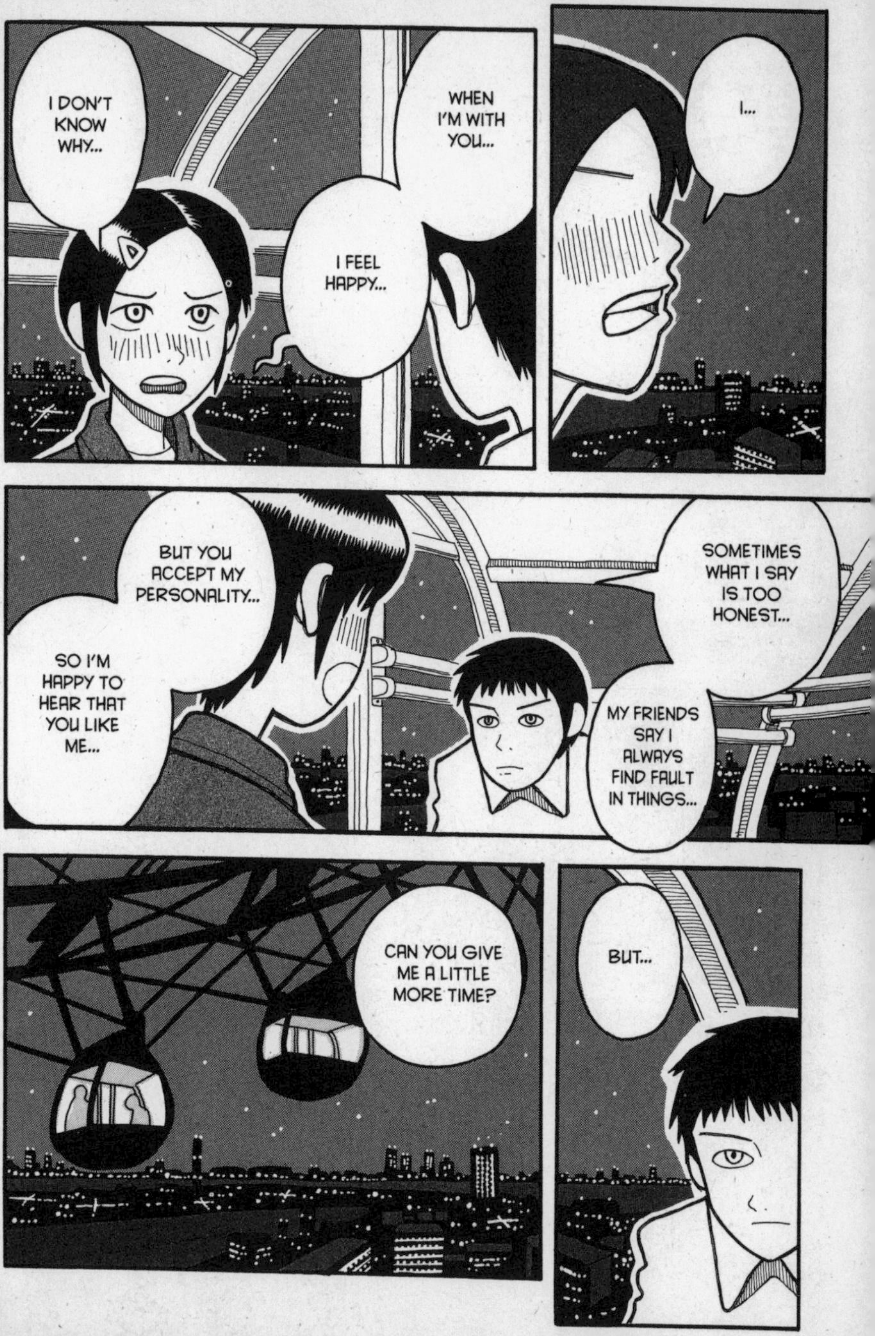
I...
WHEN I'M WITH YOU...
I FEEL HAPPY...
I DON'T KNOW WHY...
SOMETIMES WHAT I SAY IS TOO HONEST...
MY FRIENDS SAY I ALWAYS FIND FAULT IN THINGS...
BUT YOU ACCEPT MY PERSONALITY...
SO I'M HAPPY TO HEAR THAT YOU LIKE ME...
BUT...
CAN YOU GIVE ME A LITTLE MORE TIME?

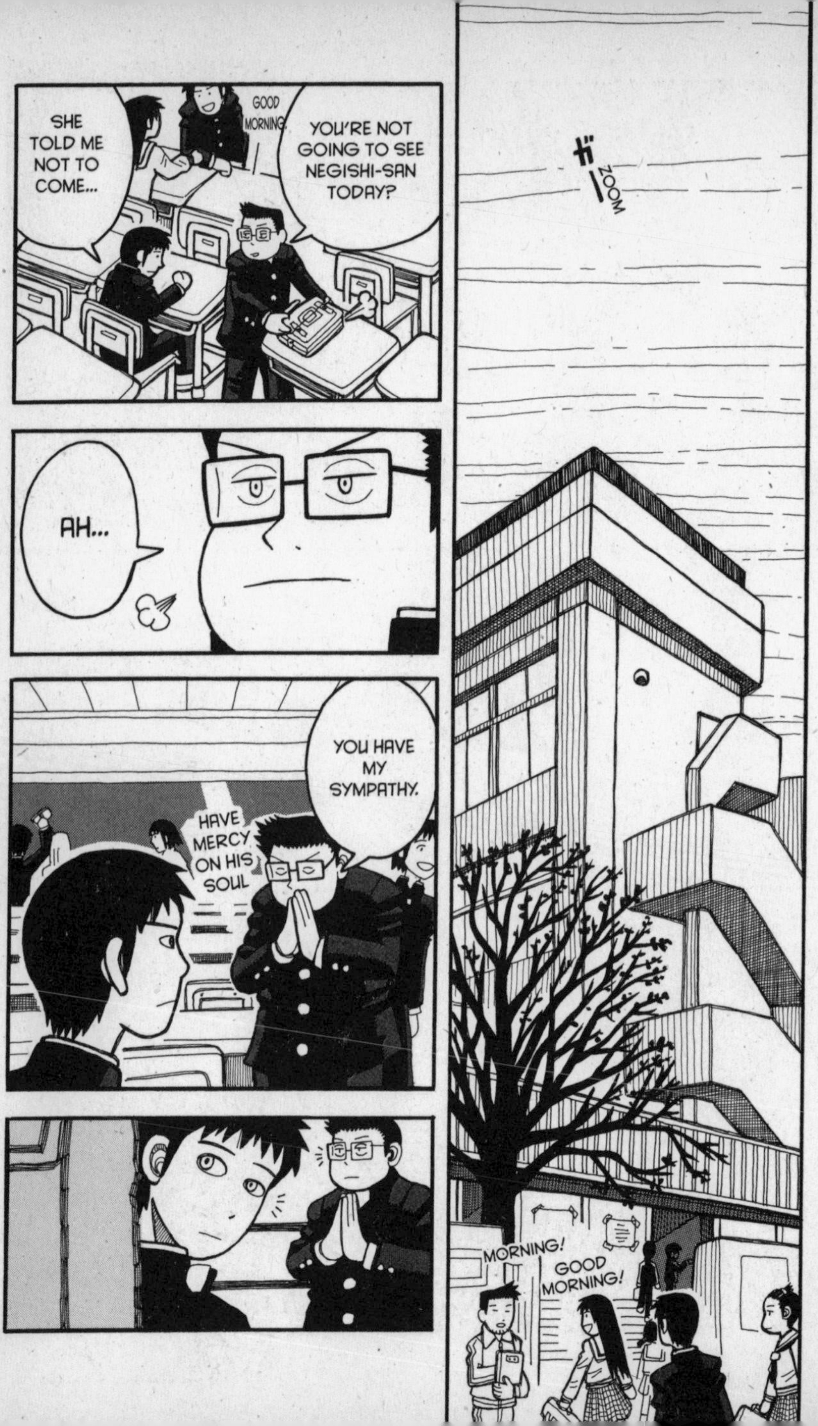
ガ
ZOOM
GOOD MORNING!
MORNING!
YOU'RE NOT GOING TO SEE NEGISHI-SAN TODAY?
GOOD MORNING.
SHE TOLD ME NOT TO COME...
AH...
YOU HAVE MY SYMPATHY.
HAVE MERCY ON HIS SOUL

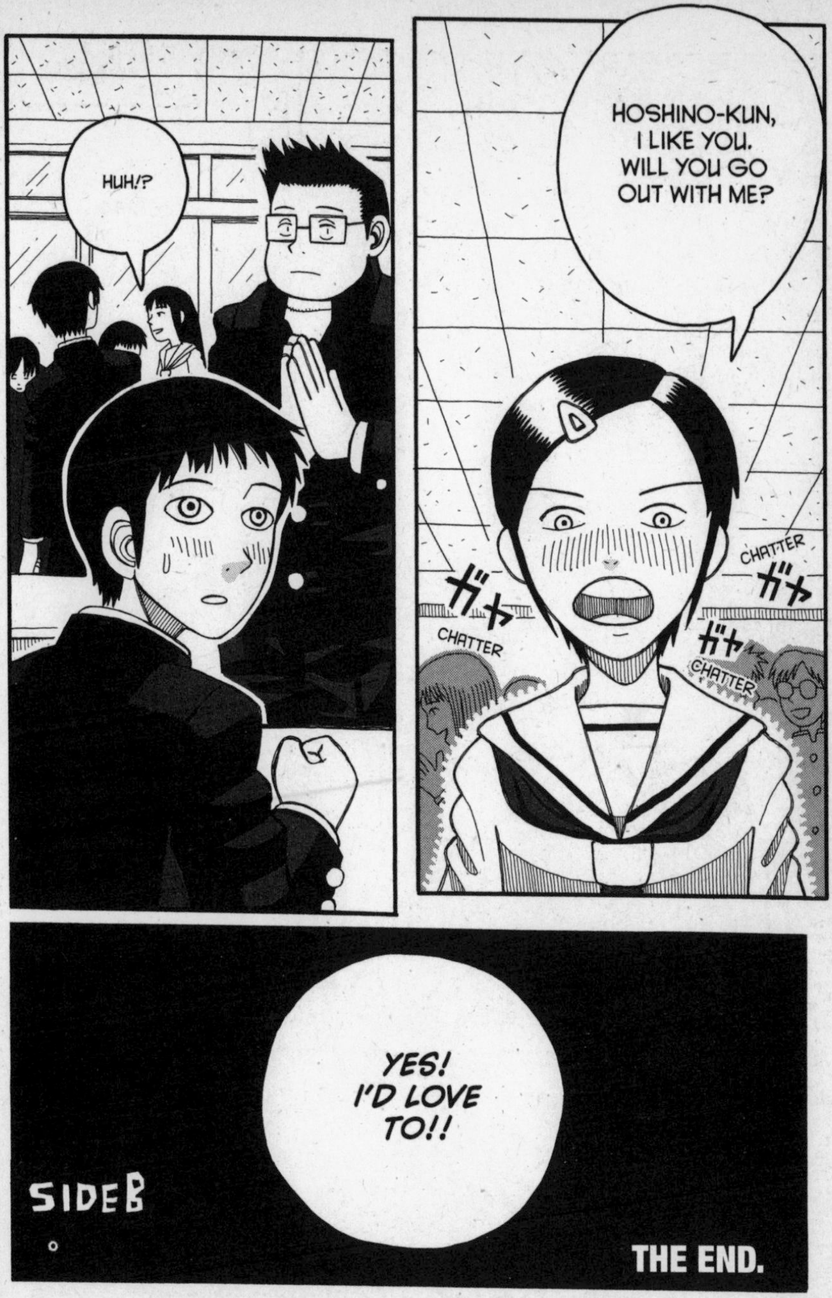
HOSHINO-KUN, I LIKE YOU. WILL YOU GO OUT WITH ME?
CHATTER
ガヤ
ガヤ
CHATTER
ガヤ
CHATTER
HUH!?
YES! I'D LOVE TO!!
SIDE B
THE END.

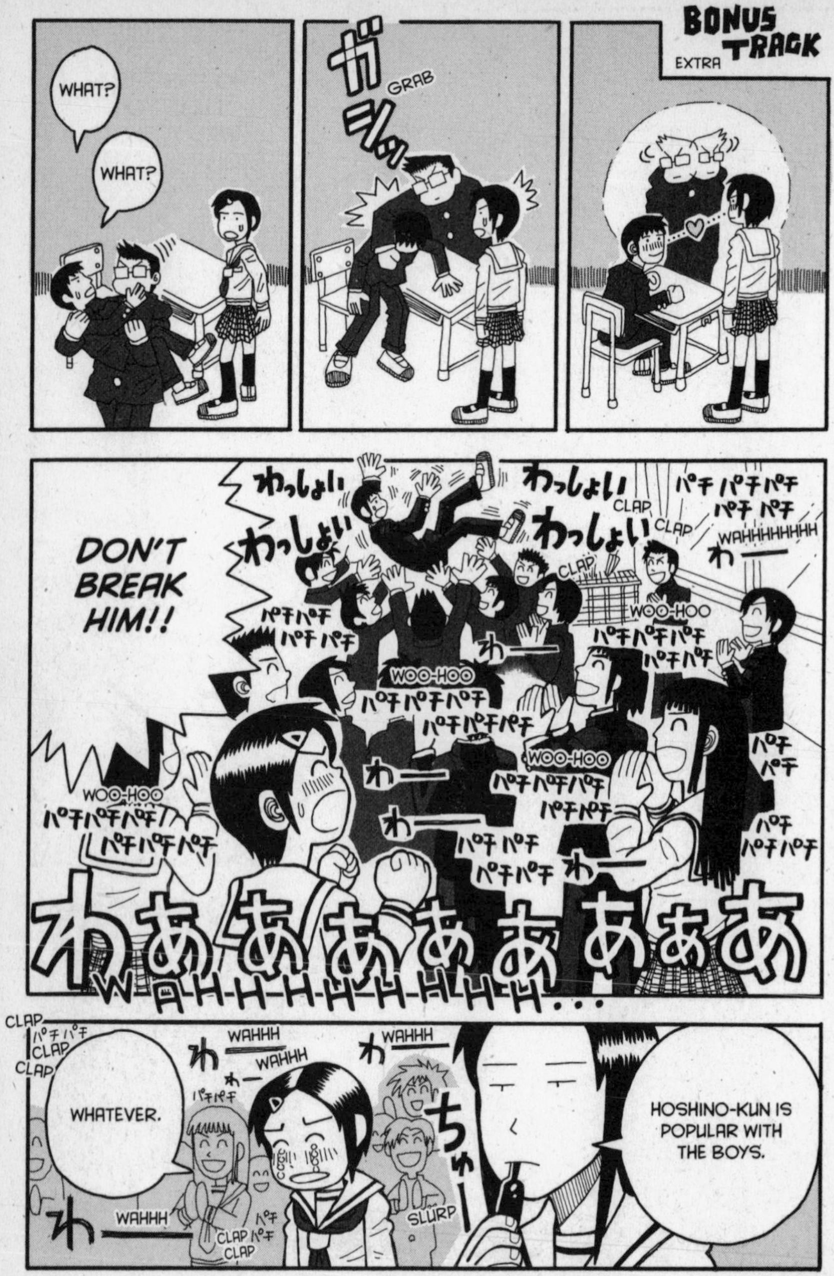
BONUS TRACK
EXTRA
ガシッ
GRAB
WHAT?
WHAT?
わっしょい
わっしょい
わっしょい
わっしょい
パチパチパチ
パチパチ
CLAP
CLAP
WAHHHHHHHHH
わー
CLAP
WOO-HOO
パチパチパチ
パチパチ
DON'T BREAK HIM!!
パチパチ
パチパチ
WOO-HOO
パチパチパチ
パチパチパチ
パチ
パチ
WOO-HOO
パチパチパチ
パチパチ
パチ
パチパチ
WOO-HOO
パチパチパチ
パチパチパチ
わー
パチパチ
パチパチ
わー
わー
わあぁあぁあぁあぁあ
WAHHHHHHHHHHH...
HOSHINO-KUN IS POPULAR WITH THE BOYS.
ちゅー
SLURP
わ WAHHH
わ WAHHH
わー WAHHH
パチパチ
WHATEVER.
パチパチ
CLAP
CLAP
わー
WAHHH
CLAP
パチパチ
CLAP
CLAP

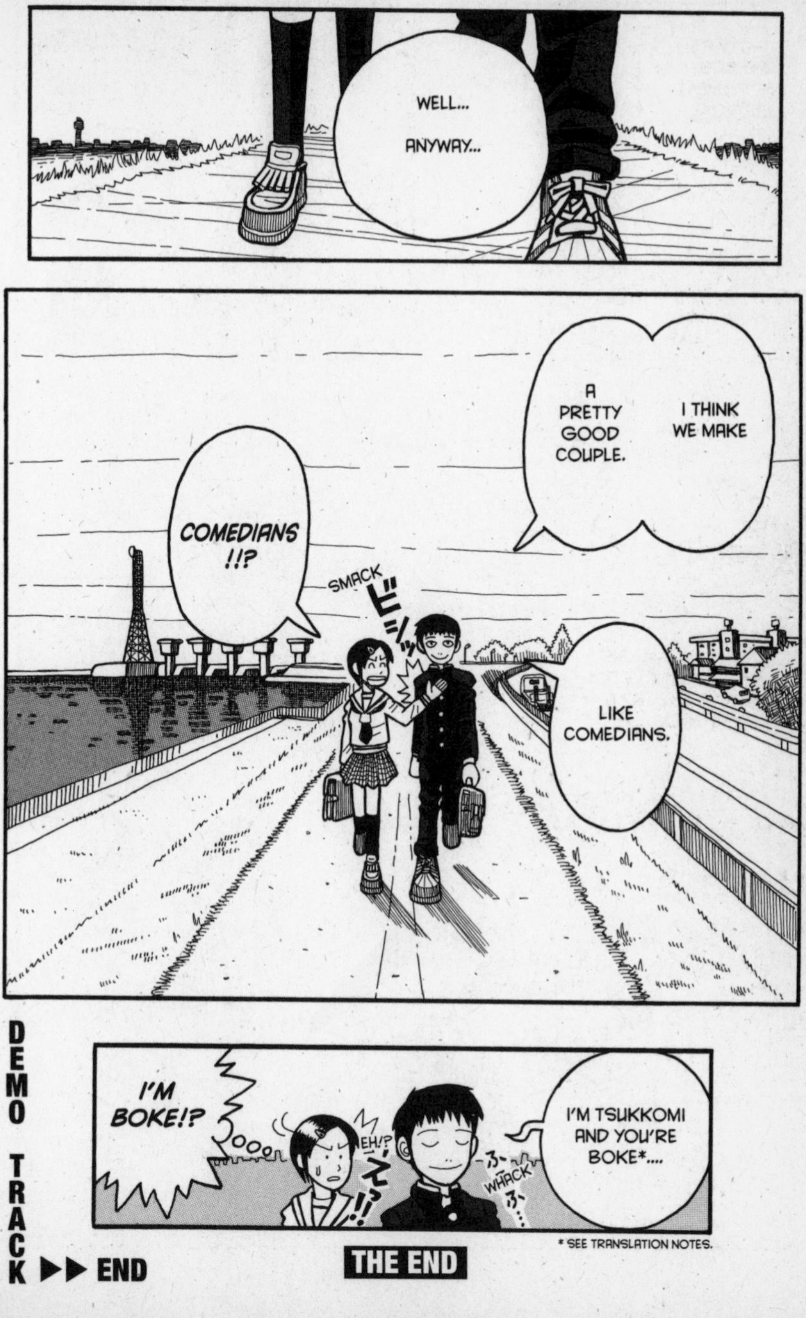
WELL...
ANYWAY...
I THINK WE MAKE A PRETTY GOOD COUPLE.
LIKE COMEDIANS.
COMEDIANS !!?
SMACK
ビシッ
I'M TSUKKOMI AND YOU'RE BOKE*....
ふーふー...
WHACK
EH!?
え!?
I'M BOKE!?

DEMO TRACK ▶▶ END

* SEE TRANSLATION NOTES.

THE END

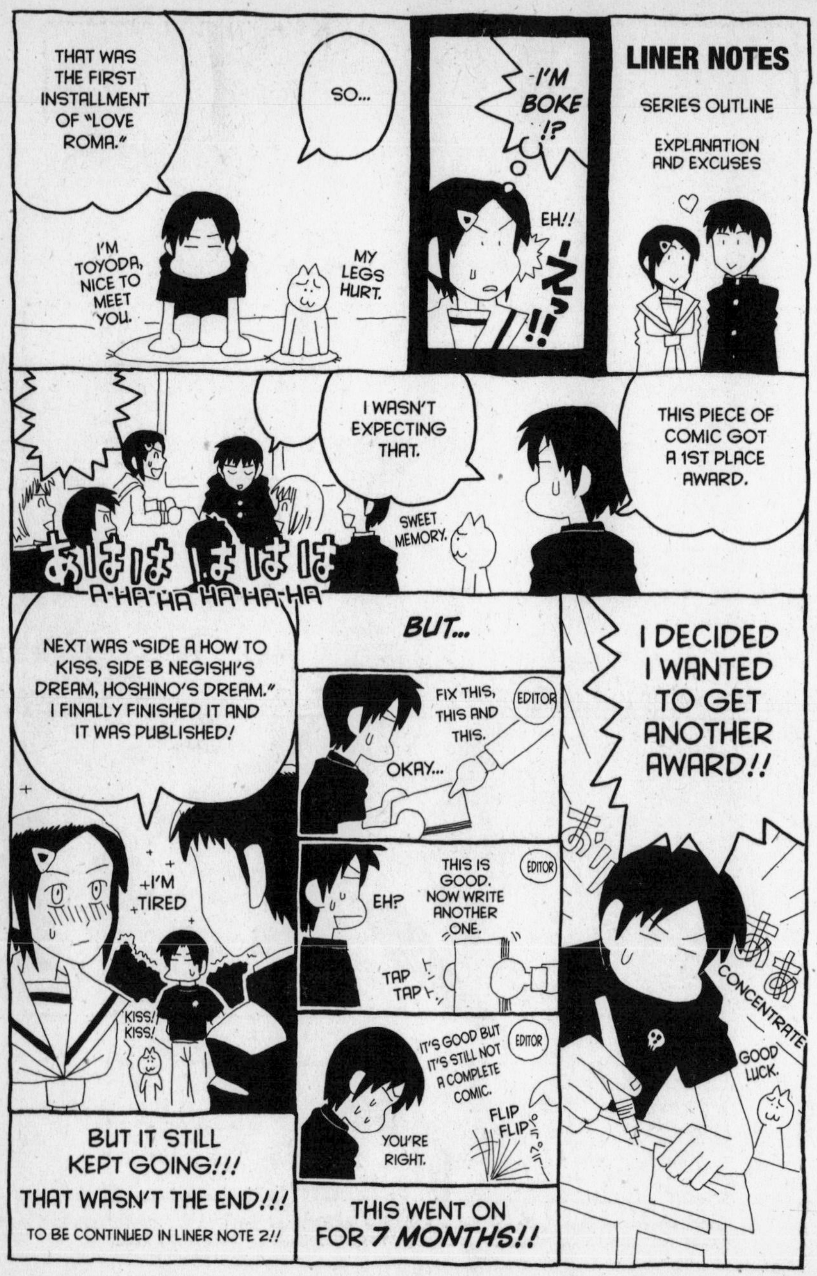
LINER NOTES
SERIES OUTLINE
EXPLANATION AND EXCUSES
-I'M BOKE !?
EH!!
えっ!!
SO...
THAT WAS THE FIRST INSTALLMENT OF "LOVE ROMA."
MY LEGS HURT.
I'M TOYODA, NICE TO MEET YOU.
THIS PIECE OF COMIC GOT A 1ST PLACE AWARD.
I WASN'T EXPECTING THAT.
SWEET MEMORY.
あはは ははは
A-HA-HA HA-HA-HA
I DECIDED I WANTED TO GET ANOTHER AWARD!!
CONCENTRATE
GOOD LUCK.
BUT...
EDITOR
FIX THIS, THIS AND THIS.
OKAY...
EDITOR
THIS IS GOOD. NOW WRITE ANOTHER ONE.
EH?
TAP TAP
EDITOR
IT'S GOOD BUT IT'S STILL NOT A COMPLETE COMIC.
FLIP FLIP
YOU'RE RIGHT.
THIS WENT ON FOR 7 MONTHS!!
NEXT WAS "SIDE A HOW TO KISS, SIDE B NEGISHI'S DREAM, HOSHINO'S DREAM." I FINALLY FINISHED IT AND IT WAS PUBLISHED!
I'M TIRED
KISS! KISS!
BUT IT STILL KEPT GOING!!! THAT WASN'T THE END!!!
TO BE CONTINUED IN LINER NOTE 2!!

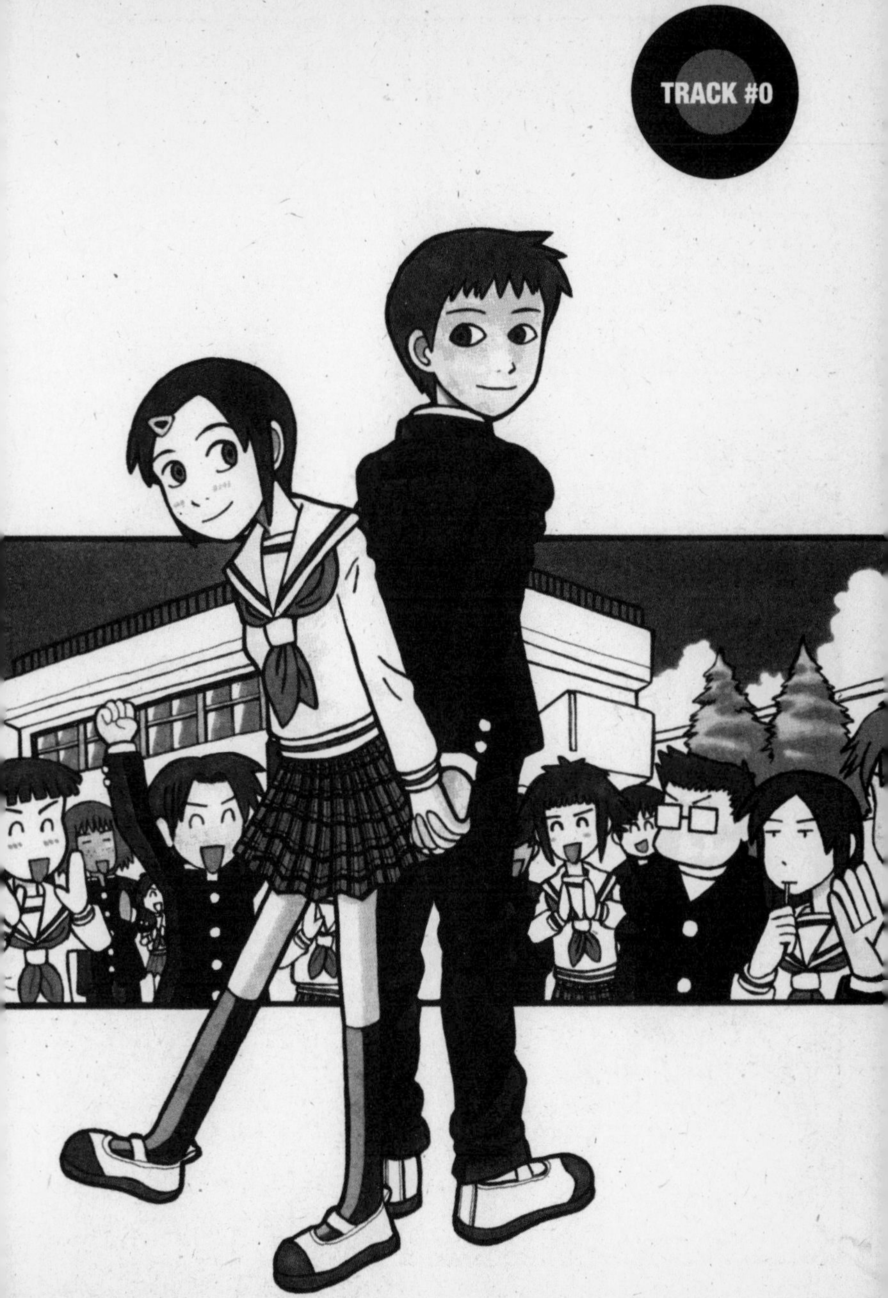

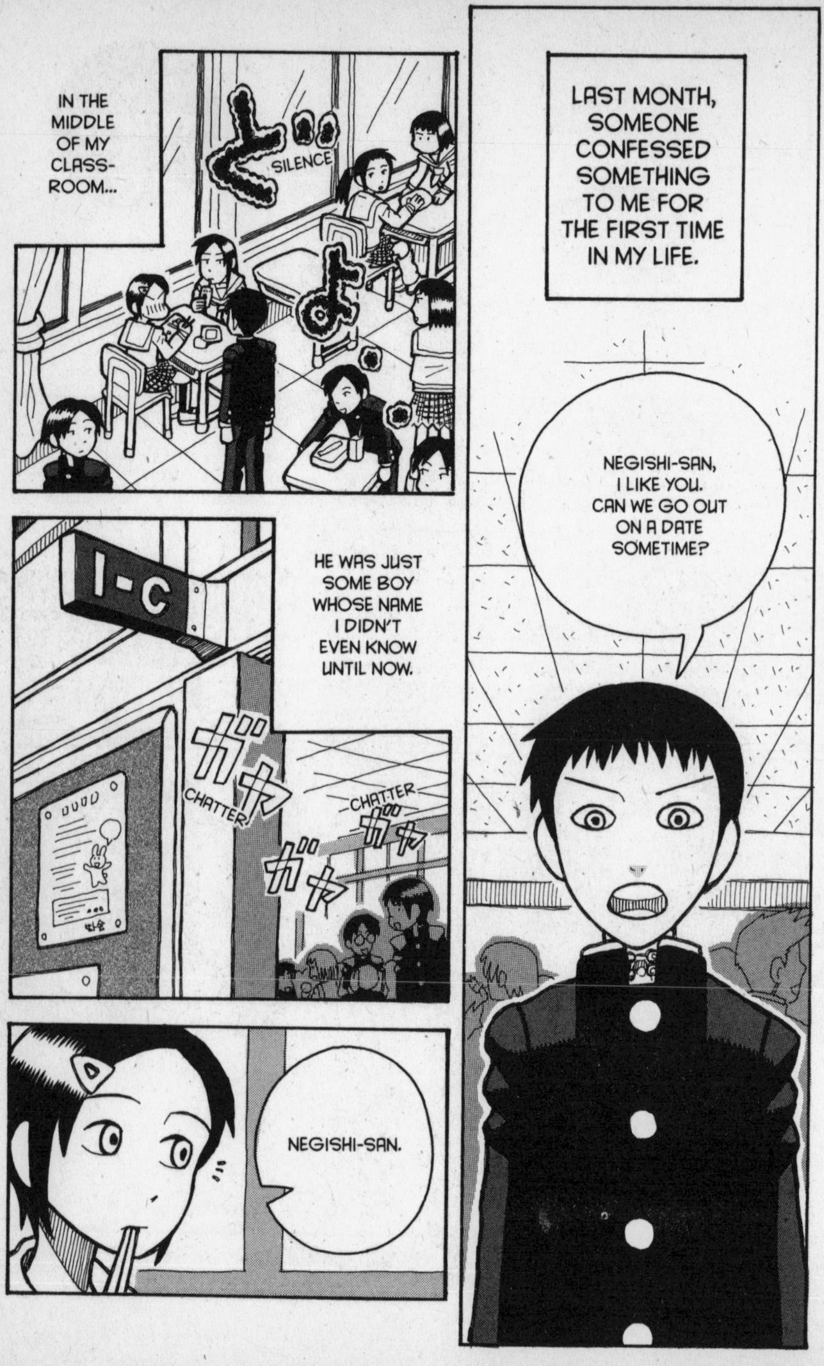
LAST MONTH, SOMEONE CONFESSED SOMETHING TO ME FOR THE FIRST TIME IN MY LIFE.
NEGISHI-SAN, I LIKE YOU. CAN WE GO OUT ON A DATE SOMETIME?
IN THE MIDDLE OF MY CLASS-ROOM...
SILENCE
1-C
HE WAS JUST SOME BOY WHOSE NAME I DIDN'T EVEN KNOW UNTIL NOW.
CHATTER
CHATTER
NEGISHI-SAN.

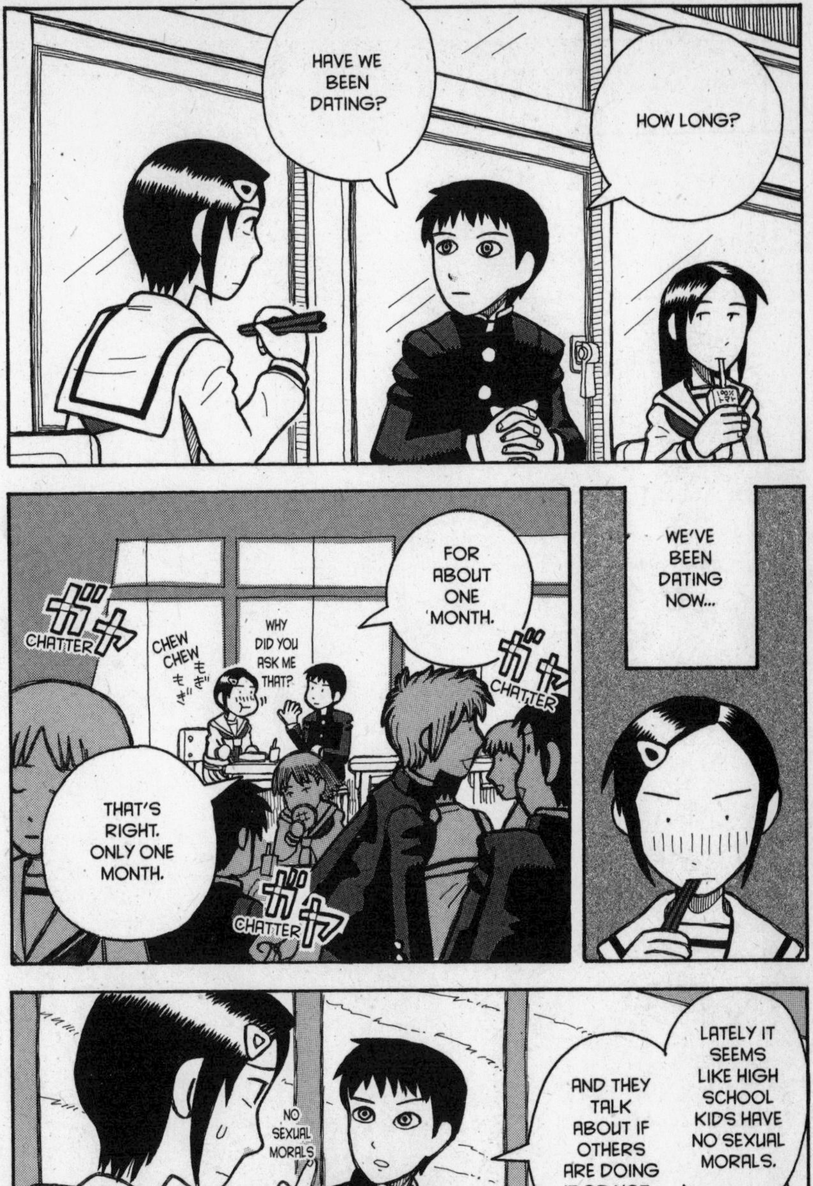
HOW LONG?
HAVE WE BEEN DATING?
WE'VE BEEN DATING NOW...
FOR ABOUT ONE MONTH.
ガヤ CHATTER
WHY DID YOU ASK ME THAT?
CHEW CHEW もぎもぎ
ガヤ CHATTER
THAT'S RIGHT. ONLY ONE MONTH.
ガヤ CHATTER
LATELY IT SEEMS LIKE HIGH SCHOOL KIDS HAVE NO SEXUAL MORALS.
AND THEY TALK ABOUT IF OTHERS ARE DOING IT OR NOT...
NO SEXUAL MORALS

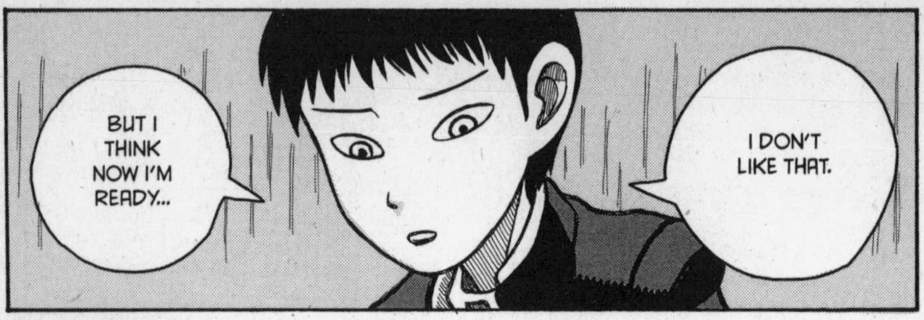
I DON'T LIKE THAT.
BUT I THINK NOW I'M READY...

TRACK #0 **SIDE A** **HOW TO KISS**

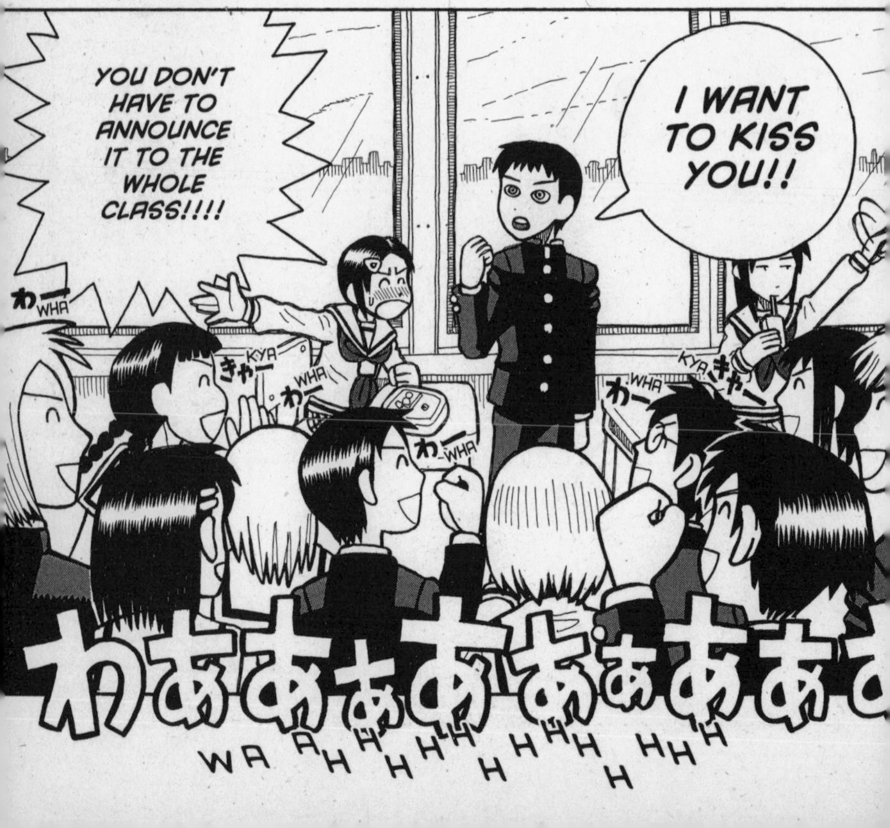
I WANT TO KISS YOU!!
YOU DON'T HAVE TO ANNOUNCE IT TO THE WHOLE CLASS!!!!
きゃー KYA
わー WHA
わー WHA
きゃー KYA
わー WHA
わー WHA
わああああああああああ
WAAHHHHHHHHHHHHHH

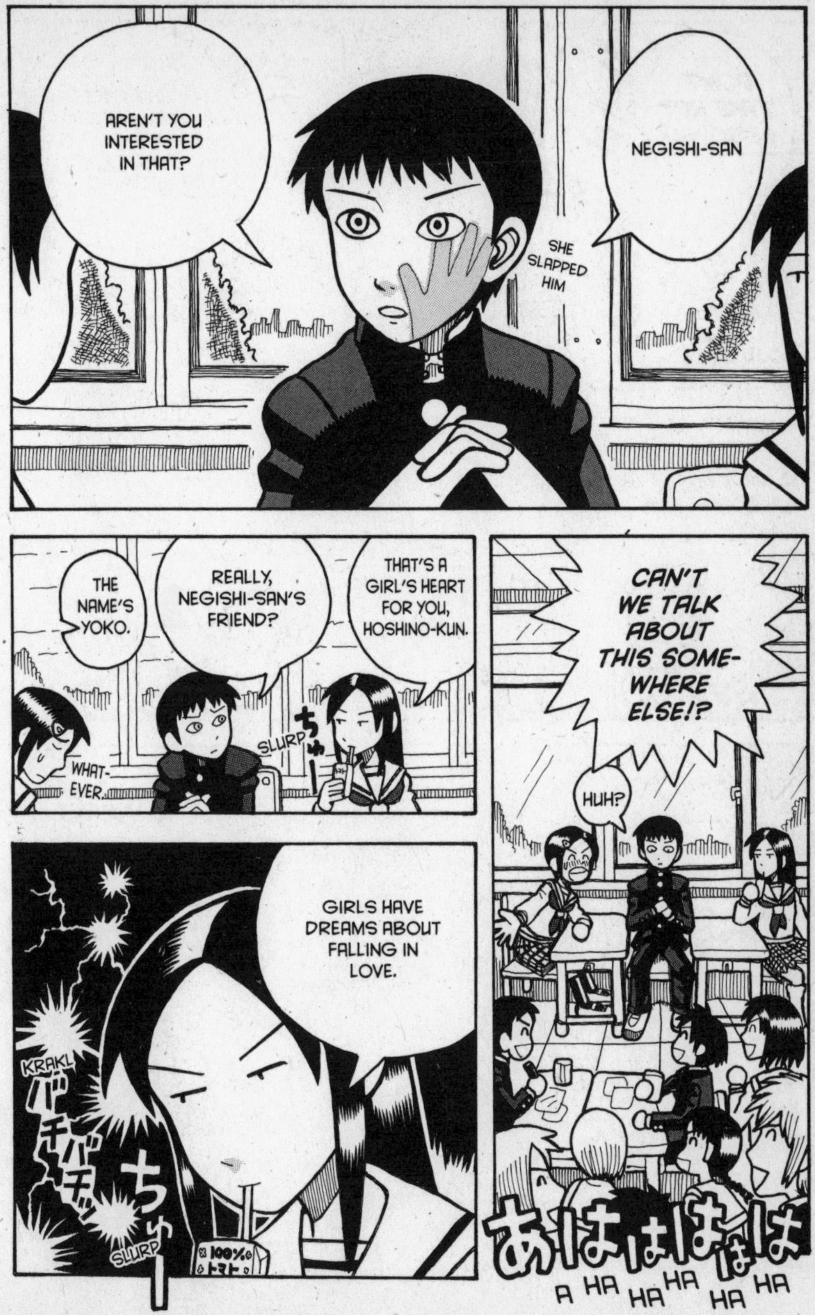
NEGISHI-SAN
SHE SLAPPED HIM
AREN'T YOU INTERESTED IN THAT?
CAN'T WE TALK ABOUT THIS SOME-WHERE ELSE!?
HUH?
あははははは
A HA HA HA HA HA
THAT'S A GIRL'S HEART FOR YOU, HOSHINO-KUN.
ちゅー
SLURP
REALLY, NEGISHI-SAN'S FRIEND?
THE NAME'S YOKO.
WHAT-EVER.
GIRLS HAVE DREAMS ABOUT FALLING IN LOVE.
ちゅー
SLURP
100% トマト
バチバチッ
KRAKL

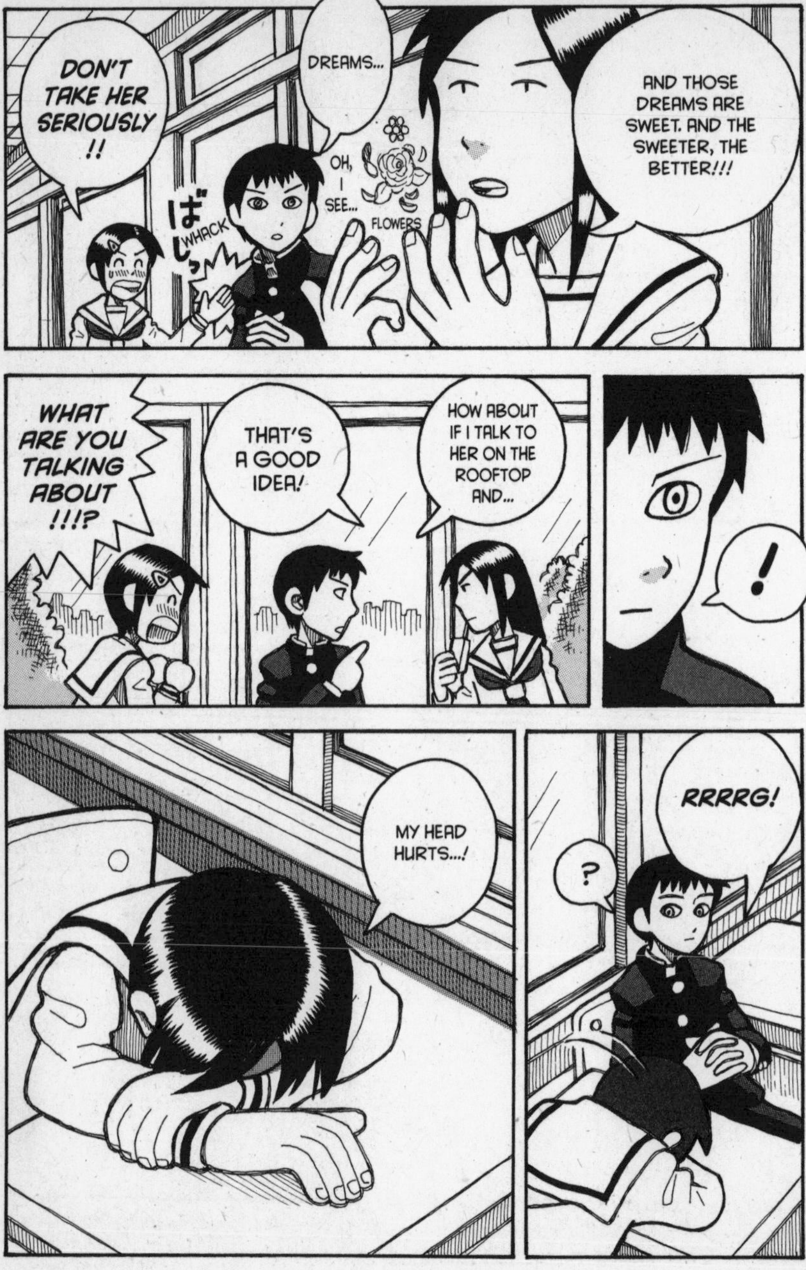
AND THOSE DREAMS ARE SWEET. AND THE SWEETER, THE BETTER!!!
FLOWERS
OH, I SEE...
DREAMS...
DON'T TAKE HER SERIOUSLY !!
ばじっ WHACK
!
HOW ABOUT IF I TALK TO HER ON THE ROOFTOP AND...
THAT'S A GOOD IDEA!
WHAT ARE YOU TALKING ABOUT !!!?
RRRRG!
?
MY HEAD HURTS...!

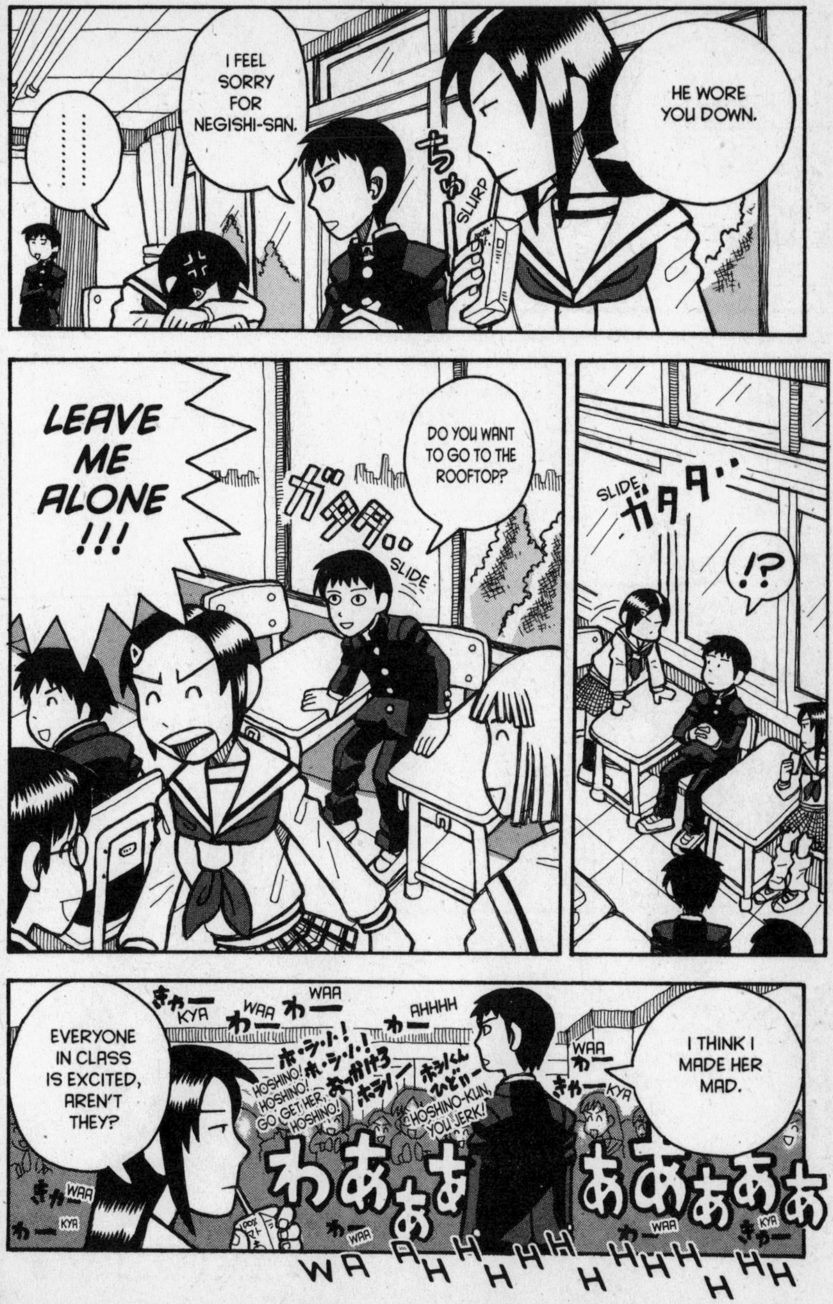
HE WORE YOU DOWN.
ちゅ
SLURP
I FEEL SORRY FOR NEGISHI-SAN.
......
ガタッ
SLIDE
!?
DO YOU WANT TO GO TO THE ROOFTOP?
ガタタ
SLIDE
LEAVE ME ALONE!!!
I THINK I MADE HER MAD.
わー WAA
きゃー KYA
ホシノくんひどーい
HOSHINO-KUN, YOU JERK!
ホシノ!
ホシノ! ホシノ!
やっつけろホシノ!
HOSHINO! HOSHINO! GO GET HER, HOSHINO!
わー WAA
わー WAA
かー AHHHH
きゃー KYA
わああぁあ ああああぁああ
WAAHHHHHHHHHHH
EVERYONE IN CLASS IS EXCITED, AREN'T THEY?

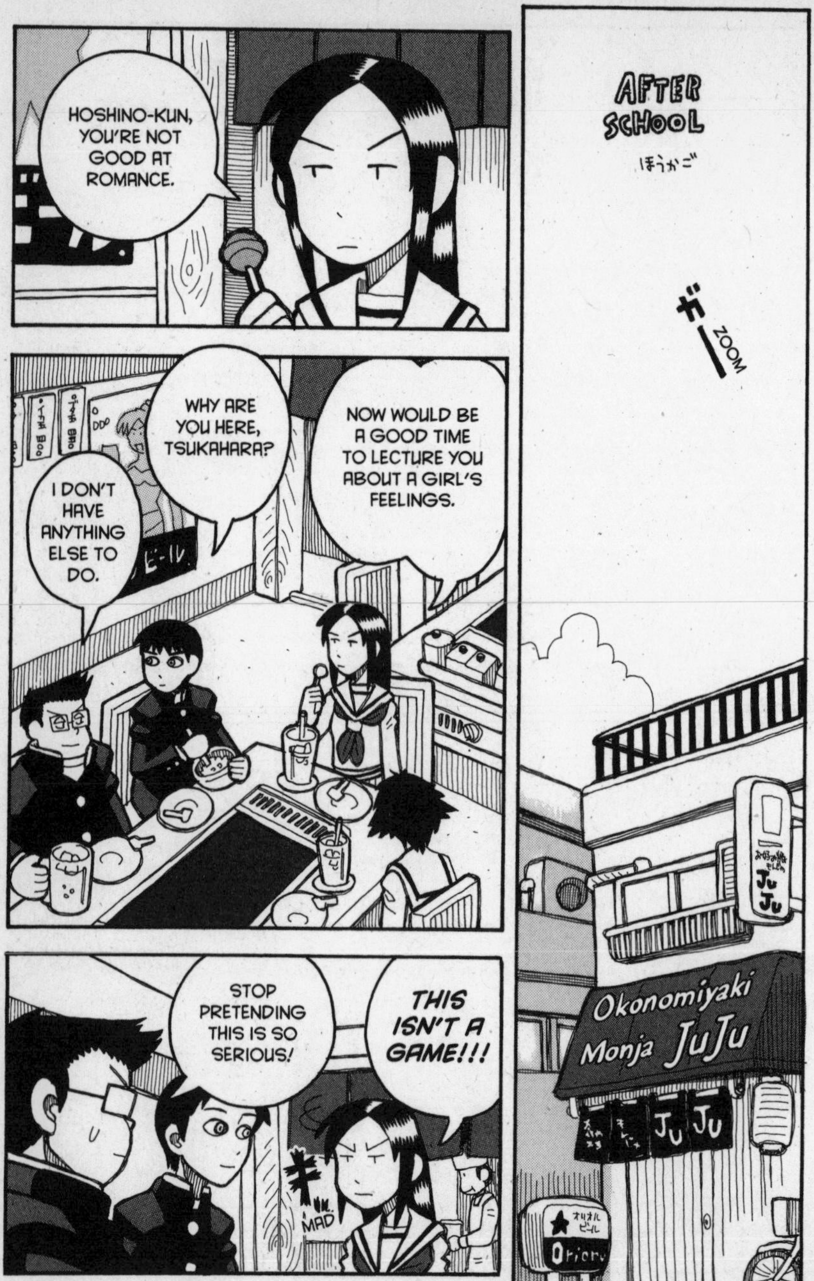

AFTER SCHOOL
ほうかご
ガー
ZOOM
Okonomiyaki Monja JuJu
JU JU
HOSHINO-KUN, YOU'RE NOT GOOD AT ROMANCE.
NOW WOULD BE A GOOD TIME TO LECTURE YOU ABOUT A GIRL'S FEELINGS.
WHY ARE YOU HERE, TSUKAHARA?
I DON'T HAVE ANYTHING ELSE TO DO.
THIS ISN'T A GAME!!!
STOP PRETENDING THIS IS SO SERIOUS!
MAD

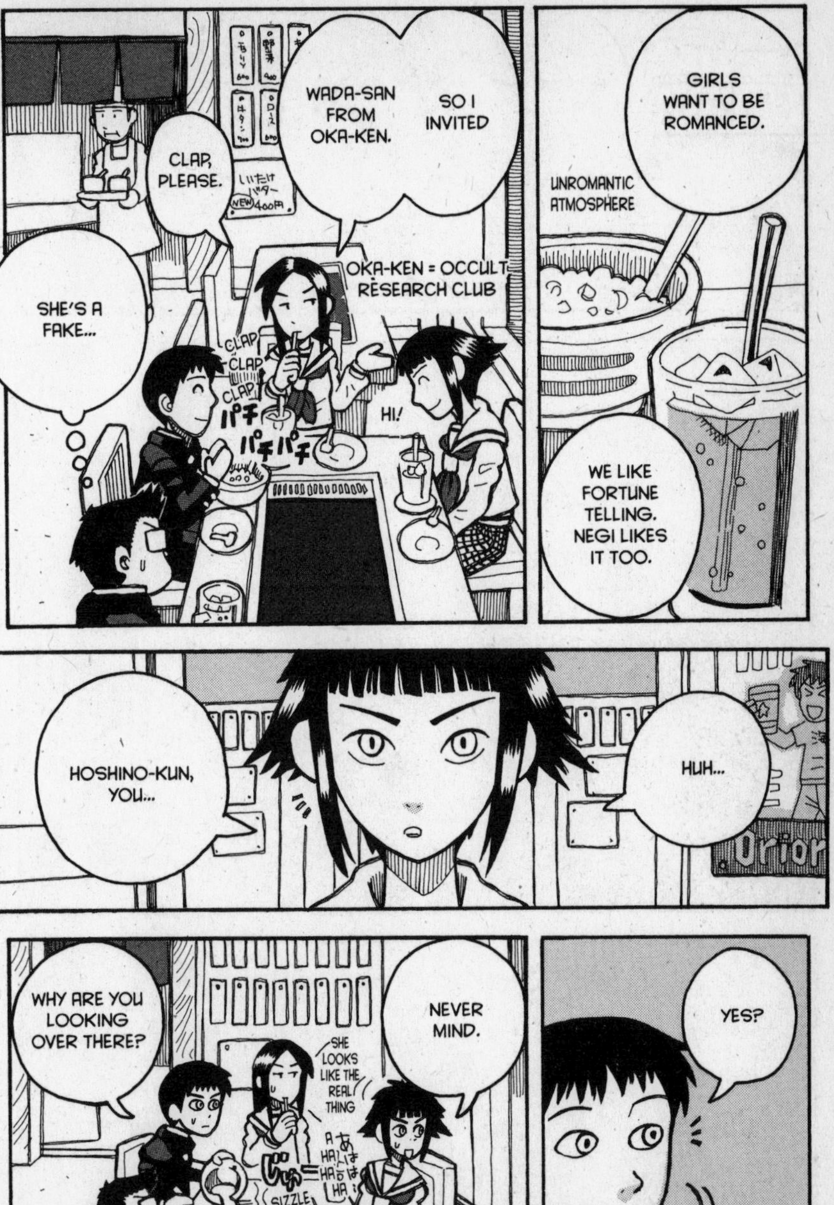
GIRLS WANT TO BE ROMANCED.
UNROMANTIC ATMOSPHERE
WE LIKE FORTUNE TELLING. NEGI LIKES IT TOO.
SO I INVITED WADA-SAN FROM OKA-KEN.
CLAP, PLEASE.
OKA-KEN = OCCULT RESEARCH CLUB
SHE'S A FAKE...
CLAP CLAP CLAP
パチ パチパチ
HI!
HUH...
HOSHINO-KUN, YOU...
YES?
NEVER MIND.
SHE LOOKS LIKE THE REAL THING
WHY ARE YOU LOOKING OVER THERE?
A HA HA HA
あはは
じゅ〜
SIZZLE

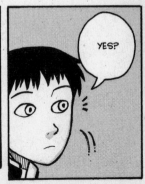

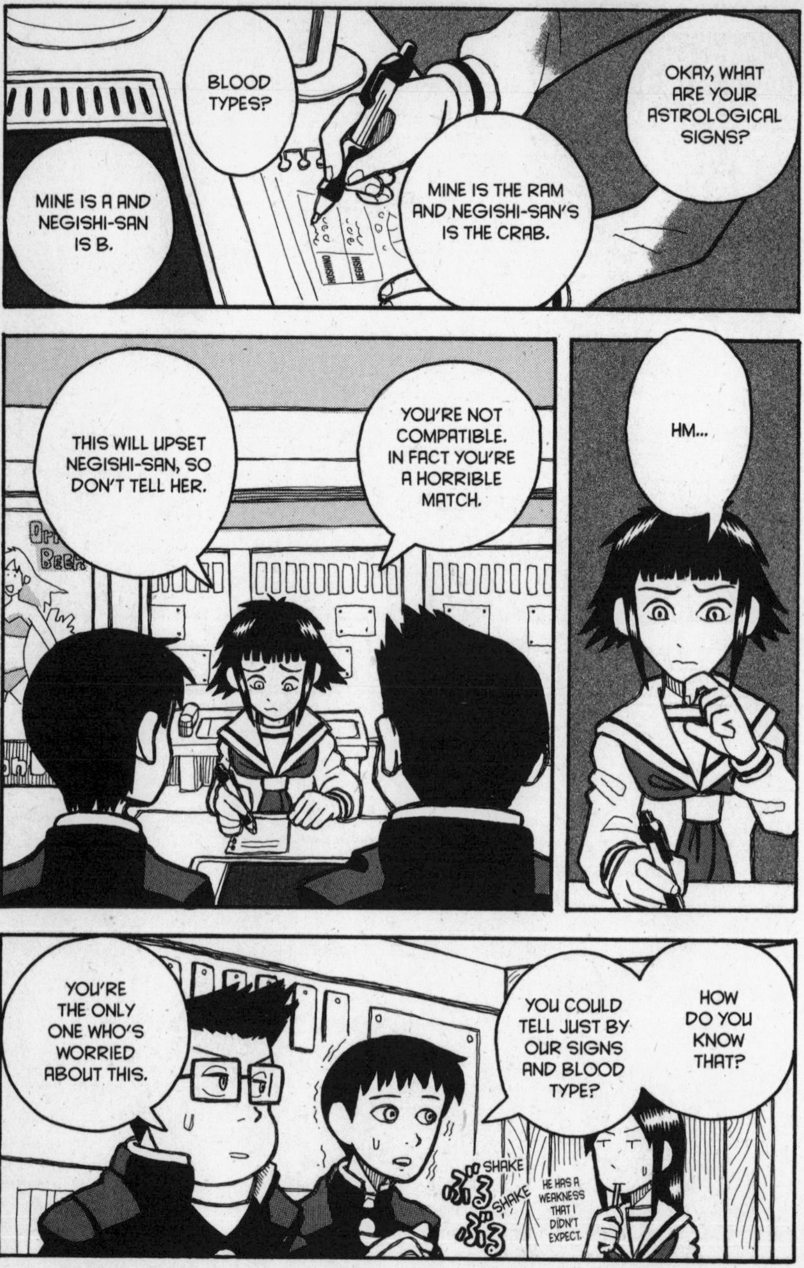
OKAY, WHAT ARE YOUR ASTROLOGICAL SIGNS?
MINE IS THE RAM AND NEGISHI-SAN'S IS THE CRAB.
BLOOD TYPES?
MINE IS A AND NEGISHI-SAN IS B.
HM...
YOU'RE NOT COMPATIBLE. IN FACT YOU'RE A HORRIBLE MATCH.
THIS WILL UPSET NEGISHI-SAN, SO DON'T TELL HER.
HOW DO YOU KNOW THAT?
YOU COULD TELL JUST BY OUR SIGNS AND BLOOD TYPE?
HE HAS A WEAKNESS THAT I DIDN'T EXPECT.
SHAKE
SHAKE
YOU'RE THE ONLY ONE WHO'S WORRIED ABOUT THIS.

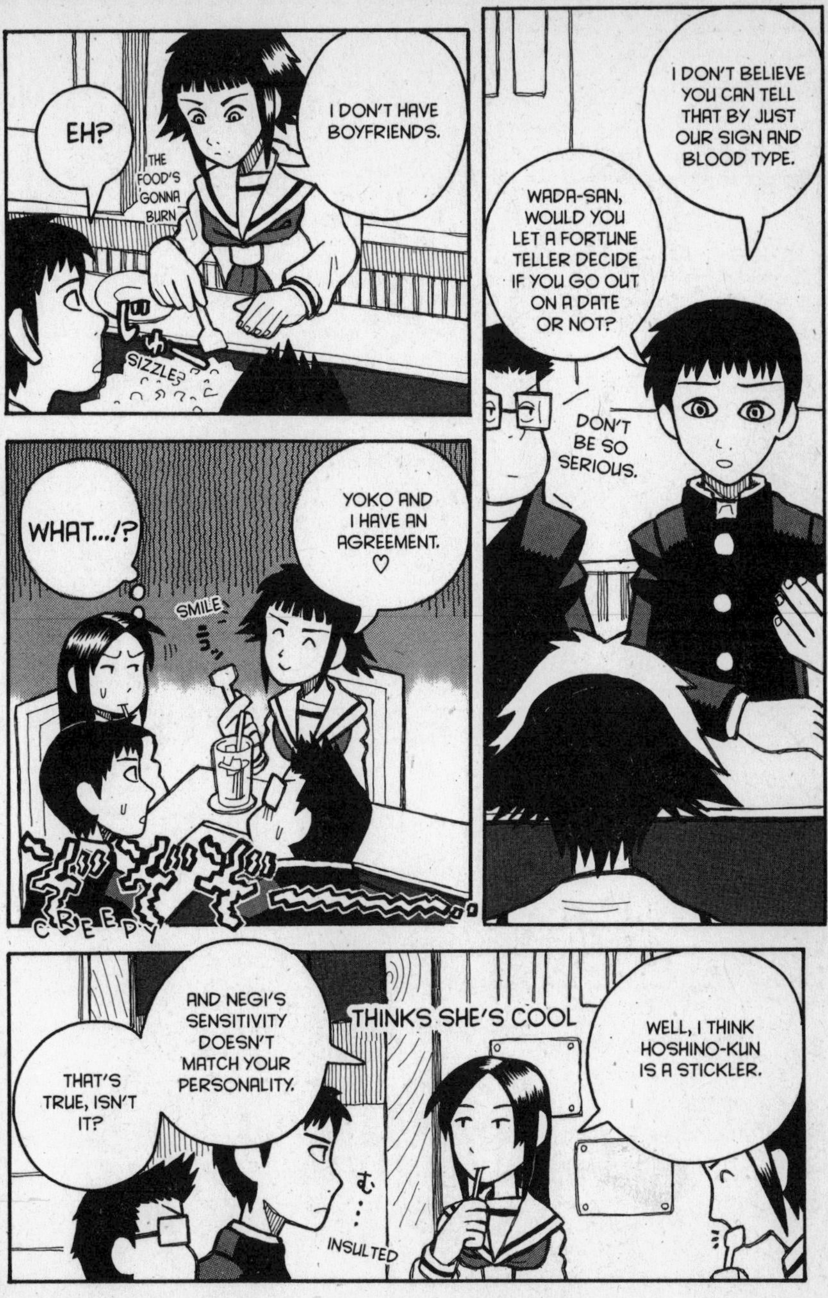

I DON'T BELIEVE YOU CAN TELL THAT BY JUST OUR SIGN AND BLOOD TYPE.
WADA-SAN, WOULD YOU LET A FORTUNE TELLER DECIDE IF YOU GO OUT ON A DATE OR NOT?
DON'T BE SO SERIOUS.
I DON'T HAVE BOYFRIENDS.
EH?
THE FOOD'S GONNA BURN
SIZZLE
YOKO AND I HAVE AN AGREEMENT. ♡
WHAT...!?
SMILE
CREEPY
WELL, I THINK HOSHINO-KUN IS A STICKLER.
THINKS SHE'S COOL
AND NEGI'S SENSITIVITY DOESN'T MATCH YOUR PERSONALITY.
THAT'S TRUE, ISN'T IT?
む…
INSULTED

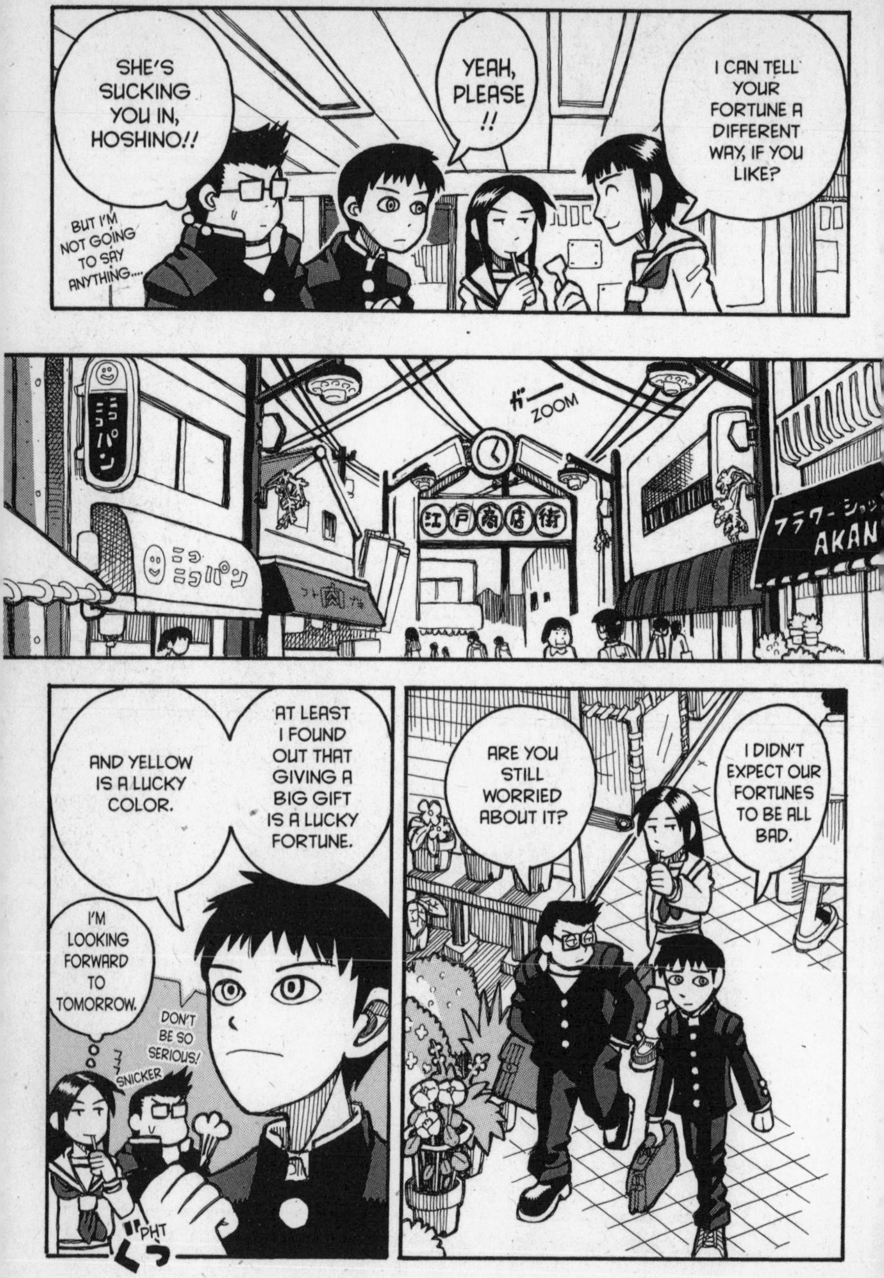
I CAN TELL YOUR FORTUNE A DIFFERENT WAY, IF YOU LIKE?
YEAH, PLEASE!!
SHE'S SUCKING YOU IN, HOSHINO!!
BUT I'M NOT GOING TO SAY ANYTHING....
ガー ZOOM
江戸商店街
フラワーショッ AKAN
ニコニコパン
I DIDN'T EXPECT OUR FORTUNES TO BE ALL BAD.
ARE YOU STILL WORRIED ABOUT IT?
AT LEAST I FOUND OUT THAT GIVING A BIG GIFT IS A LUCKY FORTUNE.
AND YELLOW IS A LUCKY COLOR.
I'M LOOKING FORWARD TO TOMORROW.
DON'T BE SO SERIOUS!
SNICKER
PHT

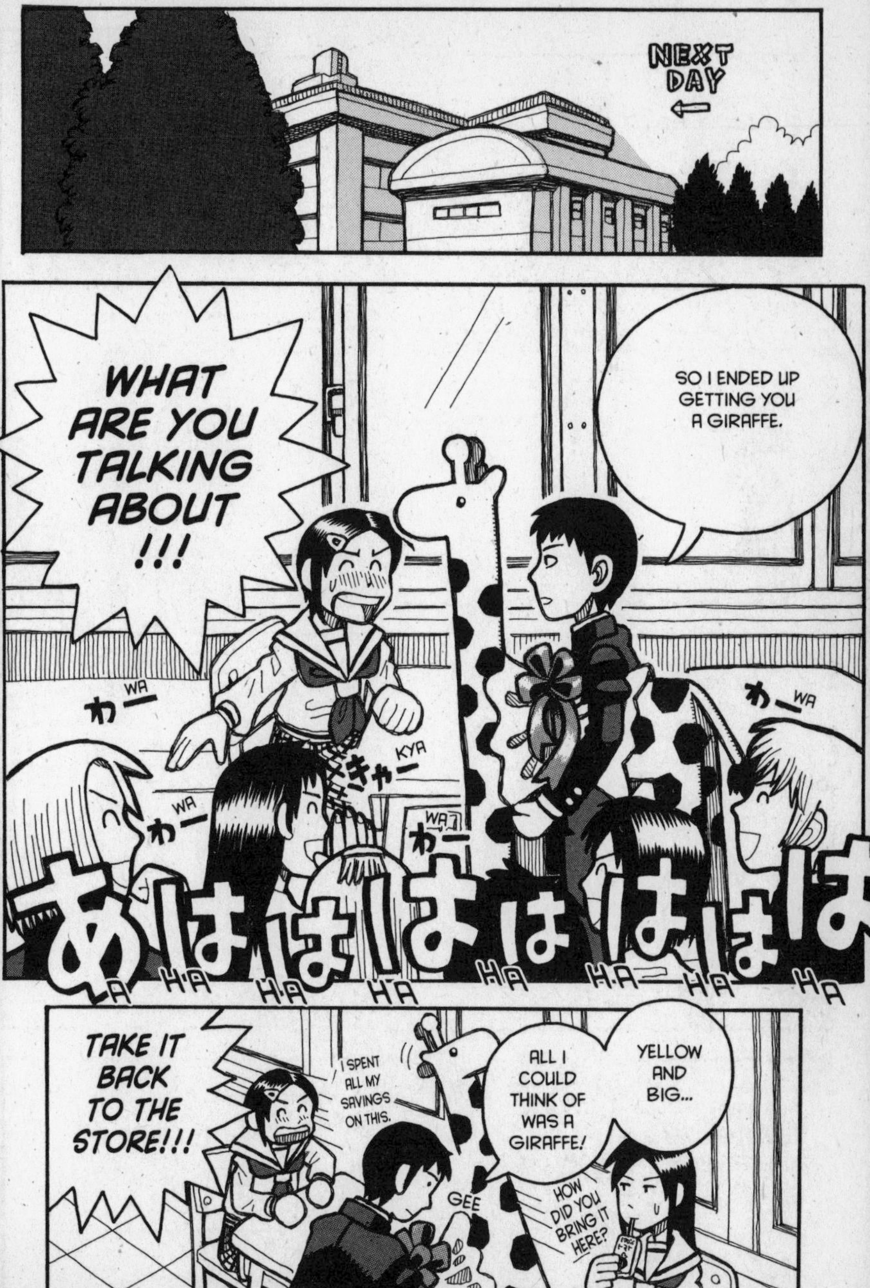
NEXT DAY
SO I ENDED UP GETTING YOU A GIRAFFE.
WHAT ARE YOU TALKING ABOUT !!!
わー WA
きゃー KYA
わー WA
わー WA
わー WA
あははははははは A HA HA HA HA HA HA HA
YELLOW AND BIG...
ALL I COULD THINK OF WAS A GIRAFFE!
I SPENT ALL MY SAVINGS ON THIS.
TAKE IT BACK TO THE STORE!!!
GEE
HOW DID YOU BRING IT HERE?

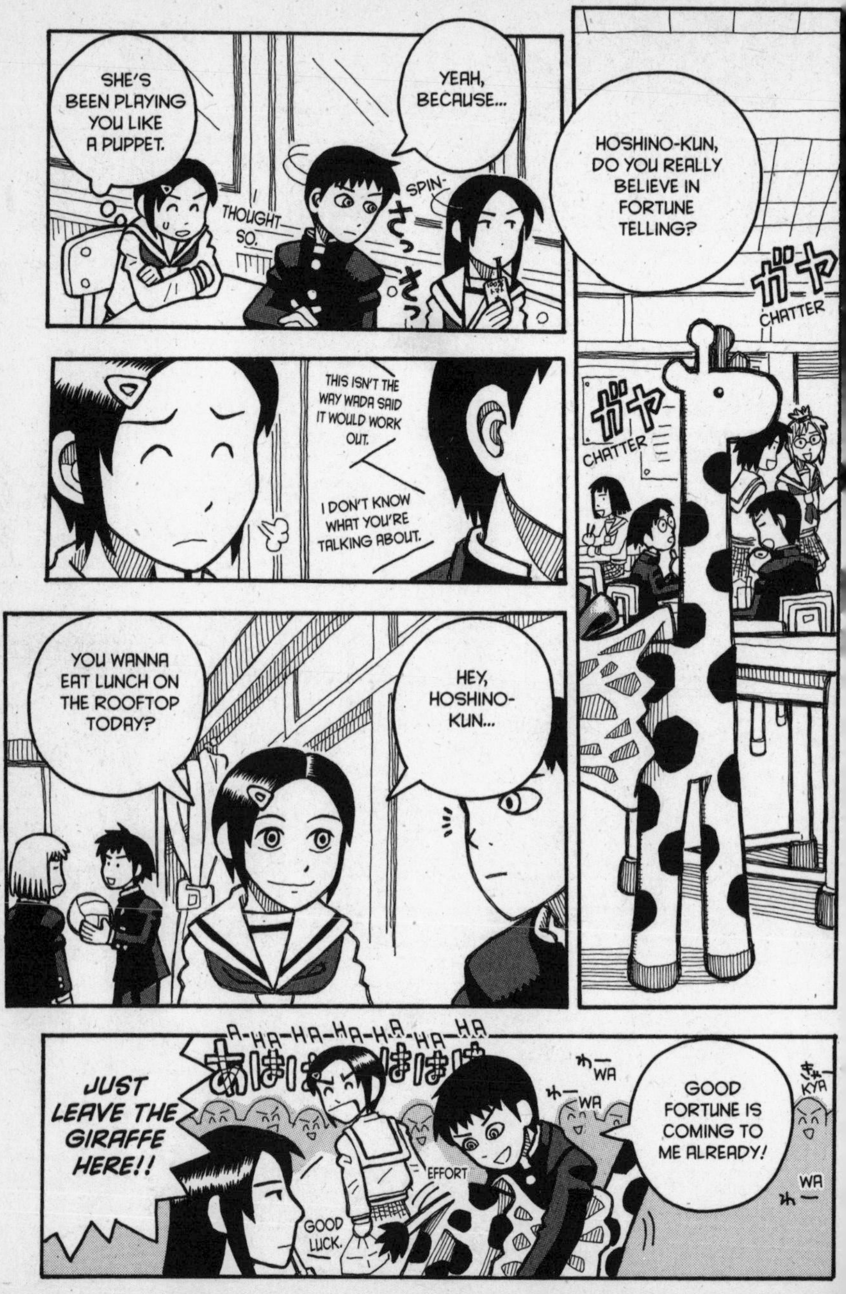
HOSHINO-KUN, DO YOU REALLY BELIEVE IN FORTUNE TELLING?
ガヤ CHATTER
ガヤ CHATTER
YEAH, BECAUSE...
SPIN- さっさっ
I THOUGHT SO.
SHE'S BEEN PLAYING YOU LIKE A PUPPET.
THIS ISN'T THE WAY WADA SAID IT WOULD WORK OUT.
I DON'T KNOW WHAT YOU'RE TALKING ABOUT.
HEY, HOSHINO-KUN...
YOU WANNA EAT LUNCH ON THE ROOFTOP TODAY?
きゃー KYA
わー WA
わー WA
GOOD FORTUNE IS COMING TO ME ALREADY!
WA わー
EFFORT
A-HA-HA-HA-HA-HA-HA-HA
GOOD LUCK.
JUST LEAVE THE GIRAFFE HERE!!

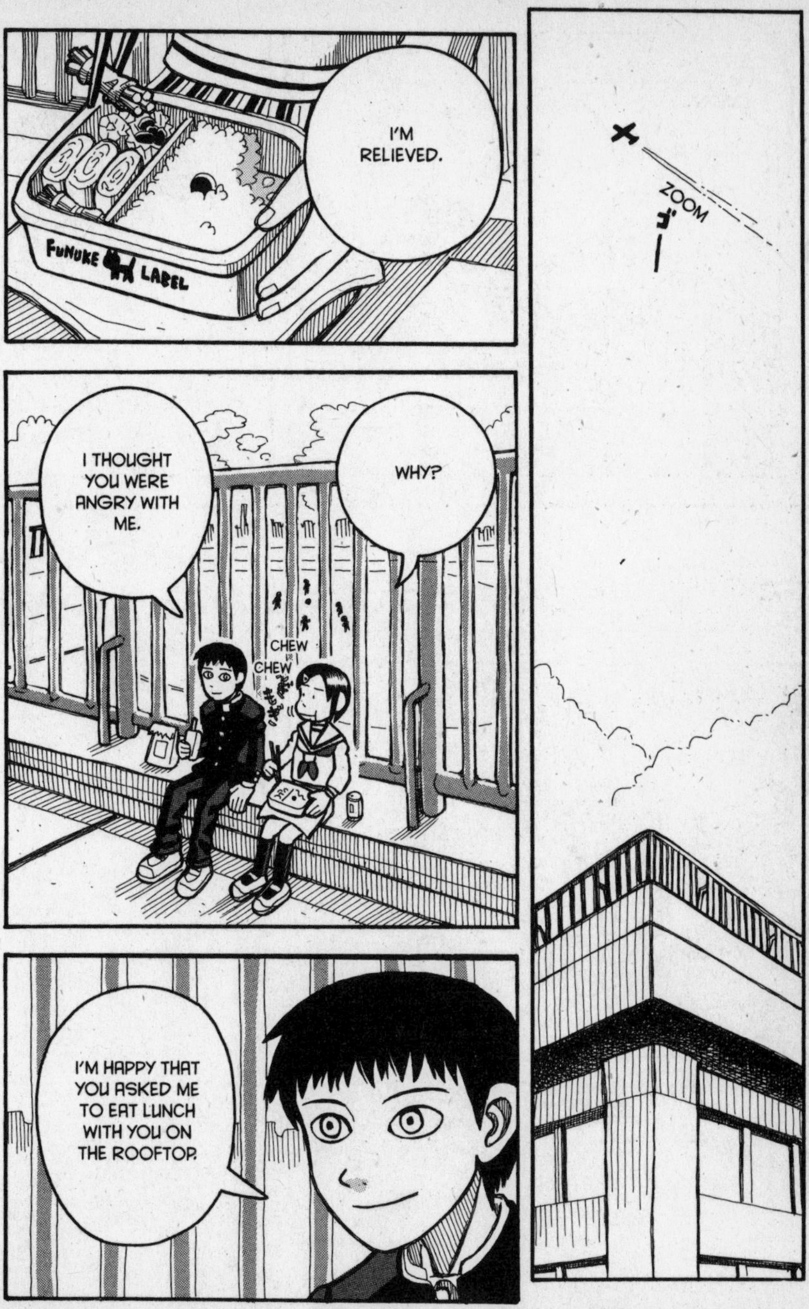
ZOOM
ゴー
FUNUKE LABEL
I'M RELIEVED.
WHY?
I THOUGHT YOU WERE ANGRY WITH ME.
CHEW CHEW
I'M HAPPY THAT YOU ASKED ME TO EAT LUNCH WITH YOU ON THE ROOFTOP.

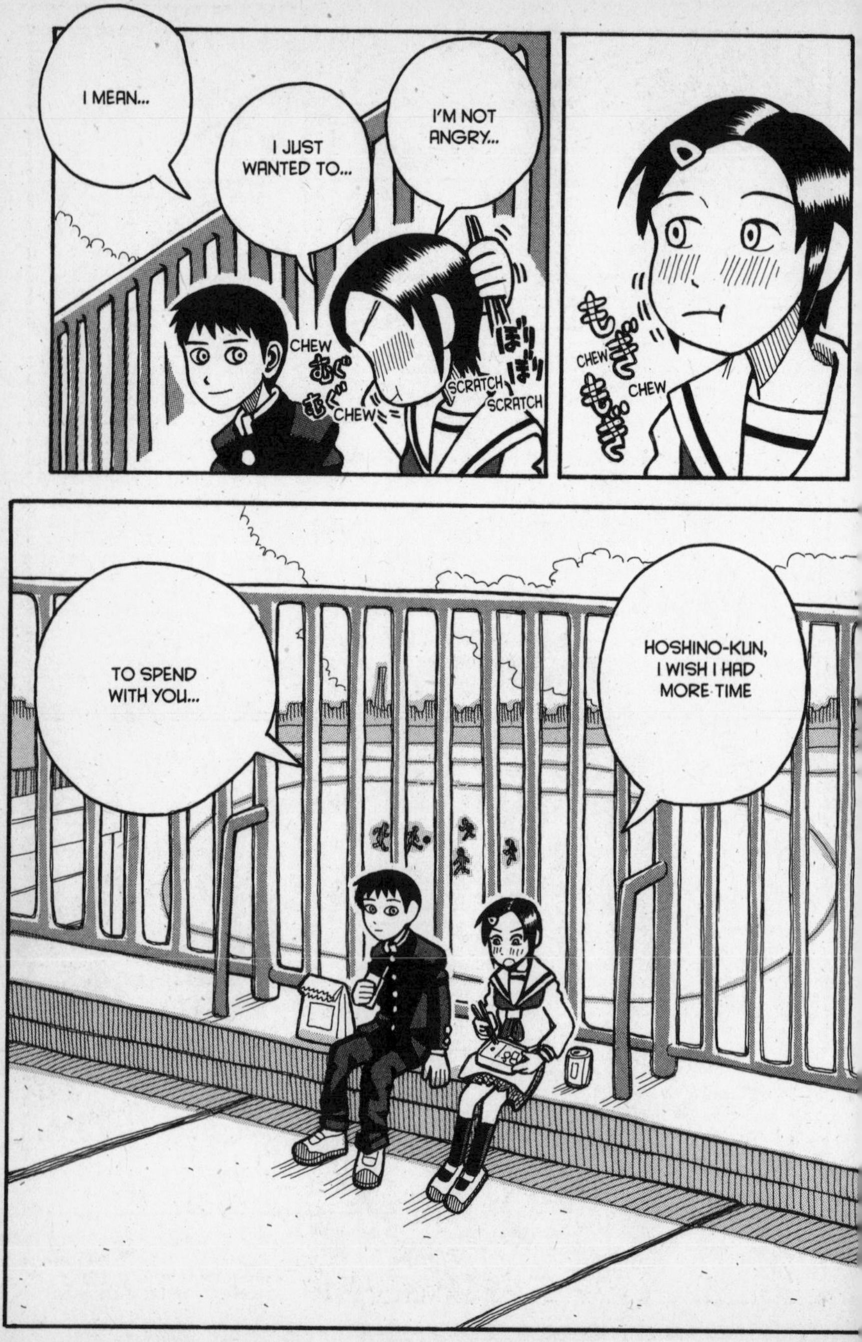
CHEW
CHEW
I'M NOT ANGRY...
I JUST WANTED TO...
I MEAN...
SCRATCH
SCRATCH
CHEW
CHEW
HOSHINO-KUN, I WISH I HAD MORE TIME
TO SPEND WITH YOU...

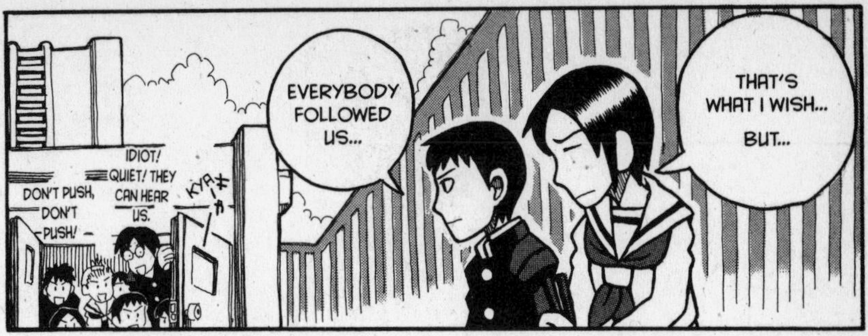
THAT'S WHAT I WISH... BUT...
EVERYBODY FOLLOWED US...
IDIOT! QUIET! THEY CAN HEAR US.
KYA キャー
DON'T PUSH, DON'T PUSH!

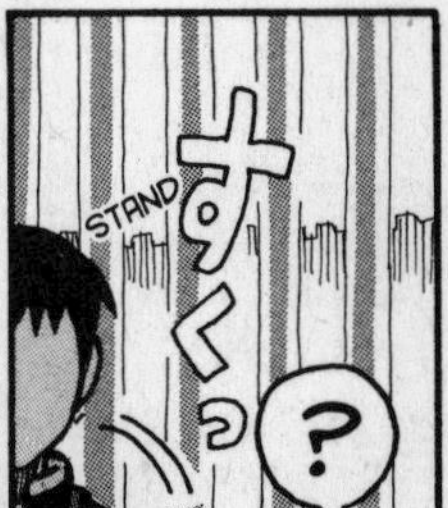
すくっ STAND
?

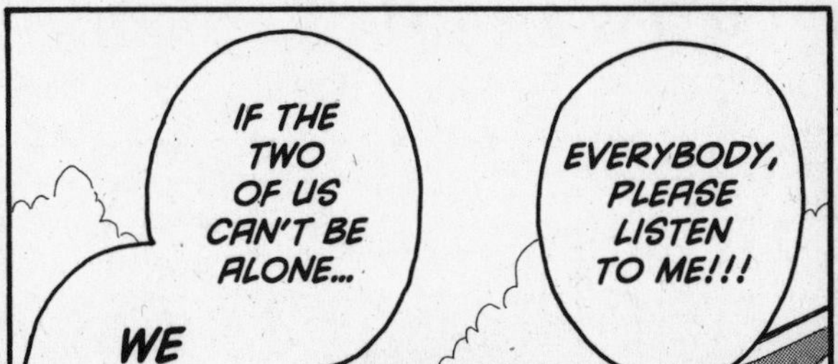
EVERYBODY, PLEASE LISTEN TO ME!!!
IF THE TWO OF US CAN'T BE ALONE...
WE CAN'T KISS!!

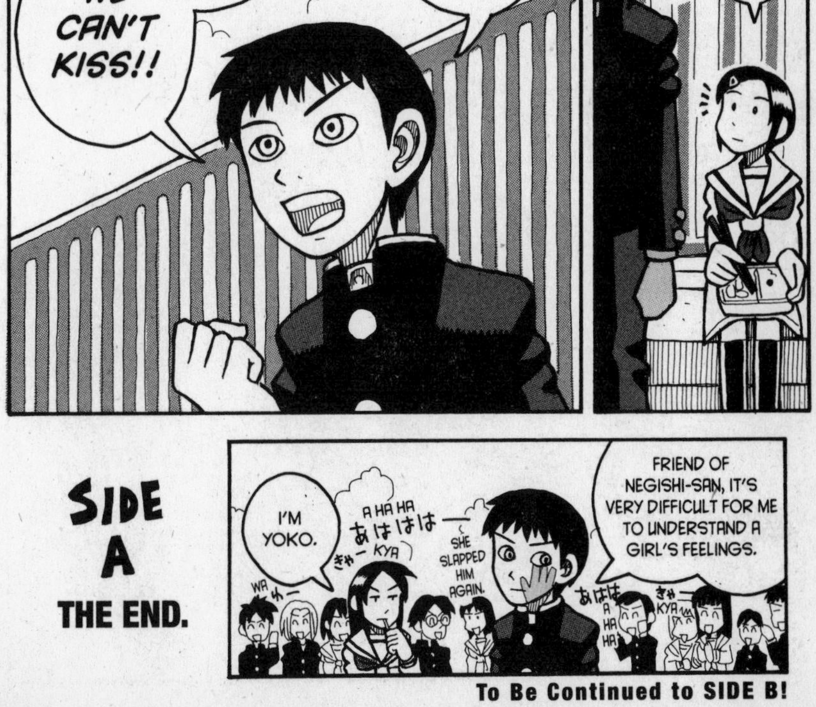
FRIEND OF NEGISHI-SAN, IT'S VERY DIFFICULT FOR ME TO UNDERSTAND A GIRL'S FEELINGS.
きゃー KYA
あはは A HA HA
SHE SLAPPED HIM AGAIN.
あははは— A HA HA
きゃー KYA
I'M YOKO.
わー WA

SIDE A

THE END.

To Be Continued to SIDE B!

TRACK #0

SIDE B

NEGISHI'S DREAM
HOSHINO'S DREAM

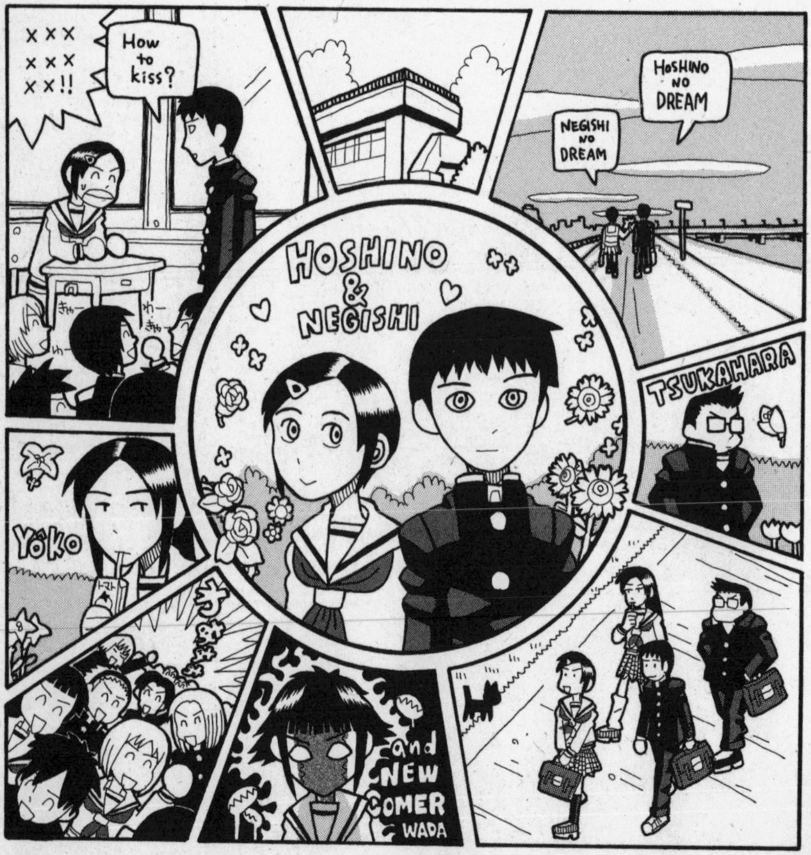
HOSHINO NO DREAM
NEGISHI NO DREAM
How to kiss?
××× ××× ××!!
HOSHINO & NEGISHI
TSUKAHARA
YŌKO
and NEW COMER WADA

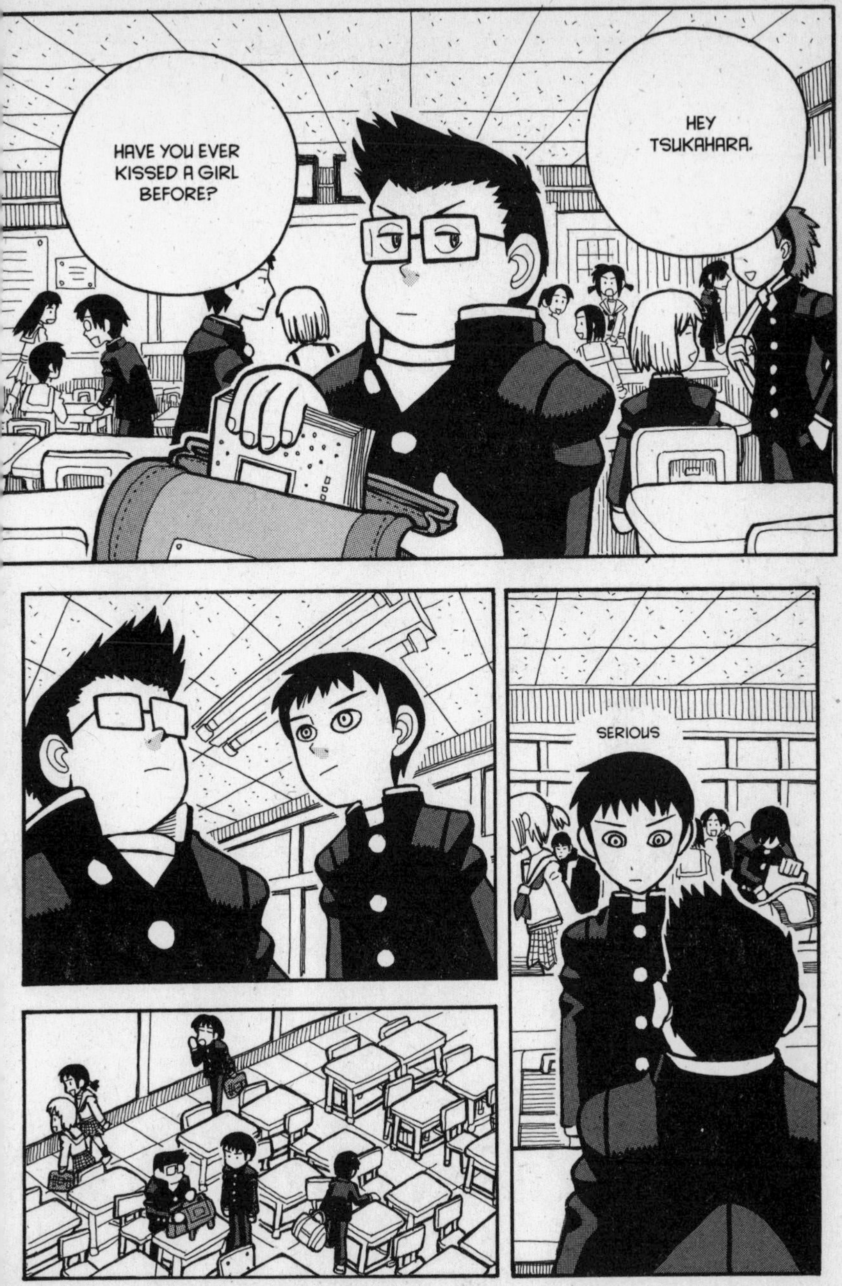
HEY TSUKAHARA.
HAVE YOU EVER KISSED A GIRL BEFORE?
SERIOUS

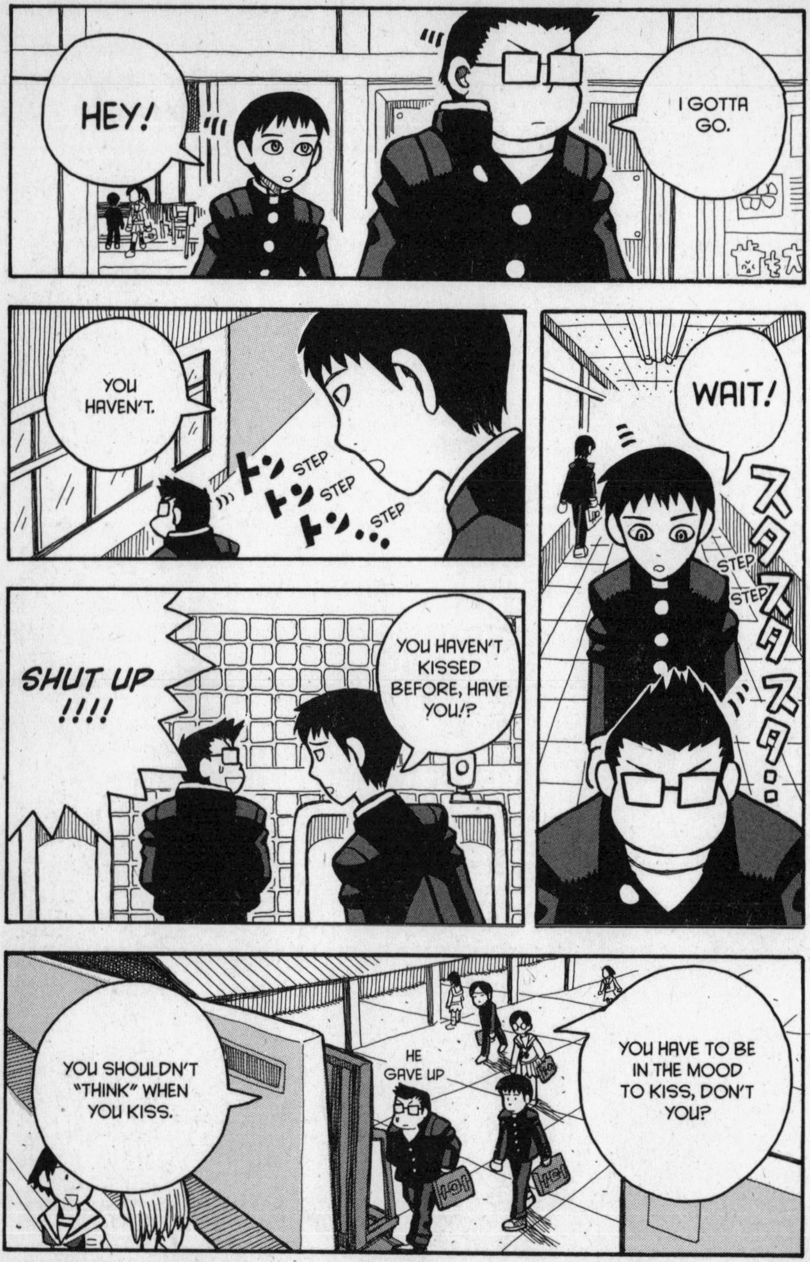
I GOTTA GO.
HEY!
WAIT!
STEP
STEP
スタスタスタ...
バ
YOU HAVEN'T.
トン STEP
トン STEP
トン... STEP
YOU HAVEN'T KISSED BEFORE, HAVE YOU!?
SHUT UP !!!!
YOU HAVE TO BE IN THE MOOD TO KISS, DON'T YOU?
HE GAVE UP
YOU SHOULDN'T "THINK" WHEN YOU KISS.

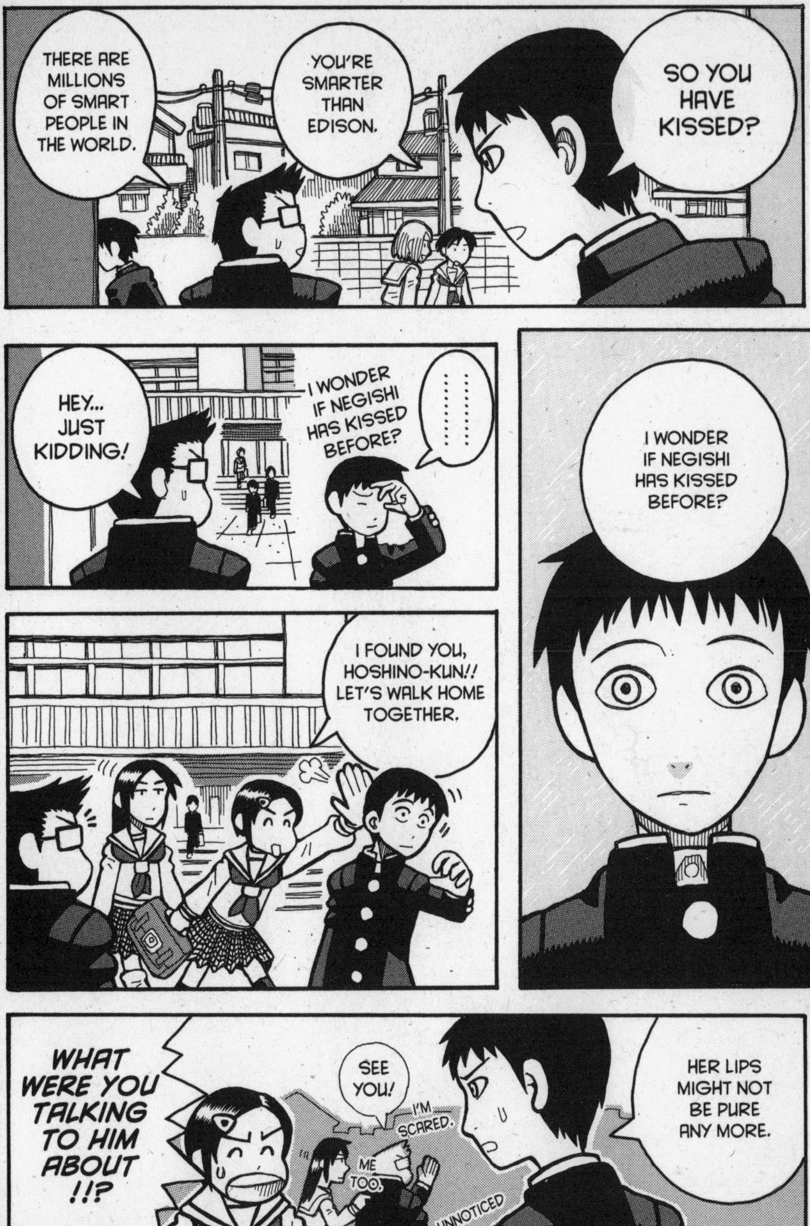
SO YOU HAVE KISSED?
YOU'RE SMARTER THAN EDISON.
THERE ARE MILLIONS OF SMART PEOPLE IN THE WORLD.
I WONDER IF NEGISHI HAS KISSED BEFORE?
......
I WONDER IF NEGISHI HAS KISSED BEFORE?
HEY... JUST KIDDING!
I FOUND YOU, HOSHINO-KUN!! LET'S WALK HOME TOGETHER.
HER LIPS MIGHT NOT BE PURE ANY MORE.
I'M SCARED.
SEE YOU!
UNNOTICED
ME TOO.
WHAT WERE YOU TALKING TO HIM ABOUT!!?

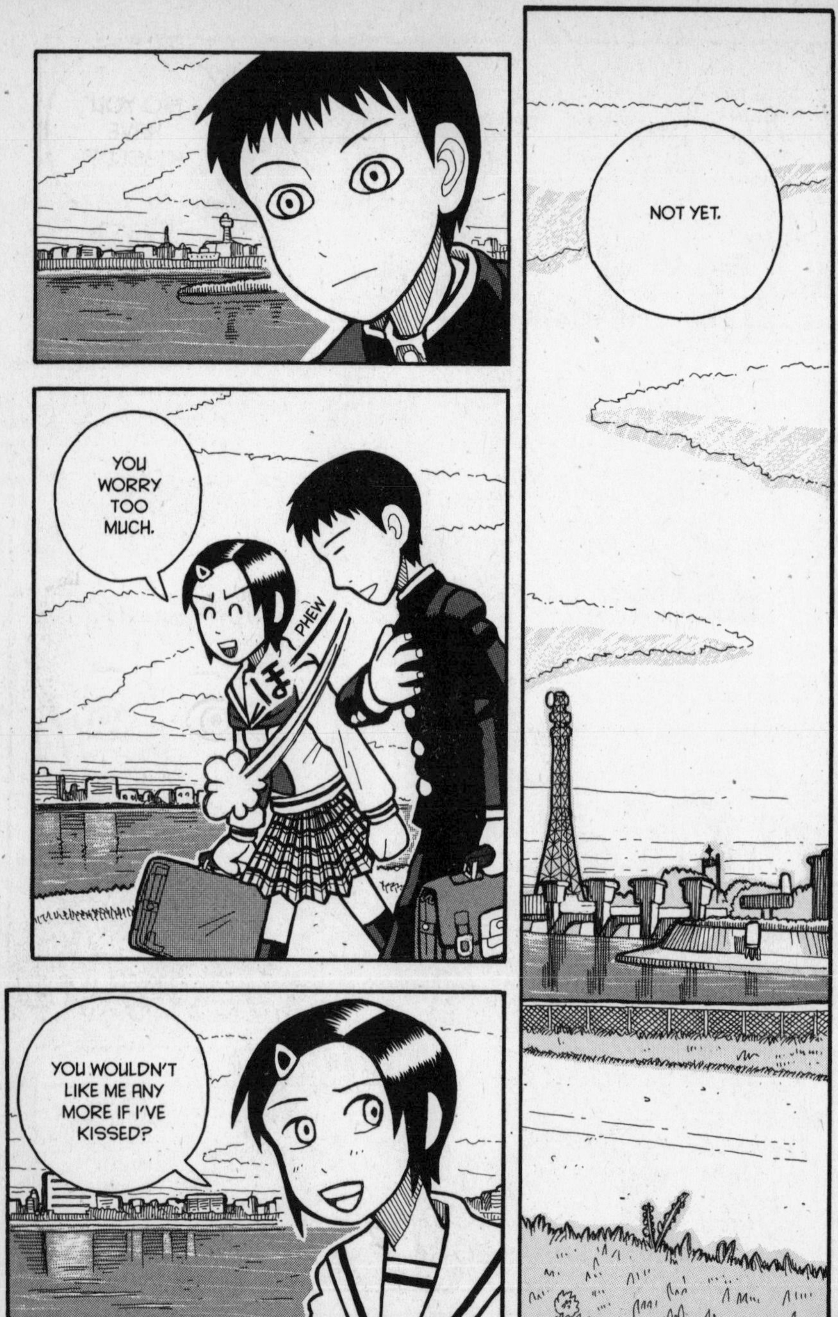
NOT YET.
YOU WORRY TOO MUCH.
PHEW
ほ
YOU WOULDN'T LIKE ME ANY MORE IF I'VE KISSED?

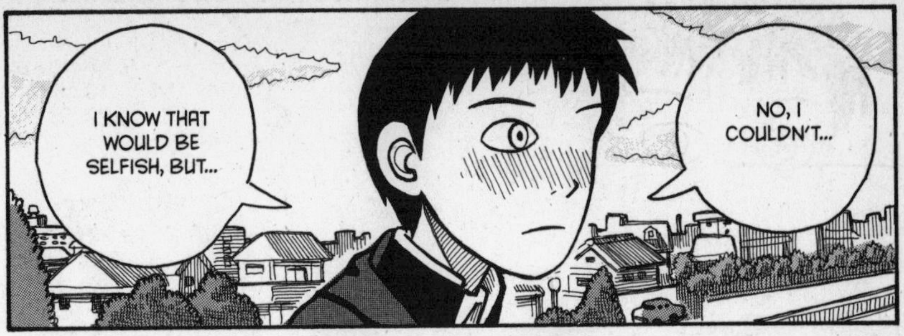
NO, I COULDN'T...
I KNOW THAT WOULD BE SELFISH, BUT...

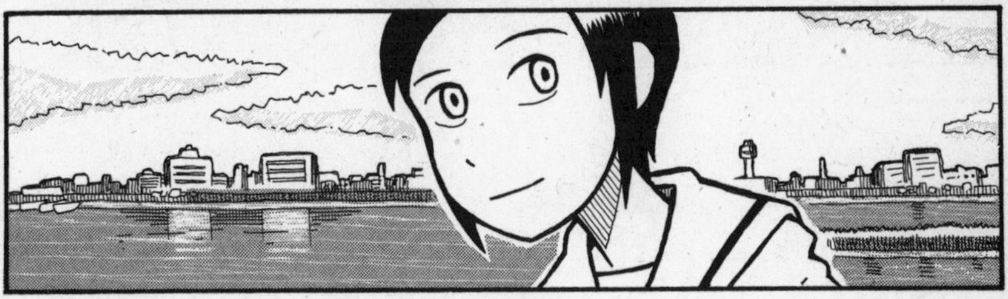

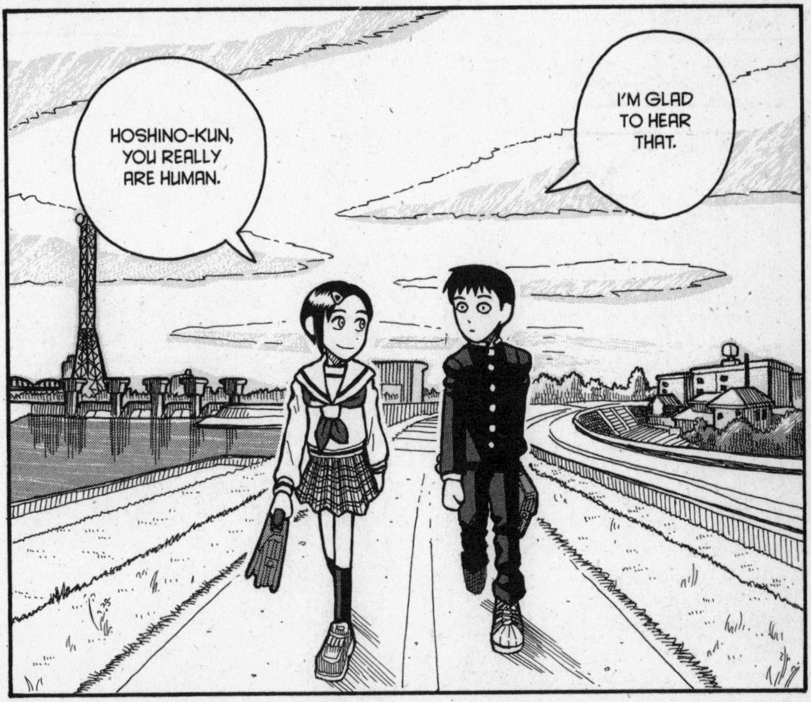
I'M GLAD TO HEAR THAT.
HOSHINO-KUN, YOU REALLY ARE HUMAN.

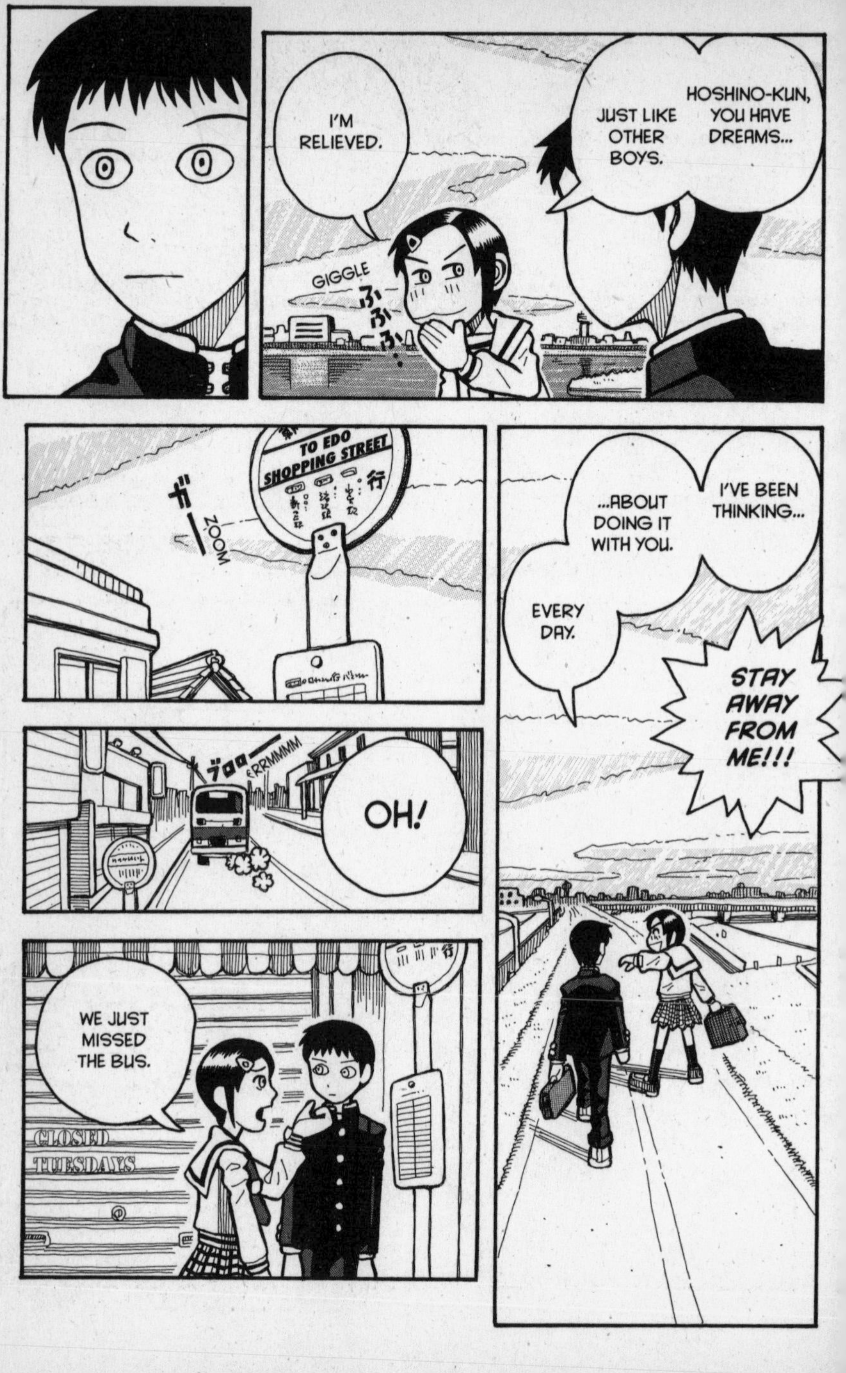
HOSHINO-KUN, YOU HAVE DREAMS...
JUST LIKE OTHER BOYS.
I'M RELIEVED.
GIGGLE
ふふふ…
I'VE BEEN THINKING...
...ABOUT DOING IT WITH YOU.
EVERY DAY.
STAY AWAY FROM ME!!!
TO EDO SHOPPING STREET
行
ガー
ZOOM
ブロロー
ERRMMMM
OH!
WE JUST MISSED THE BUS.
CLOSED TUESDAYS

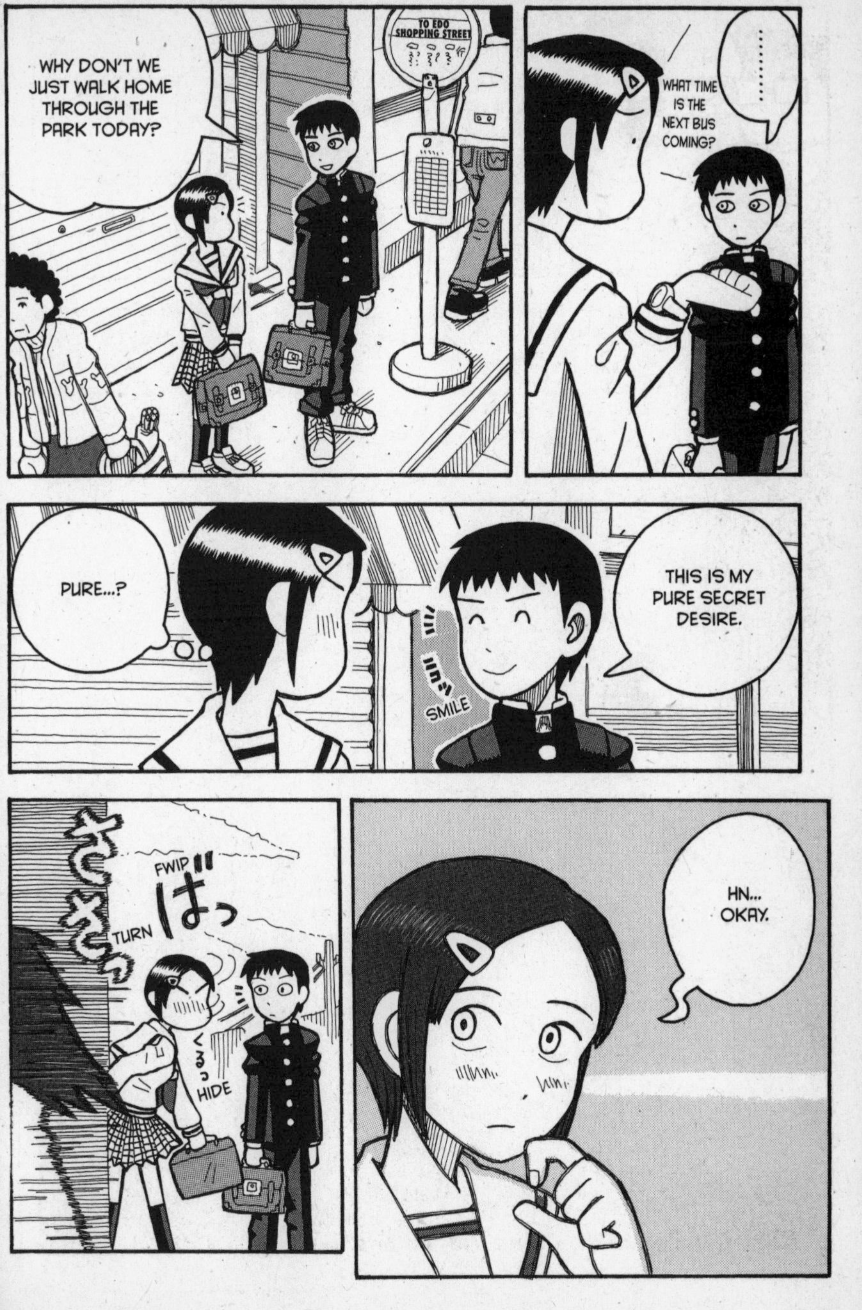
......
WHAT TIME IS THE NEXT BUS COMING?
TO EDO SHOPPING STREET
WHY DON'T WE JUST WALK HOME THROUGH THE PARK TODAY?
THIS IS MY PURE SECRET DESIRE.
SMILE
PURE...?
HN... OKAY.
ささっ
ばっ
FWIP
TURN
くるっ
HIDE

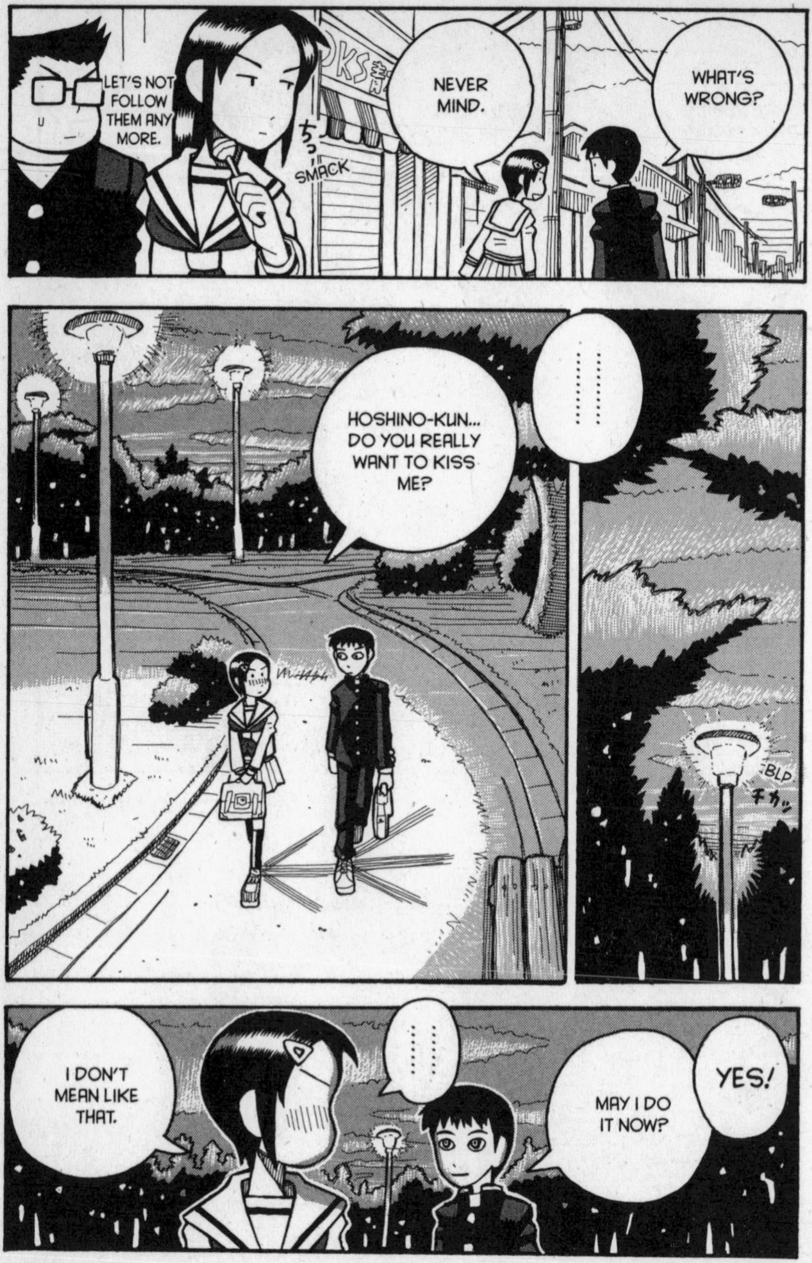
WHAT'S WRONG?
NEVER MIND.
LET'S NOT FOLLOW THEM ANY MORE.
ちっ
SMACK
.....
BLP
チカッ
HOSHINO-KUN... DO YOU REALLY WANT TO KISS ME?
YES!
MAY I DO IT NOW?
.....
I DON'T MEAN LIKE THAT.

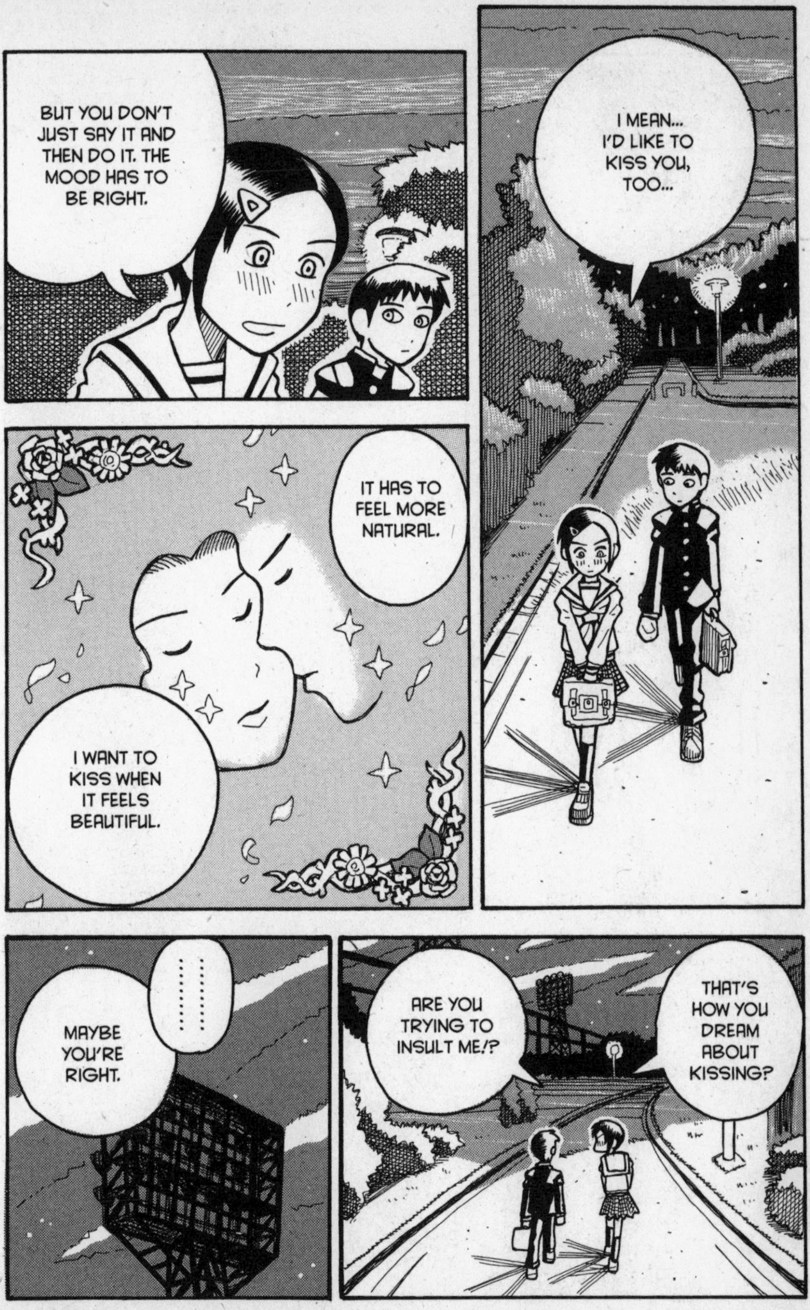
I MEAN... I'D LIKE TO KISS YOU, TOO...
BUT YOU DON'T JUST SAY IT AND THEN DO IT. THE MOOD HAS TO BE RIGHT.
IT HAS TO FEEL MORE NATURAL.
I WANT TO KISS WHEN IT FEELS BEAUTIFUL.
THAT'S HOW YOU DREAM ABOUT KISSING?
ARE YOU TRYING TO INSULT ME!?
......
MAYBE YOU'RE RIGHT.

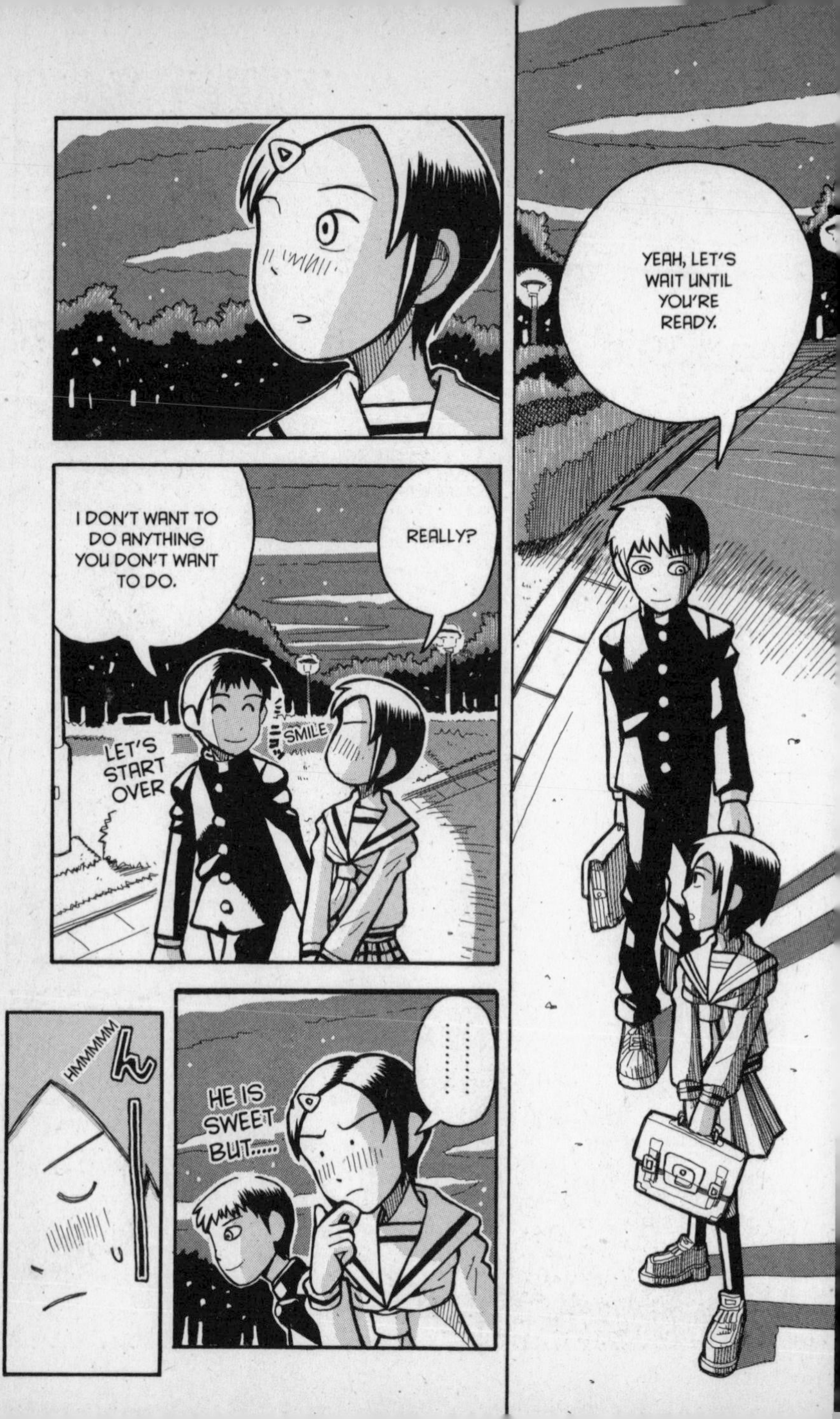
YEAH, LET'S WAIT UNTIL YOU'RE READY.
REALLY?
I DON'T WANT TO DO ANYTHING YOU DON'T WANT TO DO.
SMILE
LET'S START OVER
......
HE IS SWEET BUT.....
HMMMMM

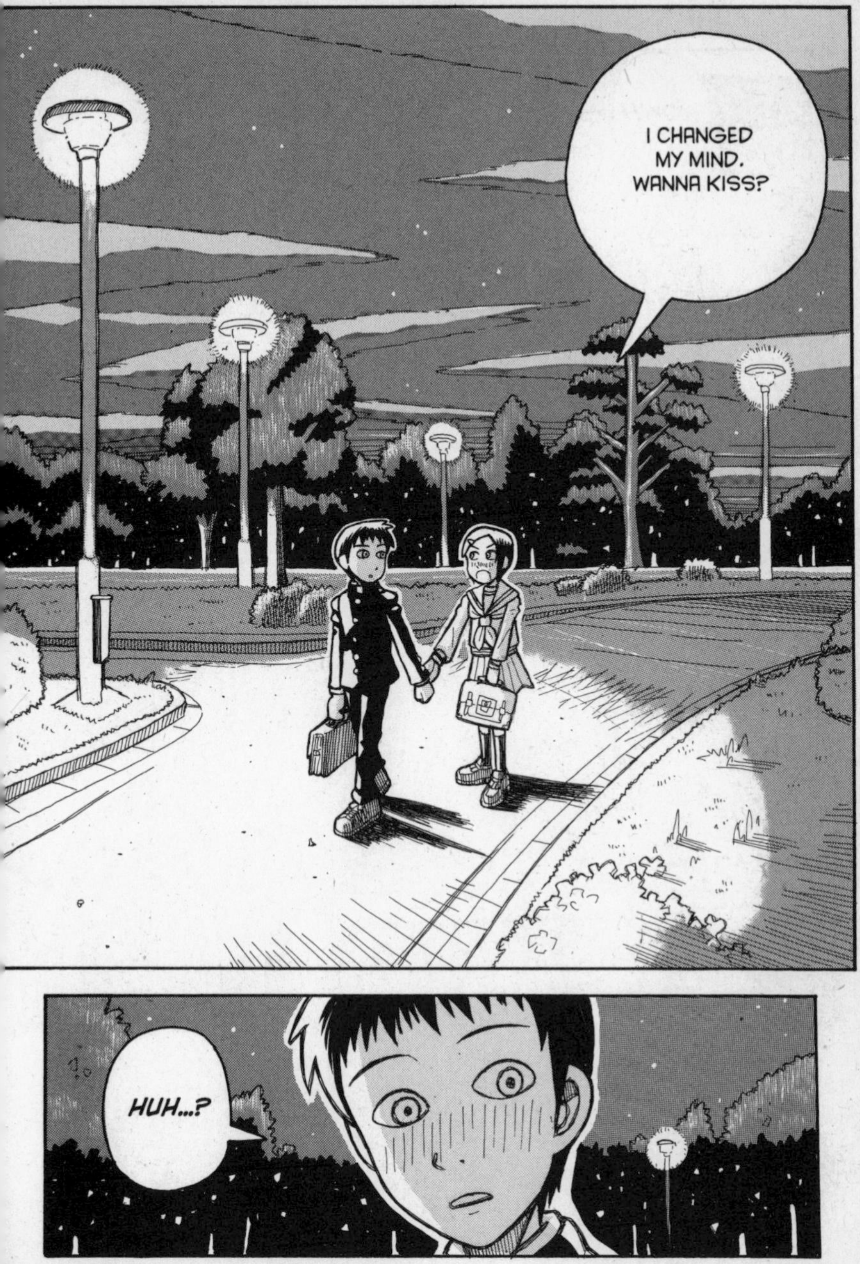
I CHANGED MY MIND. WANNA KISS?
HUH...?

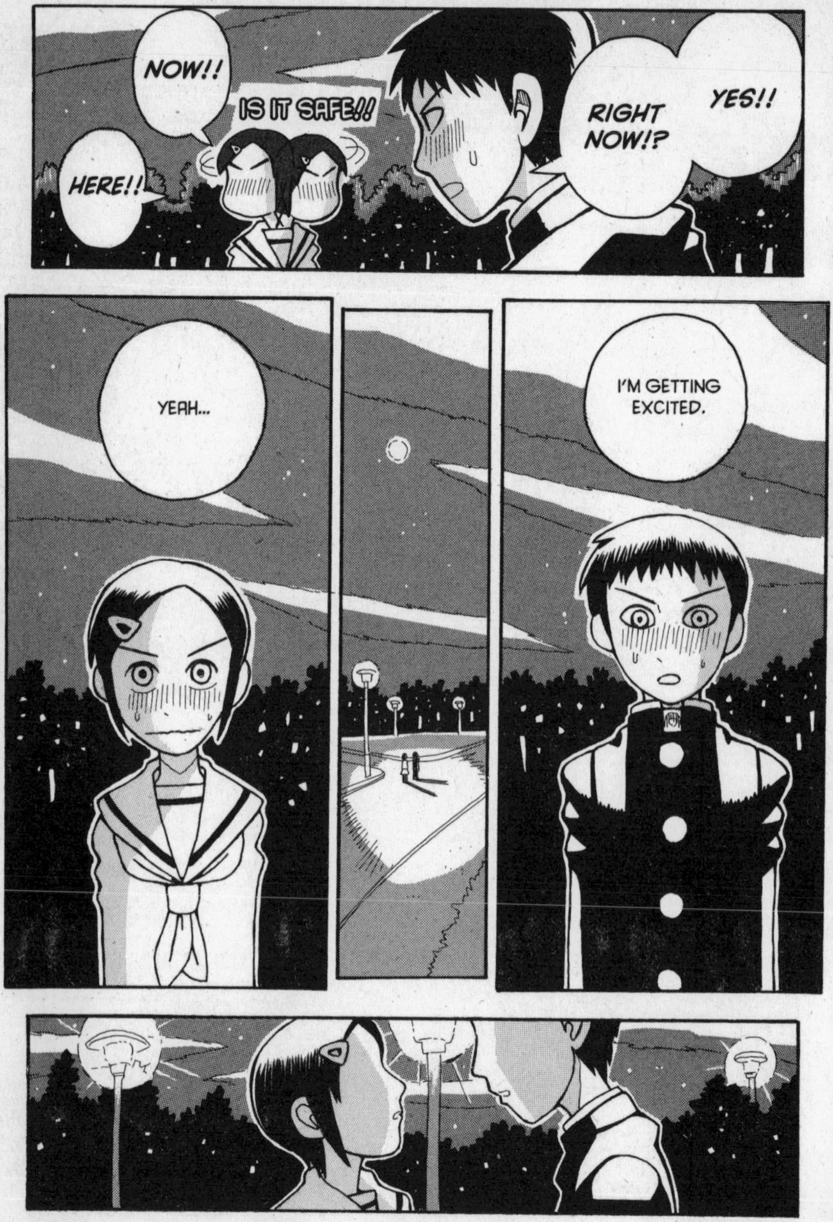
YES!!
RIGHT NOW!?
IS IT SAFE!!
NOW!!
HERE!!
I'M GETTING EXCITED.
YEAH...

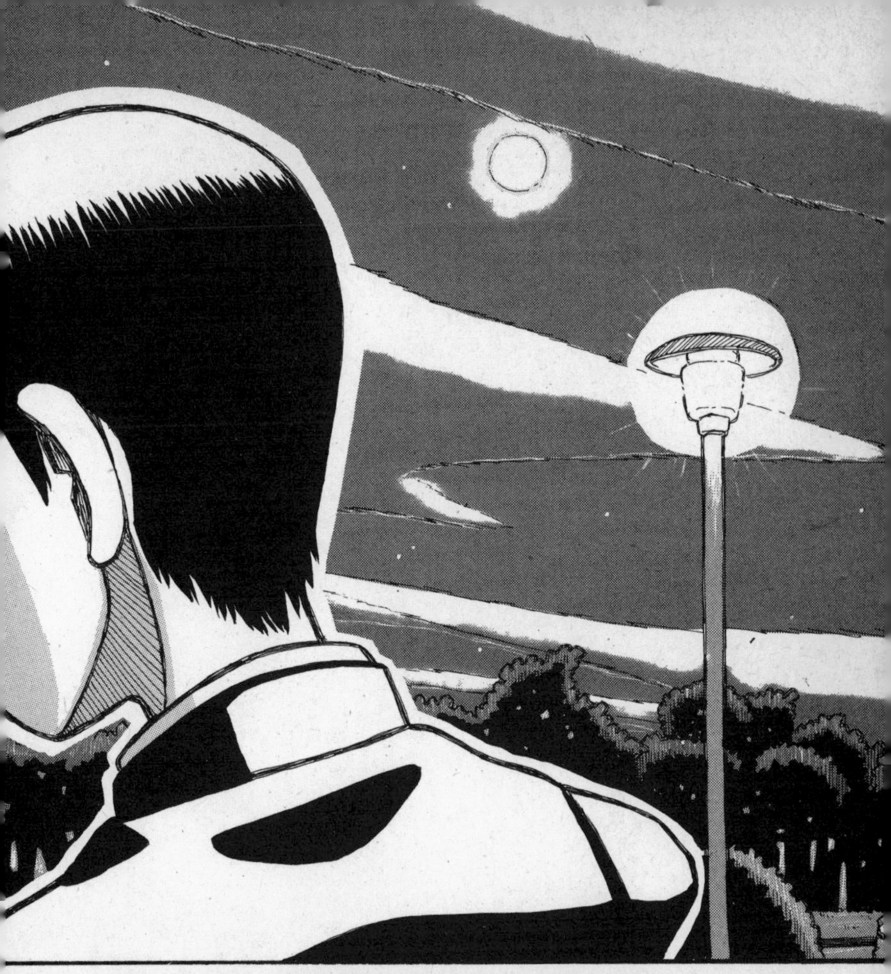
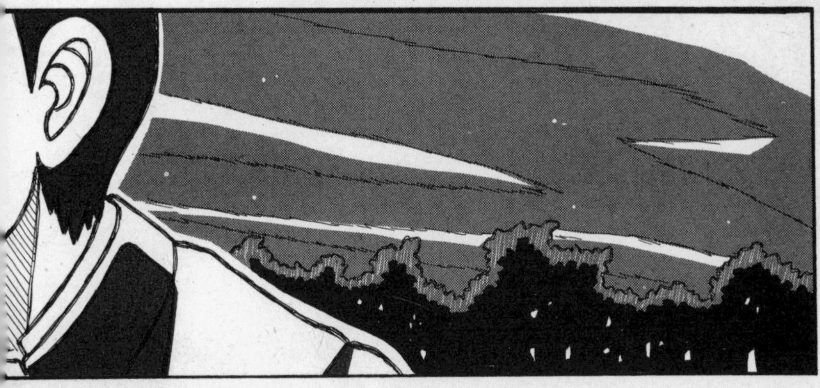

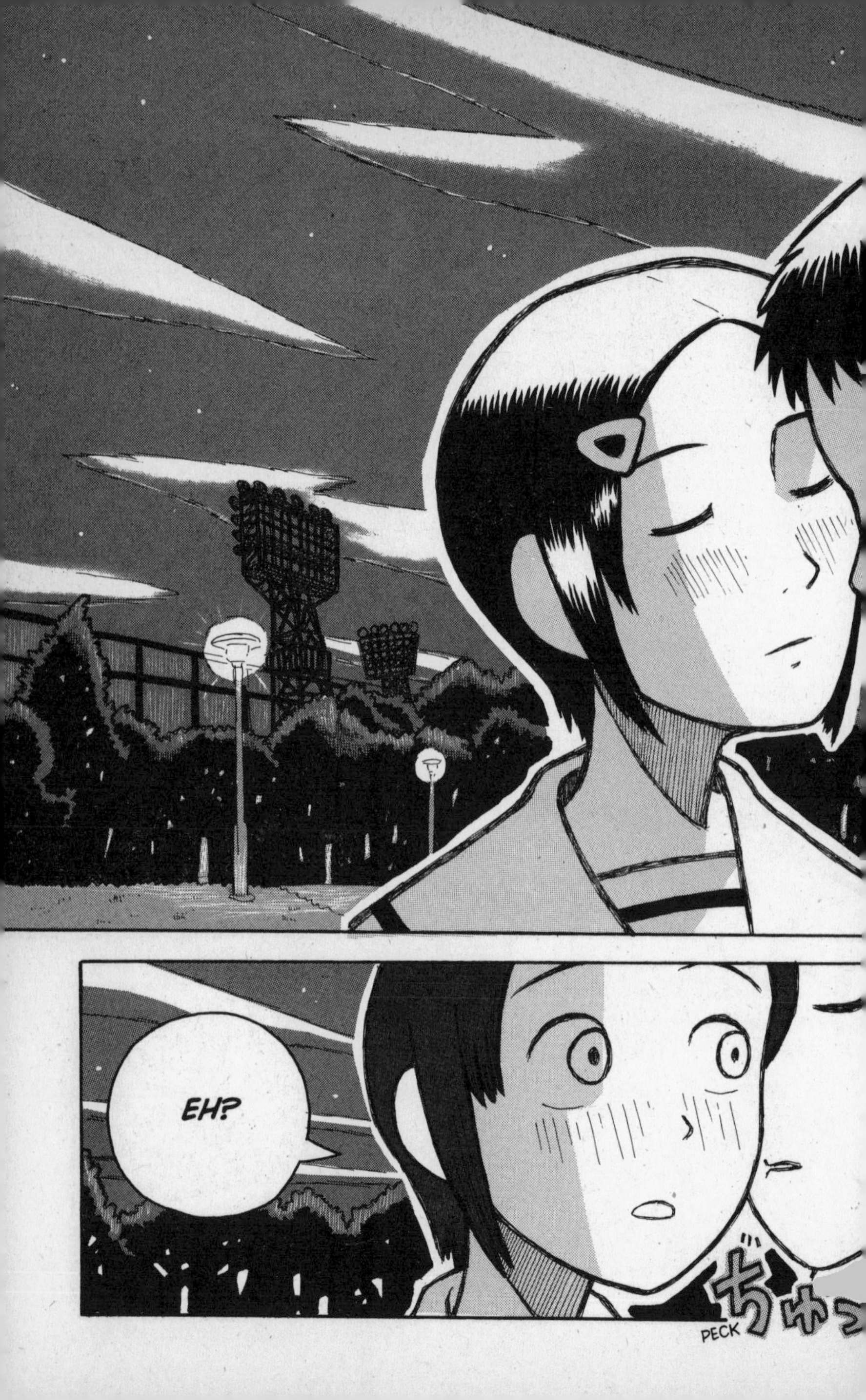
EH?
ぢゅっ
PECK

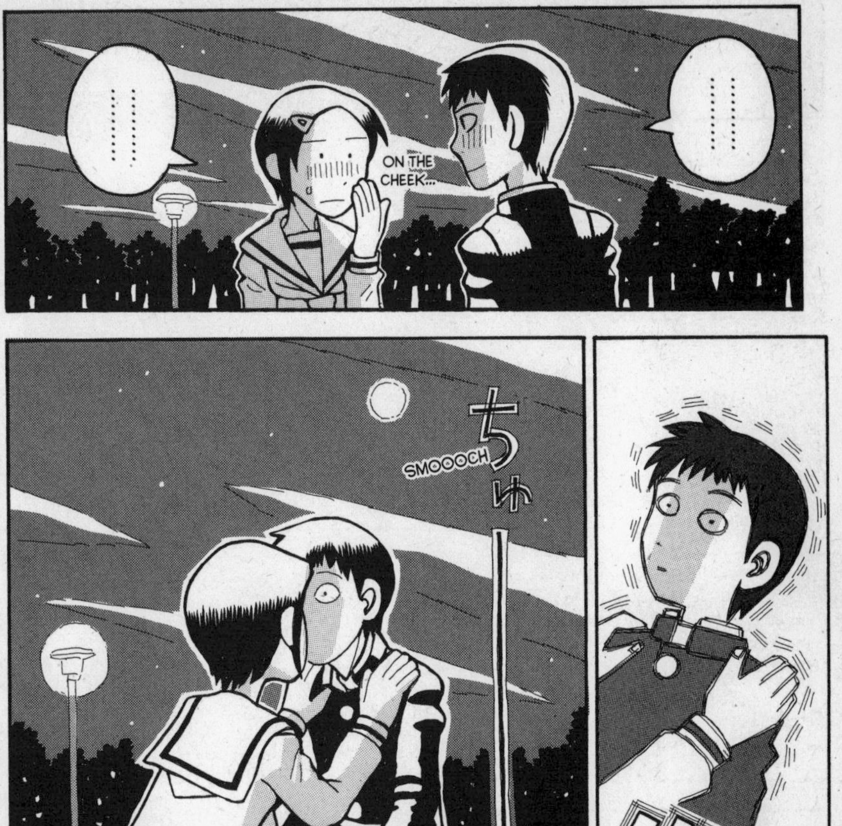
......
ON THE CHEEK...
......
ガシッ
TENSE
ちゅー
SMOOOCH
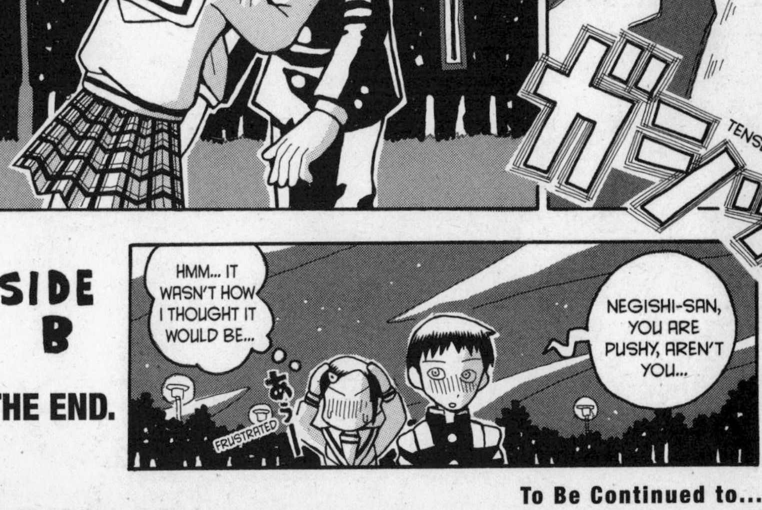
NEGISHI-SAN, YOU ARE PUSHY, AREN'T YOU...
HMM... IT WASN'T HOW I THOUGHT IT WOULD BE...
あう
FRUSTRATED

SIDE B

THE END.

To Be Continued to...

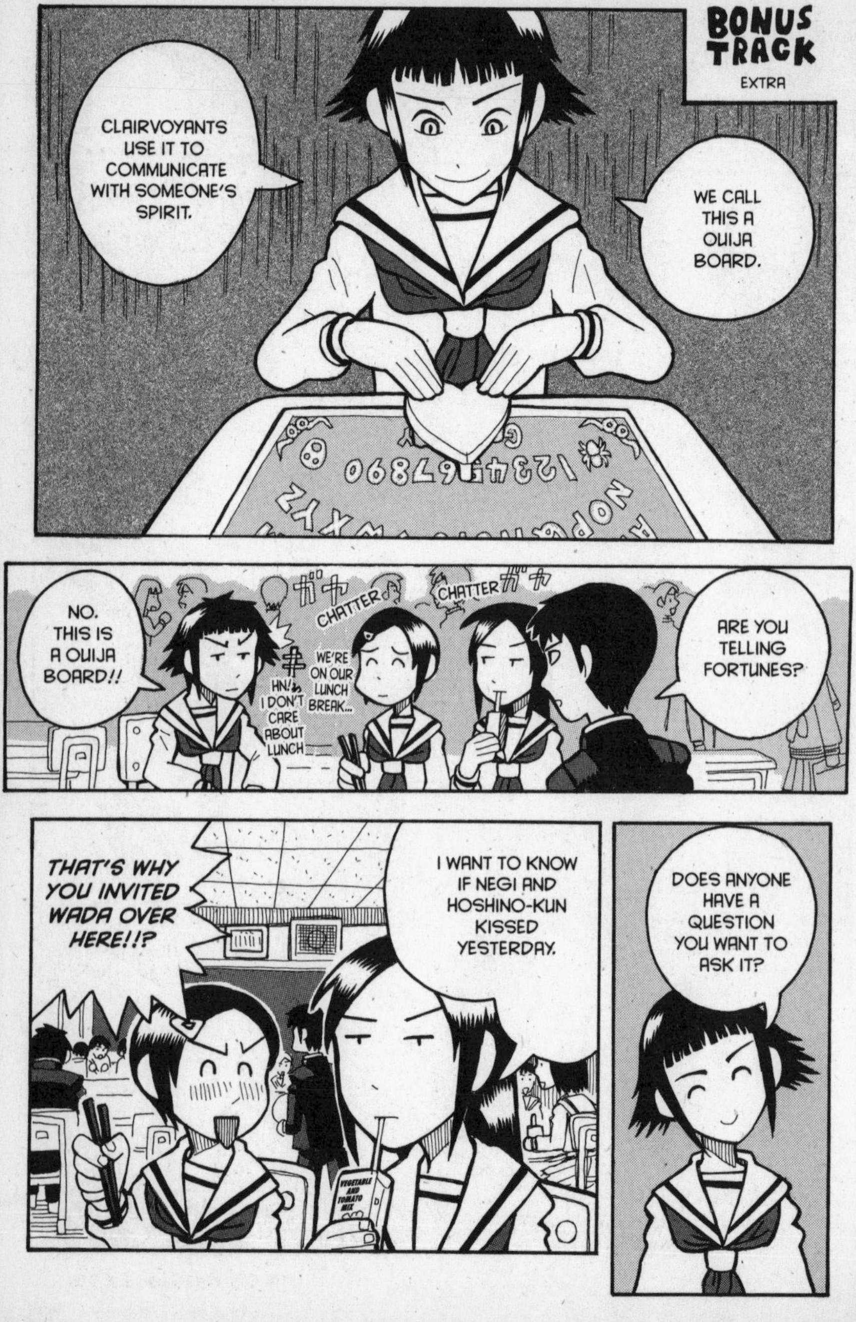
BONUS TRACK
EXTRA
WE CALL THIS A OUIJA BOARD.
CLAIRVOYANTS USE IT TO COMMUNICATE WITH SOMEONE'S SPIRIT.
ARE YOU TELLING FORTUNES?
CHATTER
CHATTER
NO. THIS IS A OUIJA BOARD!!
WE'RE ON OUR LUNCH BREAK...
HN! I DON'T CARE ABOUT LUNCH
DOES ANYONE HAVE A QUESTION YOU WANT TO ASK IT?
I WANT TO KNOW IF NEGI AND HOSHINO-KUN KISSED YESTERDAY.
THAT'S WHY YOU INVITED WADA OVER HERE!!?
VEGETABLE AND TOMATO MIX

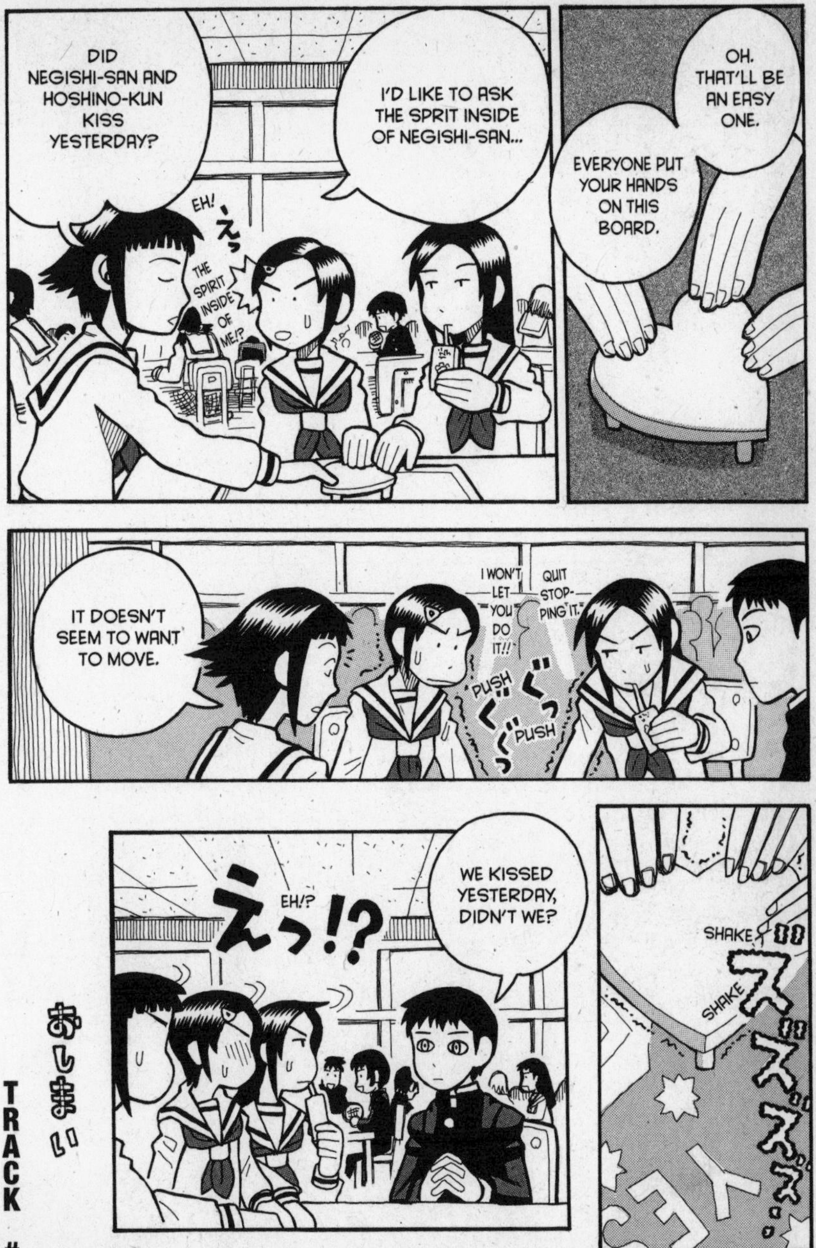
OH. THAT'LL BE AN EASY ONE.
EVERYONE PUT YOUR HANDS ON THIS BOARD.
I'D LIKE TO ASK THE SPRIT INSIDE OF NEGISHI-SAN...
DID NEGISHI-SAN AND HOSHINO-KUN KISS YESTERDAY?
EH! えっ
THE SPIRIT INSIDE OF ME!?
QUIT STOPPING IT.
I WON'T LET YOU DO IT!!
IT DOESN'T SEEM TO WANT TO MOVE.
PUSH ぐっ
PUSH ぐっ
SHAKE
SHAKE
スススス
WE KISSED YESTERDAY, DIDN'T WE?
EH!? えっ!?
おしまい
TRACK #0 ▶▶ END

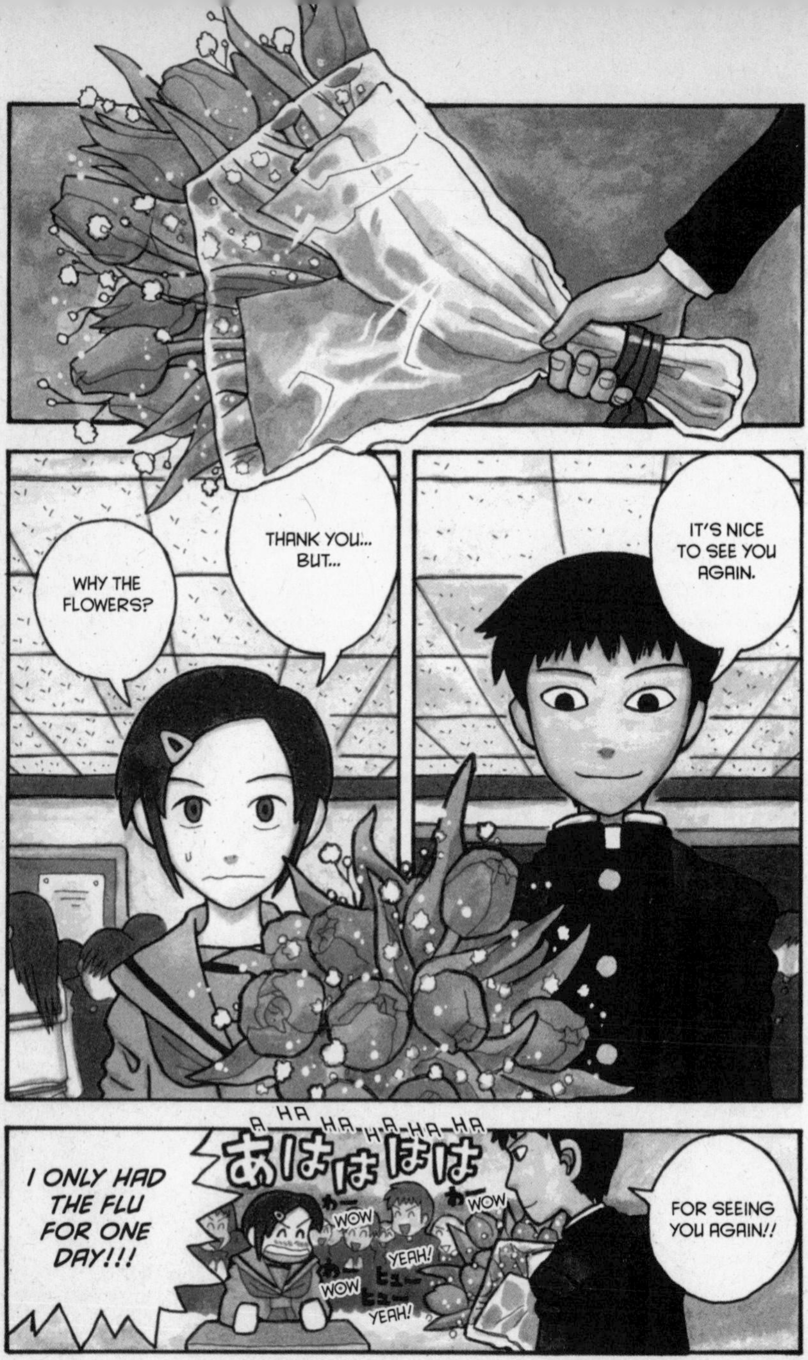

IT'S NICE TO SEE YOU AGAIN.
THANK YOU... BUT...
WHY THE FLOWERS?
FOR SEEING YOU AGAIN!!
A HA HA HA HA HA
あはははは
WOW
WOW
WOW
YEAH!
WOW
YEAH!
I ONLY HAD THE FLU FOR ONE DAY!!!

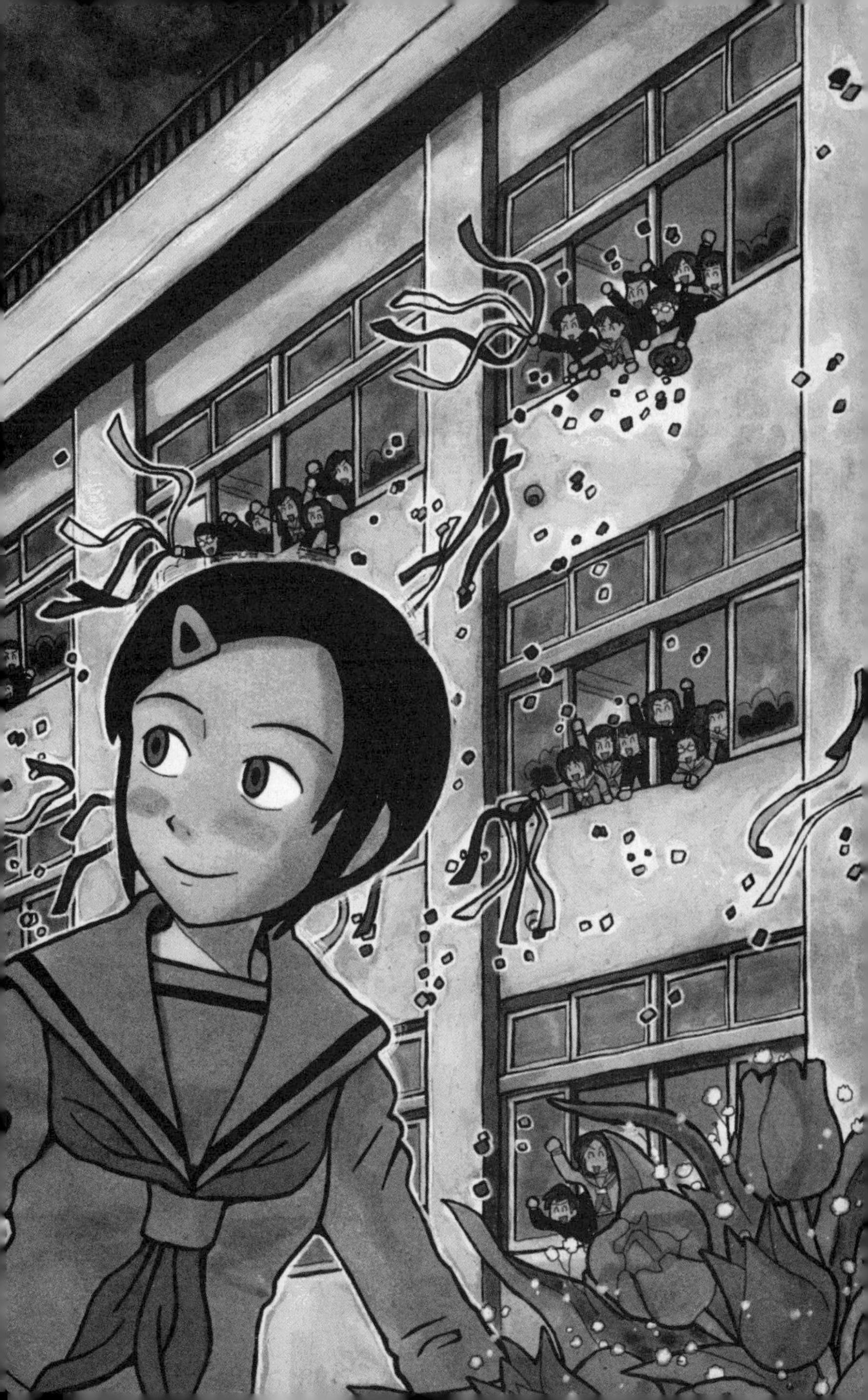

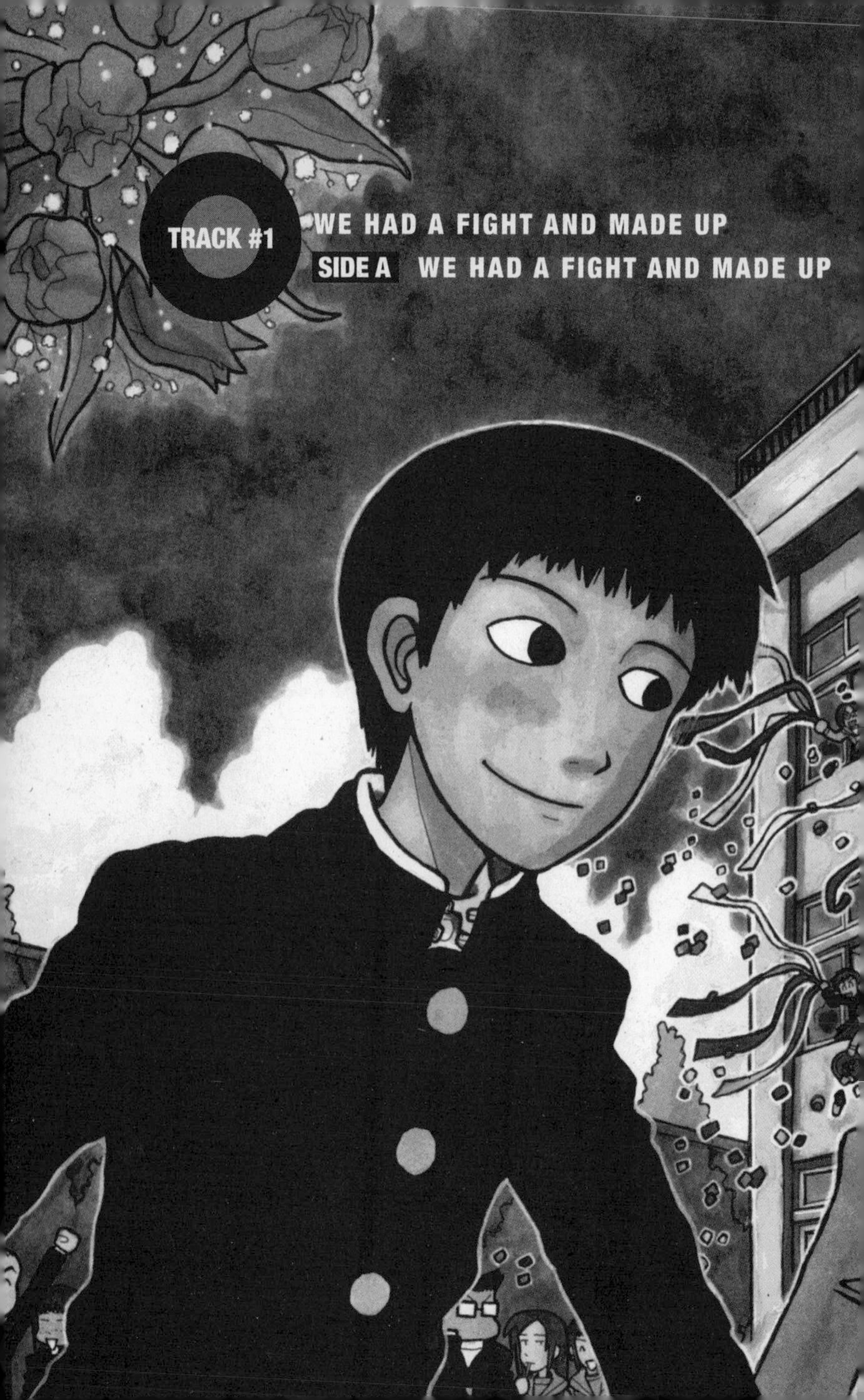
TRACK #1
WE HAD A FIGHT AND MADE UP
SIDE A WE HAD A FIGHT AND MADE UP

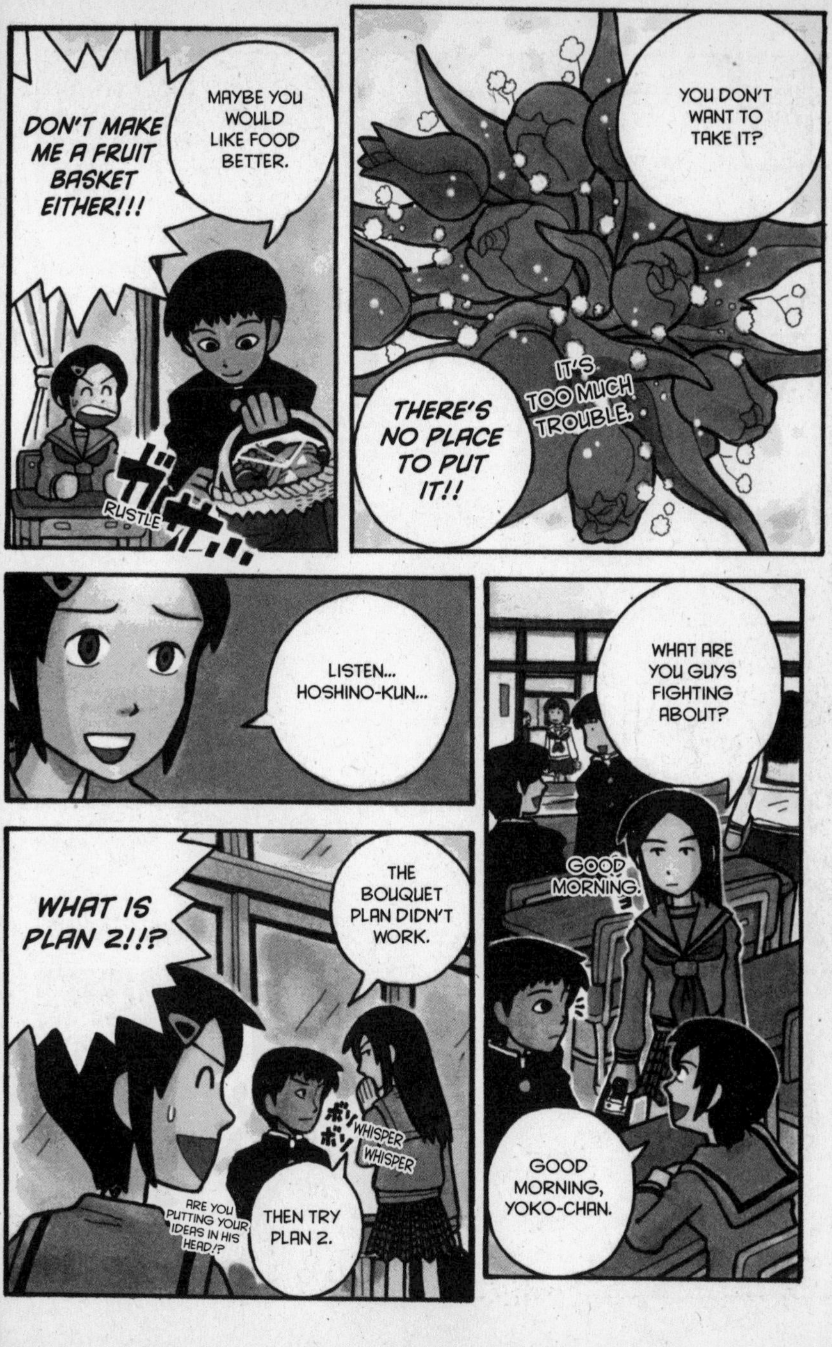
YOU DON'T WANT TO TAKE IT?
IT'S TOO MUCH TROUBLE.
THERE'S NO PLACE TO PUT IT!!
MAYBE YOU WOULD LIKE FOOD BETTER.
DON'T MAKE ME A FRUIT BASKET EITHER!!!
RUSTLE
WHAT ARE YOU GUYS FIGHTING ABOUT?
GOOD MORNING.
GOOD MORNING, YOKO-CHAN.
LISTEN... HOSHINO-KUN...
THE BOUQUET PLAN DIDN'T WORK.
WHAT IS PLAN 2!!!?
WHISPER WHISPER
THEN TRY PLAN 2.
ARE YOU PUTTING YOUR IDEAS IN HIS HEAD!?

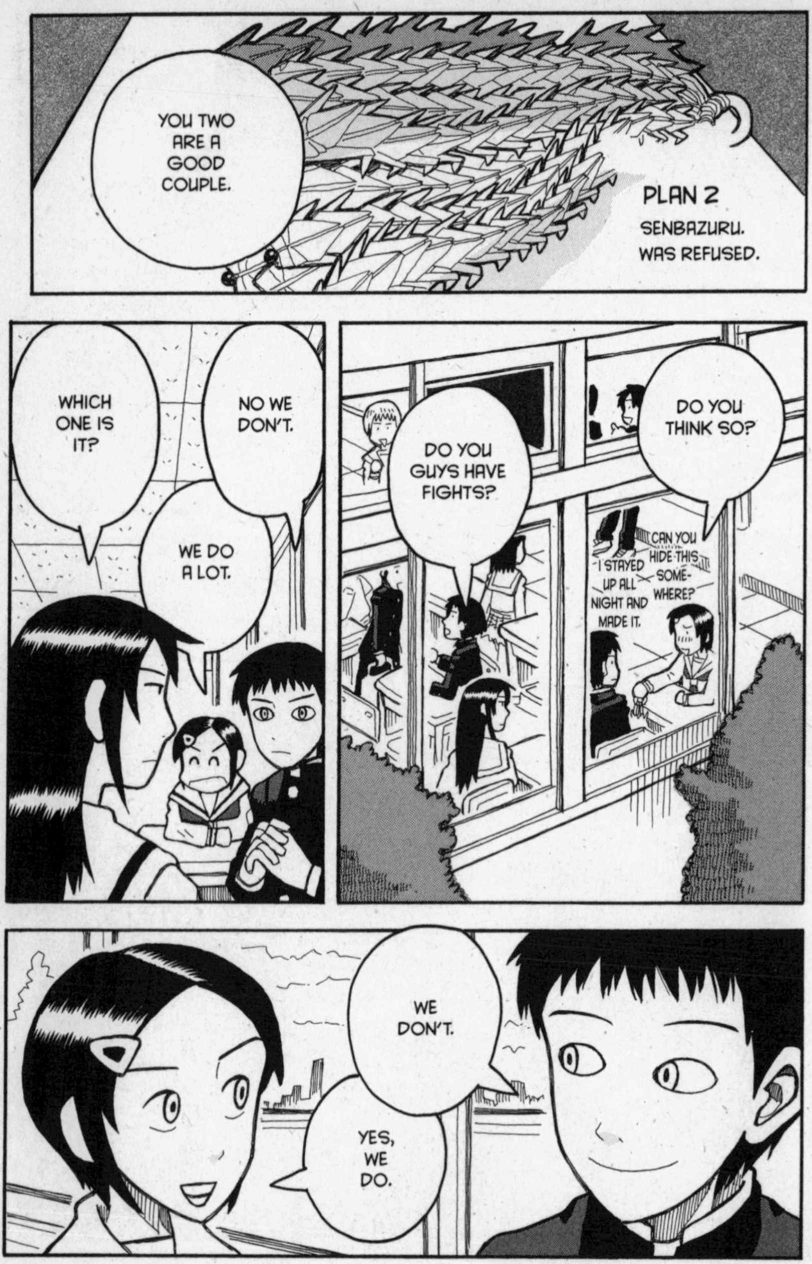
PLAN 2
SENBAZURU. WAS REFUSED.
YOU TWO ARE A GOOD COUPLE.
DO YOU THINK SO?
DO YOU GUYS HAVE FIGHTS?
CAN YOU HIDE THIS SOME-WHERE?
I STAYED UP ALL NIGHT AND MADE IT.
NO WE DON'T.
WHICH ONE IS IT?
WE DO A LOT.
WE DON'T.
YES, WE DO.

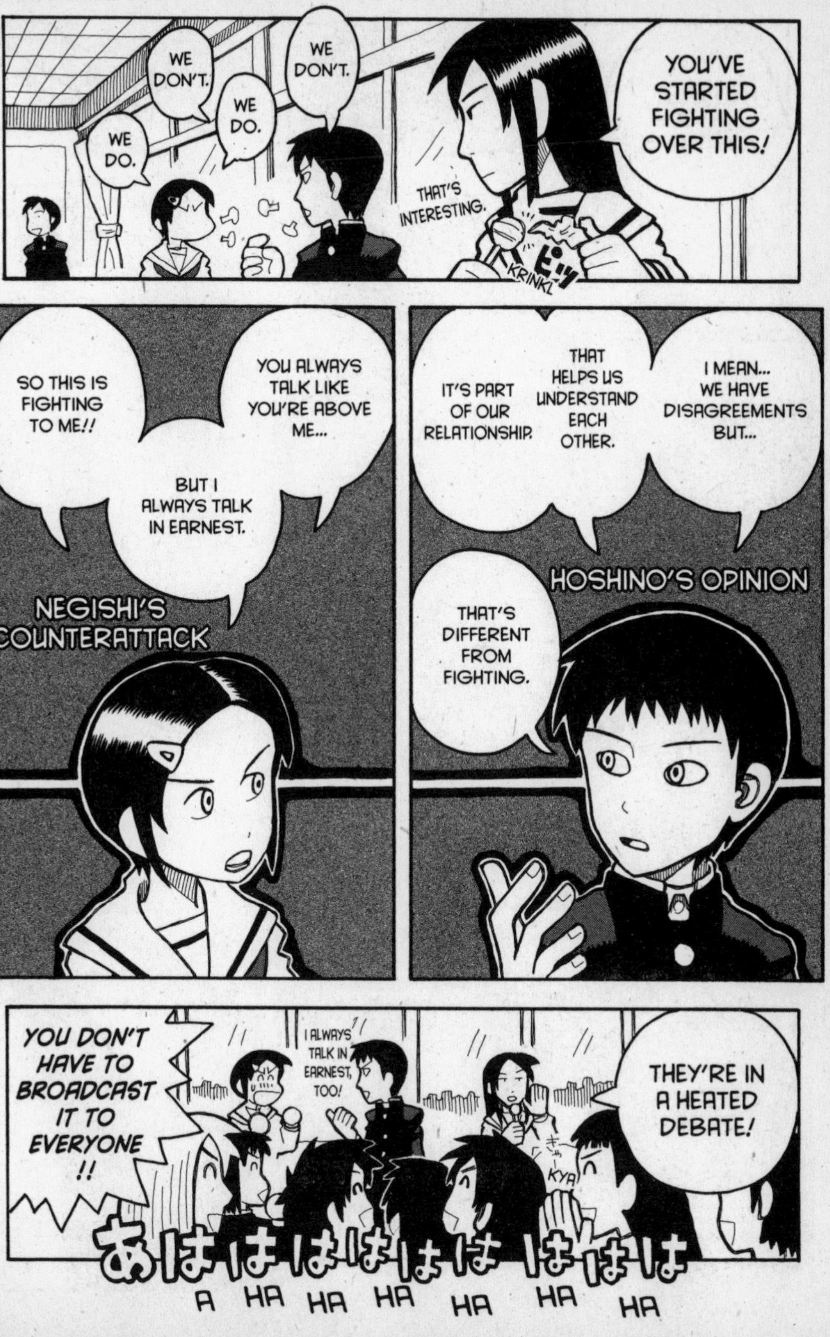
YOU'VE STARTED FIGHTING OVER THIS!
THAT'S INTERESTING.
ピッ
KRINKL
WE DON'T.
WE DO.
WE DON'T.
WE DO.
I MEAN... WE HAVE DISAGREEMENTS BUT...
THAT HELPS US UNDERSTAND EACH OTHER.
IT'S PART OF OUR RELATIONSHIP.
HOSHINO'S OPINION
THAT'S DIFFERENT FROM FIGHTING.
YOU ALWAYS TALK LIKE YOU'RE ABOVE ME...
SO THIS IS FIGHTING TO ME!!
BUT I ALWAYS TALK IN EARNEST.
NEGISHI'S COUNTERATTACK
THEY'RE IN A HEATED DEBATE!
きゃー
KYA
I ALWAYS TALK IN EARNEST, TOO!
YOU DON'T HAVE TO BROADCAST IT TO EVERYONE!!
あはははははは ははは
A HA HA HA HA HA HA

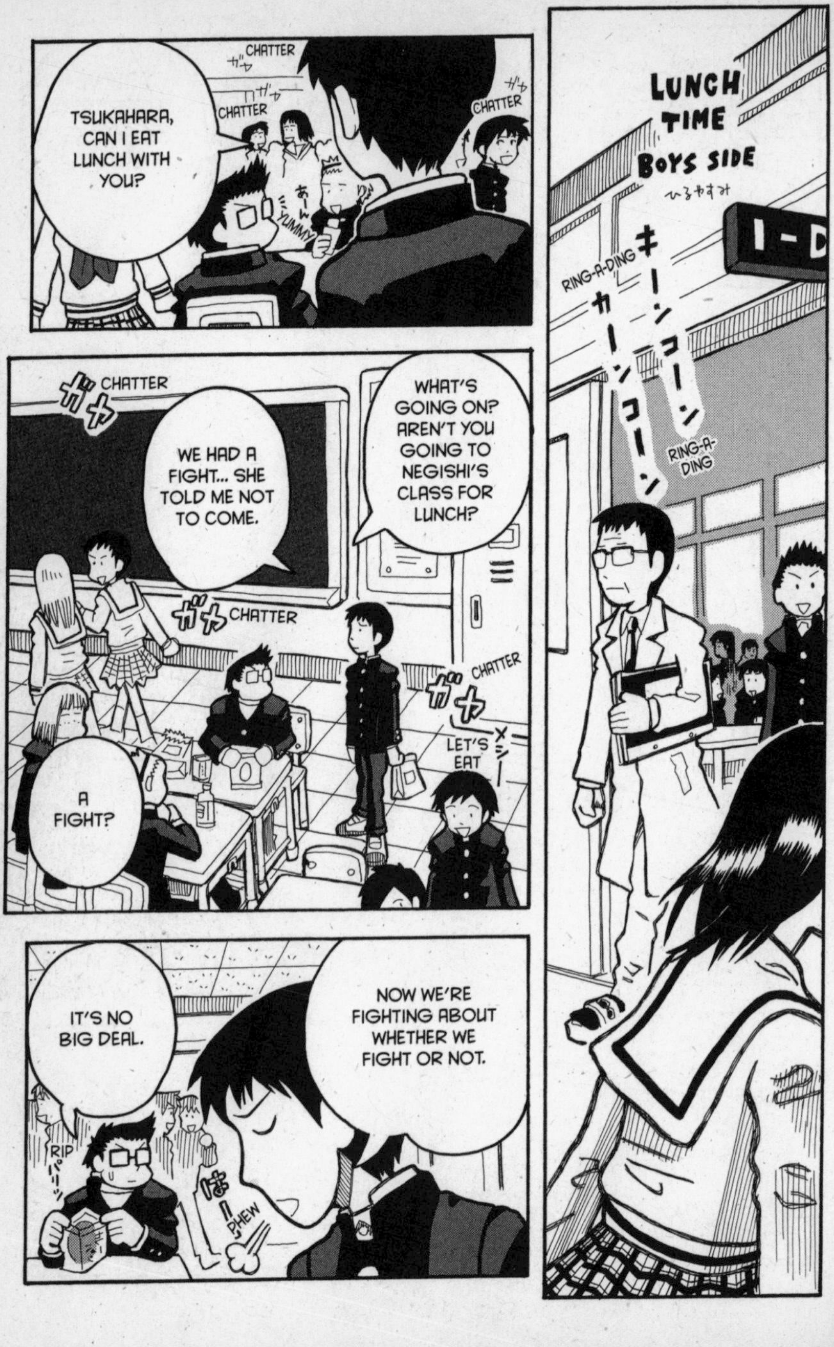
LUNCH TIME
BOYS SIDE
ひるやすみ
キーンコーン
RING-A-DING
カーンコーン
RING-A-DING
1-D
ガヤ CHATTER
ガヤ CHATTER
ガヤ CHATTER
TSUKAHARA, CAN I EAT LUNCH WITH YOU?
あーん YUMMY
WHAT'S GOING ON? AREN'T YOU GOING TO NEGISHI'S CLASS FOR LUNCH?
WE HAD A FIGHT... SHE TOLD ME NOT TO COME.
ガヤ CHATTER
ガヤ CHATTER
ガヤ CHATTER
メシー LET'S EAT
A FIGHT?
NOW WE'RE FIGHTING ABOUT WHETHER WE FIGHT OR NOT.
IT'S NO BIG DEAL.
パリッ RIP
はー PHEW

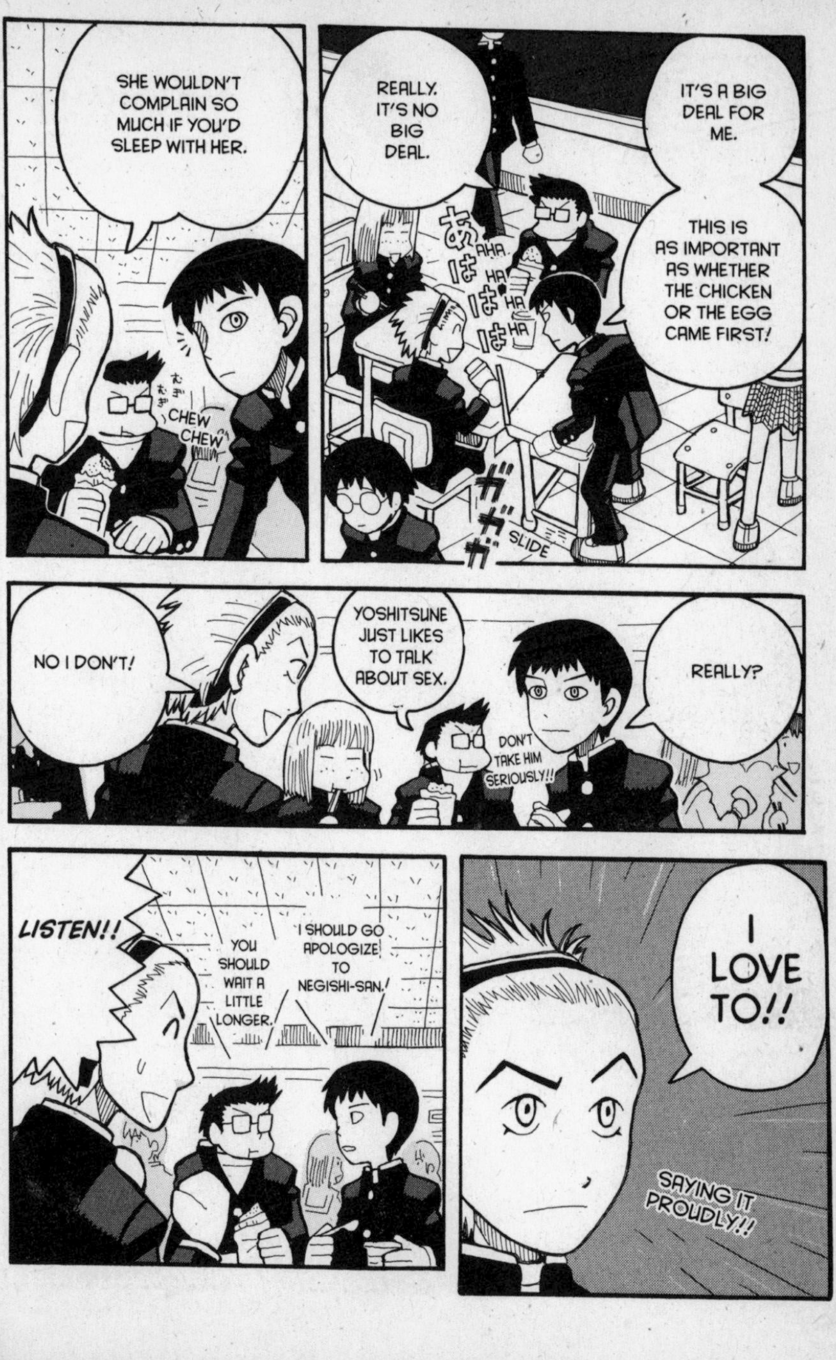
IT'S A BIG DEAL FOR ME.
THIS IS AS IMPORTANT AS WHETHER THE CHICKEN OR THE EGG CAME FIRST!
REALLY. IT'S NO BIG DEAL.
あはははは
AHA HA HA HA
ガガガ
SLIDE
SHE WOULDN'T COMPLAIN SO MUCH IF YOU'D SLEEP WITH HER.
むぎむぎ
CHEW CHEW
REALLY?
DON'T TAKE HIM SERIOUSLY!!
YOSHITSUNE JUST LIKES TO TALK ABOUT SEX.
NO I DON'T!
I LOVE TO!!
SAYING IT PROUDLY!!
I SHOULD GO APOLOGIZE TO NEGISHI-SAN.
YOU SHOULD WAIT A LITTLE LONGER.
LISTEN!!

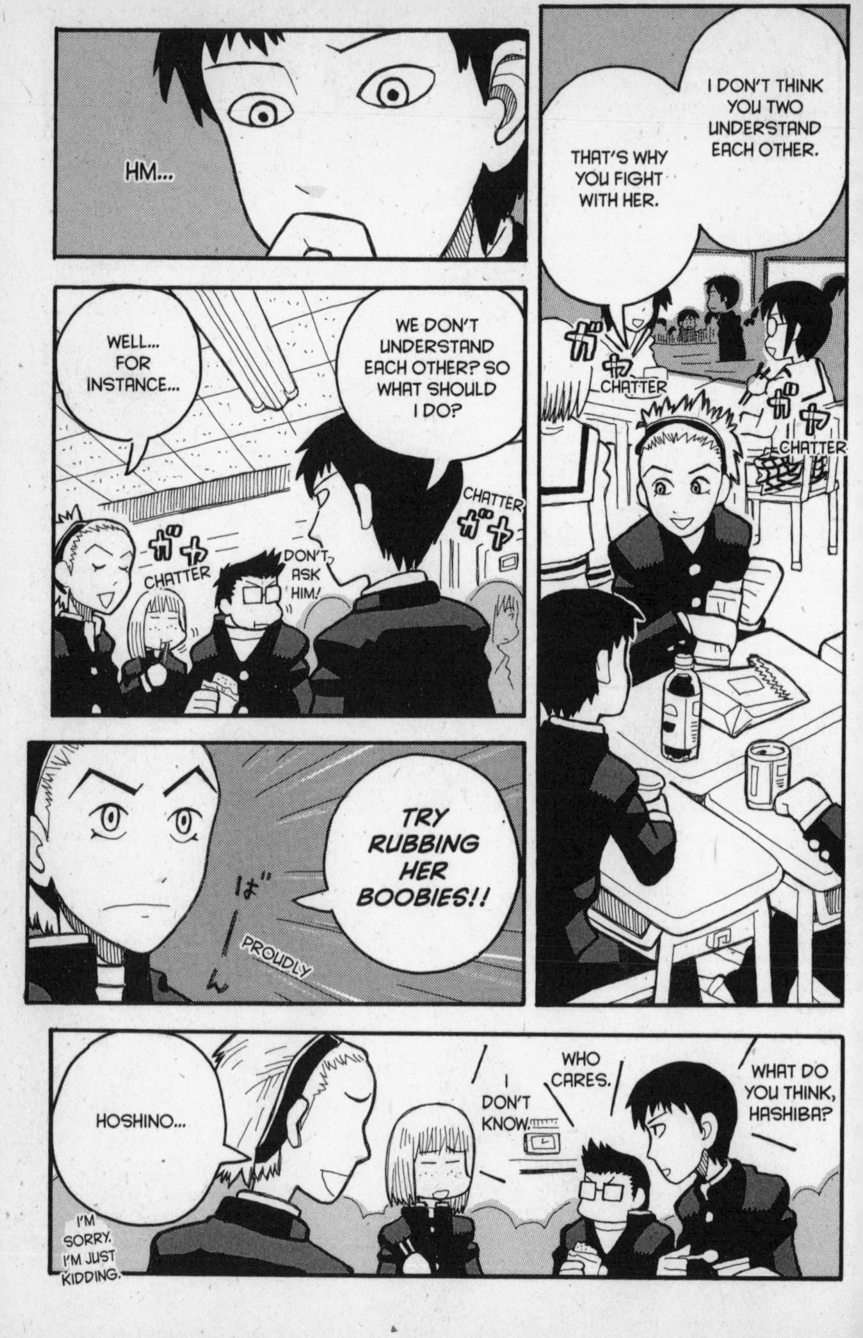
I DON'T THINK YOU TWO UNDERSTAND EACH OTHER.
THAT'S WHY YOU FIGHT WITH HER.
ガヤ
CHATTER
ガヤ
CHATTER
HM...
WE DON'T UNDERSTAND EACH OTHER? SO WHAT SHOULD I DO?
WELL... FOR INSTANCE...
CHATTER
ガヤ
DON'T ASK HIM!
ガヤ
CHATTER
TRY RUBBING HER BOOBIES!!
ば
PROUDLY
WHAT DO YOU THINK, HASHIBA?
WHO CARES.
I DON'T KNOW.
HOSHINO...
I'M SORRY. I'M JUST KIDDING.

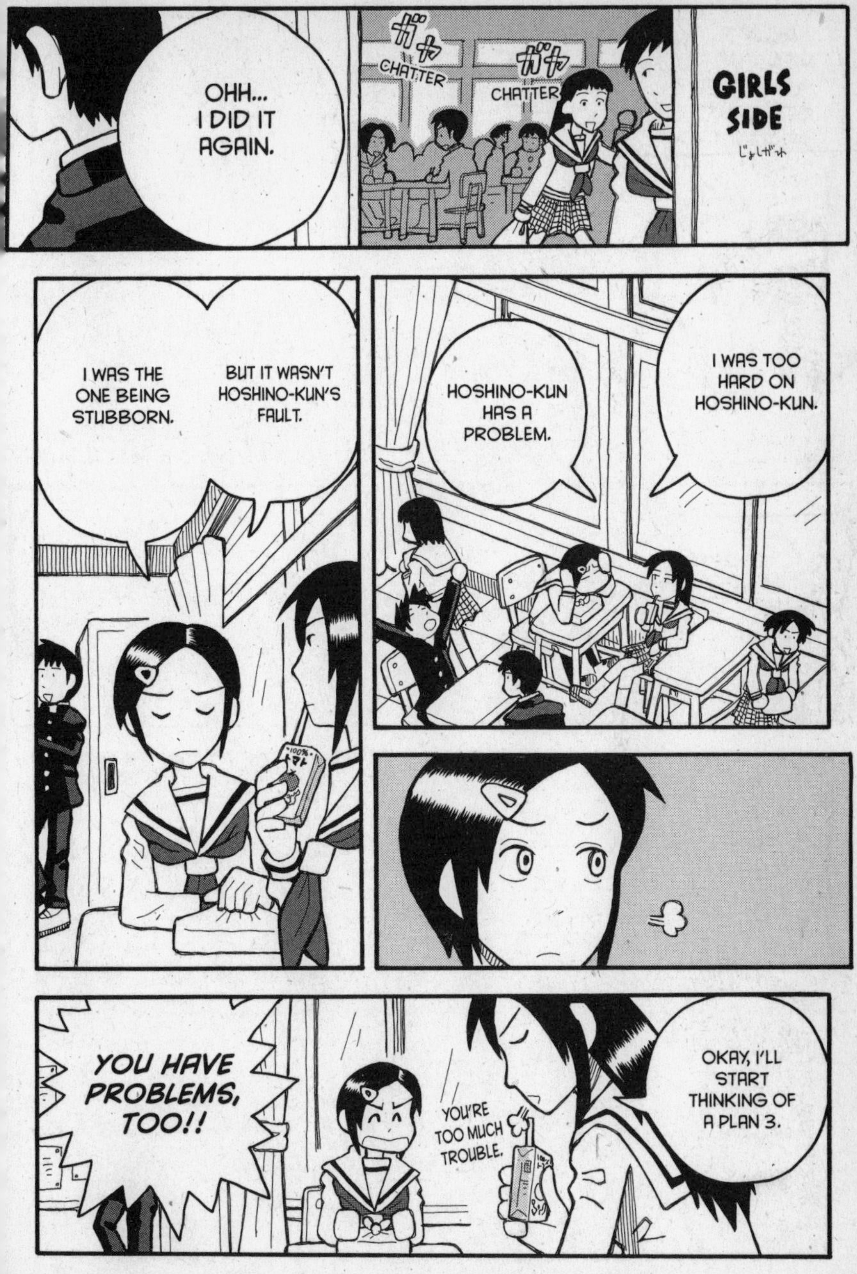
GIRLS SIDE
じょしがわ
ガヤ
CHATTER
ガヤ
CHATTER
OHH... I DID IT AGAIN.
I WAS TOO HARD ON HOSHINO-KUN.
HOSHINO-KUN HAS A PROBLEM.
BUT IT WASN'T HOSHINO-KUN'S FAULT.
I WAS THE ONE BEING STUBBORN.
OKAY, I'LL START THINKING OF A PLAN 3.
YOU'RE TOO MUCH TROUBLE.
YOU HAVE PROBLEMS, TOO!!

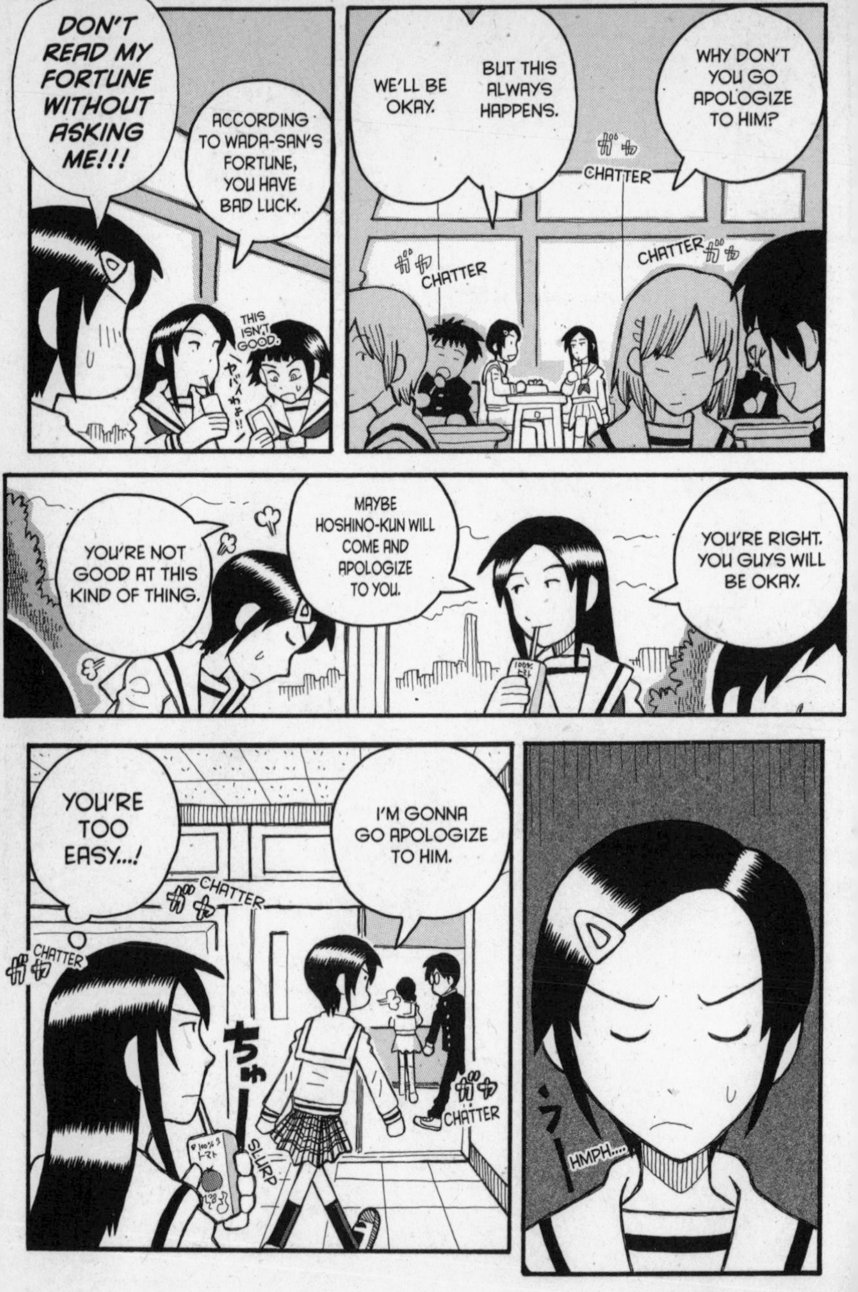
WHY DON'T YOU GO APOLOGIZE TO HIM?
CHATTER
BUT THIS ALWAYS HAPPENS.
WE'LL BE OKAY.
CHATTER
CHATTER
ACCORDING TO WADA-SAN'S FORTUNE, YOU HAVE BAD LUCK.
DON'T READ MY FORTUNE WITHOUT ASKING ME!!!
THIS ISN'T GOOD.
ヤバイわよ!!
YOU'RE RIGHT. YOU GUYS WILL BE OKAY.
MAYBE HOSHINO-KUN WILL COME AND APOLOGIZE TO YOU.
YOU'RE NOT GOOD AT THIS KIND OF THING.
う~
HMPH....
I'M GONNA GO APOLOGIZE TO HIM.
YOU'RE TOO EASY...!
CHATTER
CHATTER
CHATTER
ちゅー
SLURP

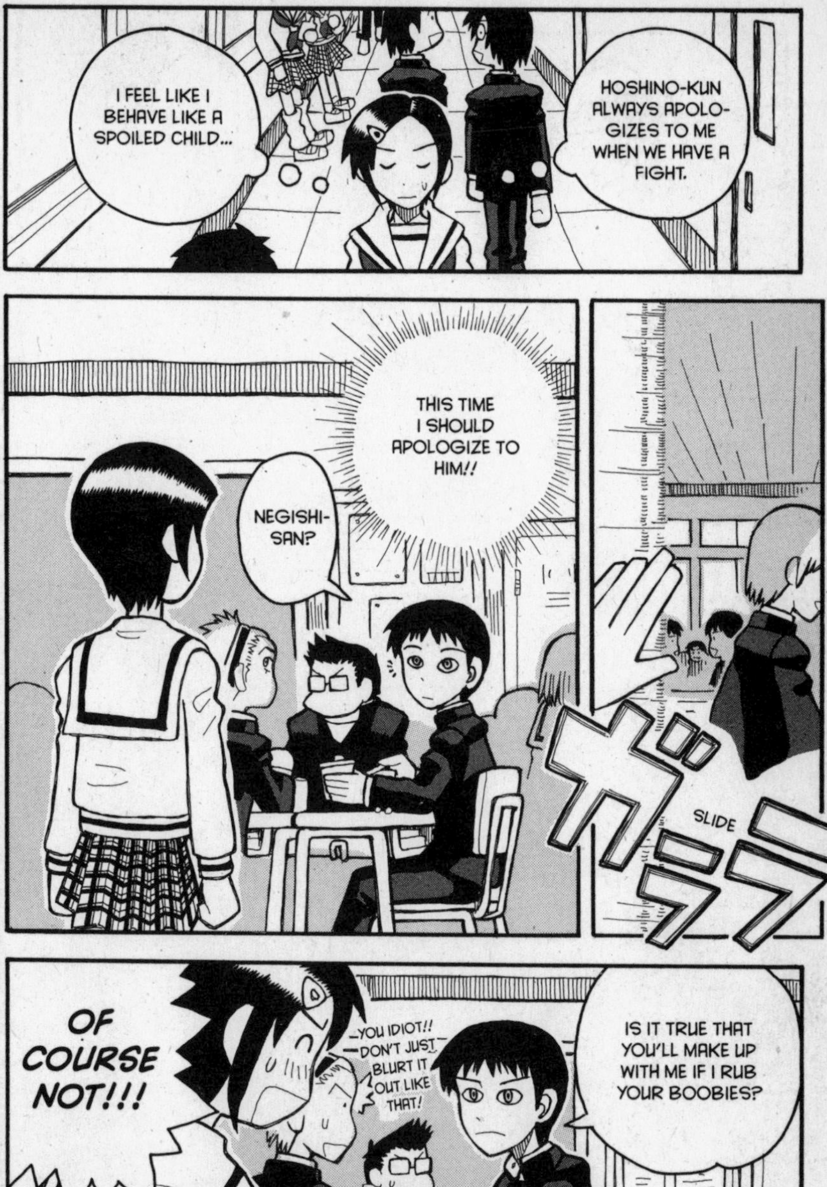
HOSHINO-KUN ALWAYS APOLOGIZES TO ME WHEN WE HAVE A FIGHT.
I FEEL LIKE I BEHAVE LIKE A SPOILED CHILD...
ガラララ
SLIDE
THIS TIME I SHOULD APOLOGIZE TO HIM!!
NEGISHI-SAN?
IS IT TRUE THAT YOU'LL MAKE UP WITH ME IF I RUB YOUR BOOBIES?
—YOU IDIOT!! —DON'T JUST BLURT IT OUT LIKE THAT!
OF COURSE NOT!!!

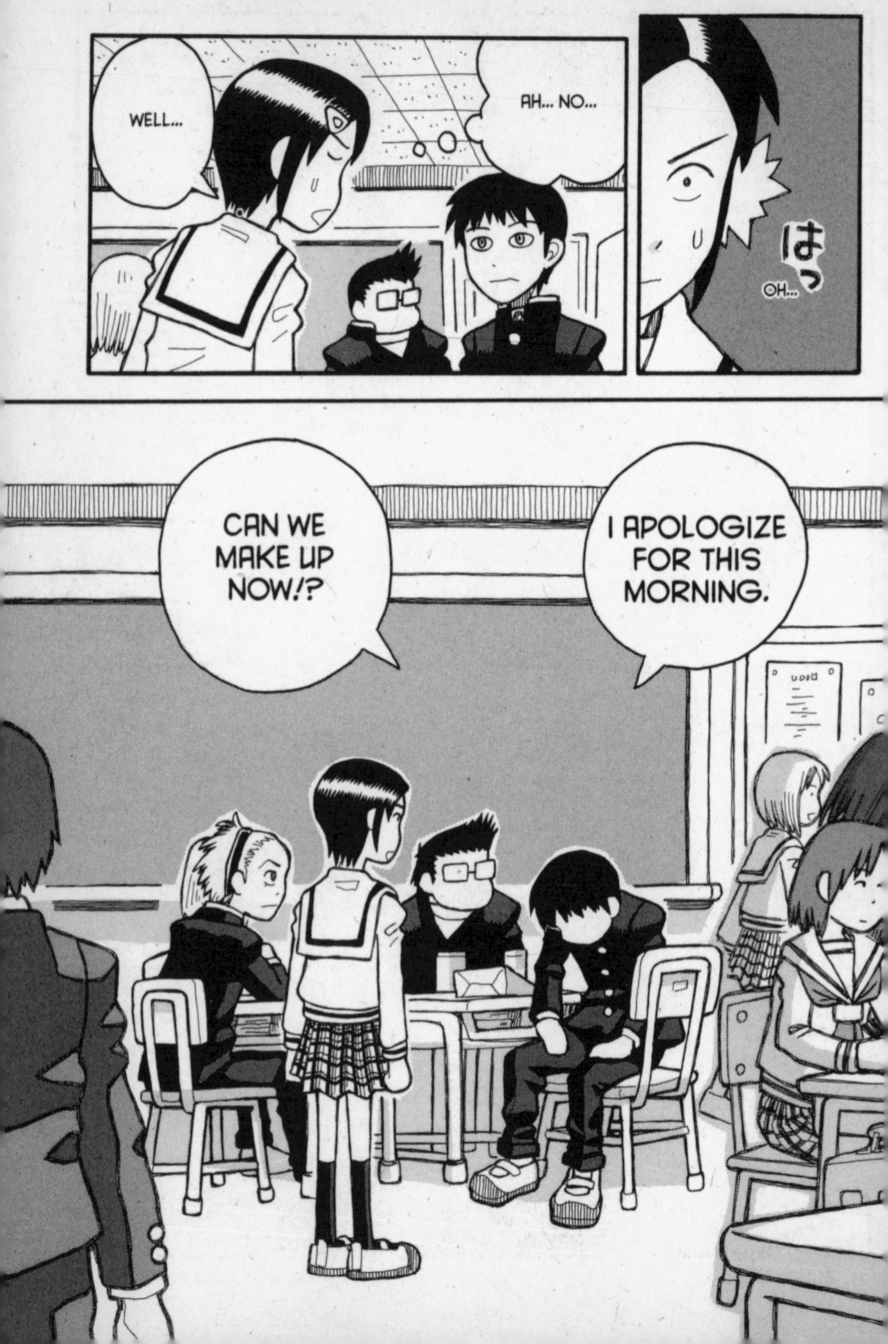
はっ
OH...
AH... NO...
WELL...
I APOLOGIZE FOR THIS MORNING.
CAN WE MAKE UP NOW!?

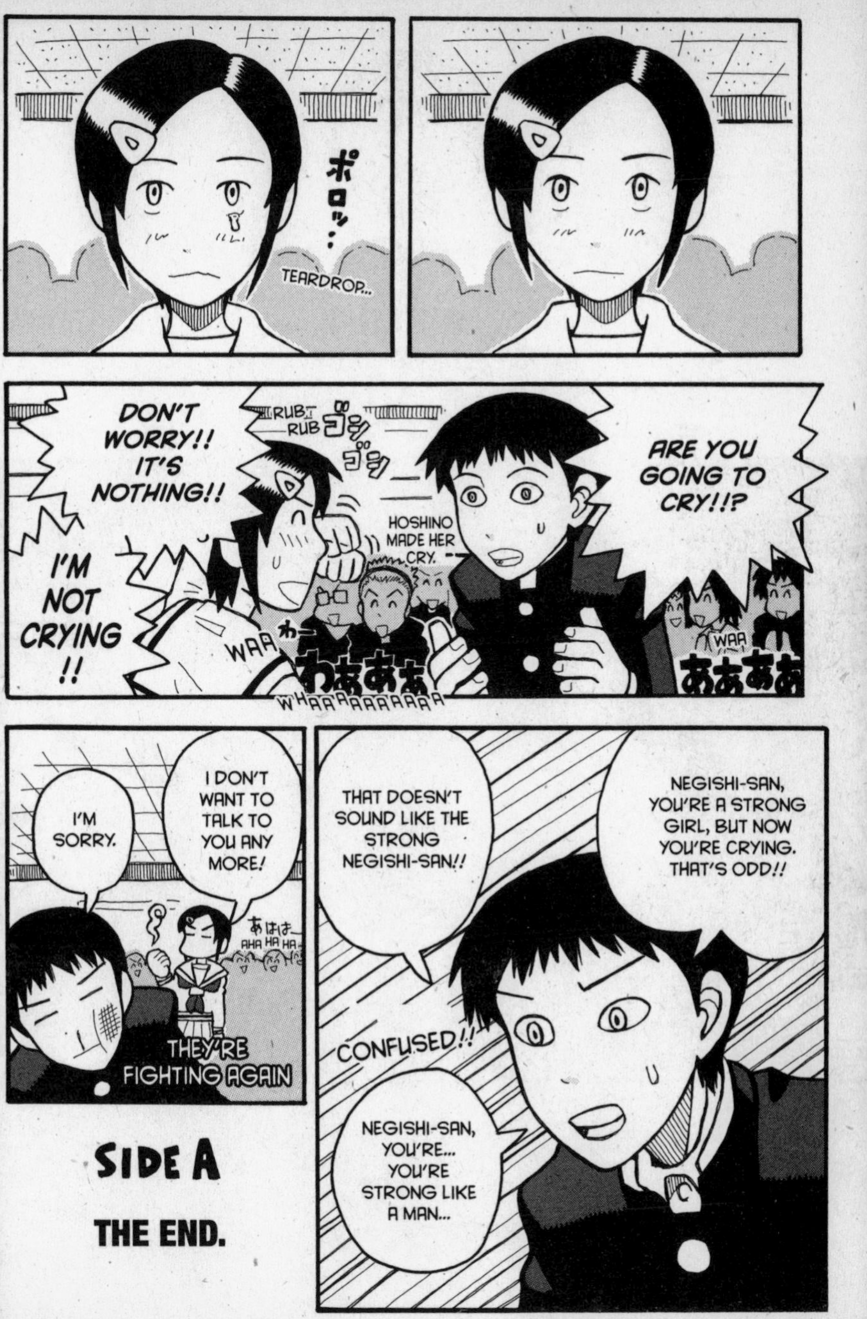
ポロッ…
TEARDROP...
ARE YOU GOING TO CRY!!?
WAA
ああああ
HOSHINO MADE HER CRY.
RUB RUB
ゴシゴシ
DON'T WORRY!! IT'S NOTHING!!
I'M NOT CRYING!!
WAA
わー
わあああ
WHAAAAAAAAAA
NEGISHI-SAN, YOU'RE A STRONG GIRL, BUT NOW YOU'RE CRYING. THAT'S ODD!!
THAT DOESN'T SOUND LIKE THE STRONG NEGISHI-SAN!!
CONFUSED!!
NEGISHI-SAN, YOU'RE... YOU'RE STRONG LIKE A MAN...
I DON'T WANT TO TALK TO YOU ANY MORE!
I'M SORRY.
あはは
AHA HA HA
THEY'RE FIGHTING AGAIN

SIDE A

THE END.

To Be Continued to SIDE B

TRACK #1

WE HAD A FIGHT AND MADE UP

SIDE B

A MATCHLESS COUPLE

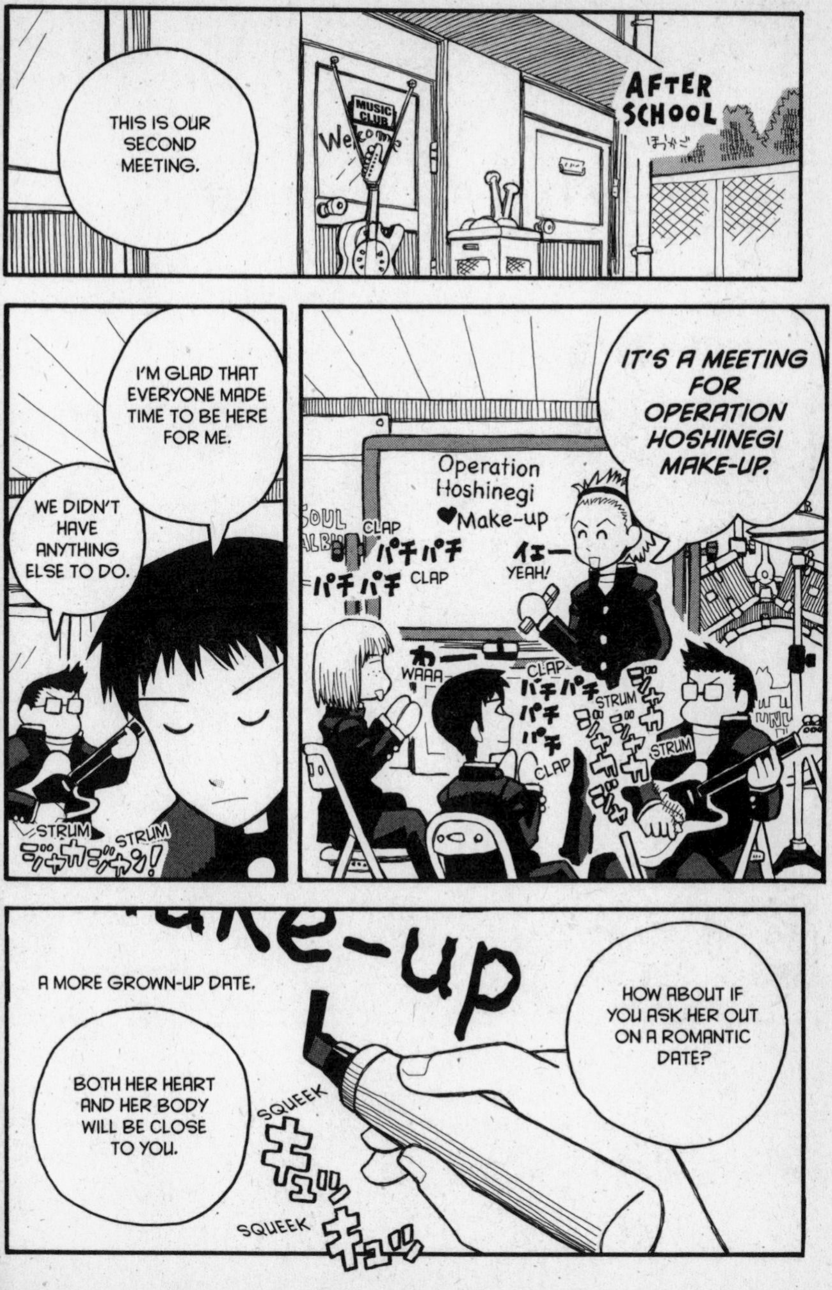
AFTER SCHOOL
ほうかご
MUSIC CLUB
THIS IS OUR SECOND MEETING.
IT'S A MEETING FOR OPERATION HOSHINEGI MAKE-UP.
Operation Hoshinegi ♥Make-up
イェー
YEAH!
CLAP
パチパチ
CLAP
パチパチ
CLAP
わー
WAAA
CLAP
パチパチ
パチ
パチ
CLAP
STRUM
STRUM
I'M GLAD THAT EVERYONE MADE TIME TO BE HERE FOR ME.
WE DIDN'T HAVE ANYTHING ELSE TO DO.
STRUM
STRUM
ジャカジャン!
HOW ABOUT IF YOU ASK HER OUT ON A ROMANTIC DATE?
A MORE GROWN-UP DATE.
BOTH HER HEART AND HER BODY WILL BE CLOSE TO YOU.
SQUEEK
キュッ
SQUEEK
キュッ

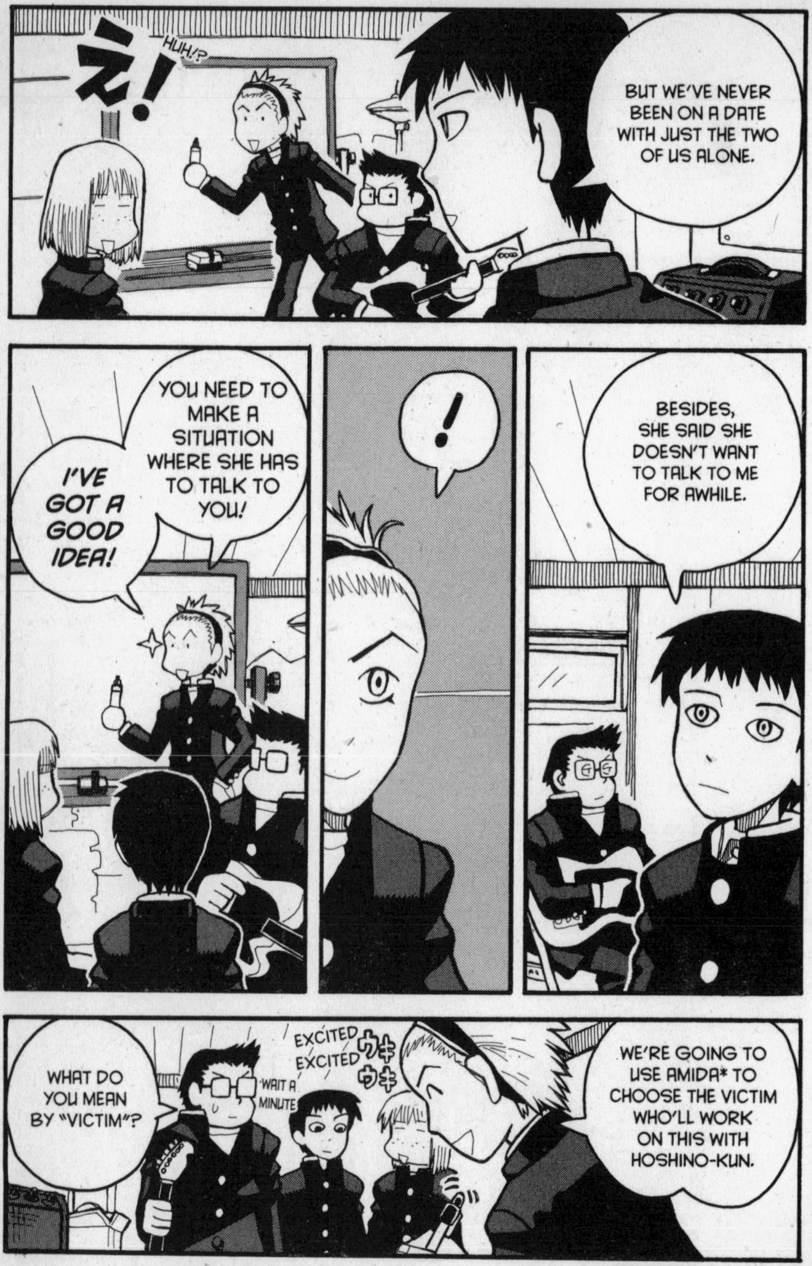
BUT WE'VE NEVER BEEN ON A DATE WITH JUST THE TWO OF US ALONE.
HUH!?
え!
BESIDES, SHE SAID SHE DOESN'T WANT TO TALK TO ME FOR AWHILE.
!
YOU NEED TO MAKE A SITUATION WHERE SHE HAS TO TALK TO YOU!
I'VE GOT A GOOD IDEA!
WE'RE GOING TO USE AMIDA* TO CHOOSE THE VICTIM WHO'LL WORK ON THIS WITH HOSHINO-KUN.
ウキウキ
EXCITED EXCITED
WAIT A MINUTE
WHAT DO YOU MEAN BY "VICTIM"?

*SEE TRANSLATION NOTES.

NEXT DAY
つぎのひ
ガー
ZOOM
I-C
ワー WAHH
パチパチ CLAP
パチパチ CLAP
ワー YEAH!
YEAH!
パチパチパチ CLAP
ガラララ CLAP
ヒュー SLIDE
?
わあああああ WAH-H-H-H-H-H-H-H
GOOD MORNING, YOKO-CHAN.
WHAT'S GOING ON?
LOOK AT THE BLACKBOARD

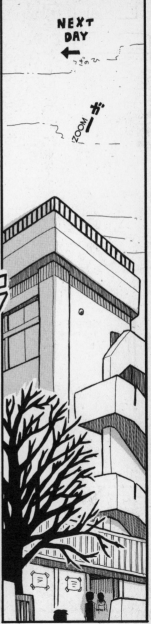

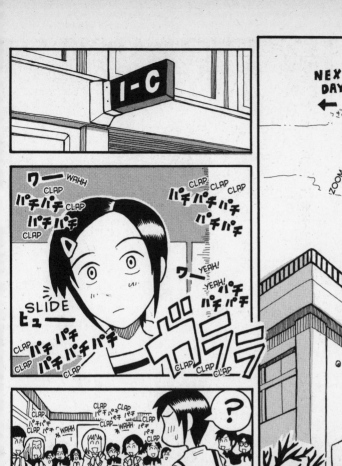

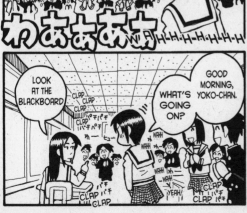

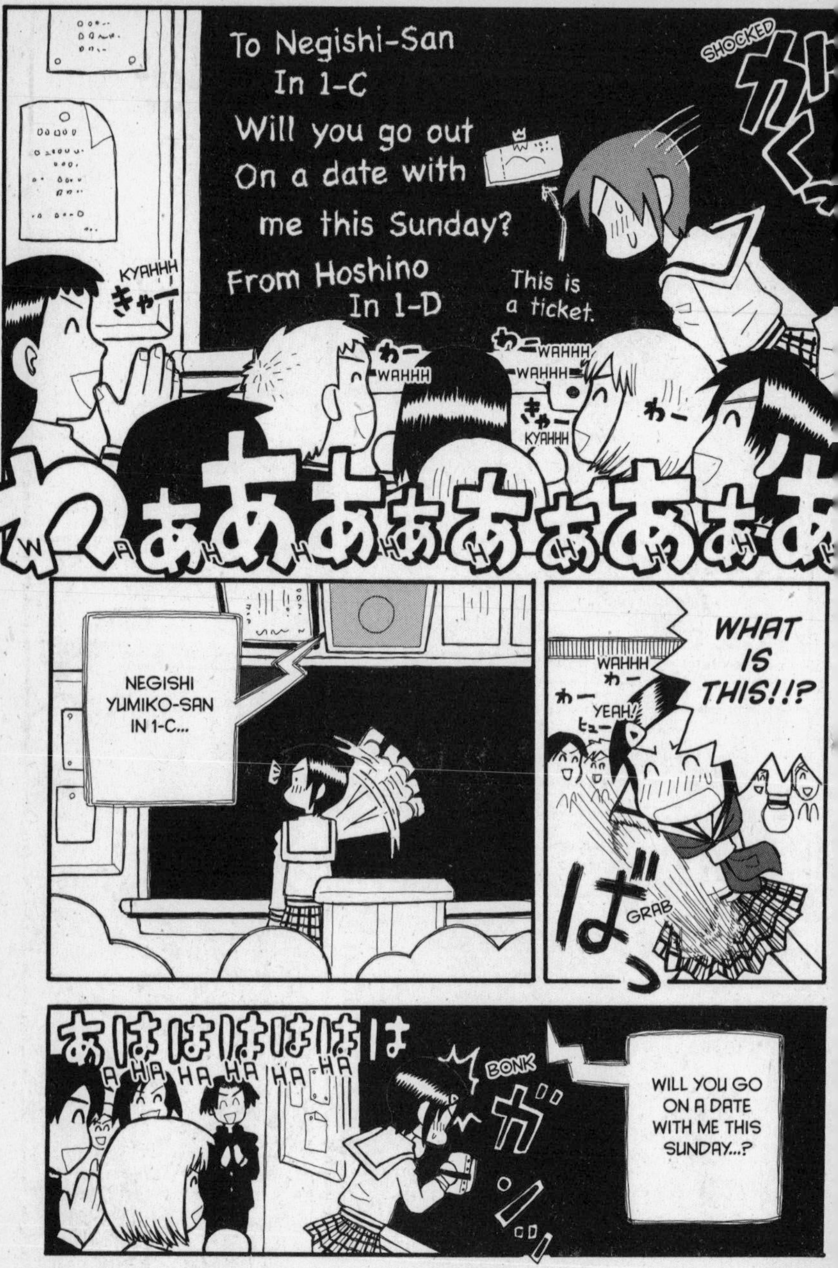

SHOCKED
がくっ
To Negishi-San
In 1-C
Will you go out
On a date with
me this Sunday?
From Hoshino
In 1-D
This is a ticket.
わー WAHHH
WAHHH
わー
WAHHH
わー WAHHH
きゃー KYAHHH
きゃー KYAHHH
わぁあああああああああ
WAHHHHHHHHH
WHAT IS THIS!!?
WAHHH
わー
わー
YEAH!
ヒュー
ばっ
GRAB
NEGISHI YUMIKO-SAN IN 1-C...
WILL YOU GO ON A DATE WITH ME THIS SUNDAY...?
BONK
ガンッ
あははははは
A HA HA HA HA HA

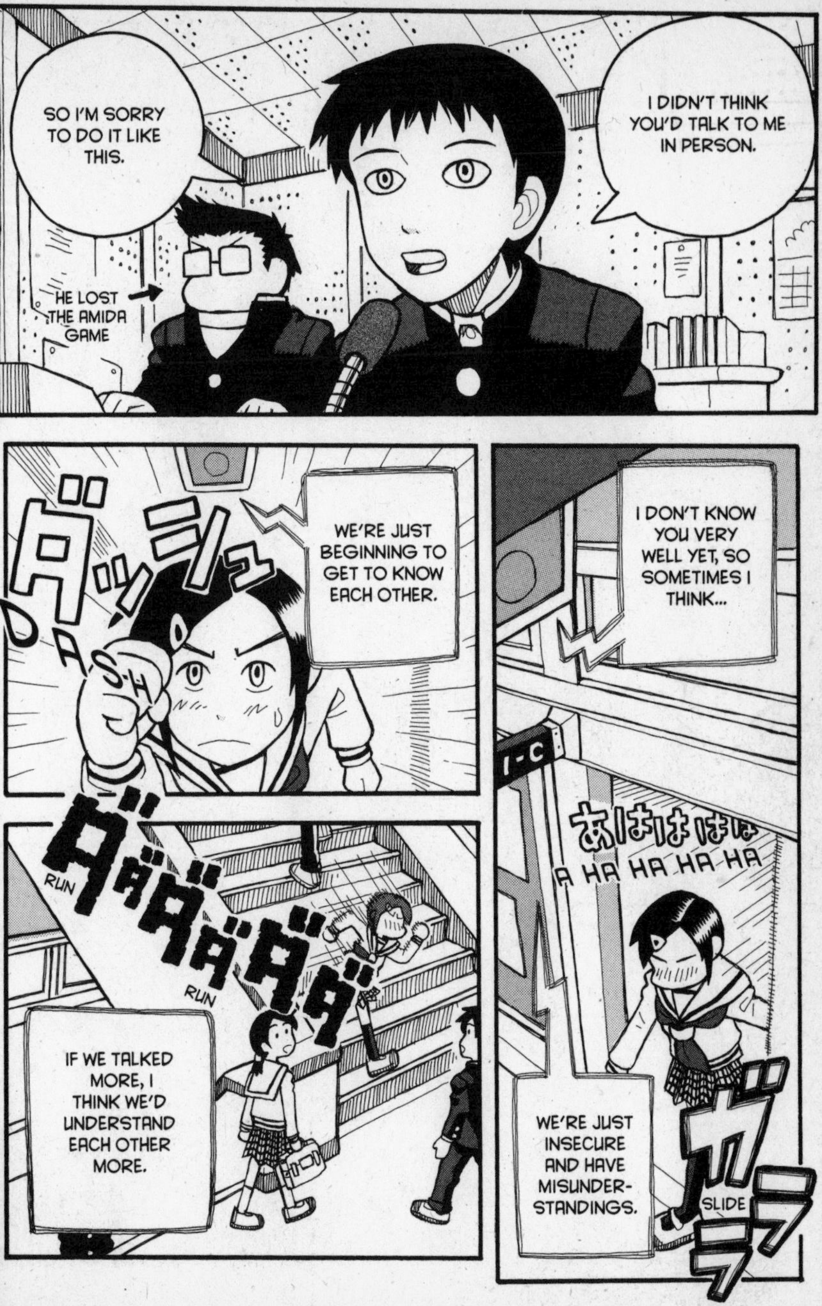
I DIDN'T THINK YOU'D TALK TO ME IN PERSON.
SO I'M SORRY TO DO IT LIKE THIS.
HE LOST THE AMIDA GAME
I DON'T KNOW YOU VERY WELL YET, SO SOMETIMES I THINK...
I-C
あははははは
A HA HA HA HA
WE'RE JUST INSECURE AND HAVE MISUNDERSTANDINGS.
ガラ
SLIDE
ダッシュ
DASH
WE'RE JUST BEGINNING TO GET TO KNOW EACH OTHER.
ダダダダダ
RUN
RUN
IF WE TALKED MORE, I THINK WE'D UNDERSTAND EACH OTHER MORE.

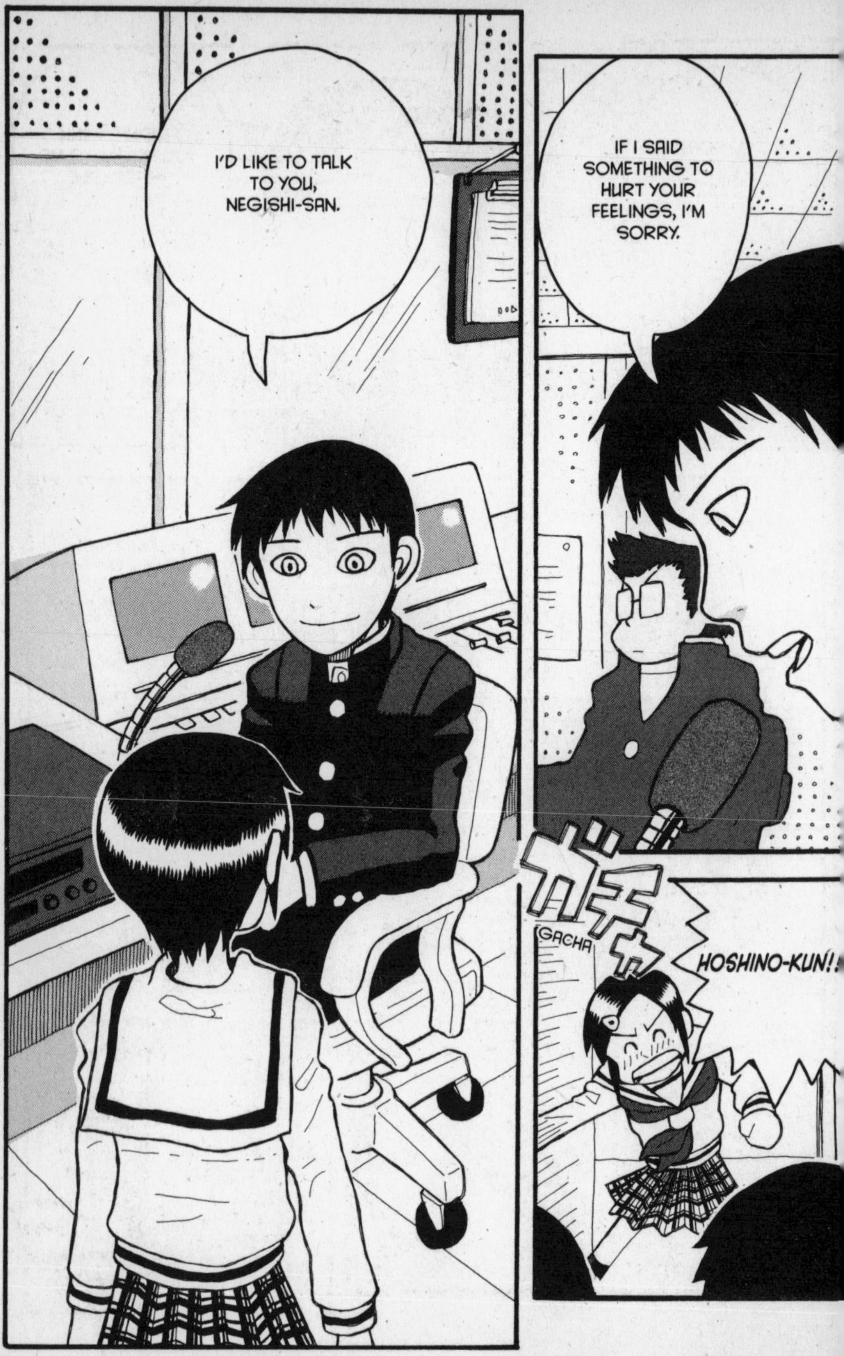
IF I SAID SOMETHING TO HURT YOUR FEELINGS, I'M SORRY.
GACHA
HOSHINO-KUN!!
I'D LIKE TO TALK TO YOU, NEGISHI-SAN.

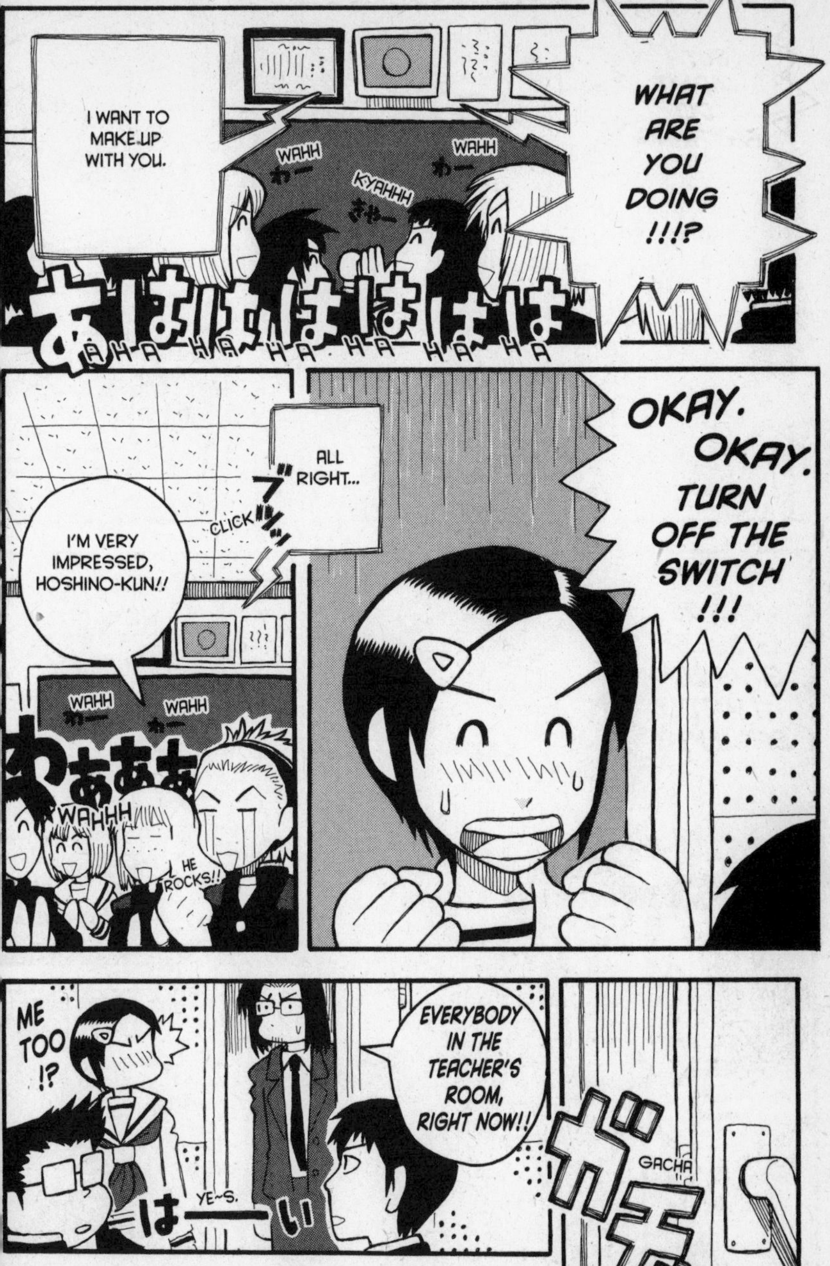
WHAT ARE YOU DOING!!!?
WAHH
わー
KYAHHH
きゃー
WAHH
わー
I WANT TO MAKE UP WITH YOU.
あははははははは
AHA HA HA HA HA HA HA
OKAY. OKAY. TURN OFF THE SWITCH!!!
ALL RIGHT...
ブツッ
CLICK
I'M VERY IMPRESSED, HOSHINO-KUN!!
WAHH
わー
WAHH
わー
わあああ
WAHHH
HE ROCKS!!
ガチャ
GACHA
EVERYBODY IN THE TEACHER'S ROOM, RIGHT NOW!!
ME TOO!?
はーーい
YE~S.

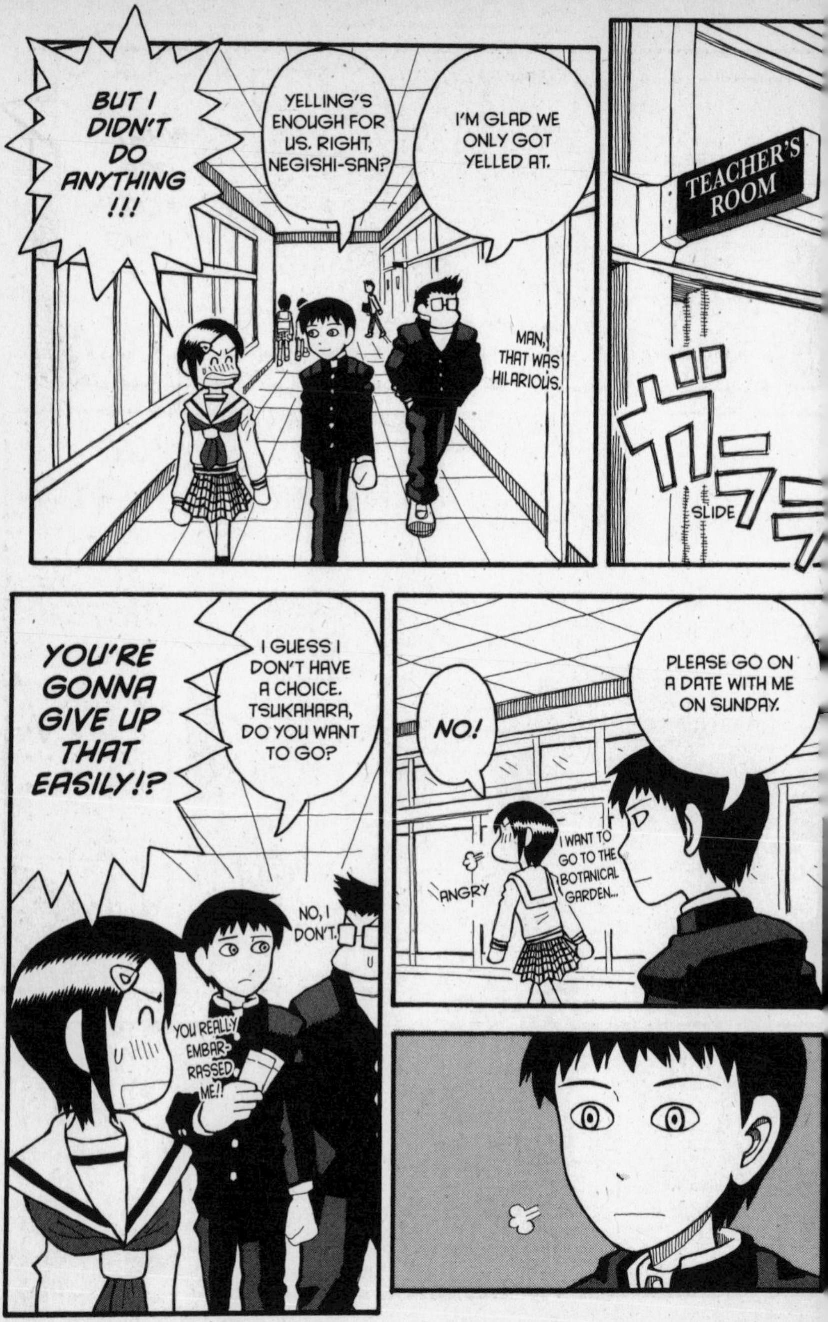
TEACHER'S ROOM
SLIDE
I'M GLAD WE ONLY GOT YELLED AT.
YELLING'S ENOUGH FOR US. RIGHT, NEGISHI-SAN?
BUT I DIDN'T DO ANYTHING !!!
MAN, THAT WAS HILARIOUS.
PLEASE GO ON A DATE WITH ME ON SUNDAY.
NO!
I WANT TO GO TO THE BOTANICAL GARDEN...
ANGRY
I GUESS I DON'T HAVE A CHOICE. TSUKAHARA, DO YOU WANT TO GO?
YOU'RE GONNA GIVE UP THAT EASILY!?
NO, I DON'T.
YOU REALLY EMBARRASSED ME!!

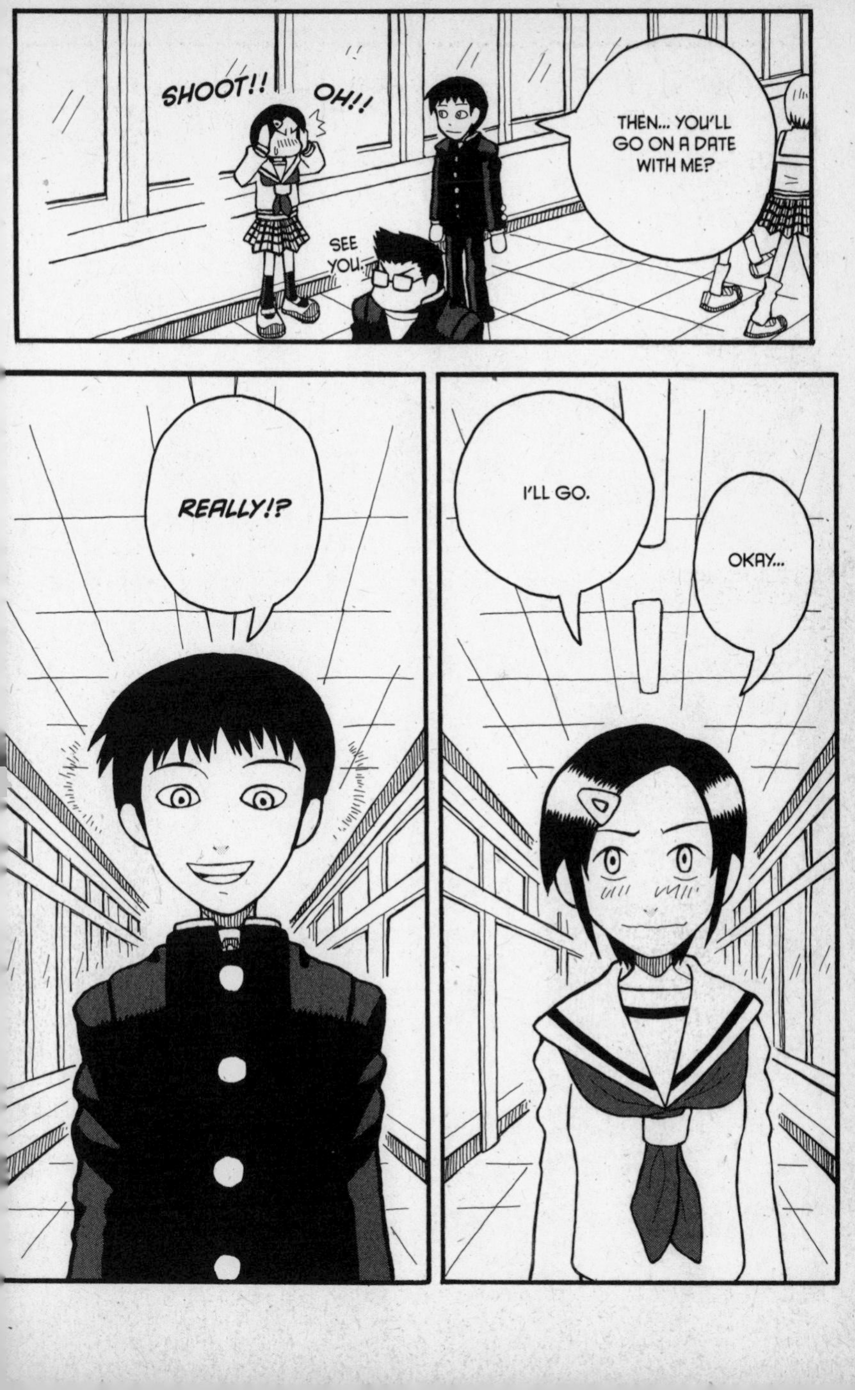
THEN... YOU'LL GO ON A DATE WITH ME?
OH!!
SHOOT!!
SEE YOU.
OKAY...
I'LL GO.
REALLY!?

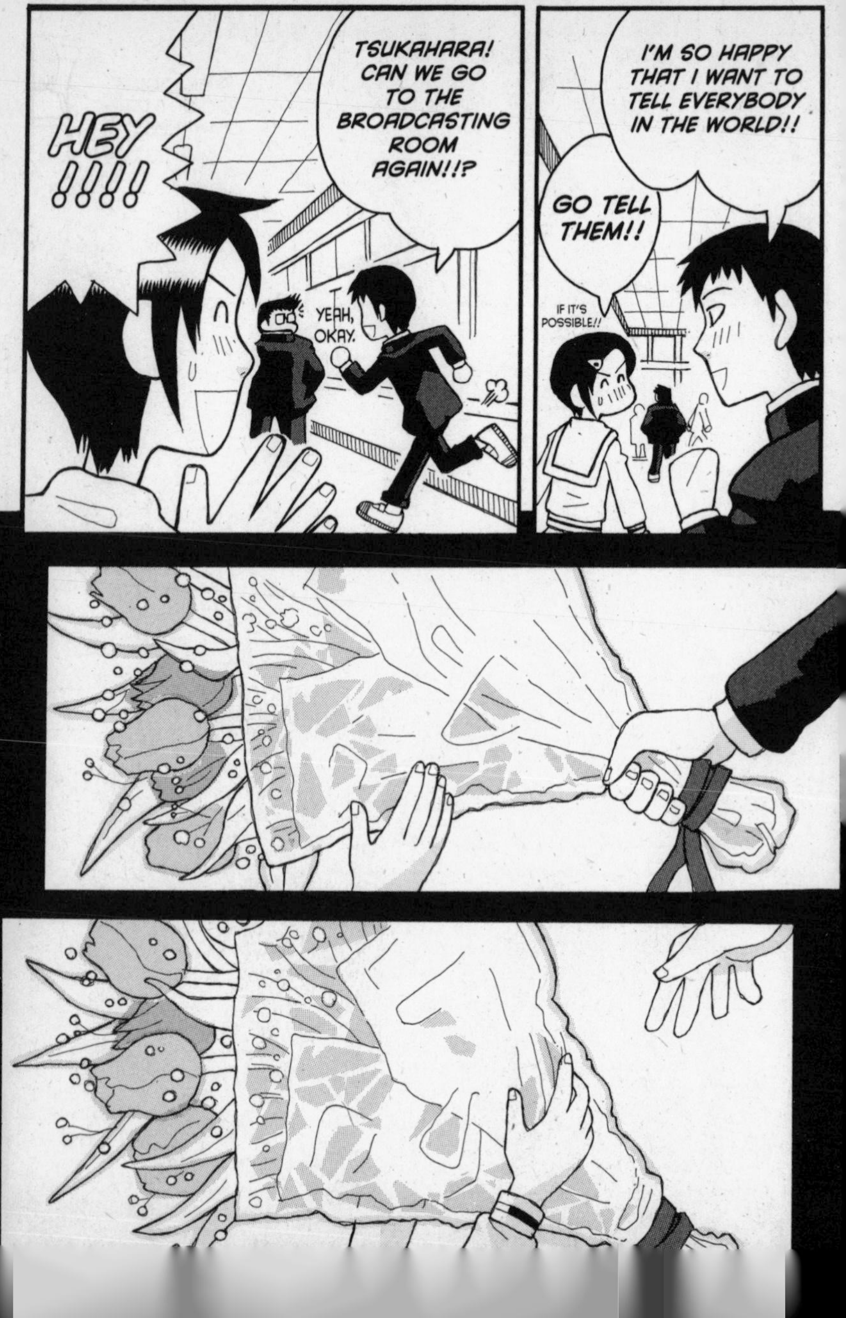
I'M SO HAPPY THAT I WANT TO TELL EVERYBODY IN THE WORLD!!
GO TELL THEM!!
IF IT'S POSSIBLE!!
TSUKAHARA! CAN WE GO TO THE BROADCASTING ROOM AGAIN!!?
YEAH, OKAY.
HEY!!!!

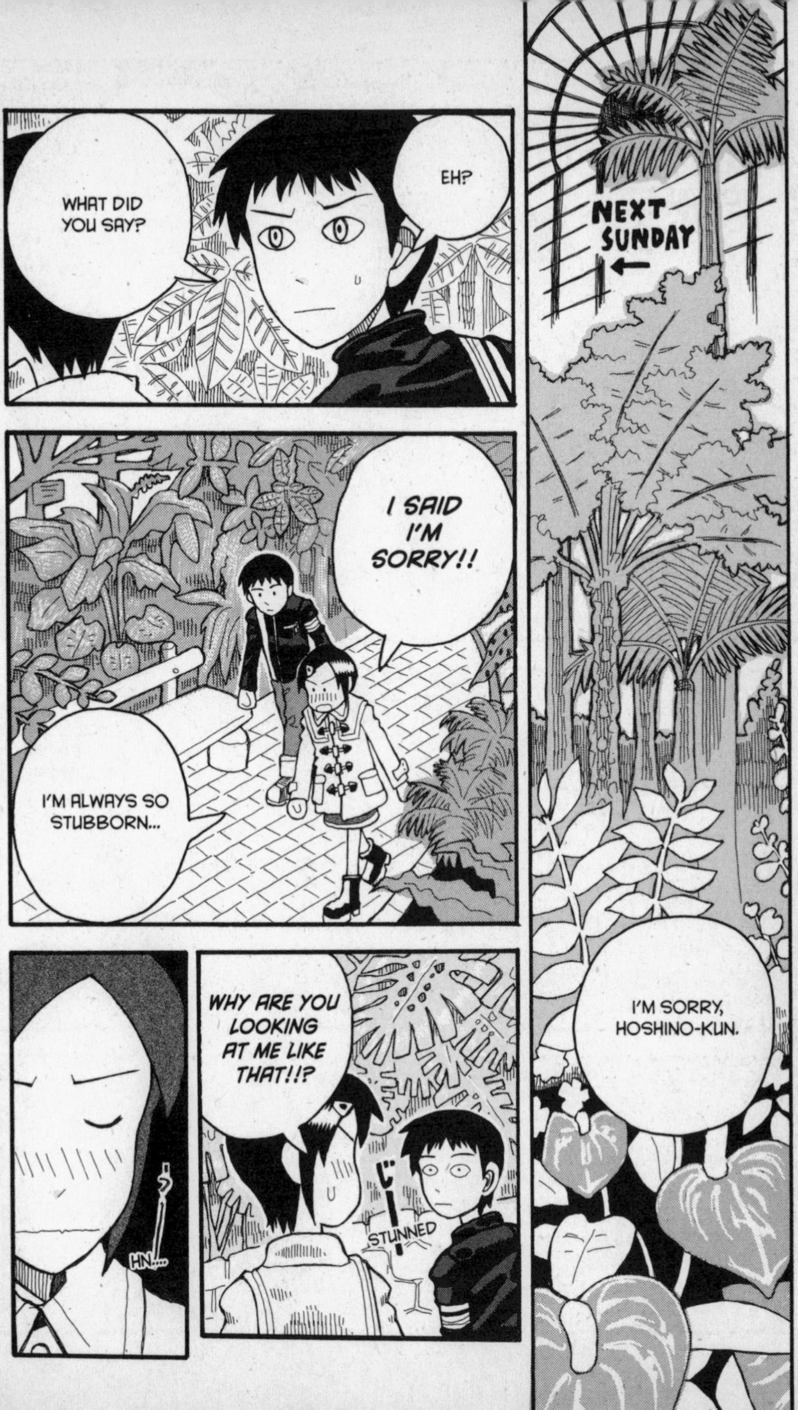
NEXT SUNDAY
I'M SORRY, HOSHINO-KUN.
EH?
WHAT DID YOU SAY?
I SAID I'M SORRY!!
I'M ALWAYS SO STUBBORN...
WHY ARE YOU LOOKING AT ME LIKE THAT!!?
STUNNED
HN...

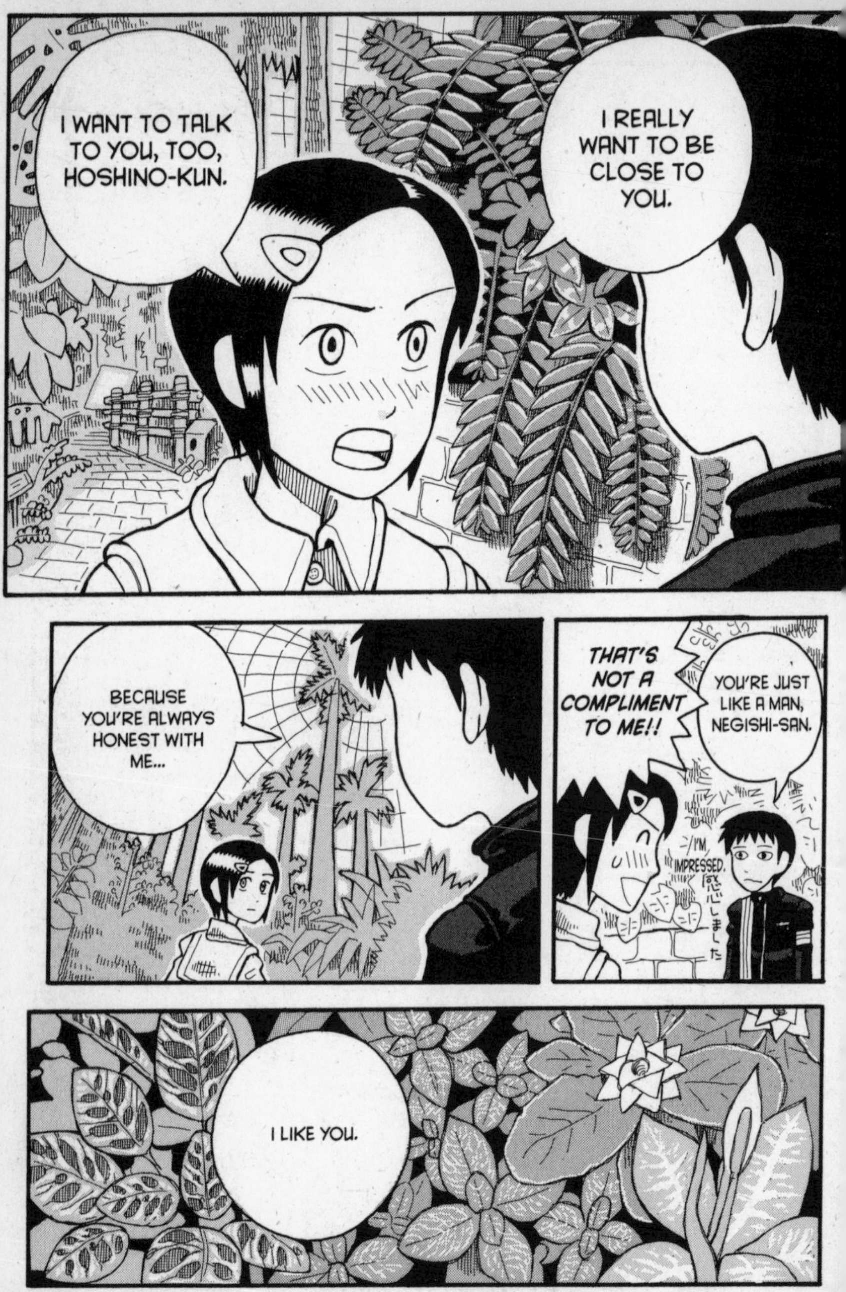
I REALLY WANT TO BE CLOSE TO YOU.
I WANT TO TALK TO YOU, TOO, HOSHINO-KUN.
YOU'RE JUST LIKE A MAN, NEGISHI-SAN.
I'M IMPRESSED.
感心しました
THAT'S NOT A COMPLIMENT TO ME!!
BECAUSE YOU'RE ALWAYS HONEST WITH ME...
I LIKE YOU.

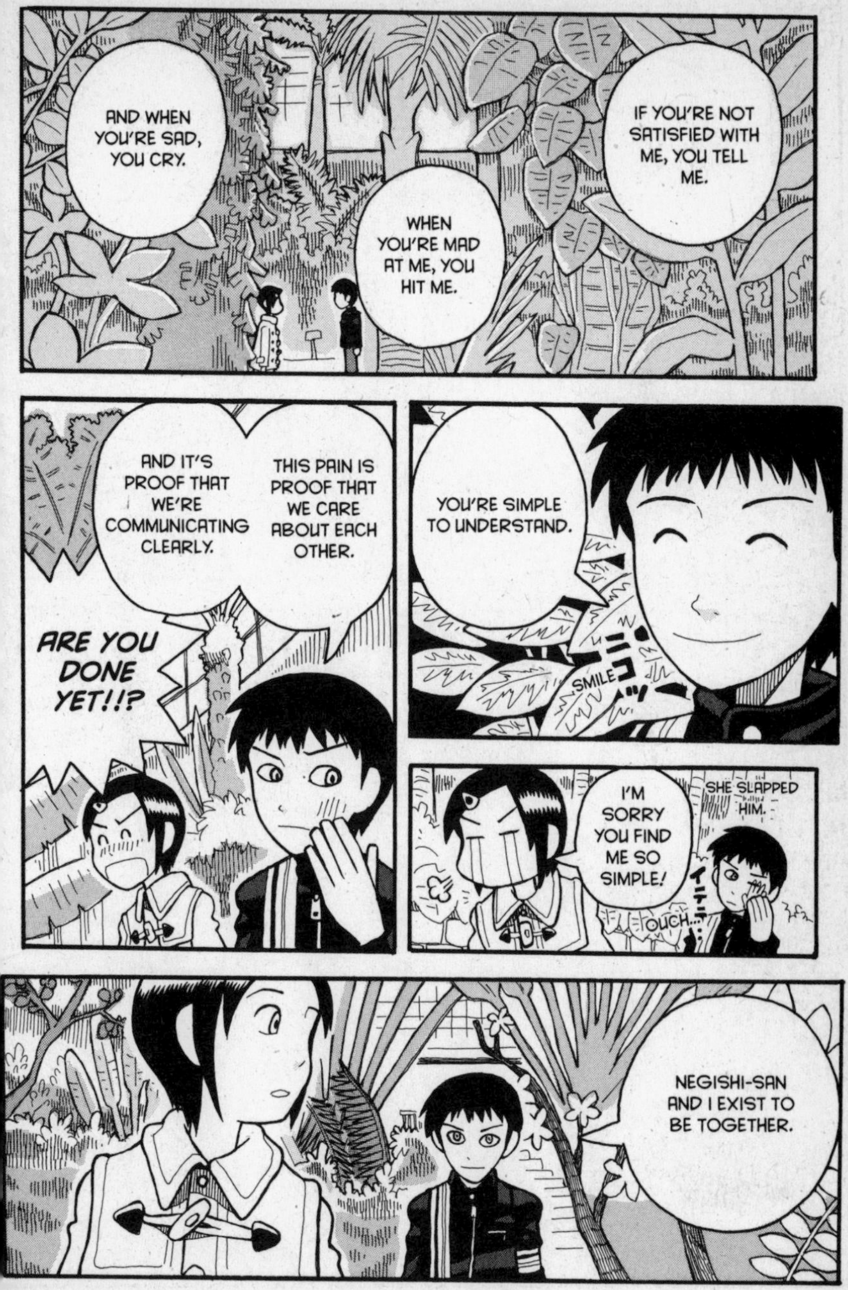
IF YOU'RE NOT SATISFIED WITH ME, YOU TELL ME.
WHEN YOU'RE MAD AT ME, YOU HIT ME.
AND WHEN YOU'RE SAD, YOU CRY.
THIS PAIN IS PROOF THAT WE CARE ABOUT EACH OTHER.
AND IT'S PROOF THAT WE'RE COMMUNICATING CLEARLY.
ARE YOU DONE YET!!?
YOU'RE SIMPLE TO UNDERSTAND.
SMILE
SHE SLAPPED HIM.
I'M SORRY YOU FIND ME SO SIMPLE!
OUCH...
NEGISHI-SAN AND I EXIST TO BE TOGETHER.

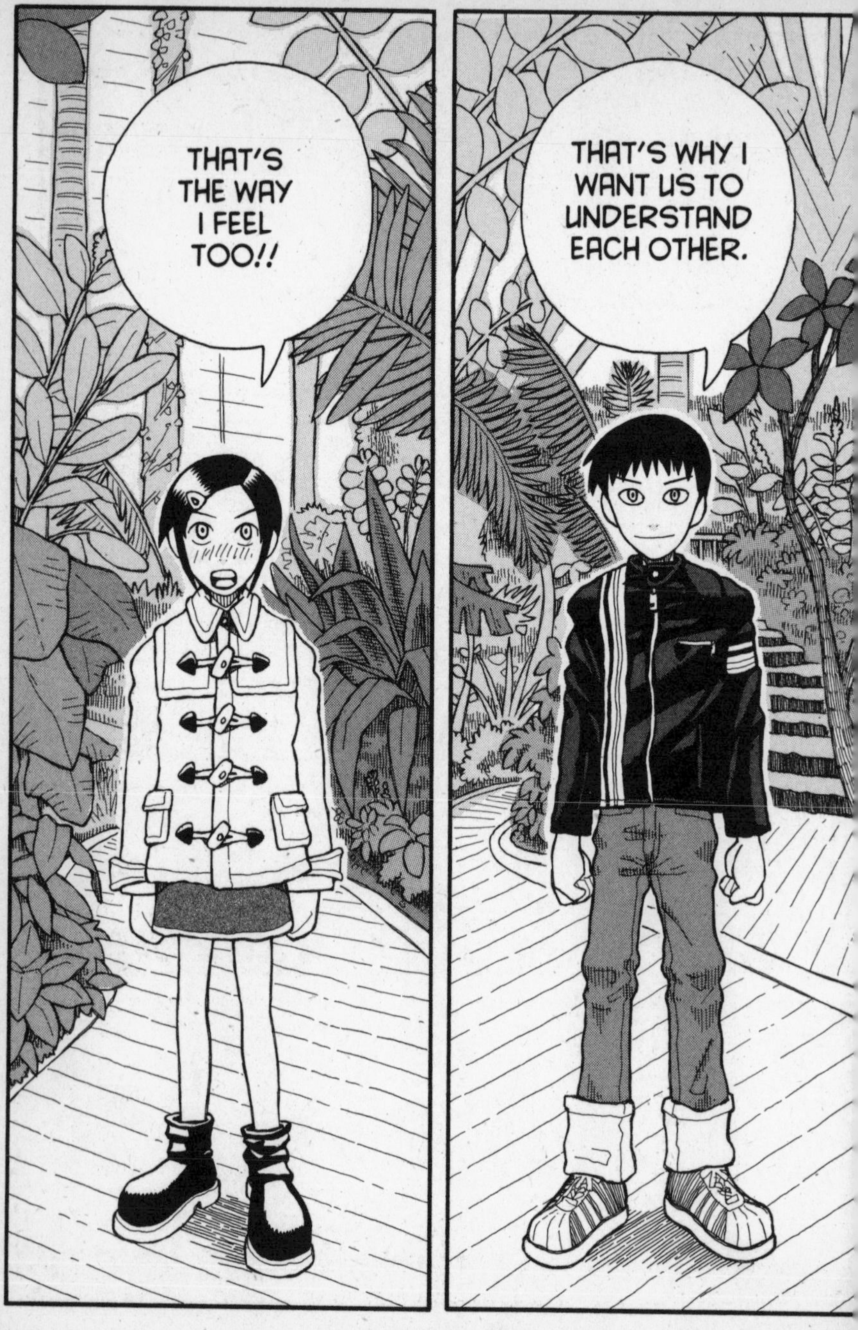
THAT'S WHY I WANT US TO UNDERSTAND EACH OTHER.
THAT'S THE WAY I FEEL TOO!!

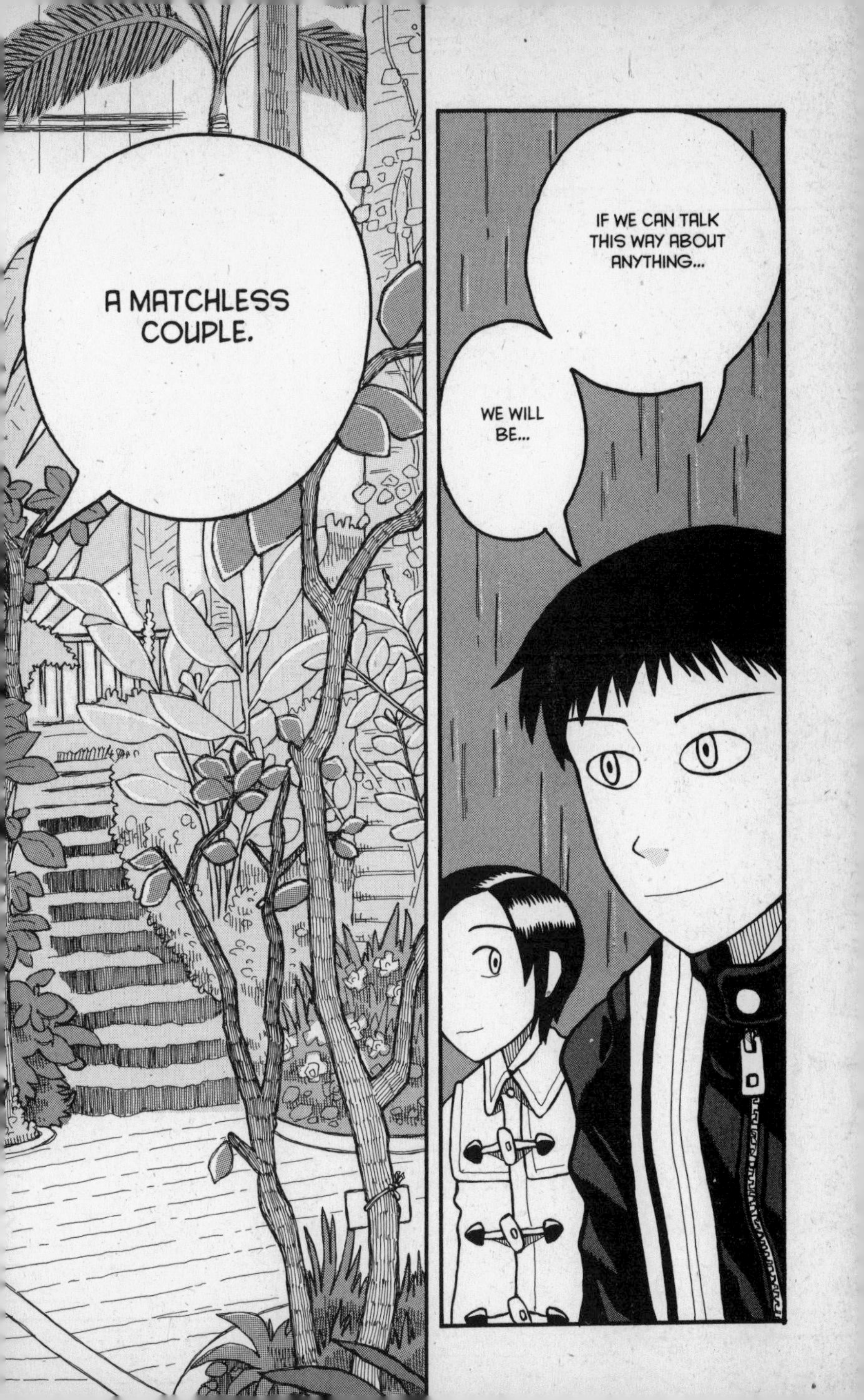
IF WE CAN TALK THIS WAY ABOUT ANYTHING...
WE WILL BE...
A MATCHLESS COUPLE.

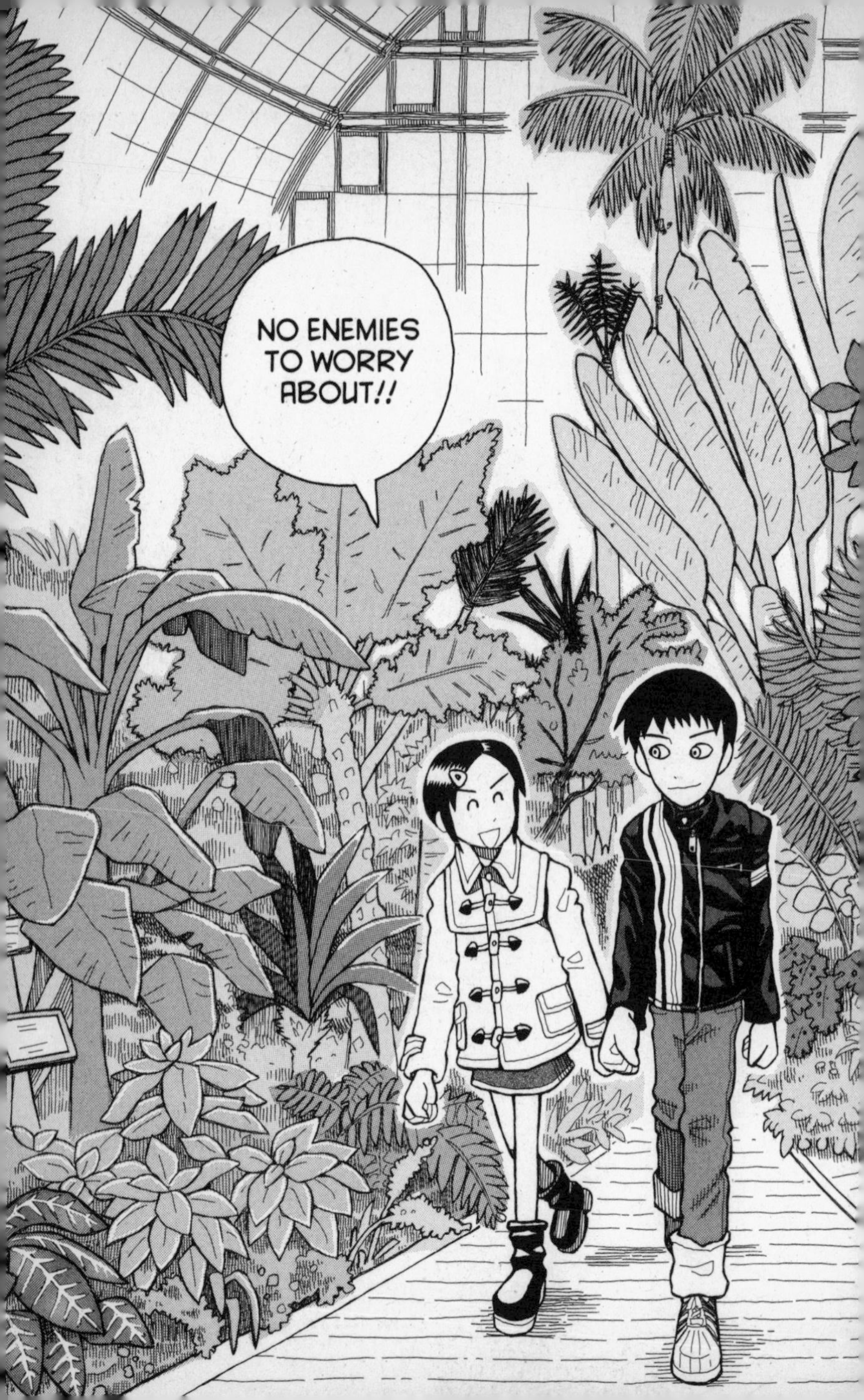
NO ENEMIES TO WORRY ABOUT!!

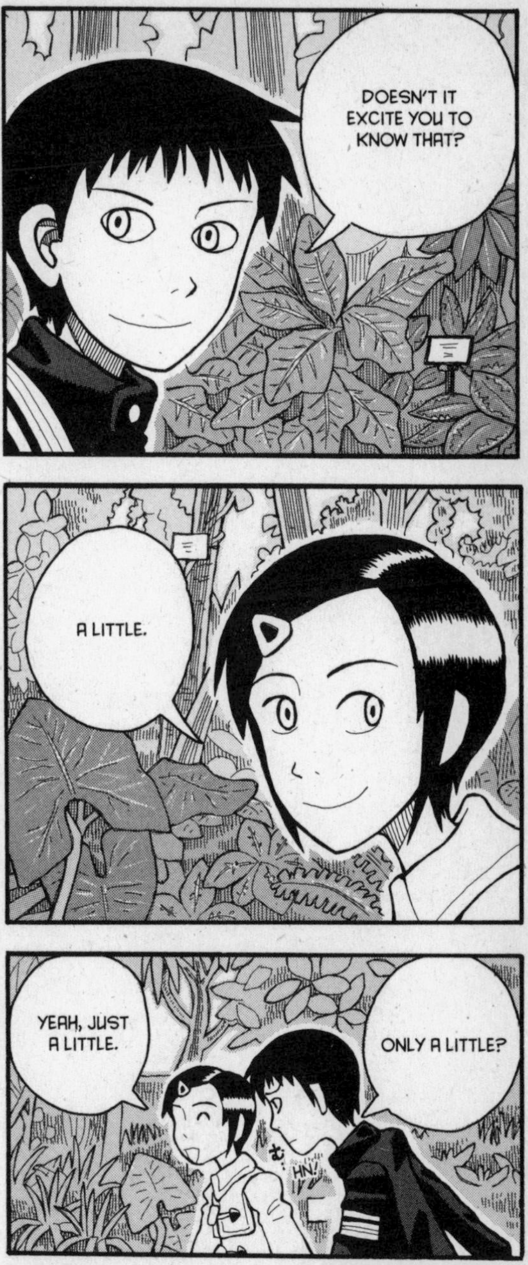
DOESN'T IT EXCITE YOU TO KNOW THAT?
A LITTLE.
ONLY A LITTLE?
YEAH, JUST A LITTLE.
HN!

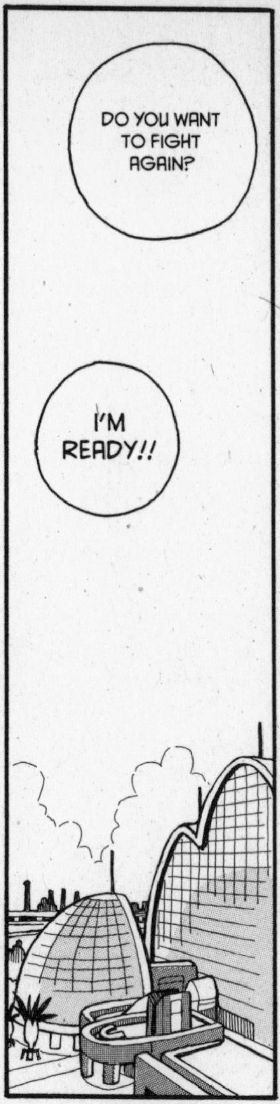
DO YOU WANT TO FIGHT AGAIN?
I'M READY!!

SIDE B

THE END.

To Be Continued to...

BONUS TRACK

おまけ

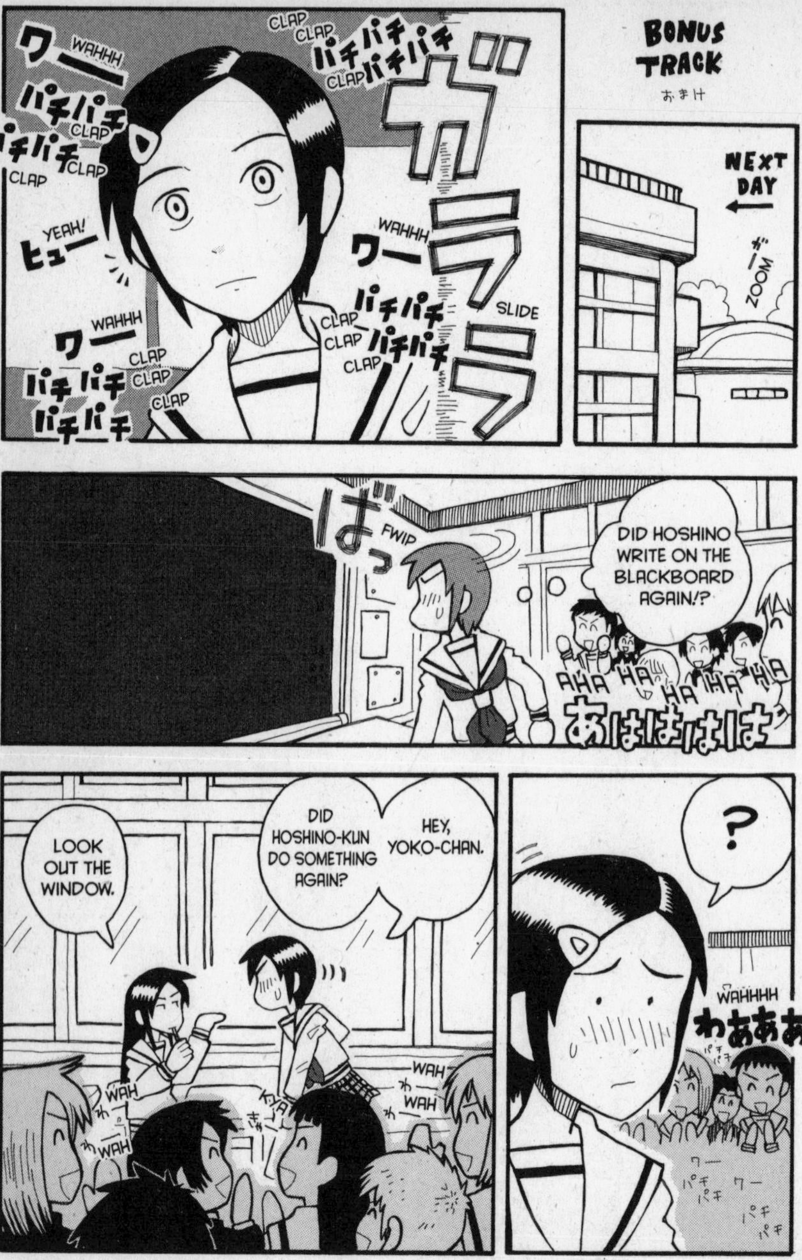
NEXT DAY
ZOOM
ガー
CLAP CLAP パチパチ パチパチ CLAP
ガラララ
SLIDE
WAHHH ワー
パチパチ パチパチ CLAP CLAP CLAP
WAHHH ワー
パチパチ CLAP
パチパチ CLAP CLAP
YEAH! ヒュー
WAHHH ワー
パチ パチ パチパチ CLAP CLAP CLAP
DID HOSHINO WRITE ON THE BLACKBOARD AGAIN!?
ばっ
FWIP
AHA HA HA HA HA
あははははは
?
WAHHHH
わあああ
ワー パチ パチ ワー パチ パチ
HEY, YOKO-CHAN.
DID HOSHINO-KUN DO SOMETHING AGAIN?
LOOK OUT THE WINDOW.
WAH
KYA
きゃー
WAH
WAH
WAH

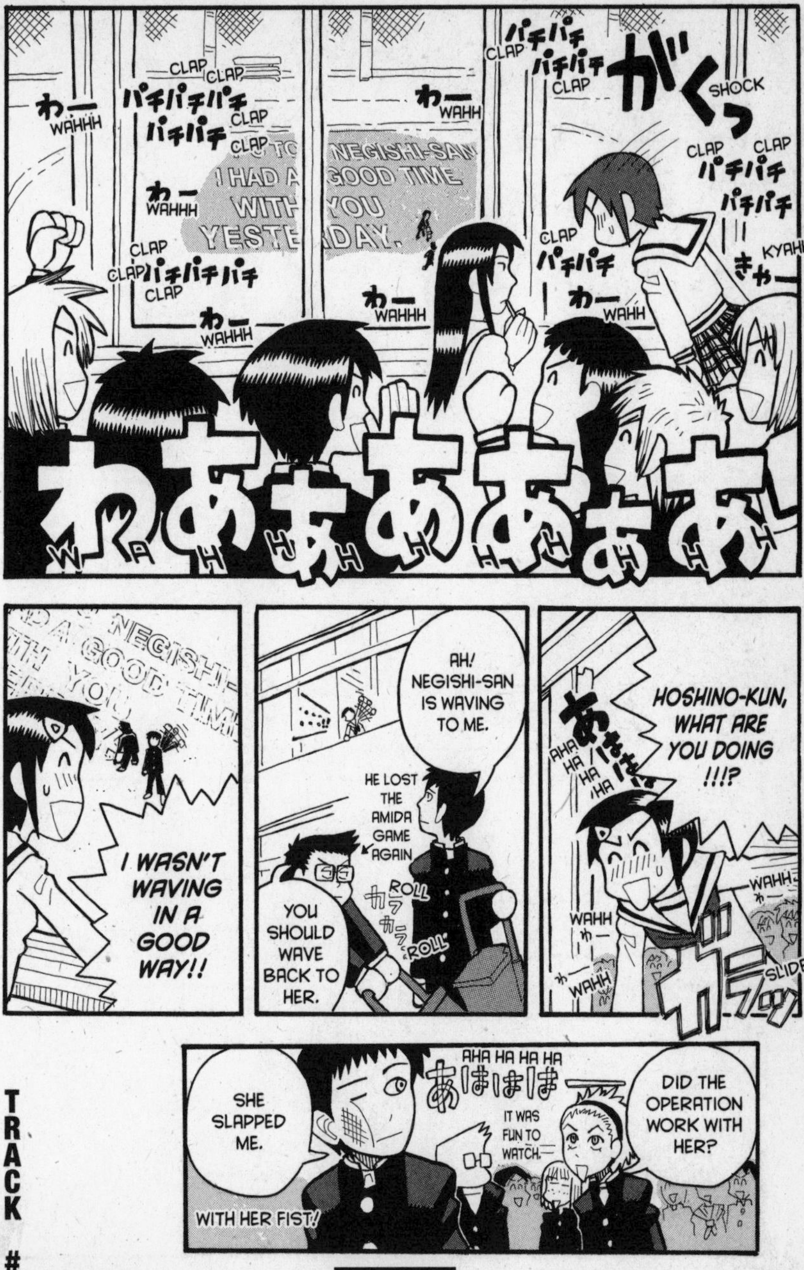

がくっ
SHOCK
パチパチ パチパチ
CLAP
CLAP
パチパチ パチパチ
CLAP CLAP
きゃー
KYAHHH
パチパチ
CLAP
わー
WAHH
わー
WAHH
TO NEGISHI-SAN
I HAD A GOOD TIME
WITH YOU
YESTERDAY.
わー
WAHHH
パチパチパチ パチパチ
CLAP CLAP CLAP CLAP
わー
WAHHH
わー
WAHHH
パチパチパチ
CLAP CLAP CLAP
わー
WAHHH
わー
WAHHH
わあああああああ
WAHHHHHHHH
HOSHINO-KUN, WHAT ARE YOU DOING !!!?
あははは
AHA HA HA HA
わー
WAHH
わー
WAHH
わー
WAHH
ガラッ
SLIDE
AH! NEGISHI-SAN IS WAVING TO ME.
HE LOST THE AMIDA GAME AGAIN
カラ カラ
ROLL ROLL
YOU SHOULD WAVE BACK TO HER.
I WASN'T WAVING IN A GOOD WAY!!
DID THE OPERATION WORK WITH HER?
あははは
AHA HA HA HA
IT WAS FUN TO WATCH.
SHE SLAPPED ME.
WITH HER FIST!

TRACK #1 ▶▶ END

THE END

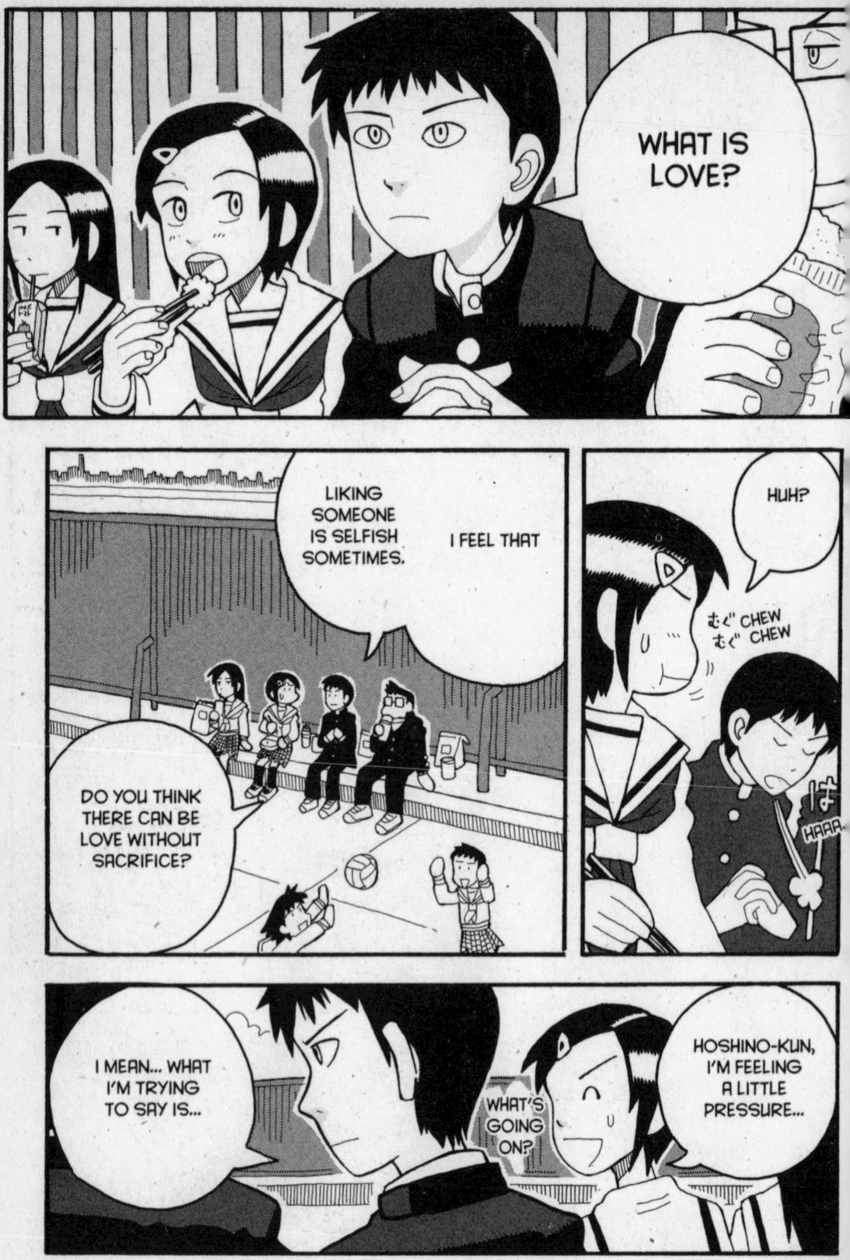
WHAT IS LOVE?
HUH?
むぐ CHEW
むぐ CHEW
は HAAA
I FEEL THAT
LIKING SOMEONE IS SELFISH SOMETIMES.
DO YOU THINK THERE CAN BE LOVE WITHOUT SACRIFICE?
HOSHINO-KUN, I'M FEELING A LITTLE PRESSURE...
WHAT'S GOING ON?
I MEAN... WHAT I'M TRYING TO SAY IS...

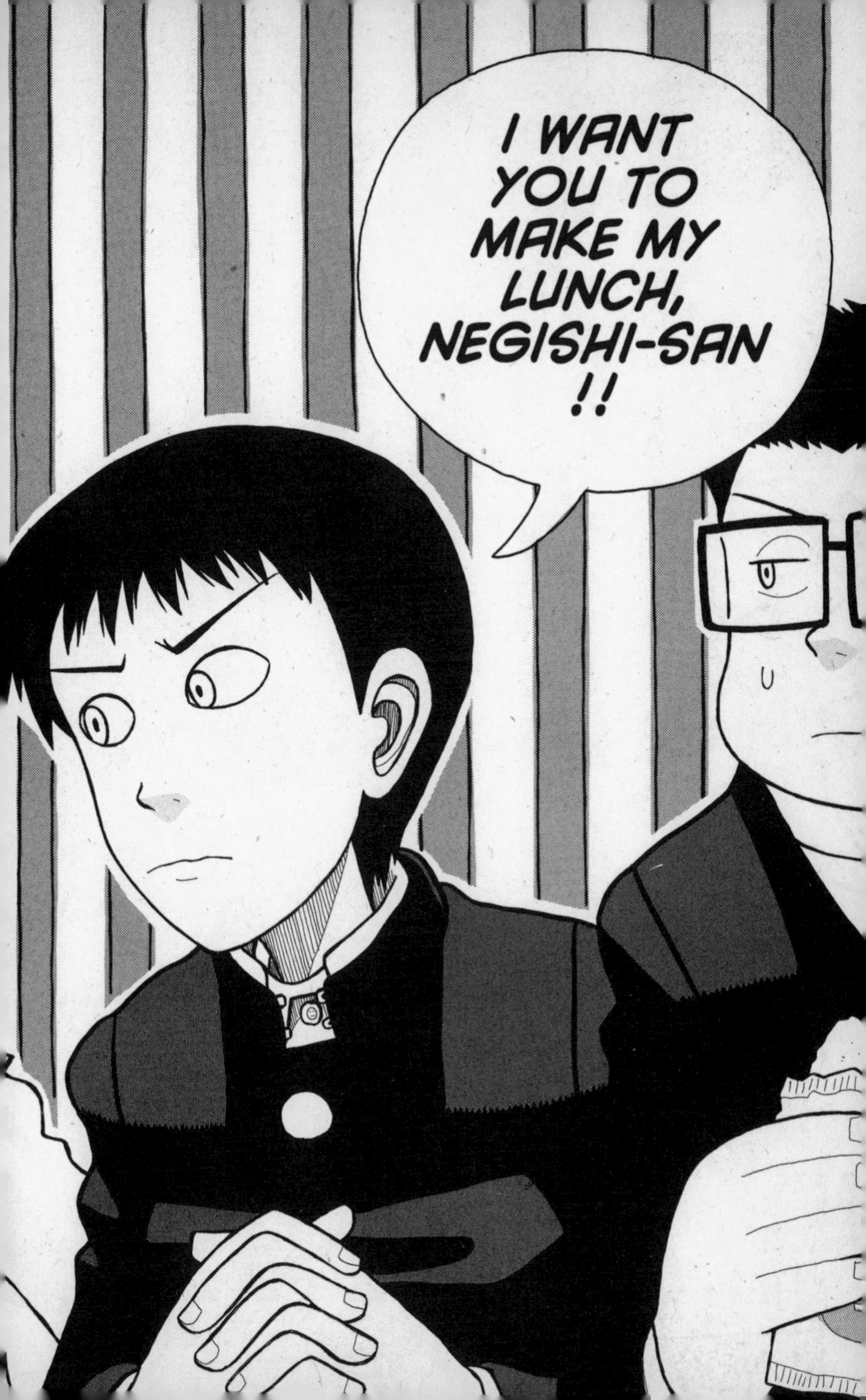
I WANT YOU TO MAKE MY LUNCH, NEGISHI-SAN !!

TRACK #2 LOVE'S LUNCHBOX

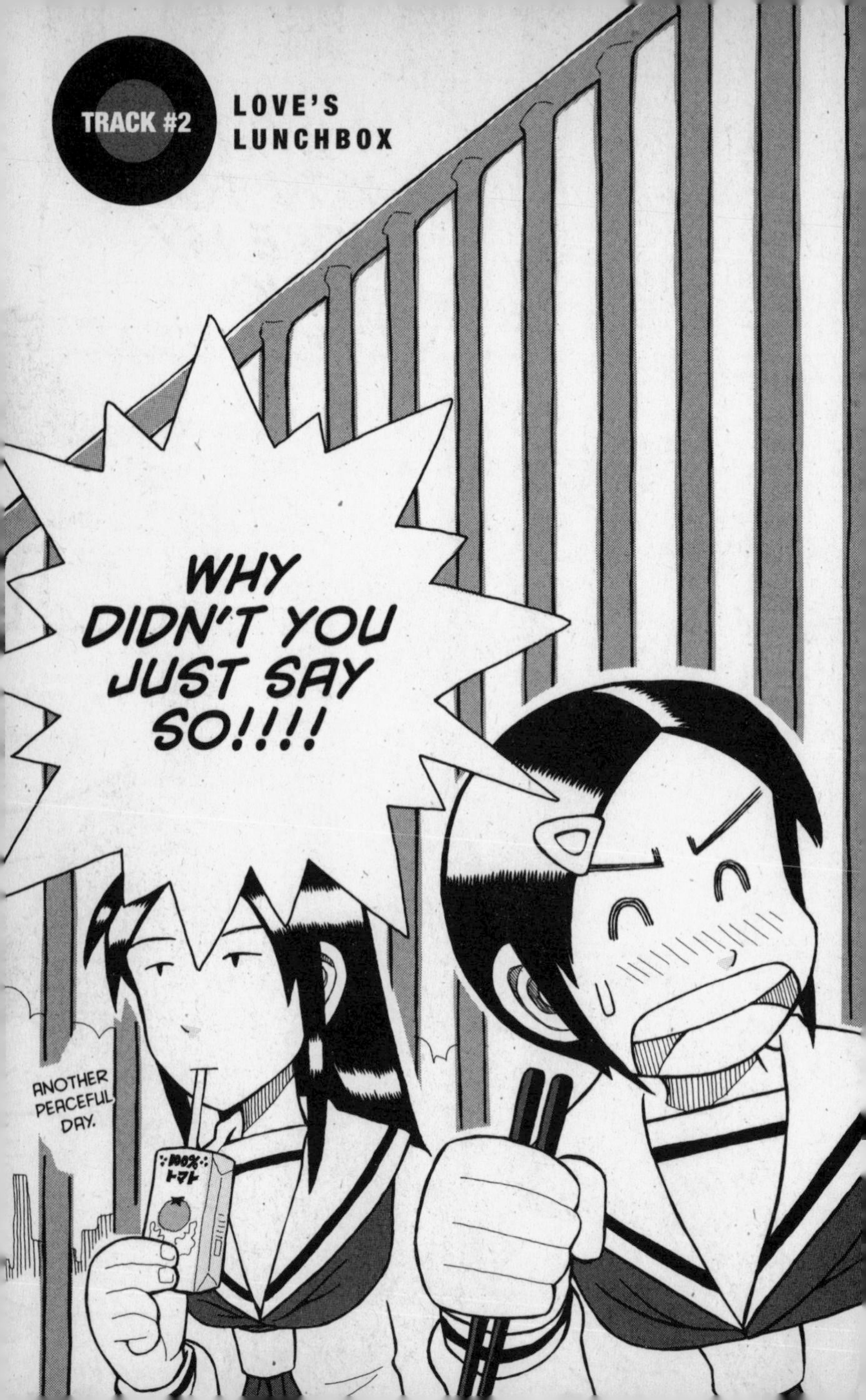
WHY DIDN'T YOU JUST SAY SO!!!!
ANOTHER PEACEFUL DAY.
100% トマト

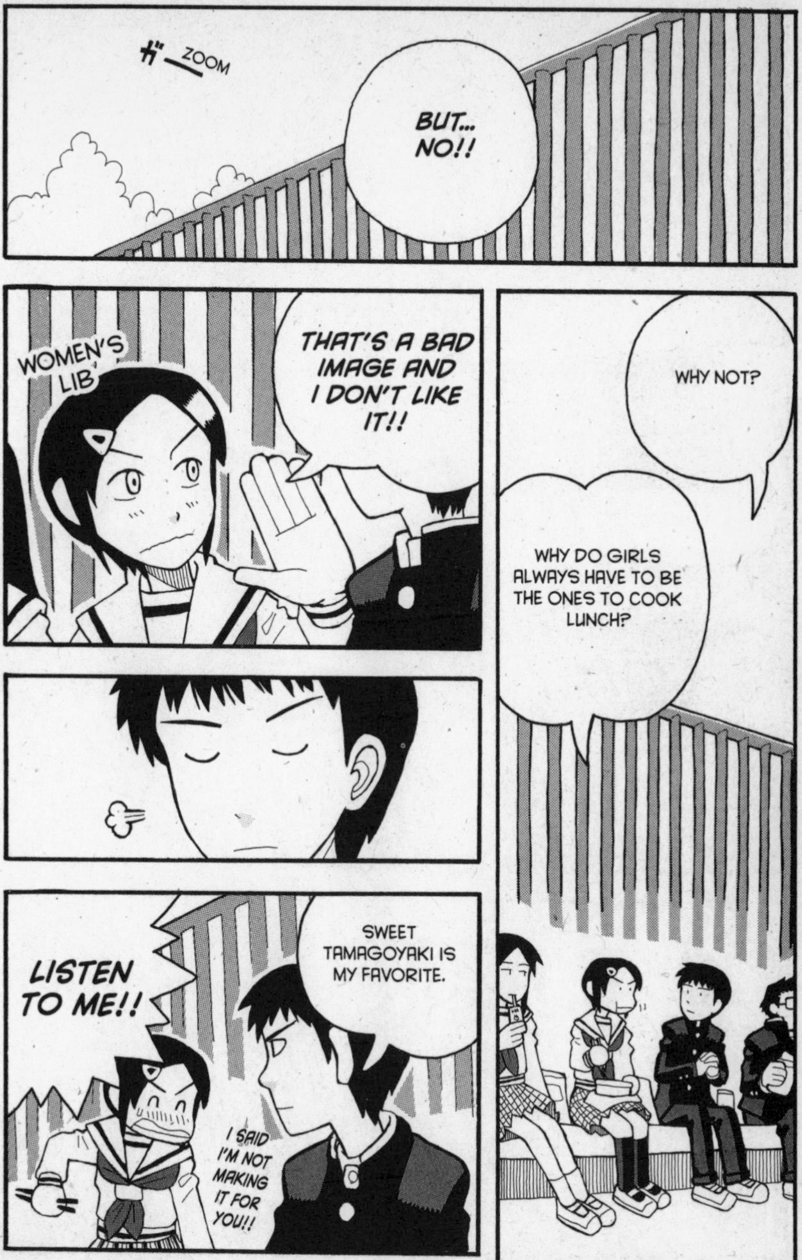
BUT... NO!!
ガー ZOOM
WHY NOT?
WHY DO GIRLS ALWAYS HAVE TO BE THE ONES TO COOK LUNCH?
THAT'S A BAD IMAGE AND I DON'T LIKE IT!!
WOMEN'S LIB
SWEET TAMAGOYAKI IS MY FAVORITE.
LISTEN TO ME!!
I SAID I'M NOT MAKING IT FOR YOU!!

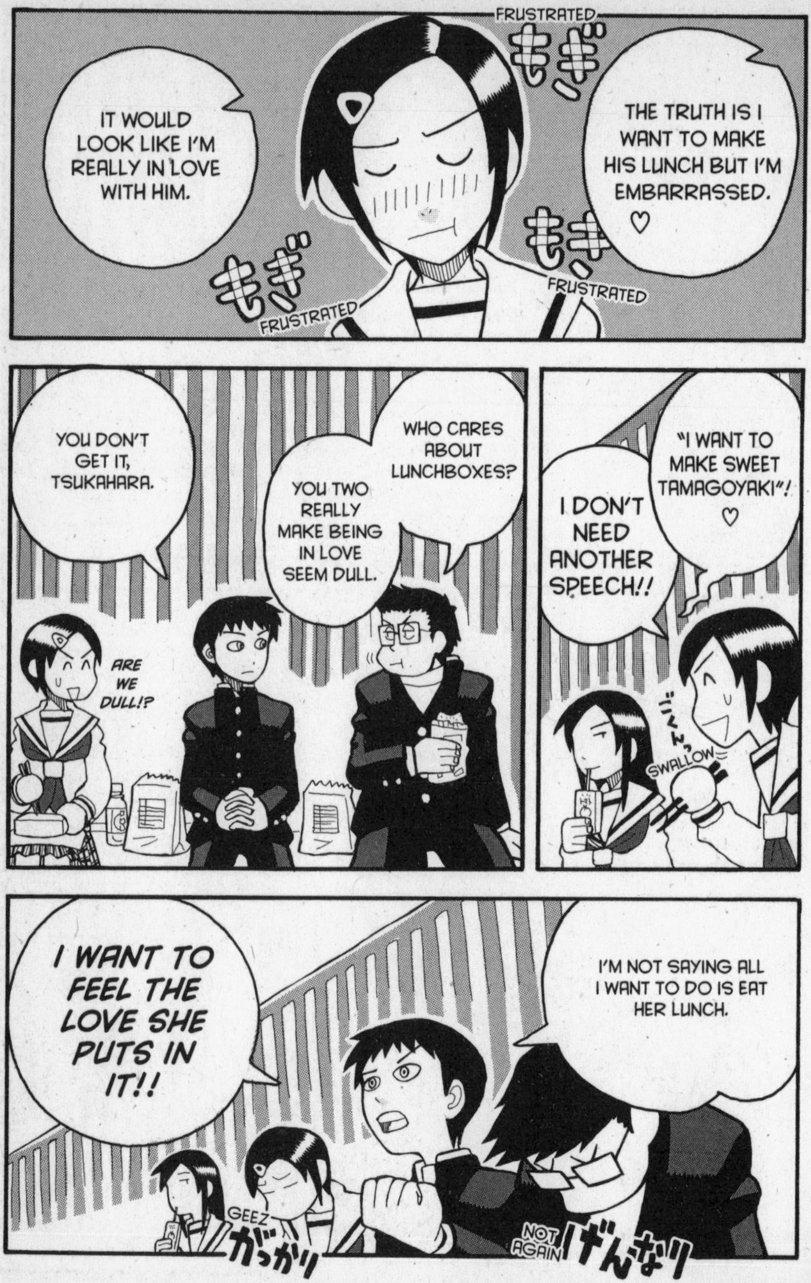
FRUSTRATED もぎ
THE TRUTH IS I WANT TO MAKE HIS LUNCH BUT I'M EMBARRASSED. ♡
FRUSTRATED もぎ
IT WOULD LOOK LIKE I'M REALLY IN LOVE WITH HIM.
FRUSTRATED もぎ
"I WANT TO MAKE SWEET TAMAGOYAKI"! ♡
I DON'T NEED ANOTHER SPEECH!!
SWALLOW
WHO CARES ABOUT LUNCHBOXES?
YOU TWO REALLY MAKE BEING IN LOVE SEEM DULL.
YOU DON'T GET IT, TSUKAHARA.
ARE WE DULL!?
I'M NOT SAYING ALL I WANT TO DO IS EAT HER LUNCH.
I WANT TO FEEL THE LOVE SHE PUTS IN IT!!
NOT AGAIN げんなり
GEEZ がっかり

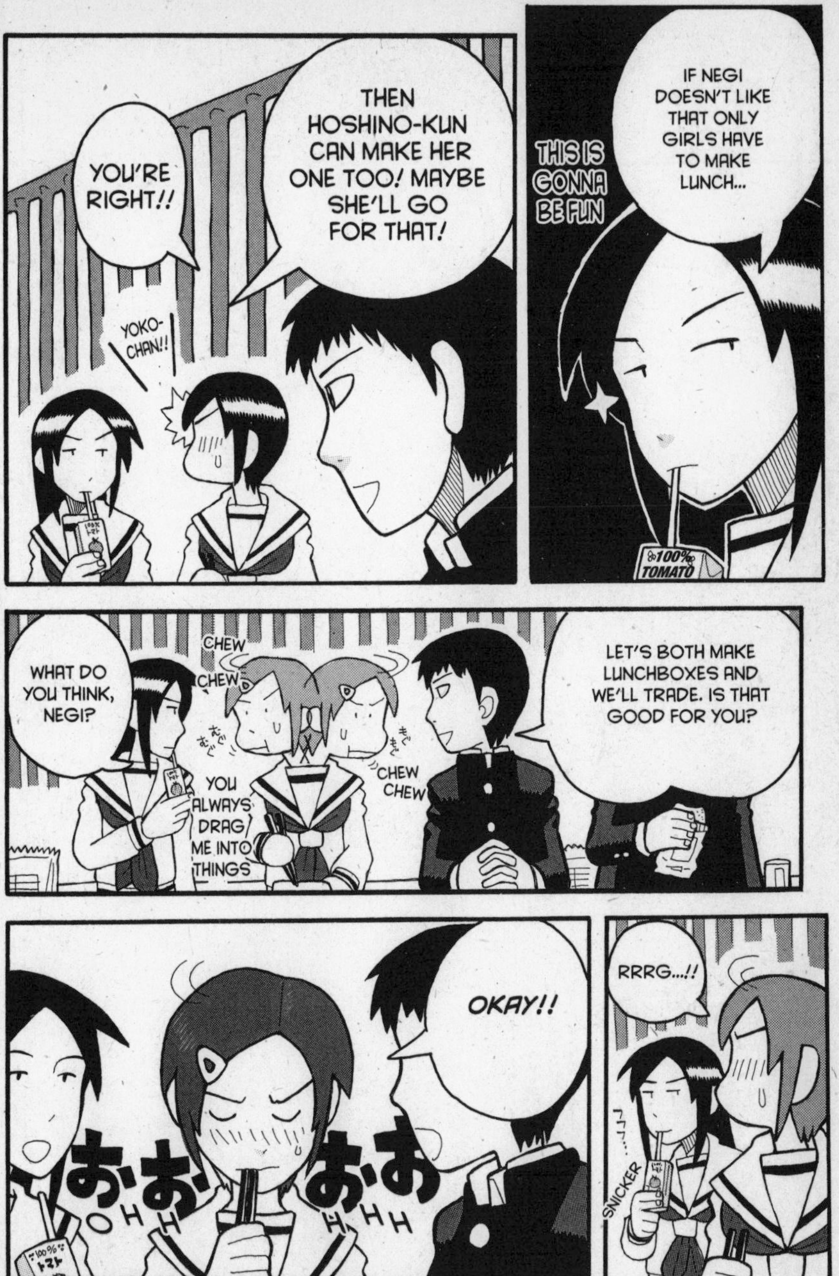
IF NEGI DOESN'T LIKE THAT ONLY GIRLS HAVE TO MAKE LUNCH...
THIS IS GONNA BE FUN
100% TOMATO
THEN HOSHINO-KUN CAN MAKE HER ONE TOO! MAYBE SHE'LL GO FOR THAT!
YOU'RE RIGHT!!
YOKO-CHAN!!
LET'S BOTH MAKE LUNCHBOXES AND WE'LL TRADE. IS THAT GOOD FOR YOU?
CHEW CHEW
YOU ALWAYS DRAG ME INTO THINGS
CHEW CHEW
WHAT DO YOU THINK, NEGI?
RRRG...!!
SNICKER
OKAY!!
おお おお
OHHH HHHH

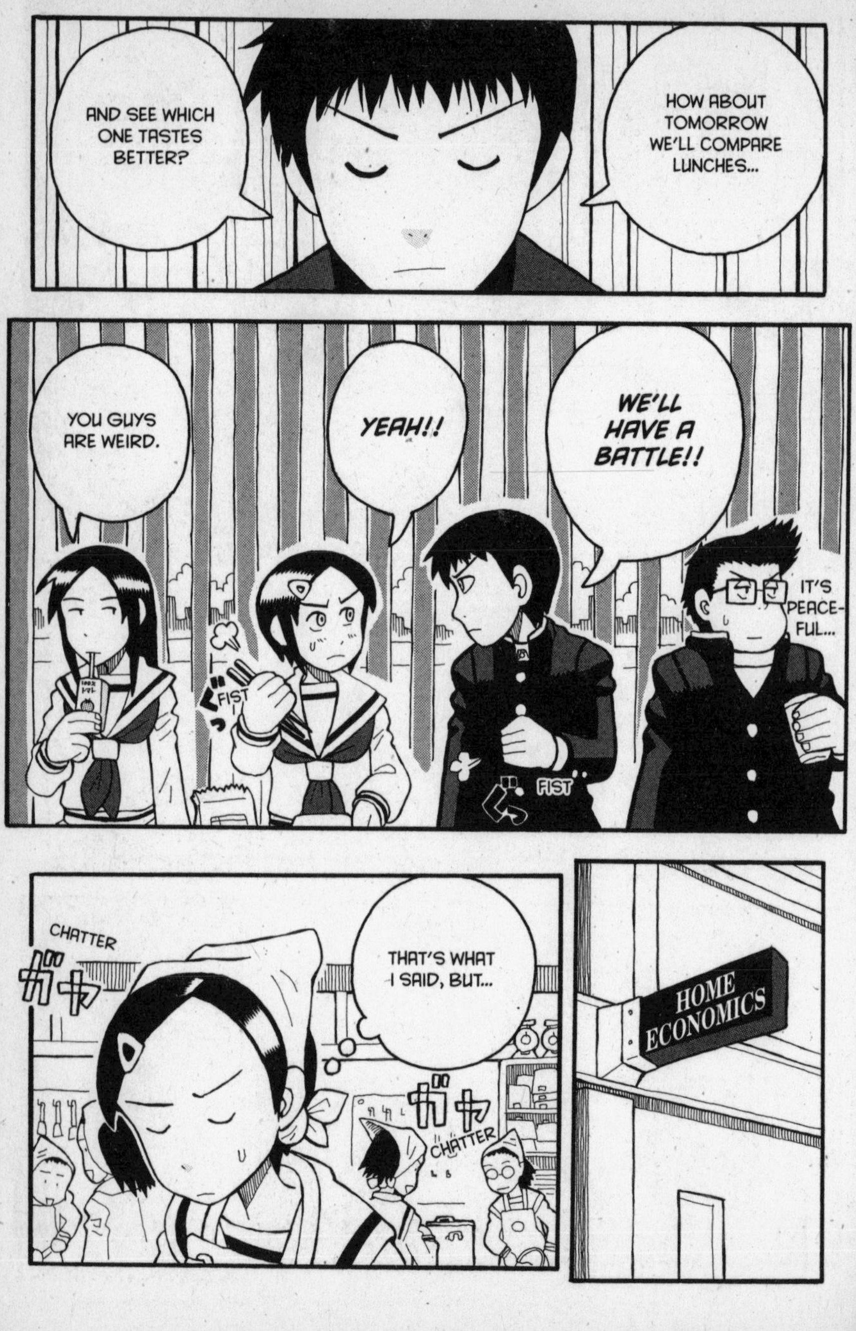
HOW ABOUT TOMORROW WE'LL COMPARE LUNCHES...
AND SEE WHICH ONE TASTES BETTER?
WE'LL HAVE A BATTLE!!
IT'S PEACE-FUL...
YEAH!!
YOU GUYS ARE WEIRD.
FIST
FIST
HOME ECONOMICS
THAT'S WHAT I SAID, BUT...
CHATTER
CHATTER

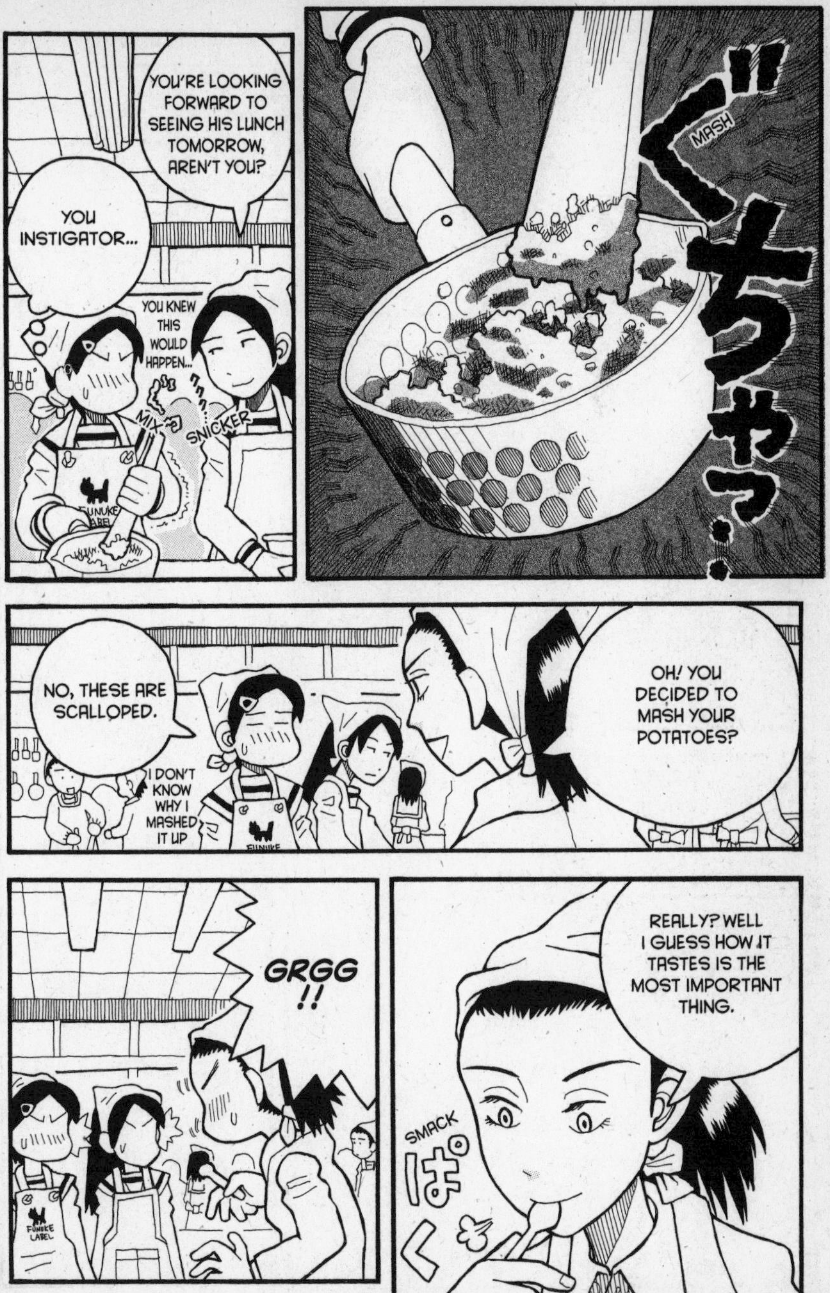
ぐちゃっ…!
MASH
YOU'RE LOOKING FORWARD TO SEEING HIS LUNCH TOMORROW, AREN'T YOU?
YOU INSTIGATOR...
YOU KNEW THIS WOULD HAPPEN...
SNICKER
MIX
OH! YOU DECIDED TO MASH YOUR POTATOES?
NO, THESE ARE SCALLOPED.
I DON'T KNOW WHY I MASHED IT UP
REALLY? WELL I GUESS HOW IT TASTES IS THE MOST IMPORTANT THING.
SMACK
ぱく
GRGG !!

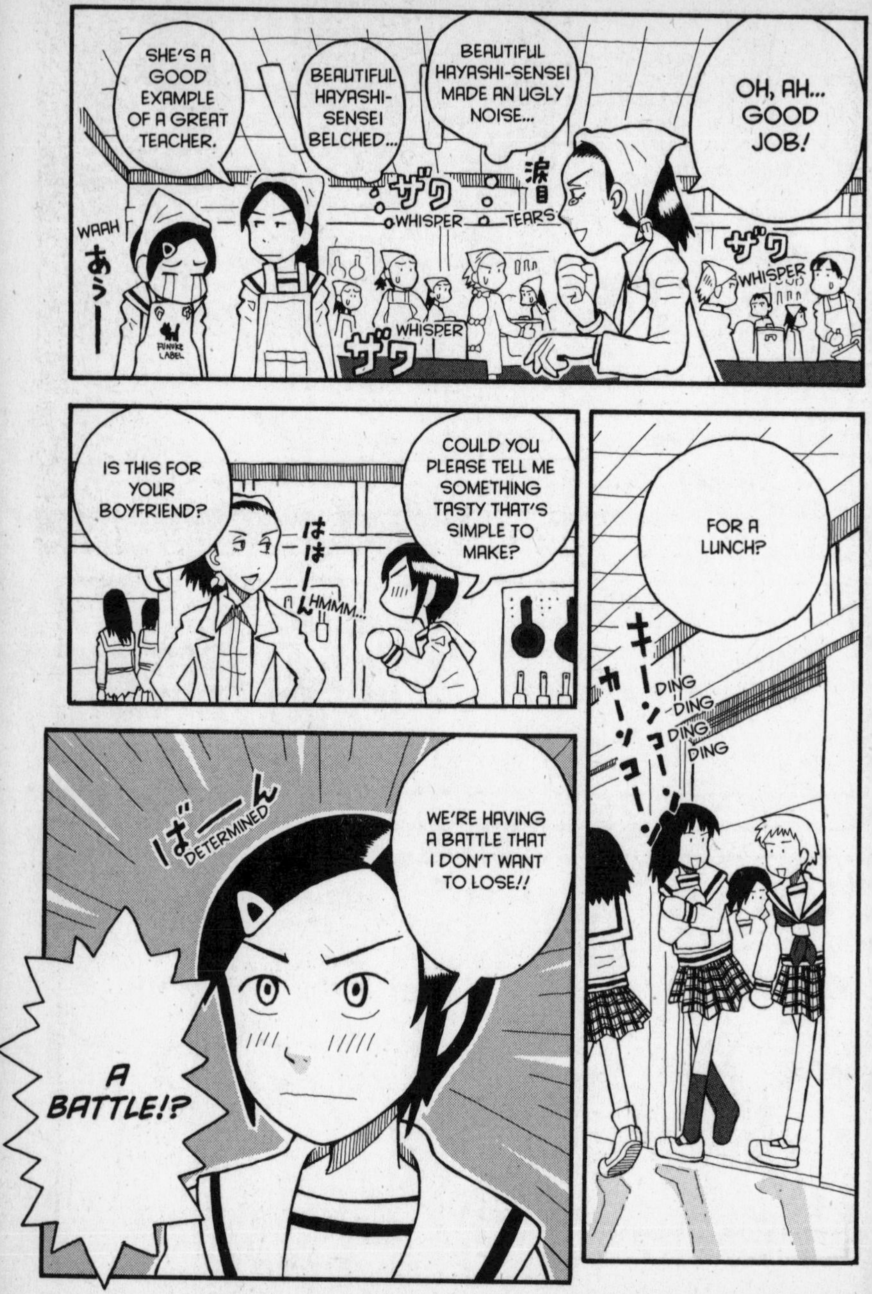
OH, AH... GOOD JOB!
ザワ WHISPER
BEAUTIFUL HAYASHI-SENSEI MADE AN UGLY NOISE...
涙 TEARS
ザワ WHISPER
BEAUTIFUL HAYASHI-SENSEI BELCHED...
ザワ WHISPER
SHE'S A GOOD EXAMPLE OF A GREAT TEACHER.
あう WAAH
FUNUKE LABEL
FOR A LUNCH?
キーンコーン カーンコーン DING DING DING DING
COULD YOU PLEASE TELL ME SOMETHING TASTY THAT'S SIMPLE TO MAKE?
ははーん HMMM...
IS THIS FOR YOUR BOYFRIEND?
WE'RE HAVING A BATTLE THAT I DON'T WANT TO LOSE!!
ばーん DETERMINED
A BATTLE!?

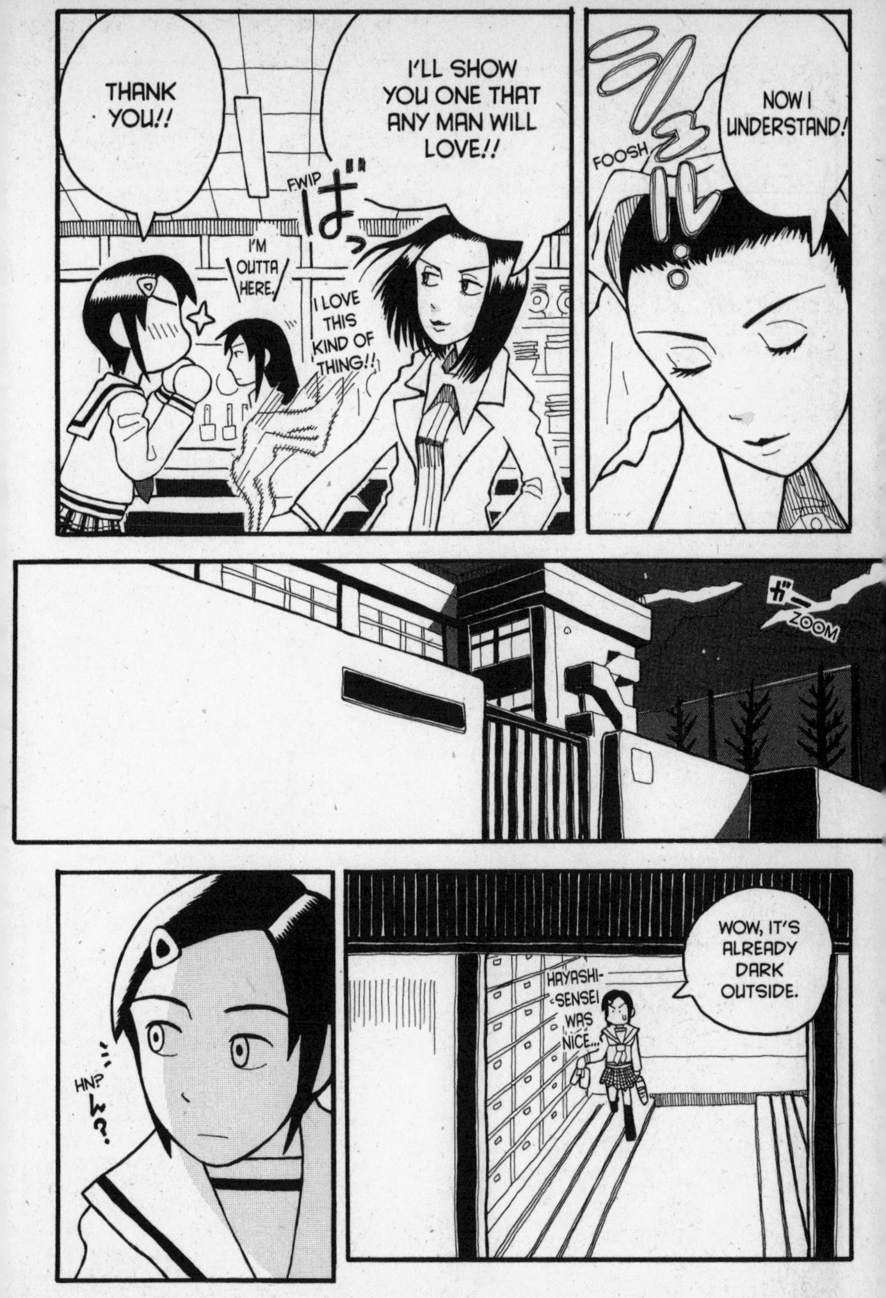
NOW I UNDERSTAND!
FOOSH
I'LL SHOW YOU ONE THAT ANY MAN WILL LOVE!!
THANK YOU!!
FWIP ばっ
I LOVE THIS KIND OF THING!!
I'M OUTTA HERE.
ガー ZOOM
WOW, IT'S ALREADY DARK OUTSIDE.
HAYASHI-SENSEI WAS NICE...
HN? ん?

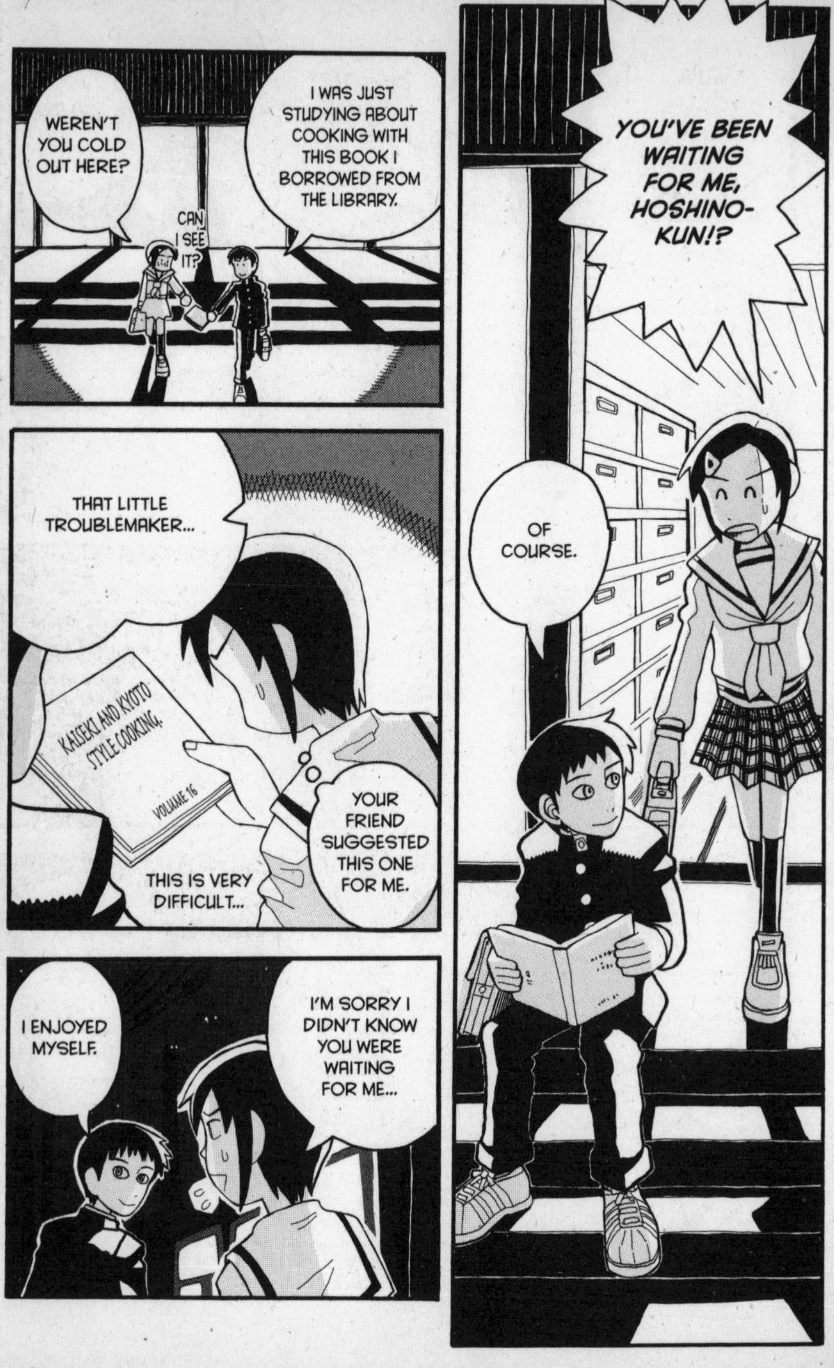
YOU'VE BEEN WAITING FOR ME, HOSHINO-KUN!?
OF COURSE.
I WAS JUST STUDYING ABOUT COOKING WITH THIS BOOK I BORROWED FROM THE LIBRARY.
WEREN'T YOU COLD OUT HERE?
CAN I SEE IT?
KAISEKI AND KYOTO STYLE COOKING.
VOLUME 16
YOUR FRIEND SUGGESTED THIS ONE FOR ME.
THIS IS VERY DIFFICULT...
THAT LITTLE TROUBLEMAKER...
I'M SORRY I DIDN'T KNOW YOU WERE WAITING FOR ME...
I ENJOYED MYSELF.

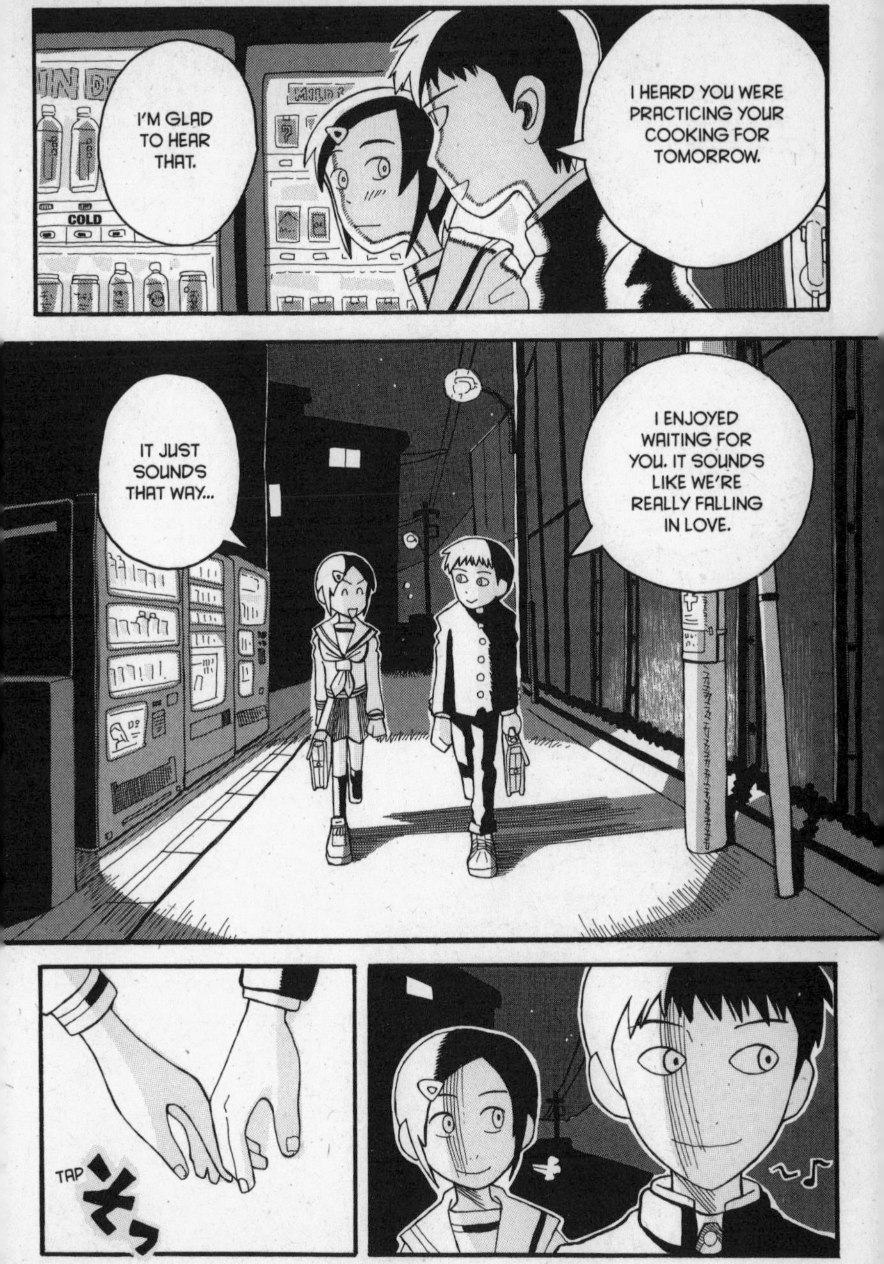
I HEARD YOU WERE PRACTICING YOUR COOKING FOR TOMORROW.
I'M GLAD TO HEAR THAT.
COLD
I ENJOYED WAITING FOR YOU. IT SOUNDS LIKE WE'RE REALLY FALLING IN LOVE.
IT JUST SOUNDS THAT WAY...
TAP
そっ

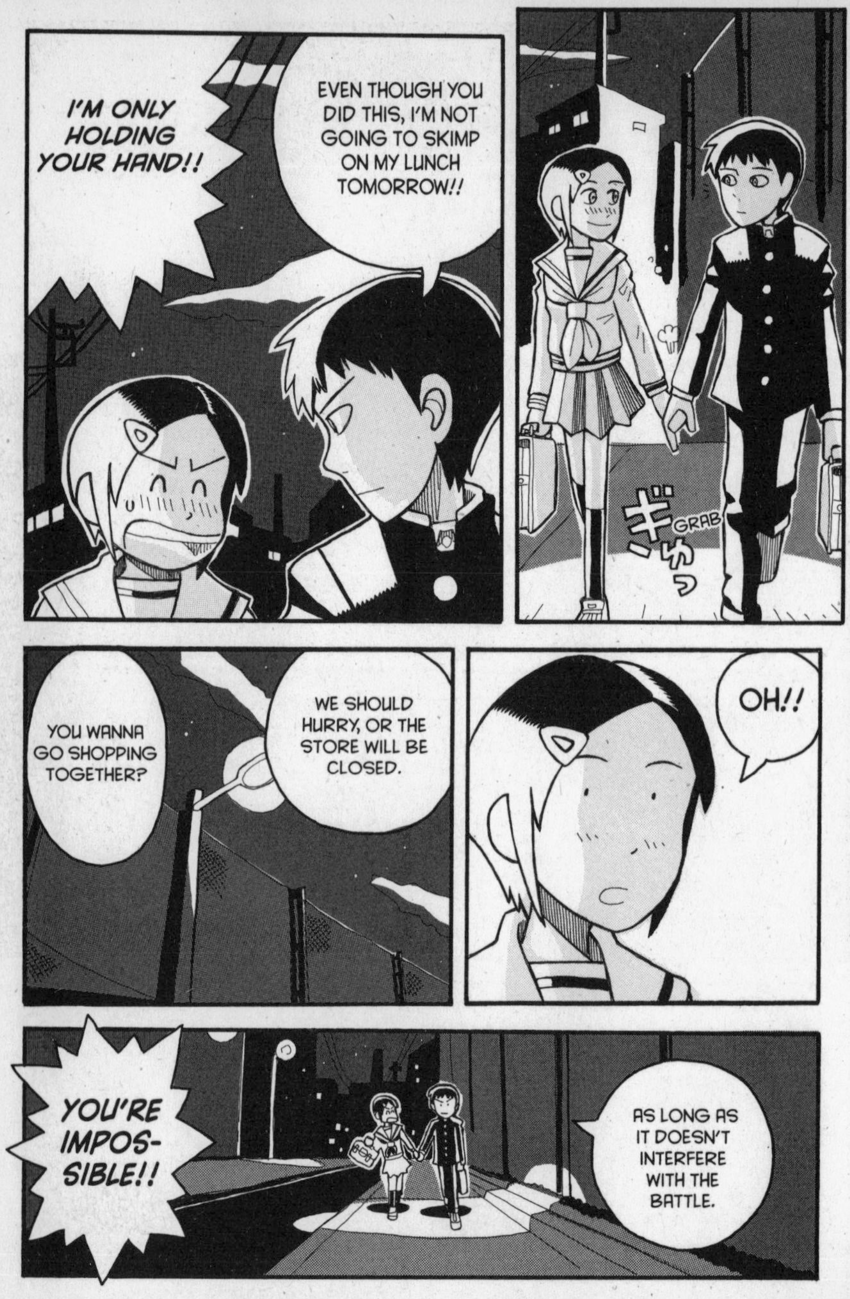
ぎゅっ
GRAB
EVEN THOUGH YOU DID THIS, I'M NOT GOING TO SKIMP ON MY LUNCH TOMORROW!!
I'M ONLY HOLDING YOUR HAND!!
OH!!
WE SHOULD HURRY, OR THE STORE WILL BE CLOSED.
YOU WANNA GO SHOPPING TOGETHER?
AS LONG AS IT DOESN'T INTERFERE WITH THE BATTLE.
YOU'RE IMPOS-SIBLE!!

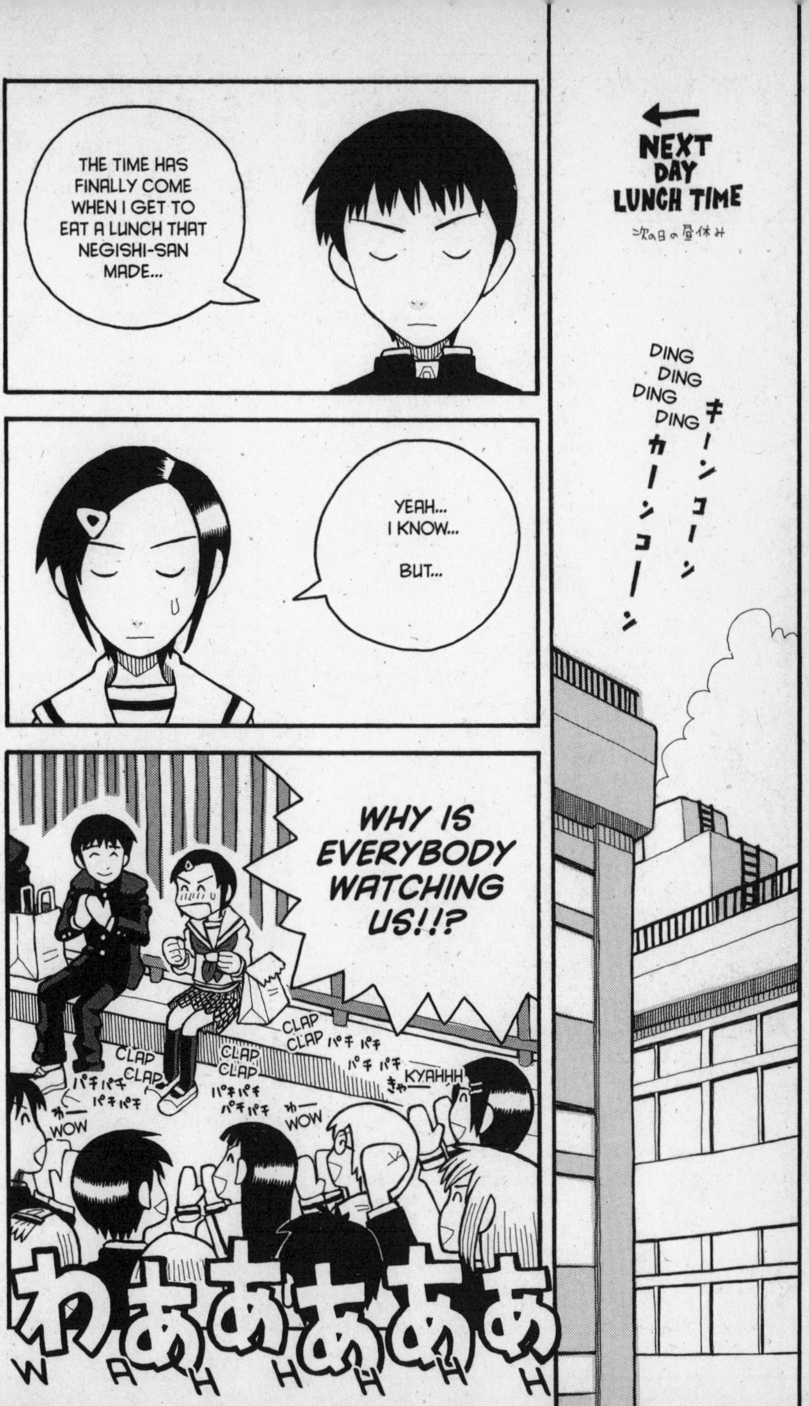
NEXT DAY LUNCH TIME
次の日の昼休み
DING DING DING DING
キーンコーン
カーンコーン
THE TIME HAS FINALLY COME WHEN I GET TO EAT A LUNCH THAT NEGISHI-SAN MADE...
YEAH... I KNOW... BUT...
WHY IS EVERYBODY WATCHING US!!?
CLAP CLAP パチ パチ
パチ パチ
CLAP CLAP
CLAP CLAP
パチパチ
パチパチ
パチパチ
パチパチ
きゃー KYAHHH
わー WOW
わー WOW
わあああああ
WAHHHHH

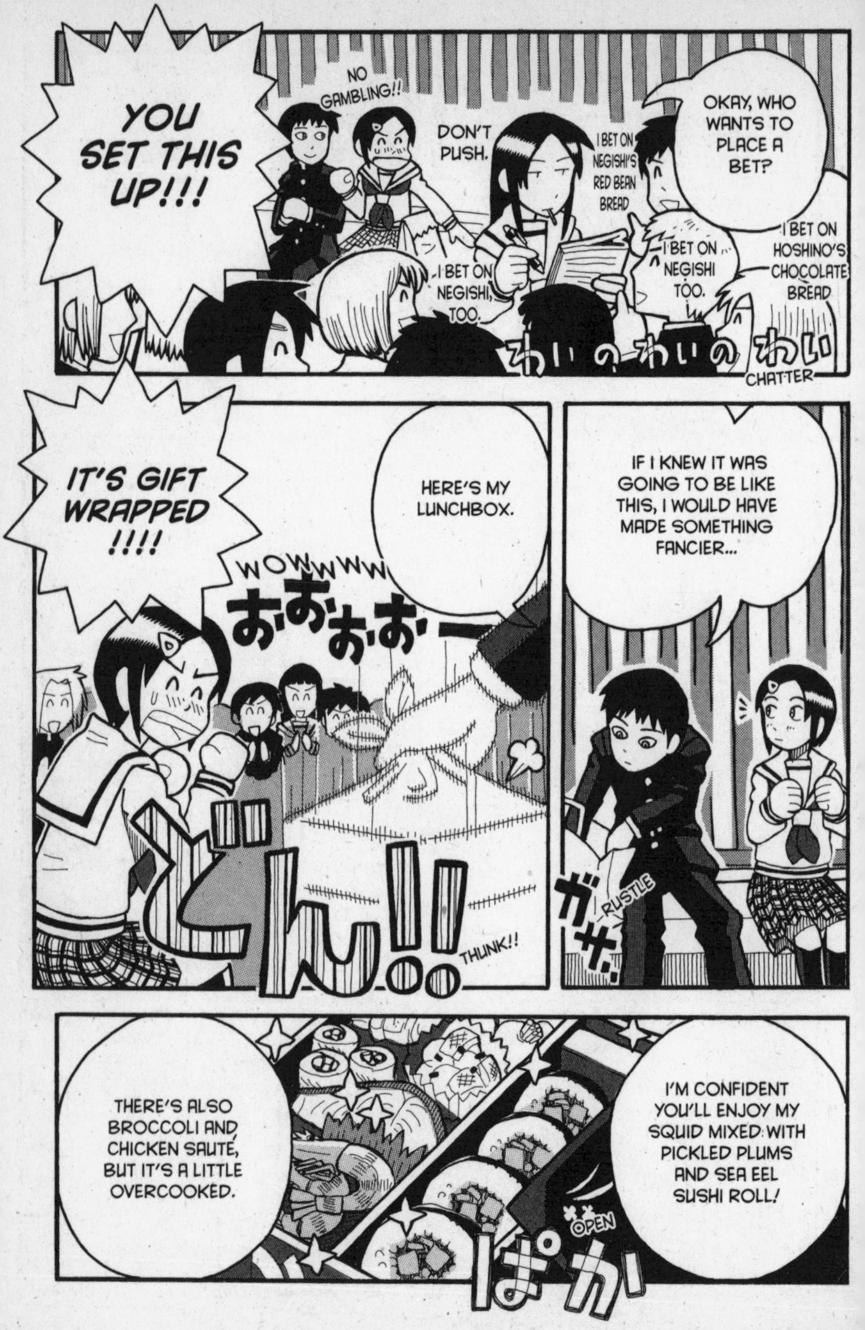
OKAY, WHO WANTS TO PLACE A BET?
I BET ON HOSHINO'S CHOCOLATE BREAD
I BET ON NEGISHI TOO.
I BET ON NEGISHI'S RED BEAN BREAD
DON'T PUSH.
I BET ON NEGISHI, TOO.
NO GAMBLING!!
YOU SET THIS UP!!!
わいのわいのわい
CHATTER
IF I KNEW IT WAS GOING TO BE LIKE THIS, I WOULD HAVE MADE SOMETHING FANCIER...
ガサ。
RUSTLE
HERE'S MY LUNCHBOX.
おおぉおー
WOWWWWW
IT'S GIFT WRAPPED!!!!
どん!!
THUNK!!
I'M CONFIDENT YOU'LL ENJOY MY SQUID MIXED WITH PICKLED PLUMS AND SEA EEL SUSHI ROLL!
THERE'S ALSO BROCCOLI AND CHICKEN SAUTE, BUT IT'S A LITTLE OVERCOOKED.
ぱかッ
OPEN

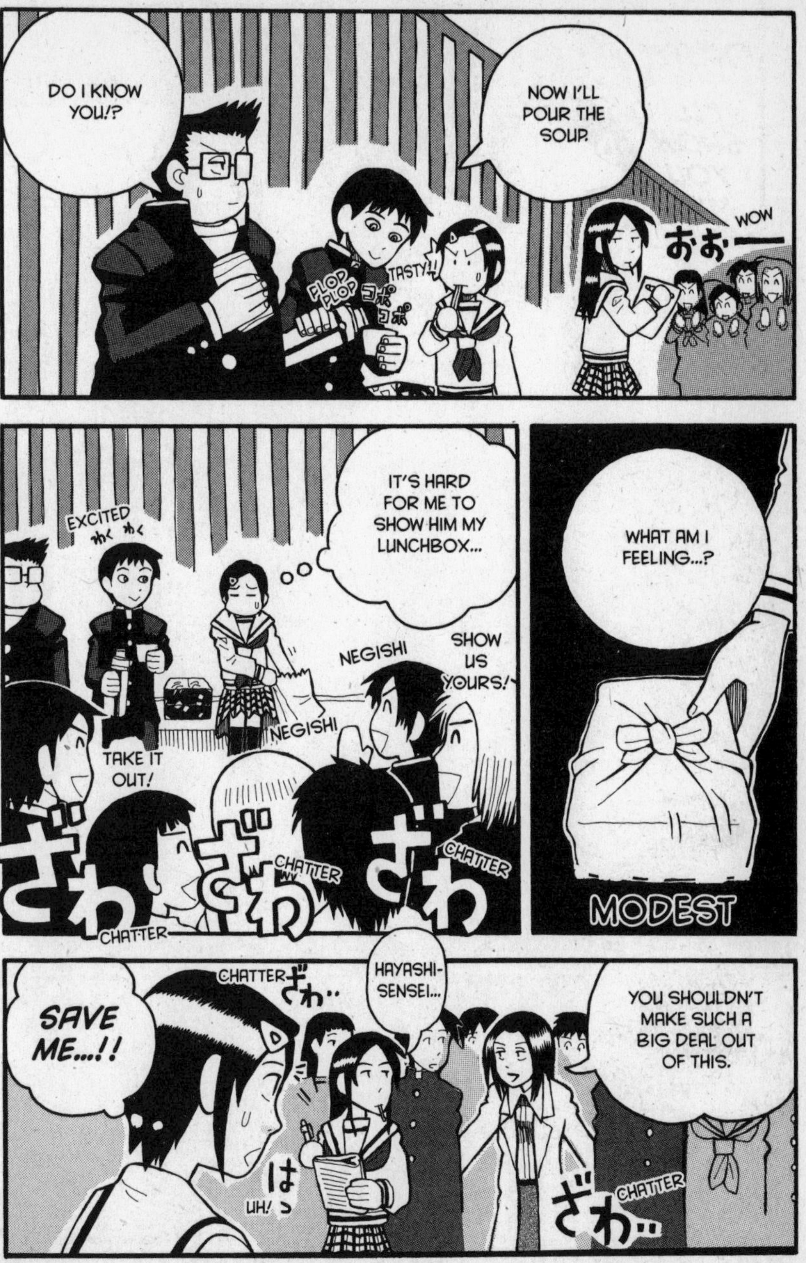
NOW I'LL POUR THE SOUP.
WOW
おおー
TASTY!!
PLOP PLOP
コポ コポ
DO I KNOW YOU!?
WHAT AM I FEELING...?
MODEST
IT'S HARD FOR ME TO SHOW HIM MY LUNCHBOX...
SHOW US YOURS!
NEGISHI
NEGISHI
EXCITED
わく わく
TAKE IT OUT!
ざわ
CHATTER
ざわ
CHATTER
ざわ
CHATTER
YOU SHOULDN'T MAKE SUCH A BIG DEAL OUT OF THIS.
HAYASHI-SENSEI...
CHATTER
ざわ..
ざわ..
CHATTER
はっ
UH!
SAVE ME...!!

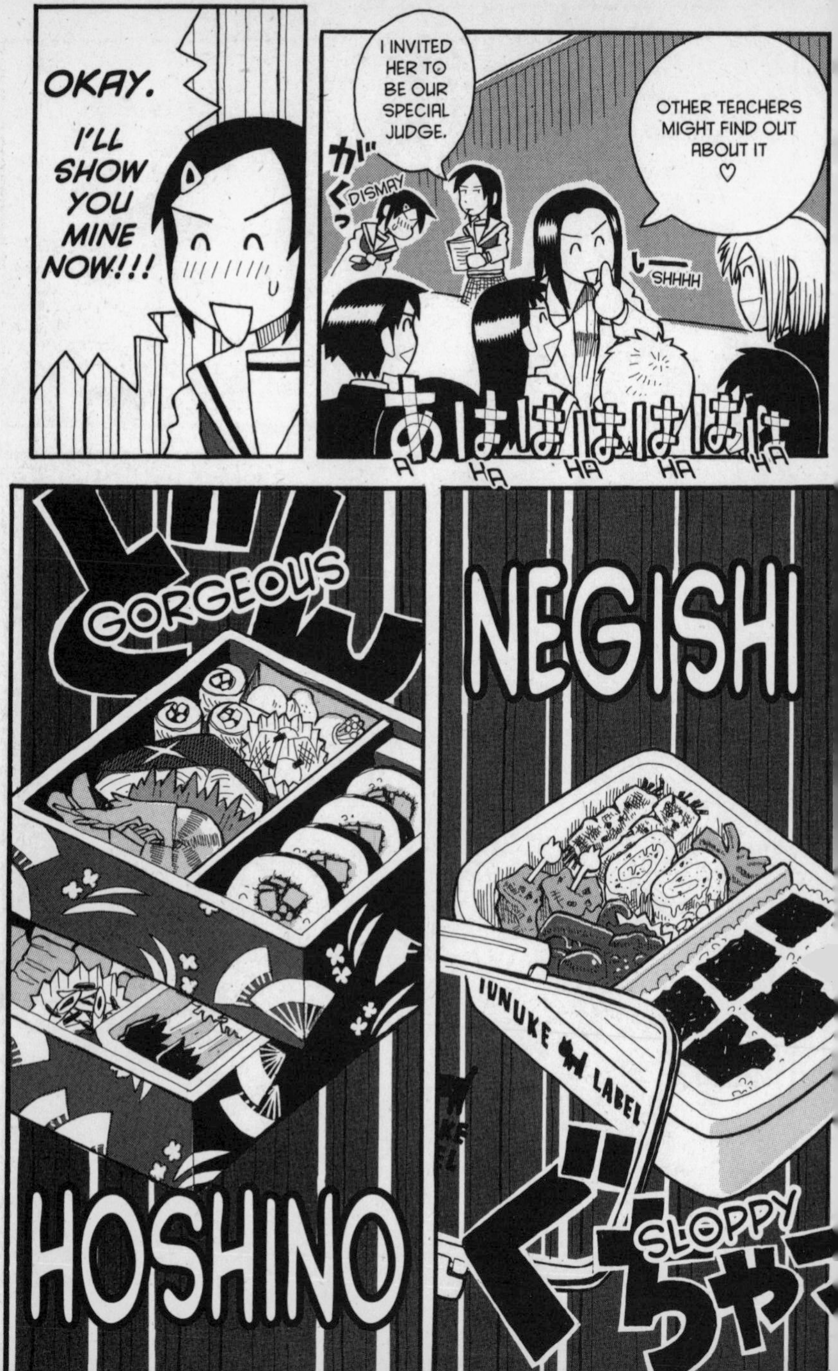
OTHER TEACHERS MIGHT FIND OUT ABOUT IT ♡
I INVITED HER TO BE OUR SPECIAL JUDGE.
がくっ DISMAY
しー SHHHH
あはははははは
A HA HA HA HA
OKAY.
I'LL SHOW YOU MINE NOW!!!
NEGISHI
IUNUKE LABEL
SLOPPY
ぐちゃ
GORGEOUS
HOSHINO

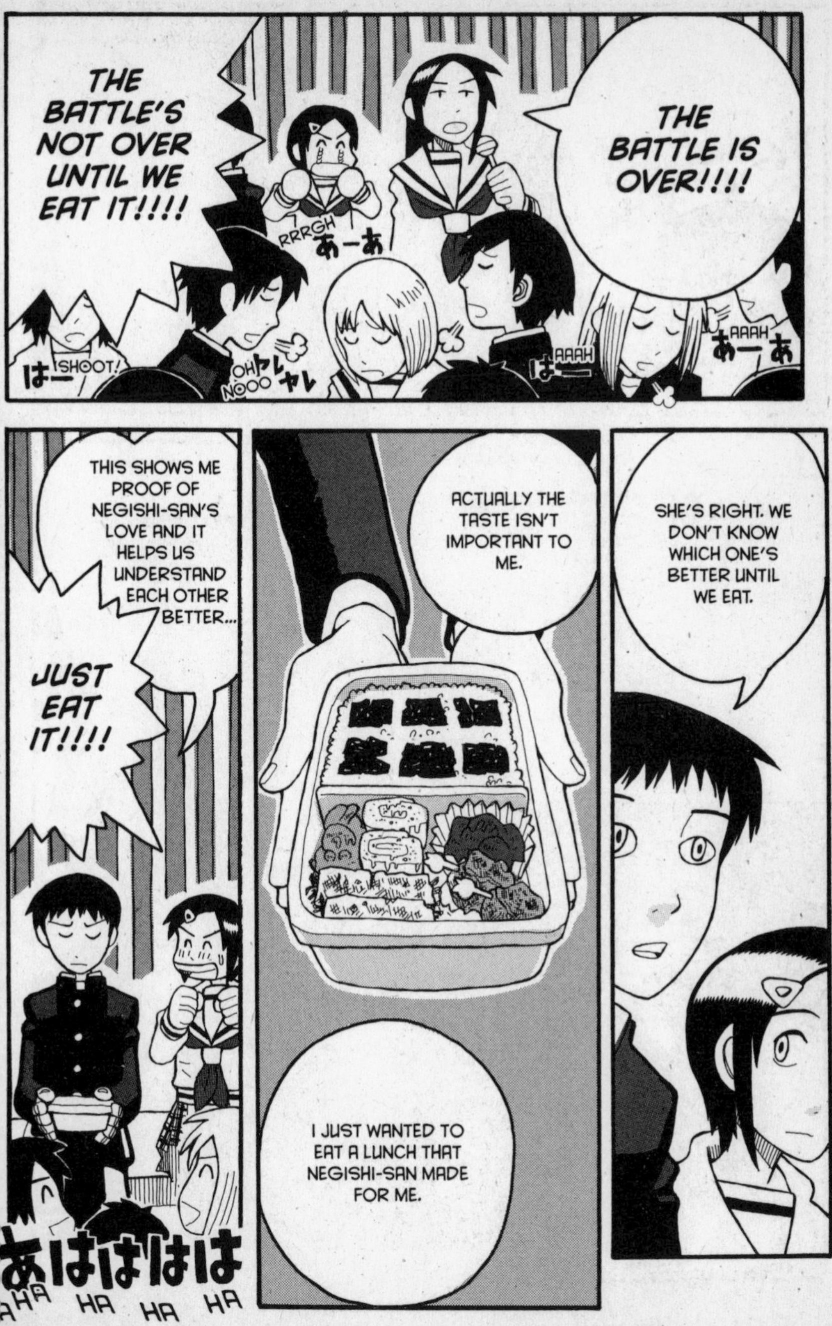
THE BATTLE IS OVER!!!!
AAAH あーあ
AAAH はー
OH NOOO ヤレヤレ
RRRGH あーあ
THE BATTLE'S NOT OVER UNTIL WE EAT IT!!!!
SHOOT! はー
SHE'S RIGHT. WE DON'T KNOW WHICH ONE'S BETTER UNTIL WE EAT.
ACTUALLY THE TASTE ISN'T IMPORTANT TO ME.
I JUST WANTED TO EAT A LUNCH THAT NEGISHI-SAN MADE FOR ME.
THIS SHOWS ME PROOF OF NEGISHI-SAN'S LOVE AND IT HELPS US UNDERSTAND EACH OTHER BETTER...
JUST EAT IT!!!!
あはははは
AHA HA HA HA

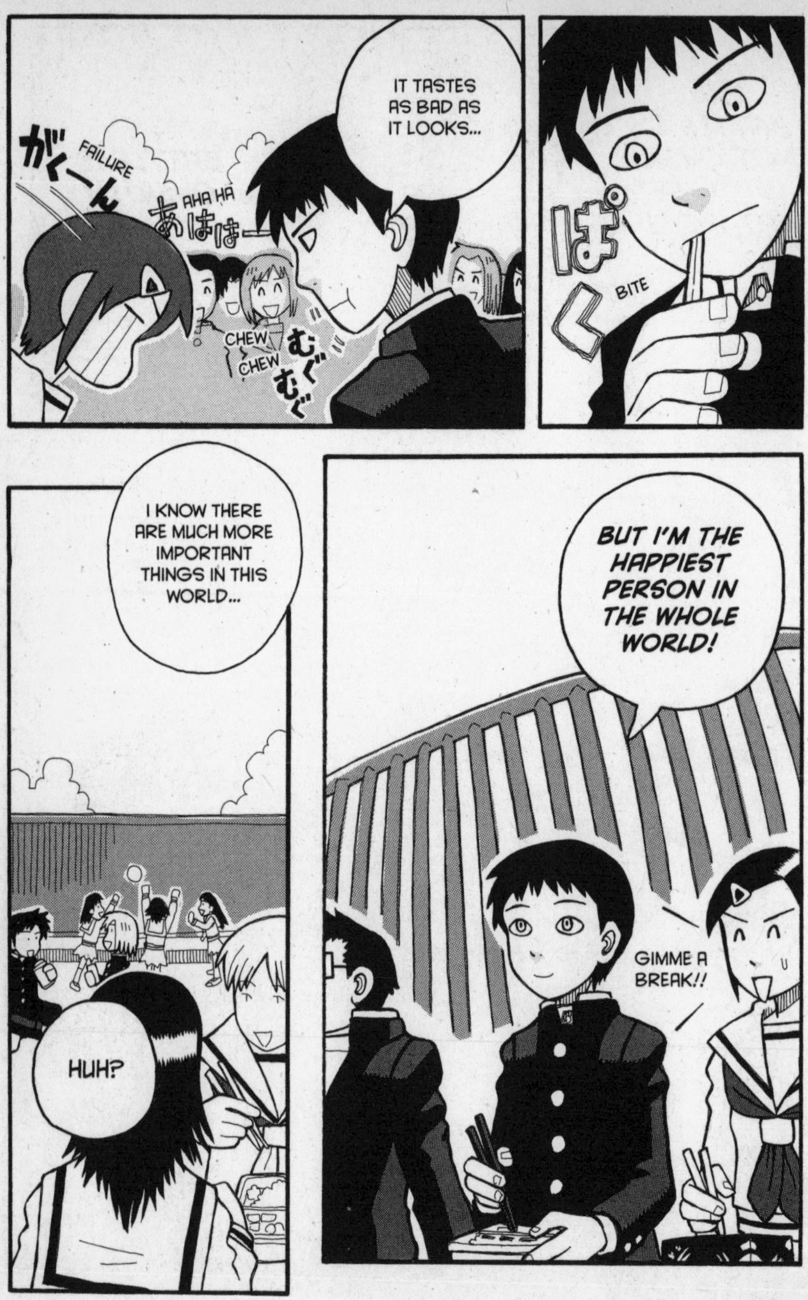
ぱく
BITE
IT TASTES AS BAD AS IT LOOKS...
あははー
AHA HA
がくーん
FAILURE
むぐむぐ
CHEW CHEW
I KNOW THERE ARE MUCH MORE IMPORTANT THINGS IN THIS WORLD...
HUH?
BUT I'M THE HAPPIEST PERSON IN THE WHOLE WORLD!
GIMME A BREAK!!

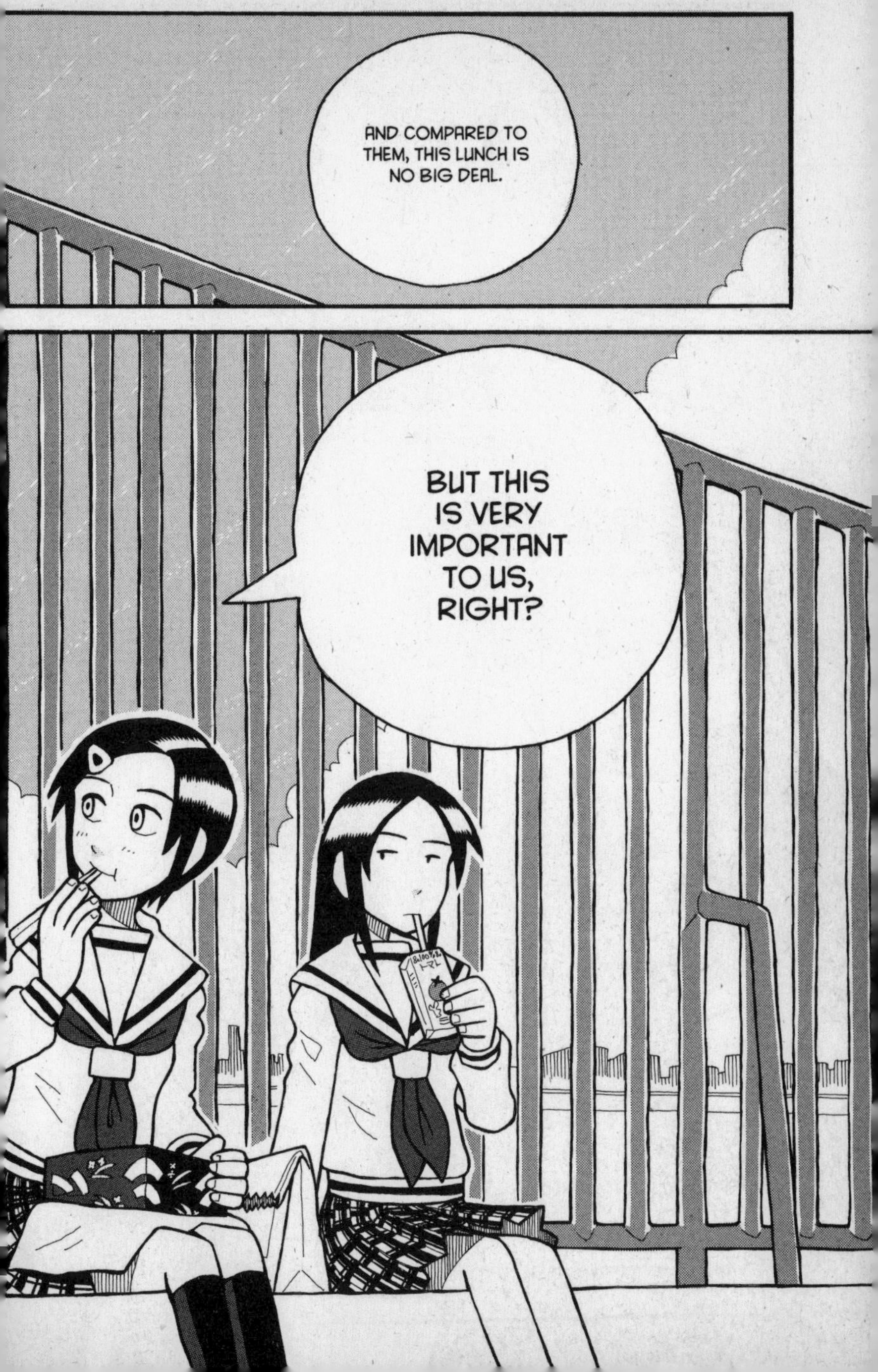
AND COMPARED TO THEM, THIS LUNCH IS NO BIG DEAL.
BUT THIS IS VERY IMPORTANT TO US, RIGHT?

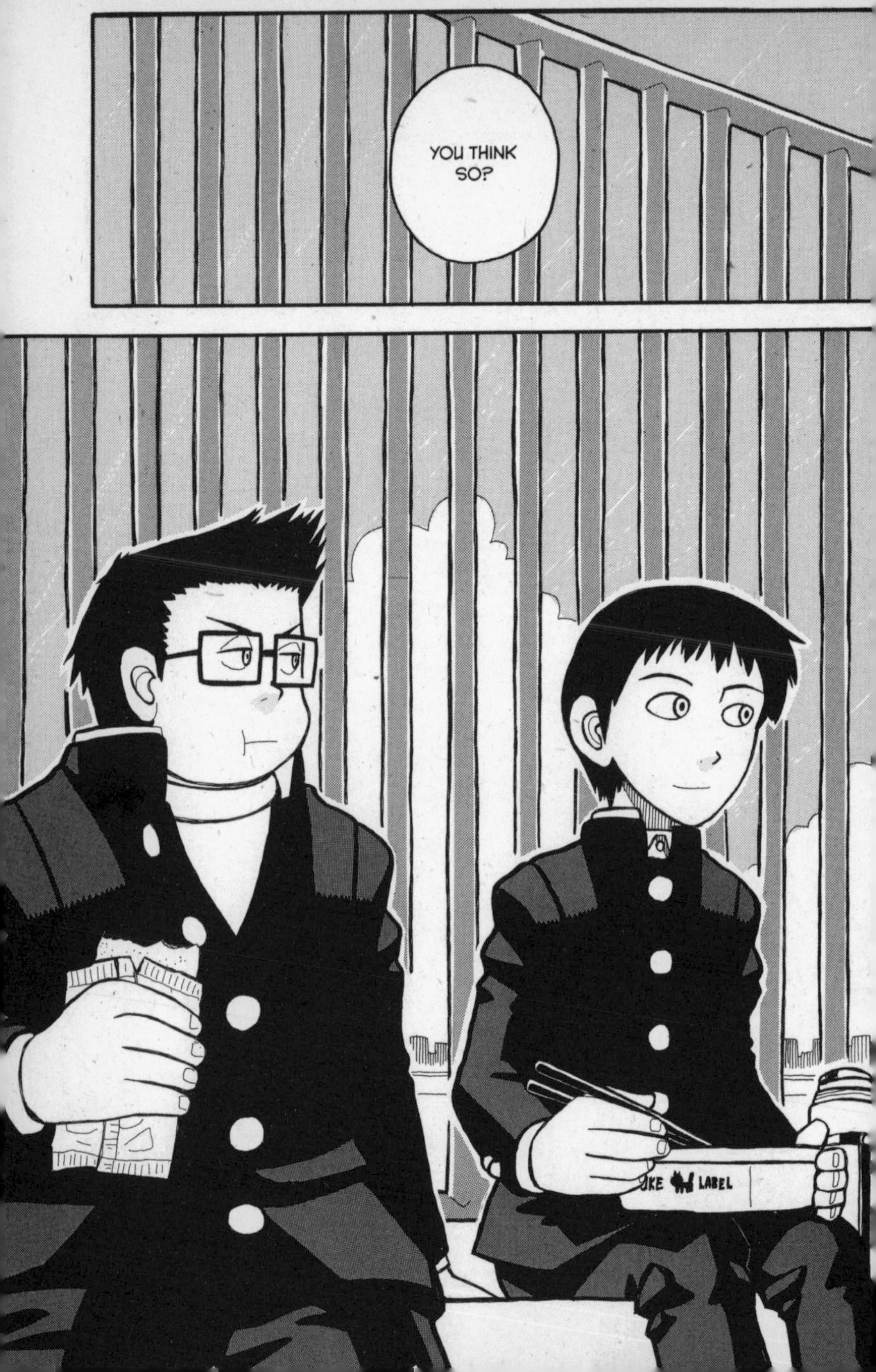
YOU THINK SO?

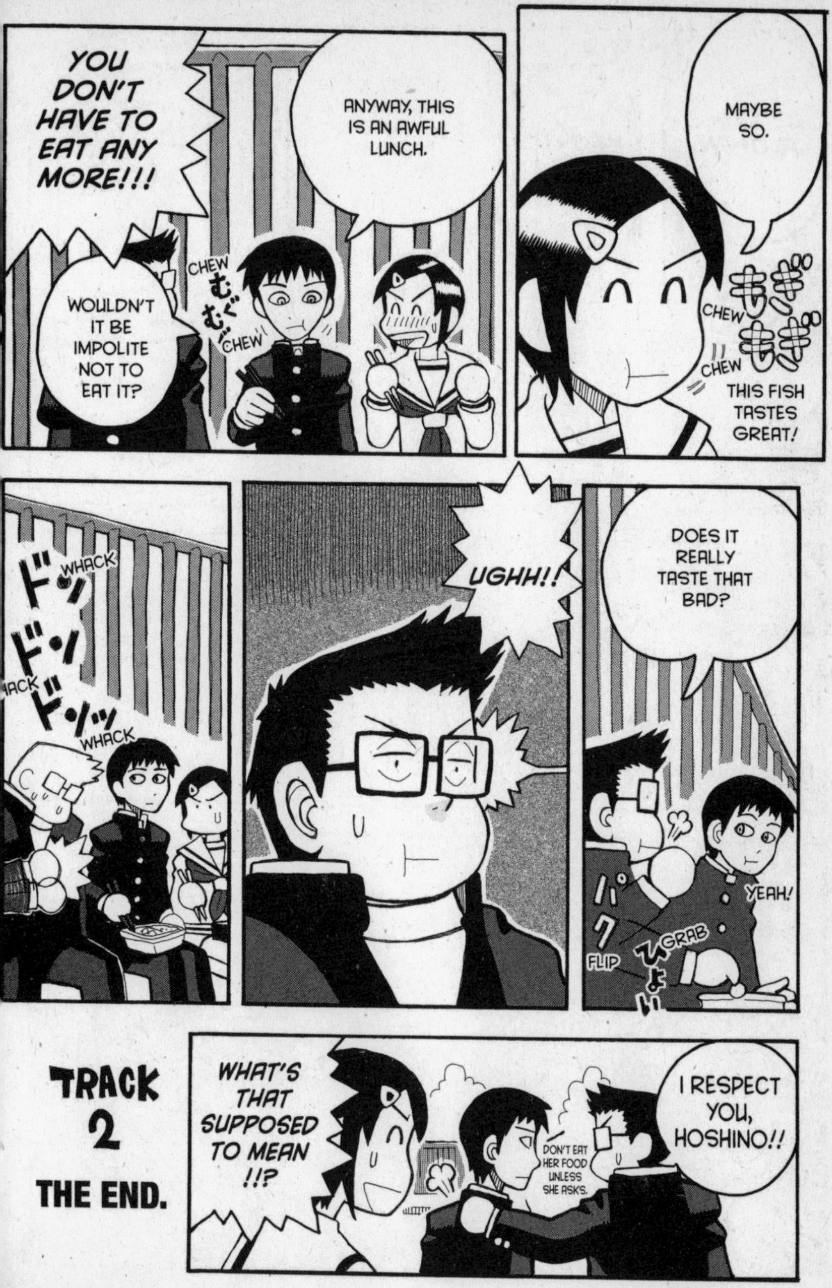
MAYBE SO.
CHEW
CHEW
THIS FISH TASTES GREAT!
ANYWAY, THIS IS AN AWFUL LUNCH.
YOU DON'T HAVE TO EAT ANY MORE!!!
CHEW
CHEW
WOULDN'T IT BE IMPOLITE NOT TO EAT IT?
DOES IT REALLY TASTE THAT BAD?
YEAH!
GRAB
FLIP
UGHH!!
WHACK
WHACK
I RESPECT YOU, HOSHINO!!
DON'T EAT HER FOOD UNLESS SHE ASKS.
WHAT'S THAT SUPPOSED TO MEAN!!?

TRACK 2 THE END.

To Be Continued to...

BONUS TRACK

EXTRA

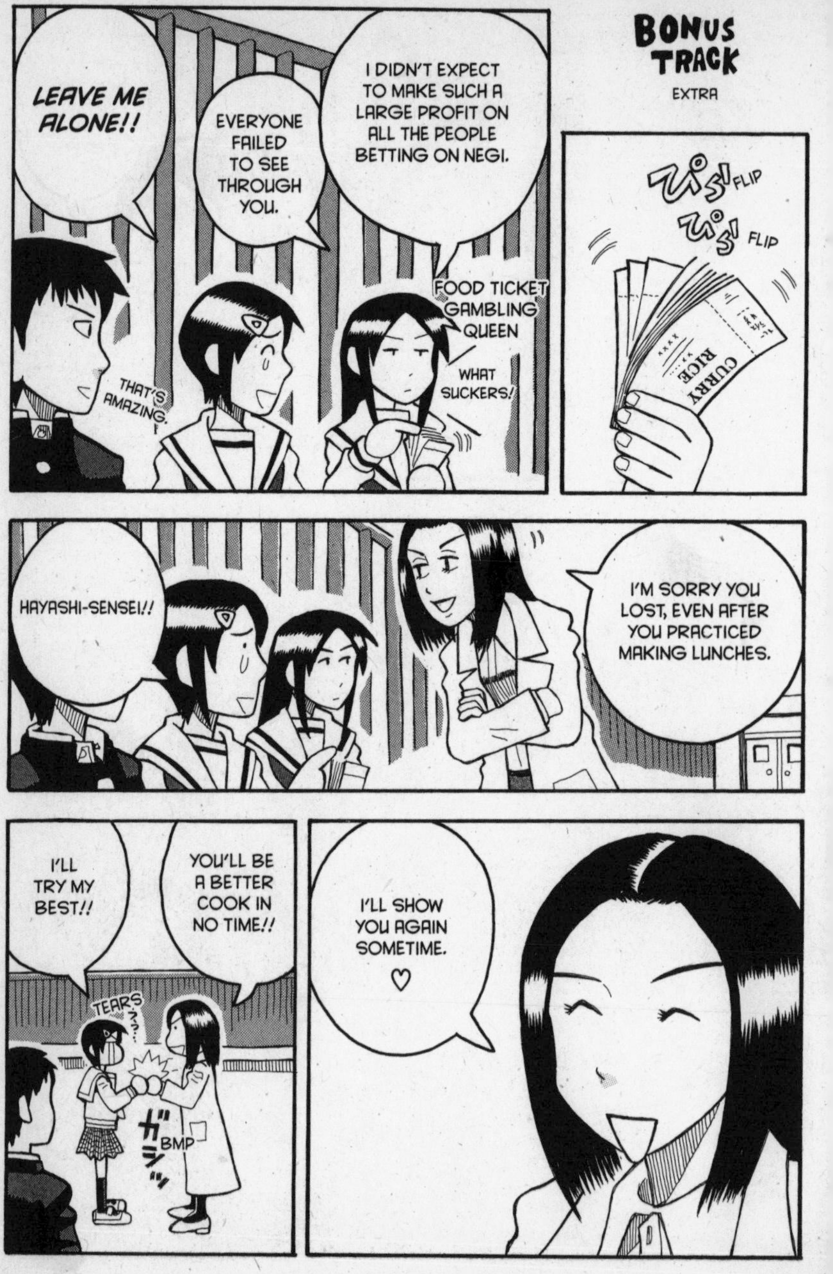
FLIP
FLIP
CURRY RICE
I DIDN'T EXPECT TO MAKE SUCH A LARGE PROFIT ON ALL THE PEOPLE BETTING ON NEGI.
FOOD TICKET GAMBLING QUEEN
WHAT SUCKERS!
EVERYONE FAILED TO SEE THROUGH YOU.
THAT'S AMAZING.
LEAVE ME ALONE!!
I'M SORRY YOU LOST, EVEN AFTER YOU PRACTICED MAKING LUNCHES.
HAYASHI-SENSEI!!
I'LL SHOW YOU AGAIN SOMETIME. ♡
YOU'LL BE A BETTER COOK IN NO TIME!!
I'LL TRY MY BEST!!
TEARS
BMP

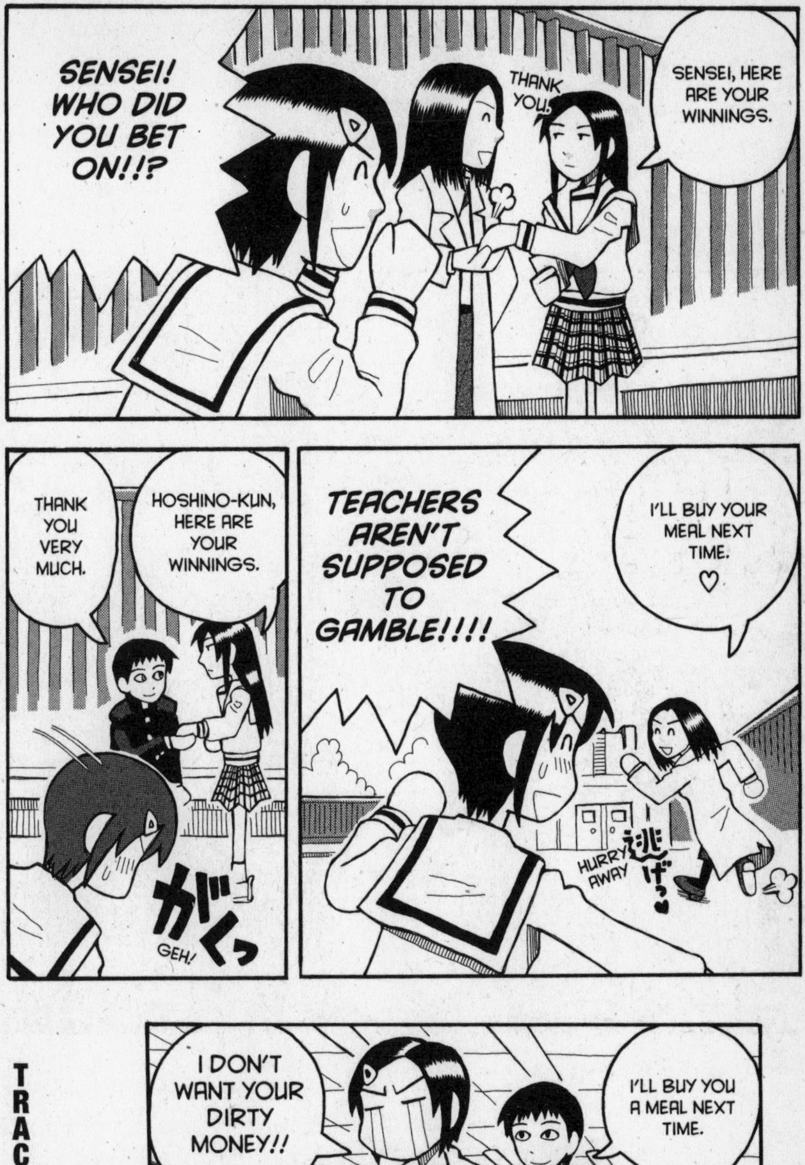
SENSEI, HERE ARE YOUR WINNINGS.
THANK YOU.
SENSEI! WHO DID YOU BET ON!!?
I'LL BUY YOUR MEAL NEXT TIME. ♡
TEACHERS AREN'T SUPPOSED TO GAMBLE!!!!
逃げっ
HURRY AWAY
HOSHINO-KUN, HERE ARE YOUR WINNINGS.
THANK YOU VERY MUCH.
がくっ
GEH!
I'LL BUY YOU A MEAL NEXT TIME.
I DON'T WANT YOUR DIRTY MONEY!!

TRACK #2 ▶▶ END

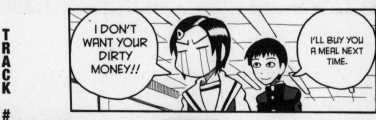

THE END

TRACK #3

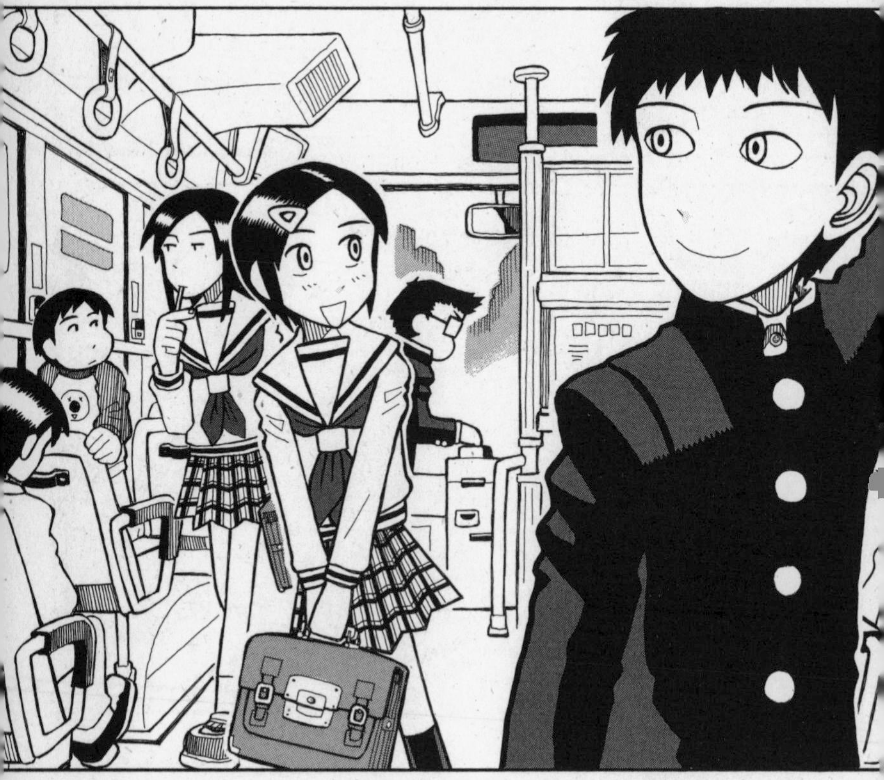

LOVE LETTER ANXIETY

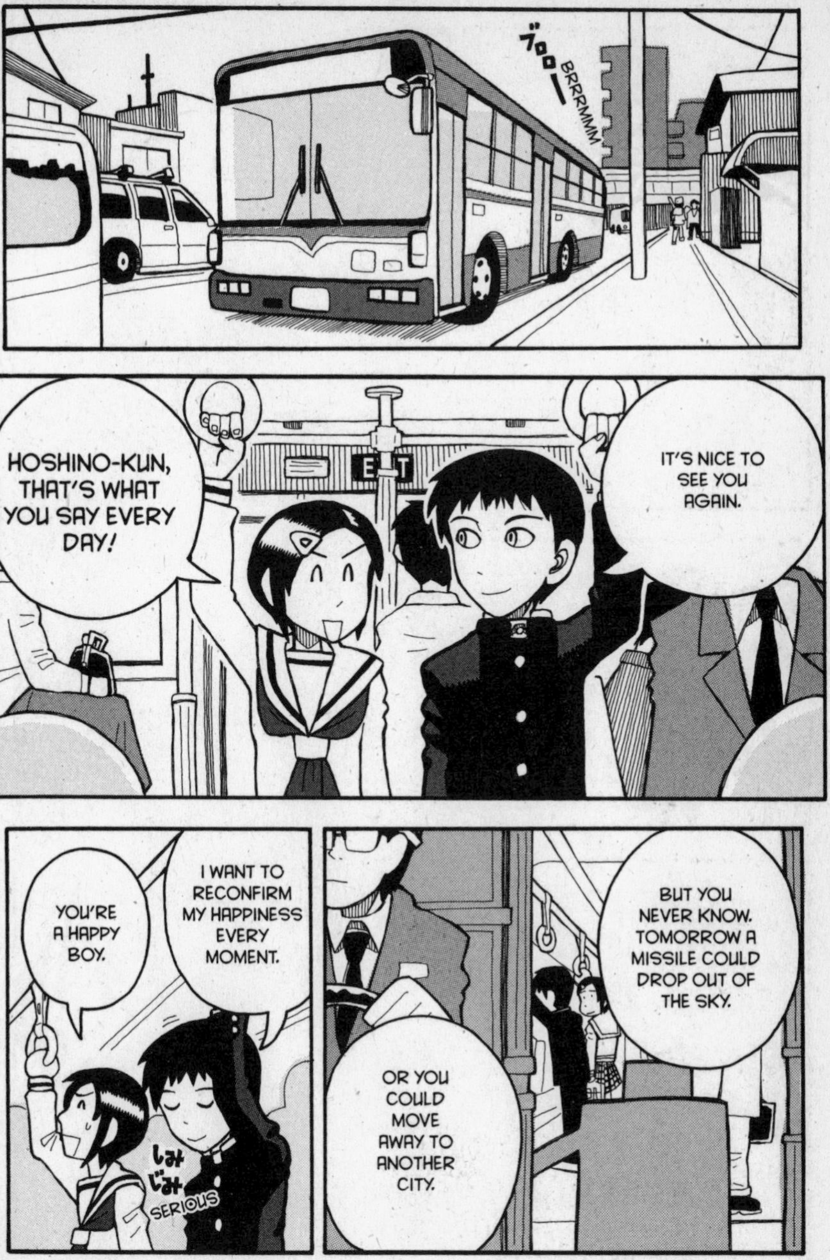
ブロロー
BRRRMMM
IT'S NICE TO SEE YOU AGAIN.
HOSHINO-KUN, THAT'S WHAT YOU SAY EVERY DAY!
BUT YOU NEVER KNOW. TOMORROW A MISSILE COULD DROP OUT OF THE SKY.
OR YOU COULD MOVE AWAY TO ANOTHER CITY.
I WANT TO RECONFIRM MY HAPPINESS EVERY MOMENT.
YOU'RE A HAPPY BOY.
しみじみ
SERIOUS

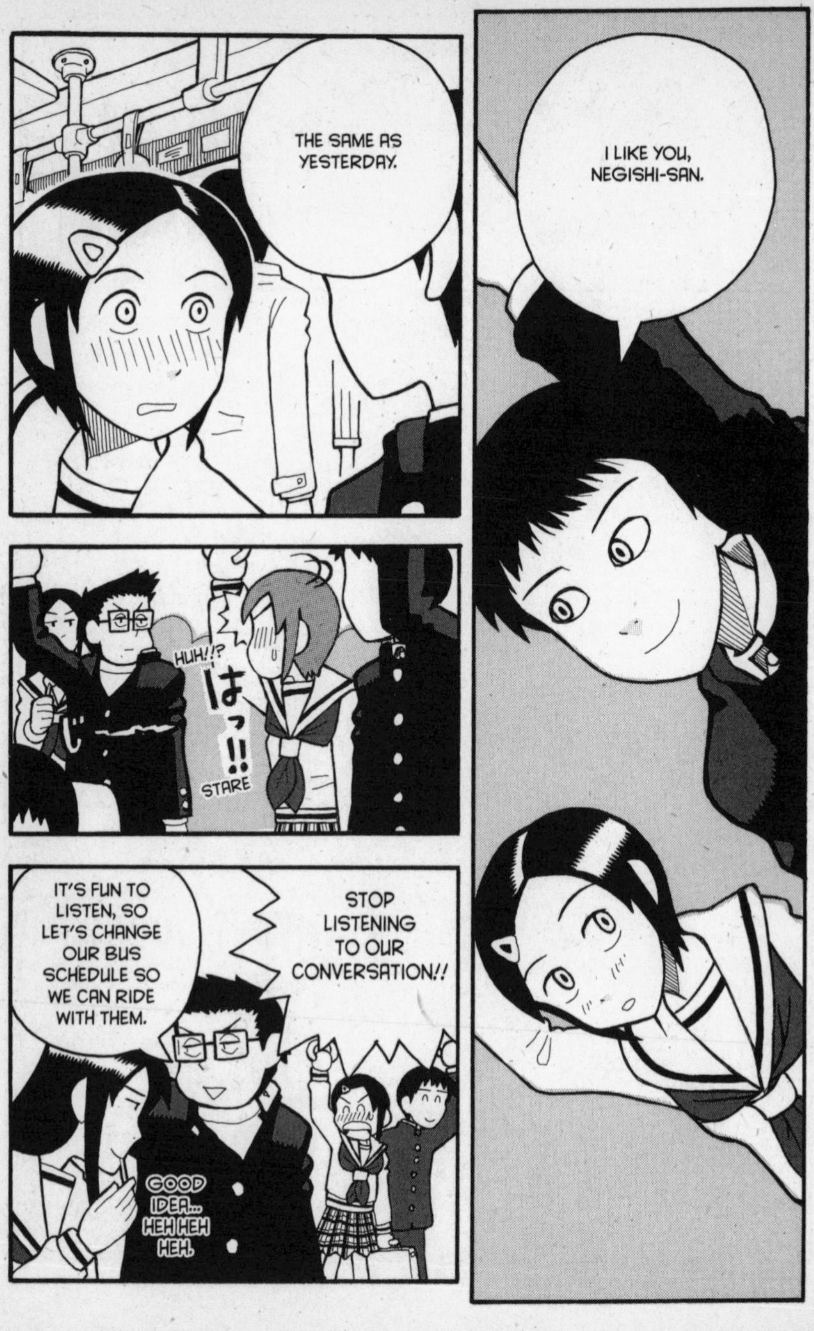
I LIKE YOU, NEGISHI-SAN.
THE SAME AS YESTERDAY.
HUH!!?
はっ!!
STARE
STOP LISTENING TO OUR CONVERSATION!!
IT'S FUN TO LISTEN, SO LET'S CHANGE OUR BUS SCHEDULE SO WE CAN RIDE WITH THEM.
GOOD IDEA... HEH HEH HEH.

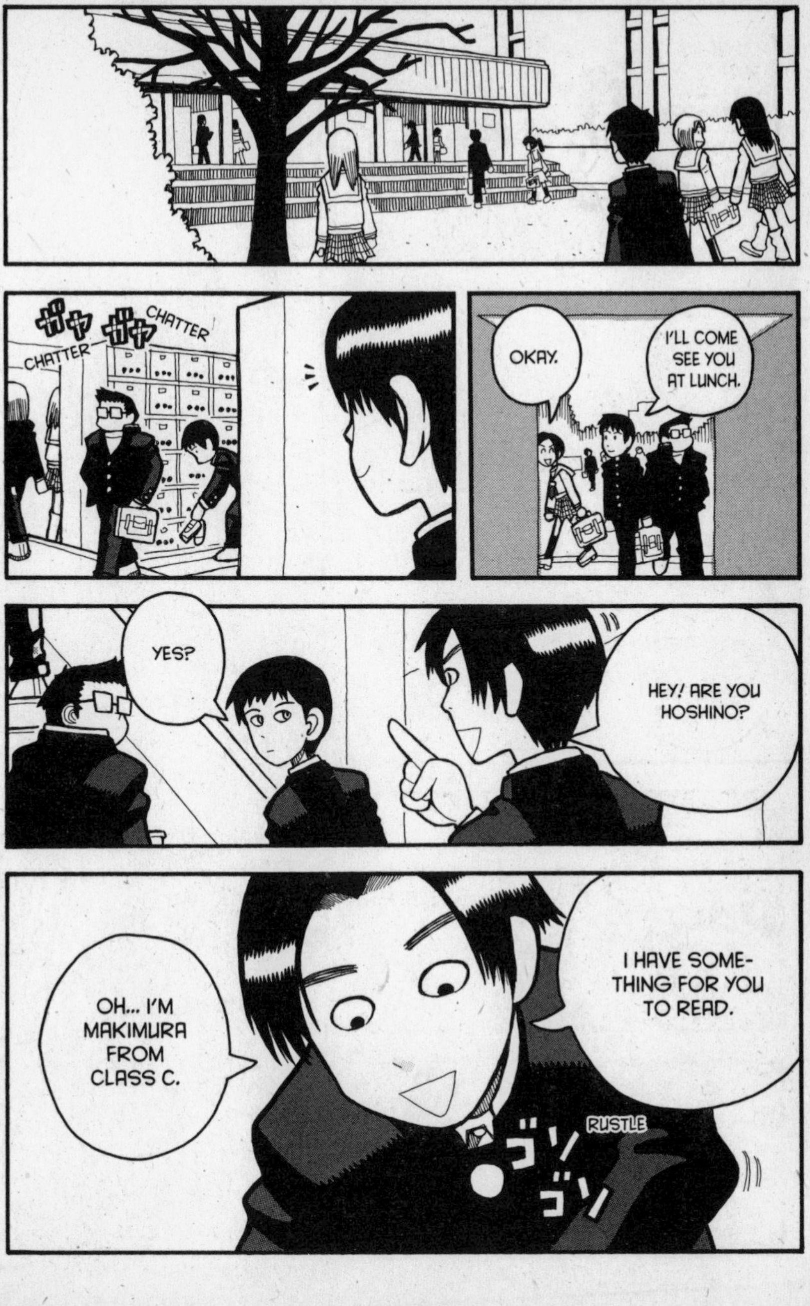
I'LL COME SEE YOU AT LUNCH.
OKAY.
CHATTER
ガヤ
ガヤ
CHATTER
HEY! ARE YOU HOSHINO?
YES?
I HAVE SOME-THING FOR YOU TO READ.
OH... I'M MAKIMURA FROM CLASS C.
RUSTLE
ゴソ
ゴソ

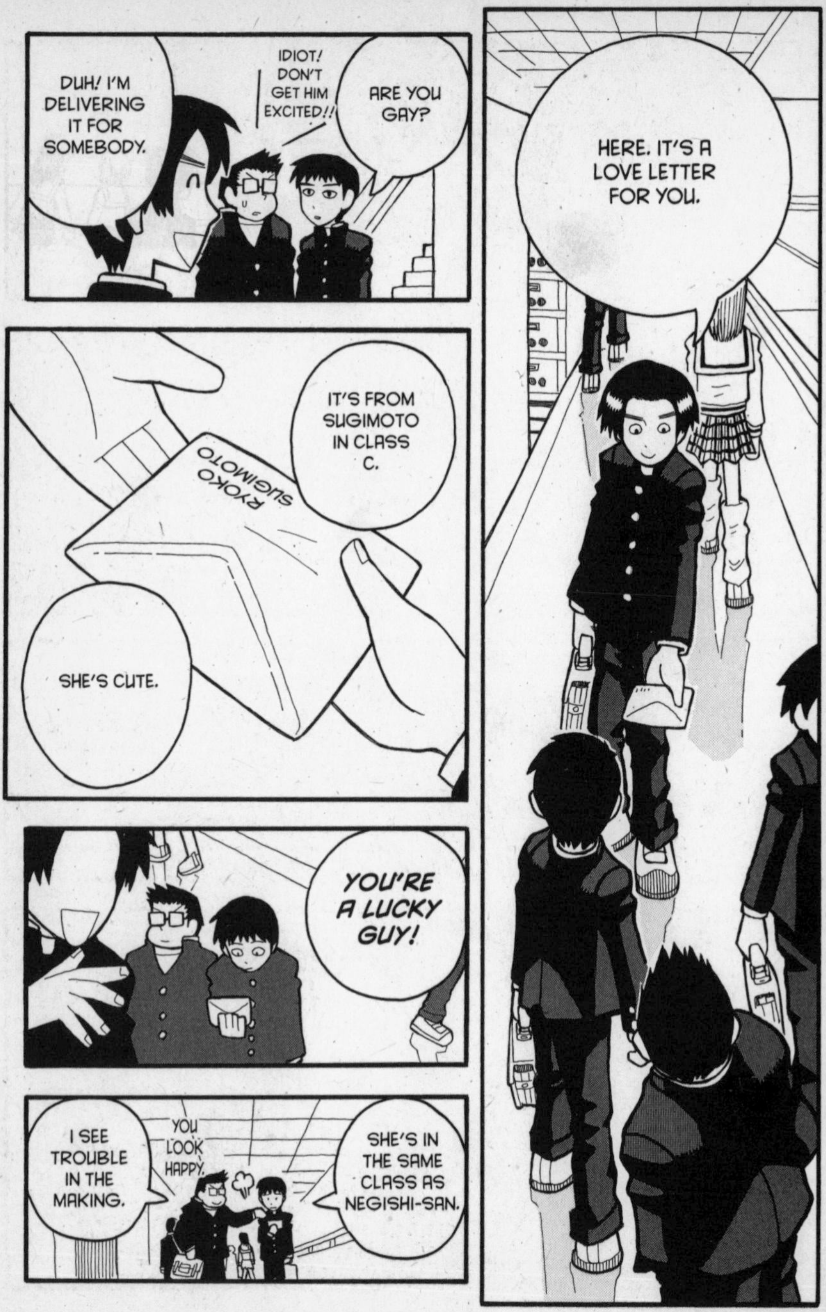
HERE. IT'S A LOVE LETTER FOR YOU.
ARE YOU GAY?
IDIOT! DON'T GET HIM EXCITED!!
DUH! I'M DELIVERING IT FOR SOMEBODY.
IT'S FROM SUGIMOTO IN CLASS C.
RYOKO SUGIMOTO
SHE'S CUTE.
YOU'RE A LUCKY GUY!
SHE'S IN THE SAME CLASS AS NEGISHI-SAN.
YOU LOOK HAPPY.
I SEE TROUBLE IN THE MAKING.

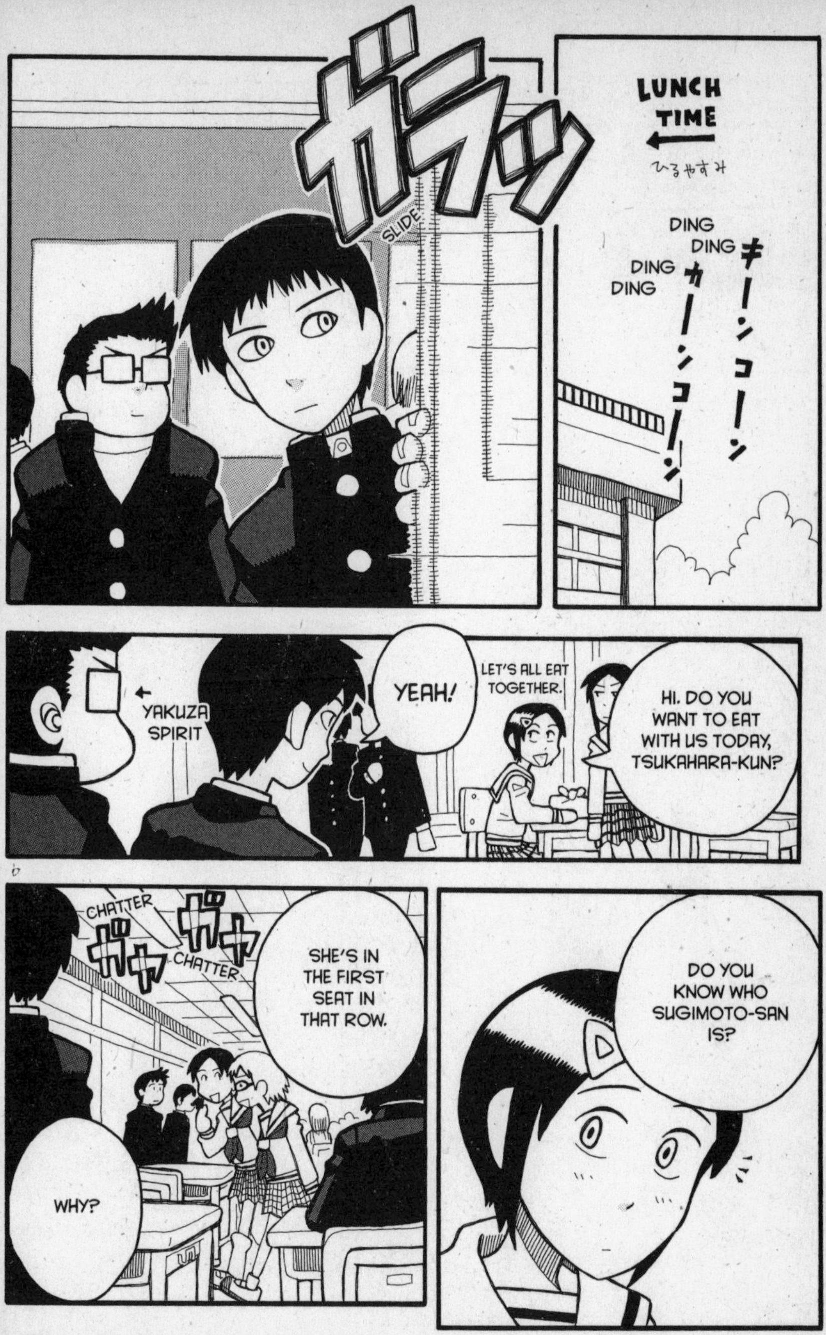

LUNCH TIME
ひるやすみ
DING DING
キーンコーン
DING DING
カーンコーン
ガラッ
SLIDE
HI. DO YOU WANT TO EAT WITH US TODAY, TSUKAHARA-KUN?
LET'S ALL EAT TOGETHER.
YEAH!
YAKUZA SPIRIT
DO YOU KNOW WHO SUGIMOTO-SAN IS?
SHE'S IN THE FIRST SEAT IN THAT ROW.
ガヤ
CHATTER
ガヤ
CHATTER
WHY?

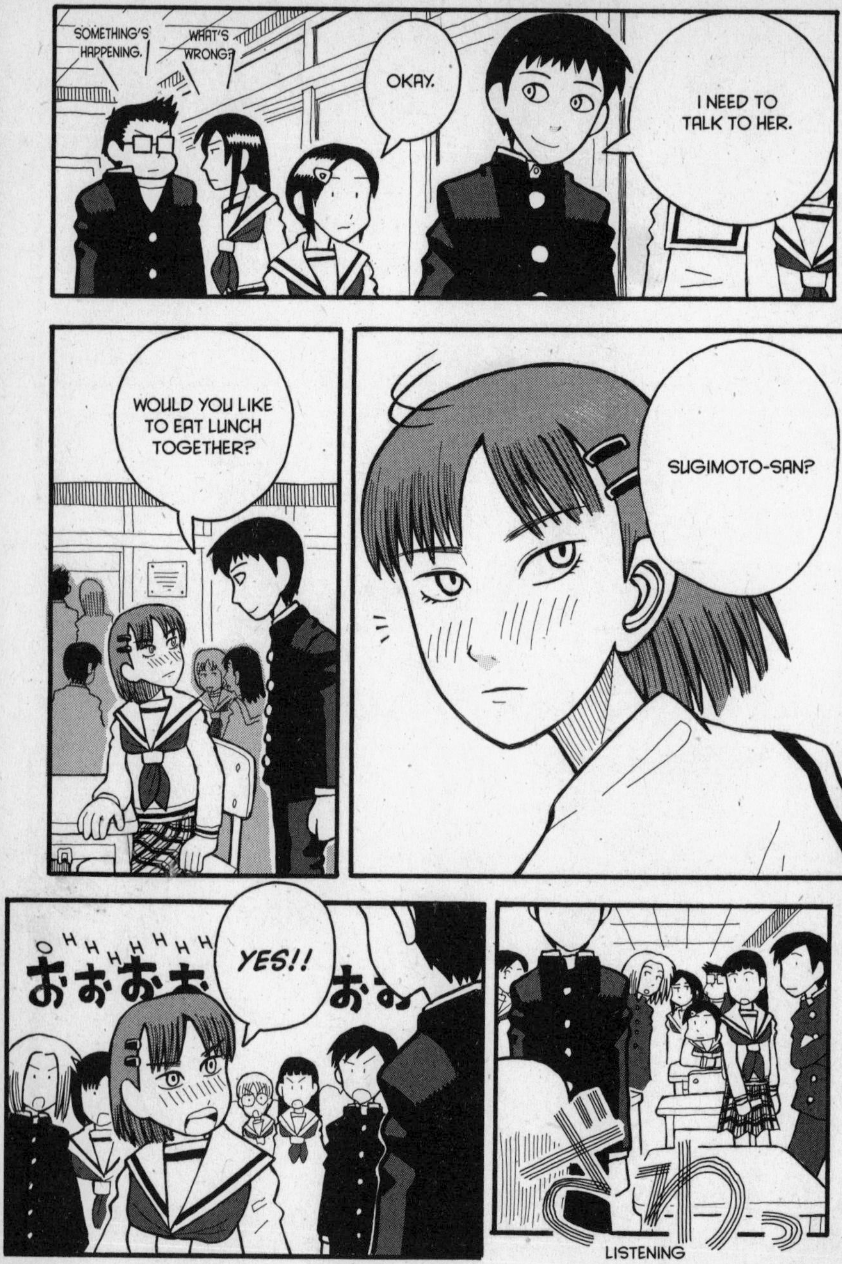
I NEED TO TALK TO HER.
OKAY.
WHAT'S WRONG?
SOMETHING'S HAPPENING.
SUGIMOTO-SAN?
WOULD YOU LIKE TO EAT LUNCH TOGETHER?
ざわっ
LISTENING
YES!!
OHHHHHHHH

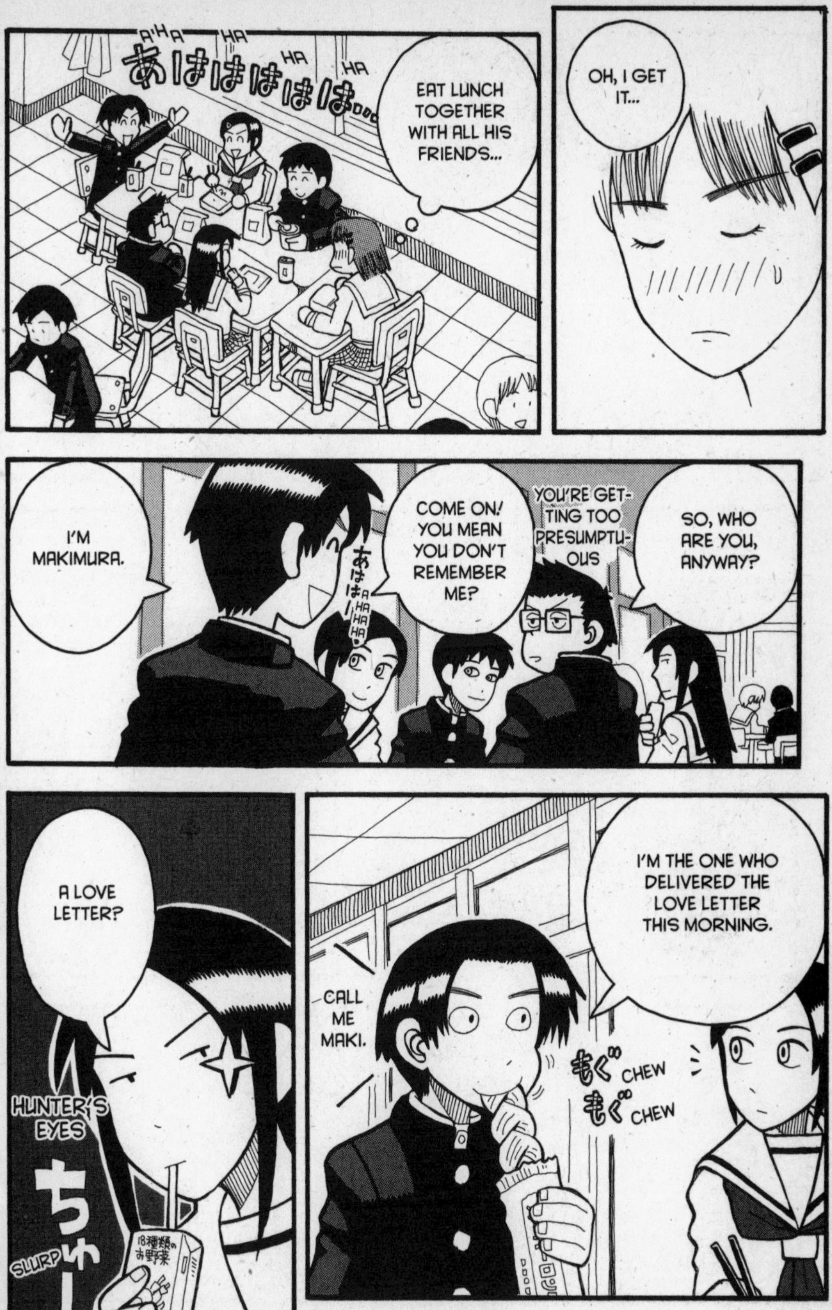
OH, I GET IT...
EAT LUNCH TOGETHER WITH ALL HIS FRIENDS...
あはははは... AHAHA HA HA HA
SO, WHO ARE YOU, ANYWAY?
YOU'RE GETTING TOO PRESUMPTUOUS
COME ON! YOU MEAN YOU DON'T REMEMBER ME?
あはは! AHAHAHA!
I'M MAKIMURA.
I'M THE ONE WHO DELIVERED THE LOVE LETTER THIS MORNING.
もぐ CHEW もぐ CHEW
CALL ME MAKI.
A LOVE LETTER?
HUNTER'S EYES
ちゅー SLURP
18種類のお野菜

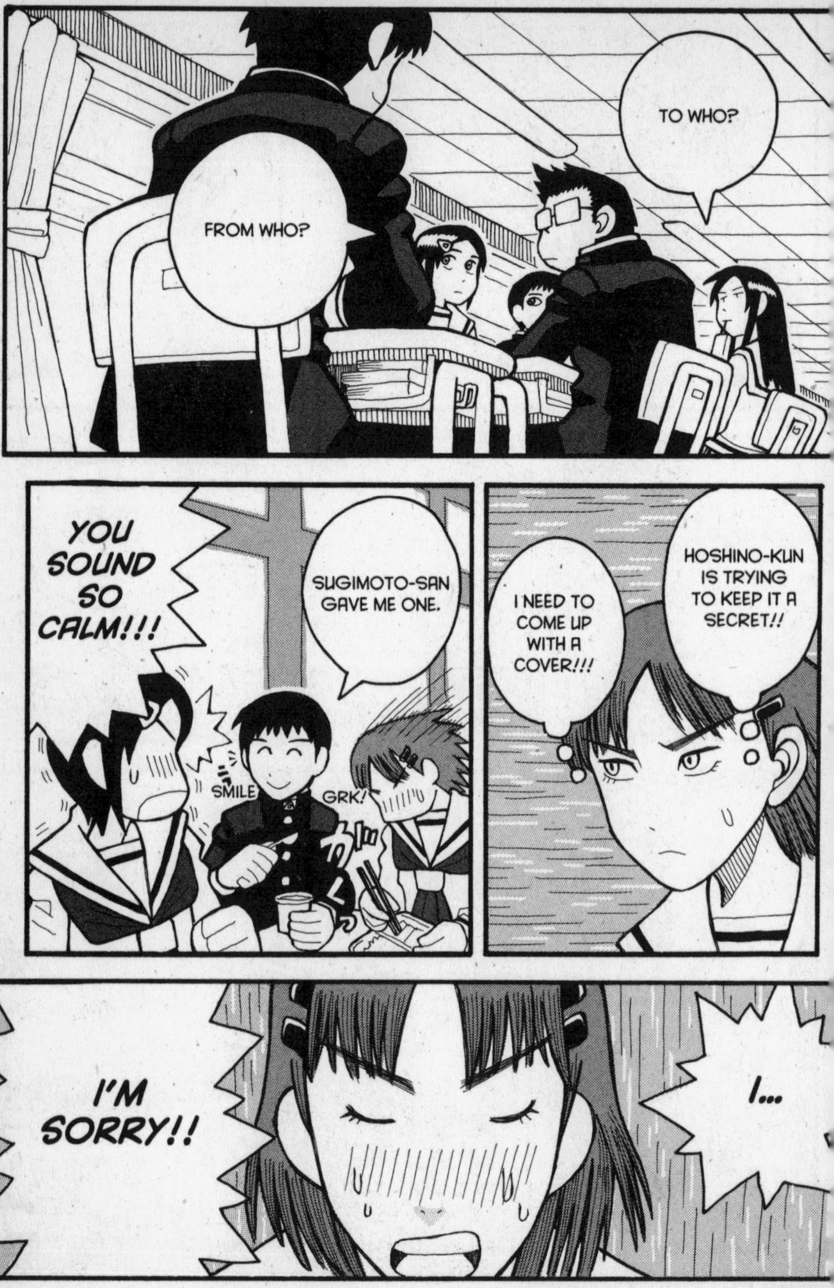
TO WHO?
FROM WHO?
HOSHINO-KUN IS TRYING TO KEEP IT A SECRET!!
I NEED TO COME UP WITH A COVER!!!
SUGIMOTO-SAN GAVE ME ONE.
YOU SOUND SO CALM!!!
SMILE
GRK!
I...
I'M SORRY!!

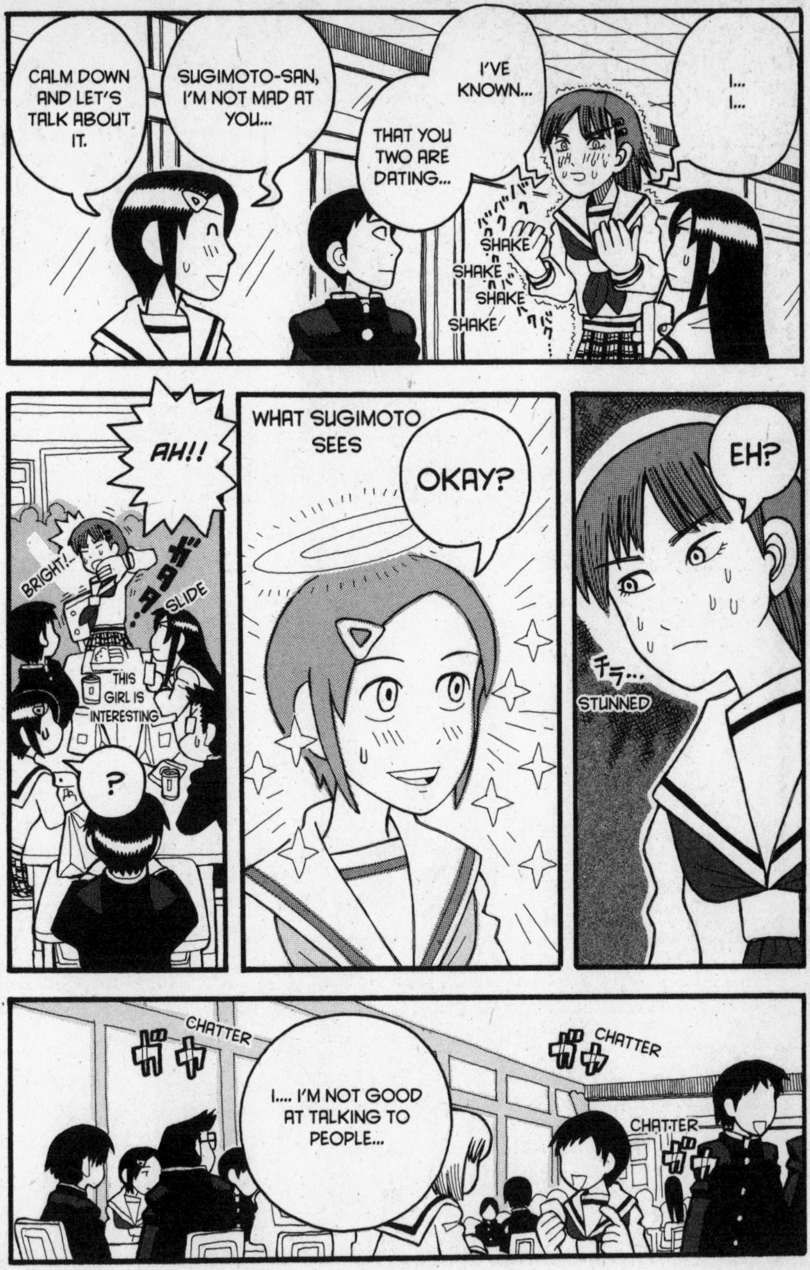
I...
I...
I'VE KNOWN...
THAT YOU TWO ARE DATING...
SHAKE
SHAKE
SHAKE
SHAKE
SUGIMOTO-SAN, I'M NOT MAD AT YOU...
CALM DOWN AND LET'S TALK ABOUT IT.
EH?
チラ...
STUNNED
WHAT SUGIMOTO SEES
OKAY?
AH!!
SLIDE
BRIGHT!
THIS GIRL IS INTERESTING
?
CHATTER
CHATTER
I.... I'M NOT GOOD AT TALKING TO PEOPLE...
CHATTER

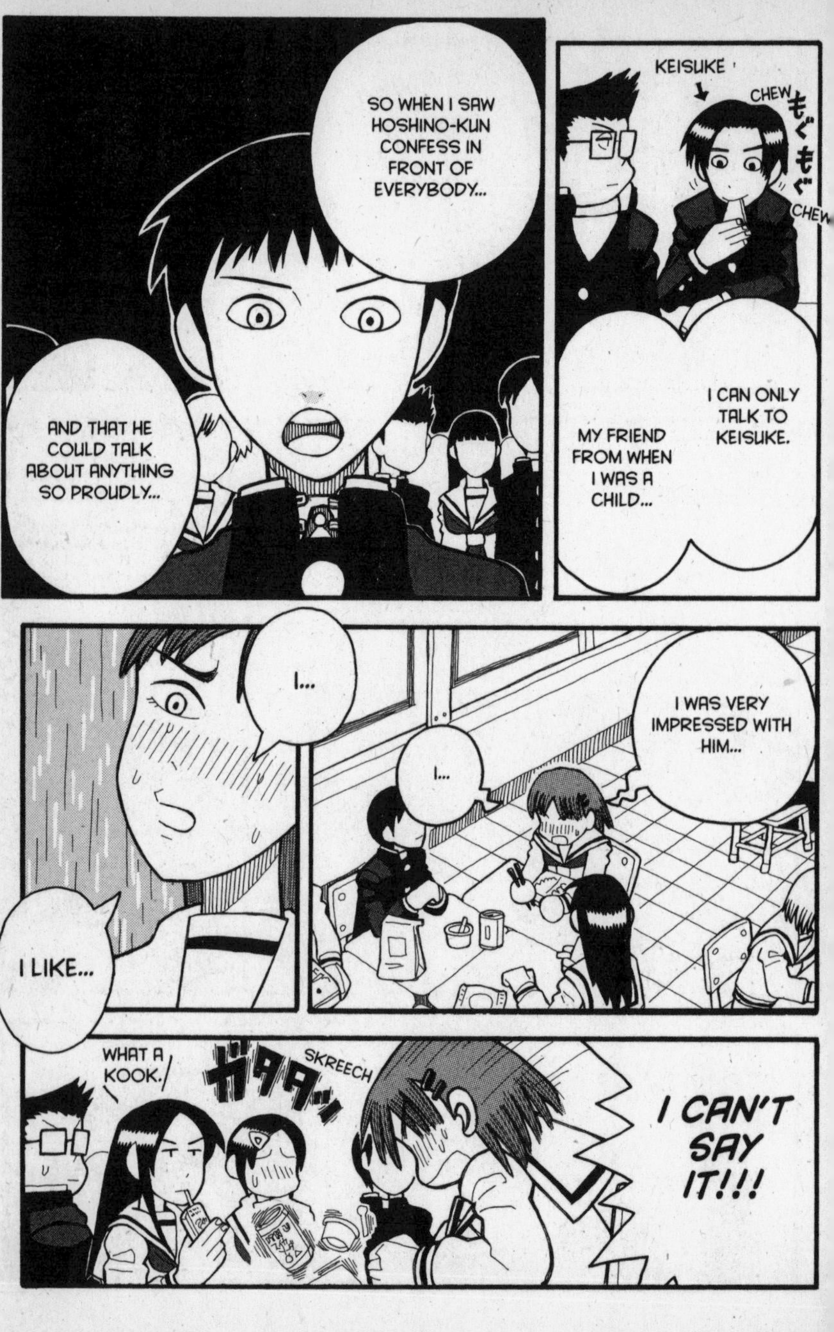
KEISUKE
CHEW もぐもぐ CHEW
I CAN ONLY TALK TO KEISUKE.
MY FRIEND FROM WHEN I WAS A CHILD...
SO WHEN I SAW HOSHINO-KUN CONFESS IN FRONT OF EVERYBODY...
AND THAT HE COULD TALK ABOUT ANYTHING SO PROUDLY...
I WAS VERY IMPRESSED WITH HIM...
I...
I...
I LIKE...
I CAN'T SAY IT!!!
ガタタッ
SKREECH
WHAT A KOOK.

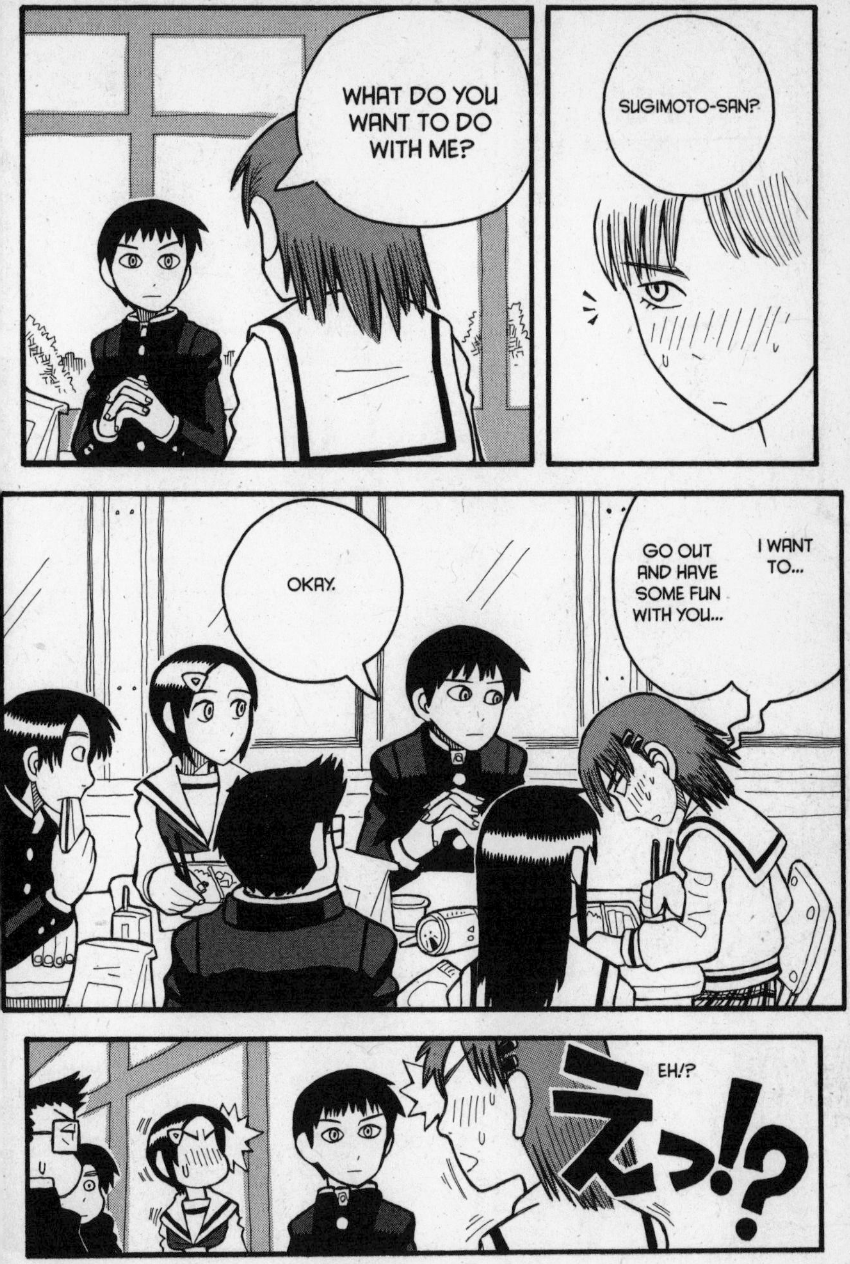
SUGIMOTO-SAN?
WHAT DO YOU WANT TO DO WITH ME?
I WANT TO...
GO OUT AND HAVE SOME FUN WITH YOU...
OKAY.
えっ!?
EH!?

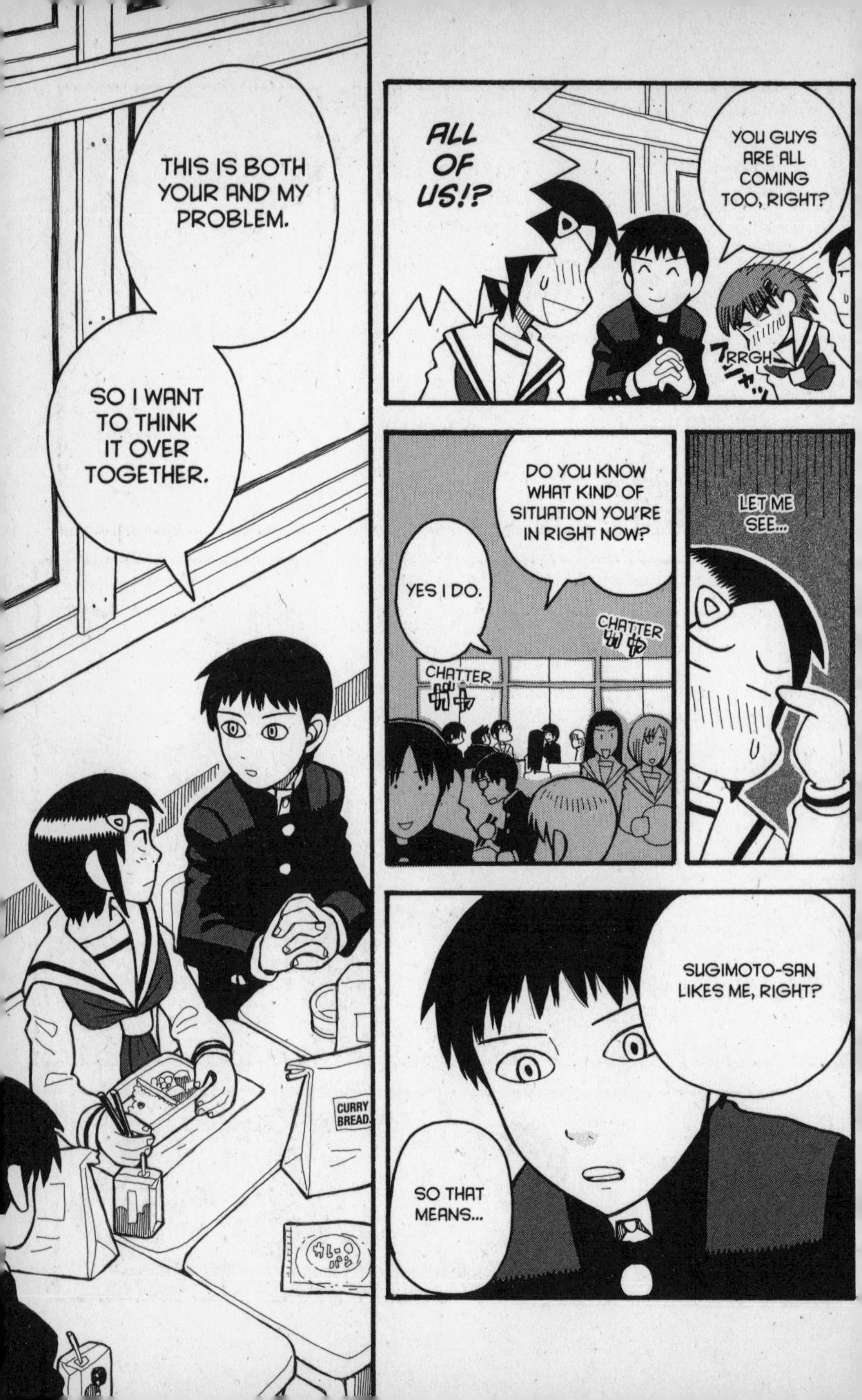
YOU GUYS ARE ALL COMING TOO, RIGHT?
ALL OF US!?
GRRGH
LET ME SEE...
DO YOU KNOW WHAT KIND OF SITUATION YOU'RE IN RIGHT NOW?
YES I DO.
CHATTER
CHATTER
SUGIMOTO-SAN LIKES ME, RIGHT?
SO THAT MEANS...
THIS IS BOTH YOUR AND MY PROBLEM.
SO I WANT TO THINK IT OVER TOGETHER.
CURRY BREAD

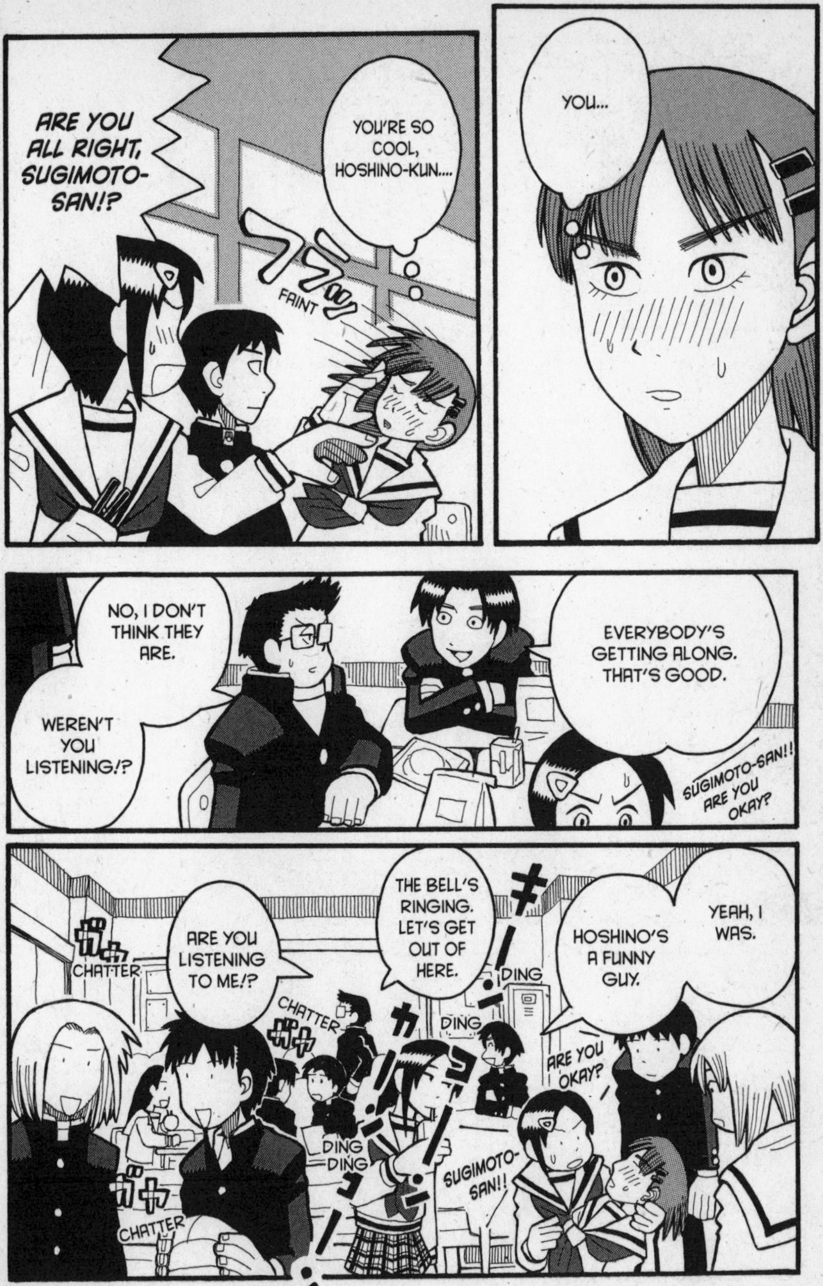
YOU...
YOU'RE SO COOL, HOSHINO-KUN....
FAINT
ARE YOU ALL RIGHT, SUGIMOTO-SAN!?
EVERYBODY'S GETTING ALONG. THAT'S GOOD.
SUGIMOTO-SAN!! ARE YOU OKAY?
NO, I DON'T THINK THEY ARE.
WEREN'T YOU LISTENING!?
YEAH, I WAS.
HOSHINO'S A FUNNY GUY.
ARE YOU OKAY?
DING
THE BELL'S RINGING. LET'S GET OUT OF HERE.
DING
SUGIMOTO-SAN!!
DING
DING
CHATTER
ARE YOU LISTENING TO ME!?
CHATTER
CHATTER

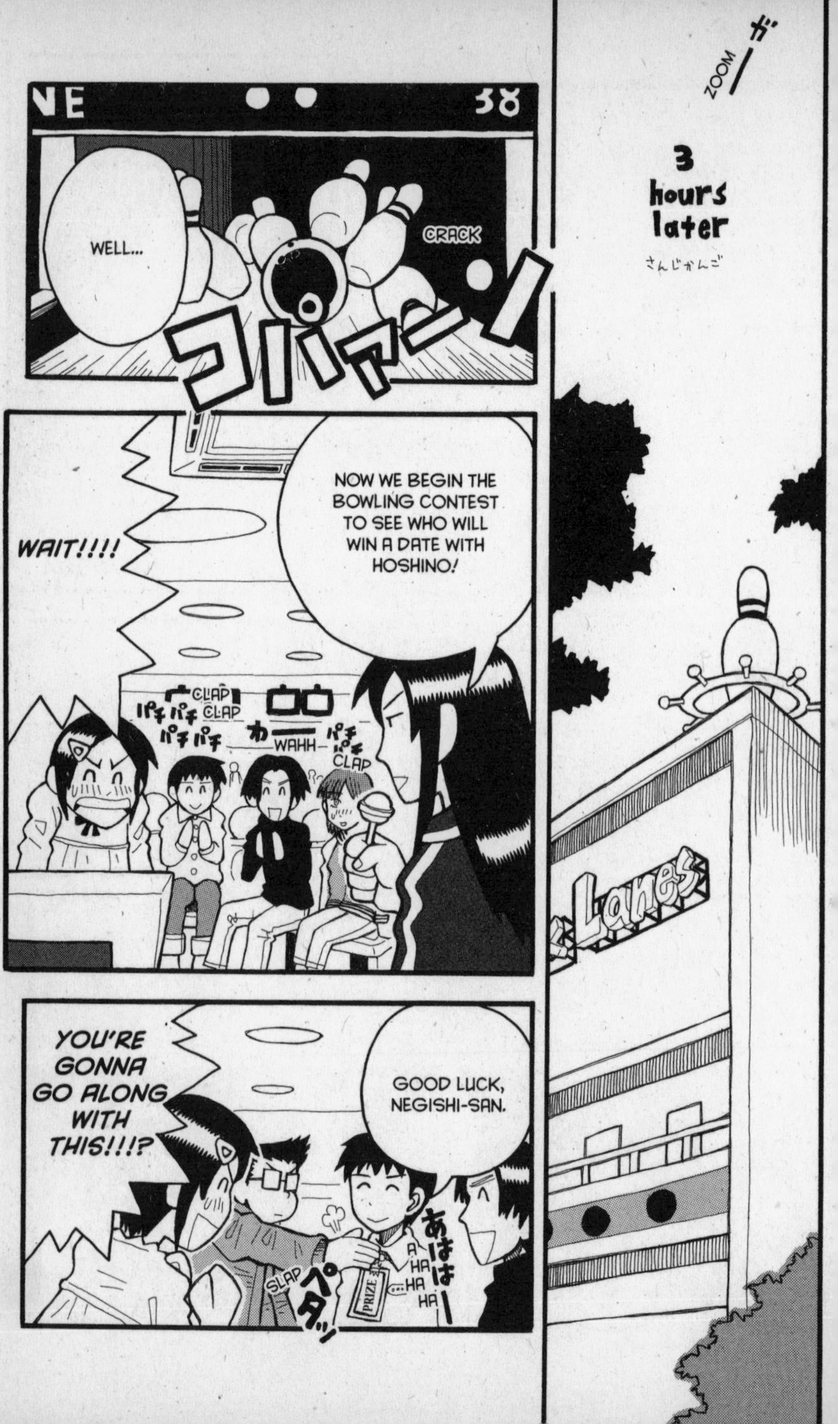
ガー
ZOOM
3 hours later
さんじかんご
Lanes
NE 38
WELL...
CRACK
コパーン
NOW WE BEGIN THE BOWLING CONTEST TO SEE WHO WILL WIN A DATE WITH HOSHINO!
WAIT!!!!
パチパチ パチパチ
CLAP CLAP
ワー
WAHH
パチパチ
CLAP
GOOD LUCK, NEGISHI-SAN.
YOU'RE GONNA GO ALONG WITH THIS!!!?
あははー
A HA HA HA
PRIZE
ペタッ
SLAP

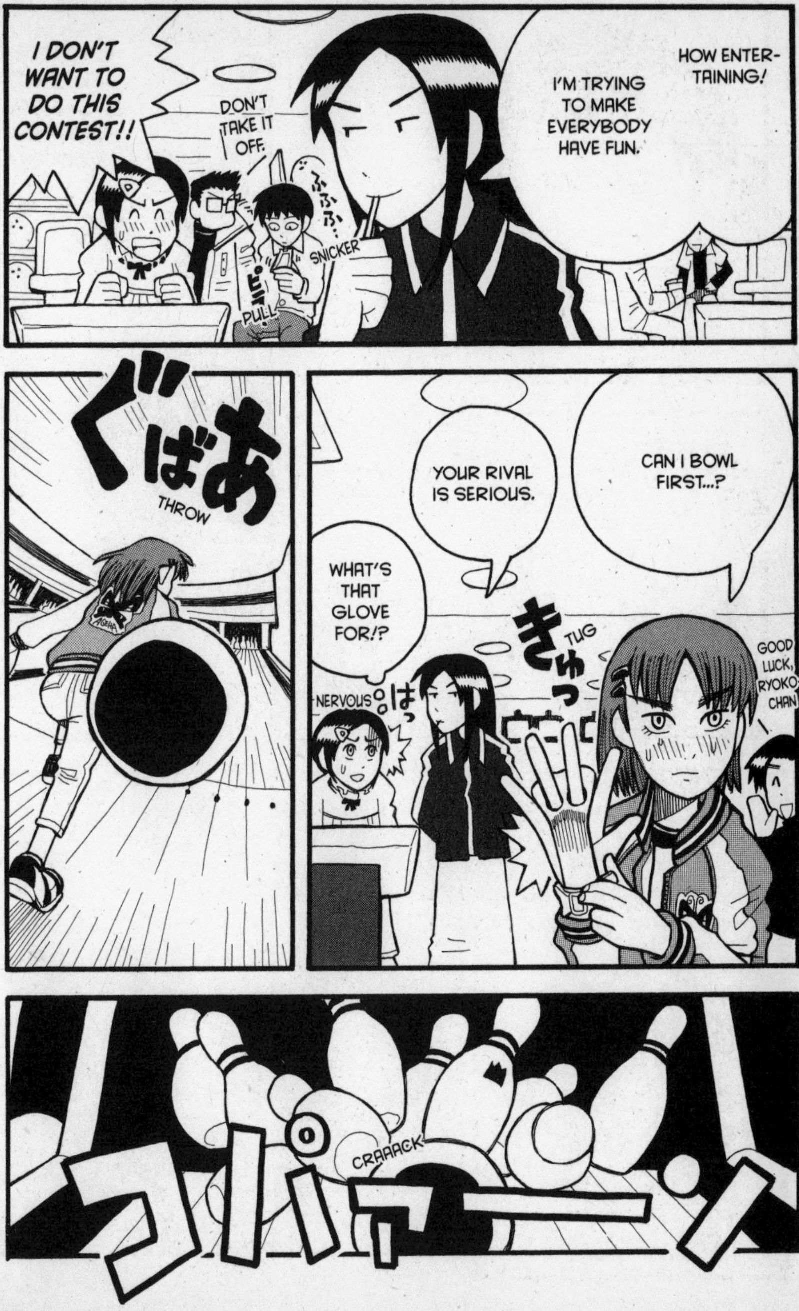
HOW ENTER-TAINING!
I'M TRYING TO MAKE EVERYBODY HAVE FUN.
ふふふ…
SNICKER
PULL
DON'T TAKE IT OFF.
I DON'T WANT TO DO THIS CONTEST!!
CAN I BOWL FIRST...?
GOOD LUCK, RYOKO-CHAN
きゅっ
TUG
YOUR RIVAL IS SERIOUS.
WHAT'S THAT GLOVE FOR!?
はっ
NERVOUS
ぐばあ
THROW
CRAAACK

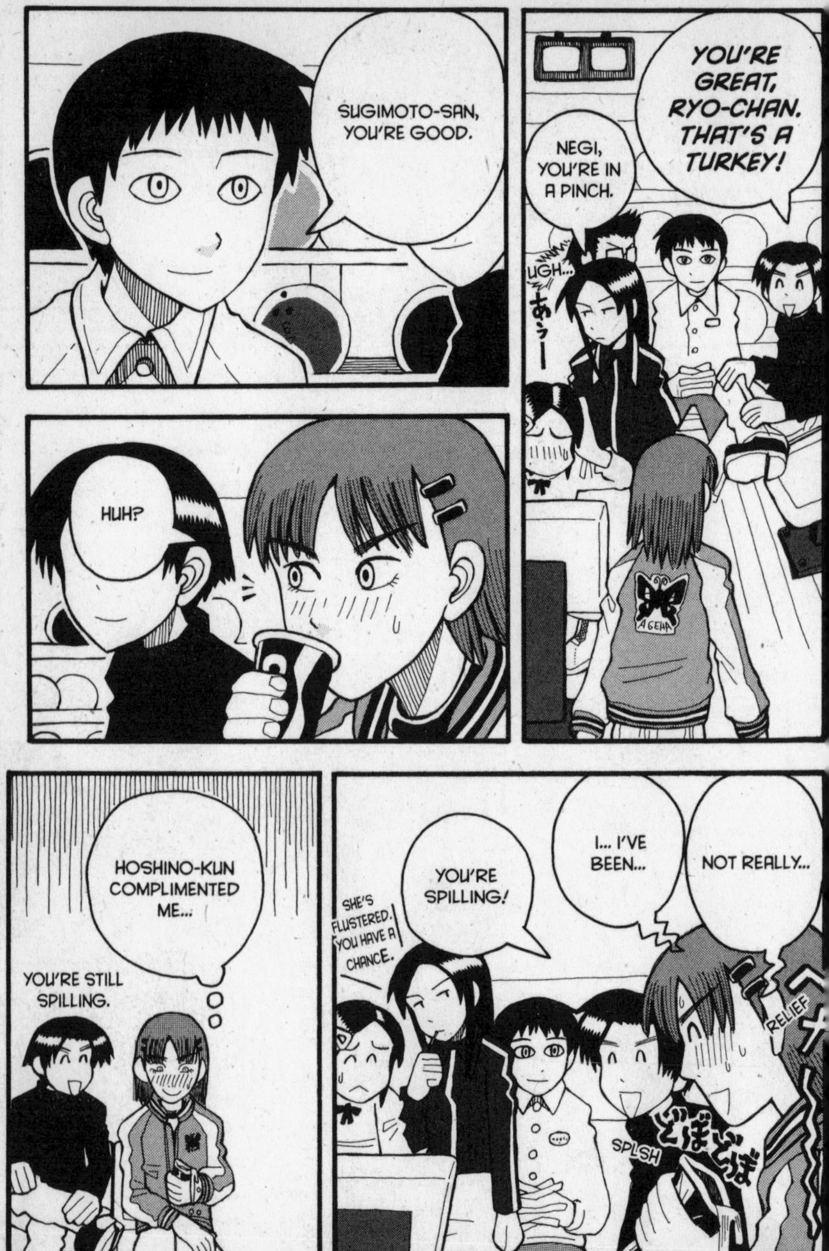
YOU'RE GREAT, RYO-CHAN. THAT'S A TURKEY!
NEGI, YOU'RE IN A PINCH.
UGH...
SUGIMOTO-SAN, YOU'RE GOOD.
HUH?
NOT REALLY...
I... I'VE BEEN...
YOU'RE SPILLING!
SHE'S FLUSTERED. YOU HAVE A CHANCE.
RELIEF
SPLSH
HOSHINO-KUN COMPLIMENTED ME...
YOU'RE STILL SPILLING.

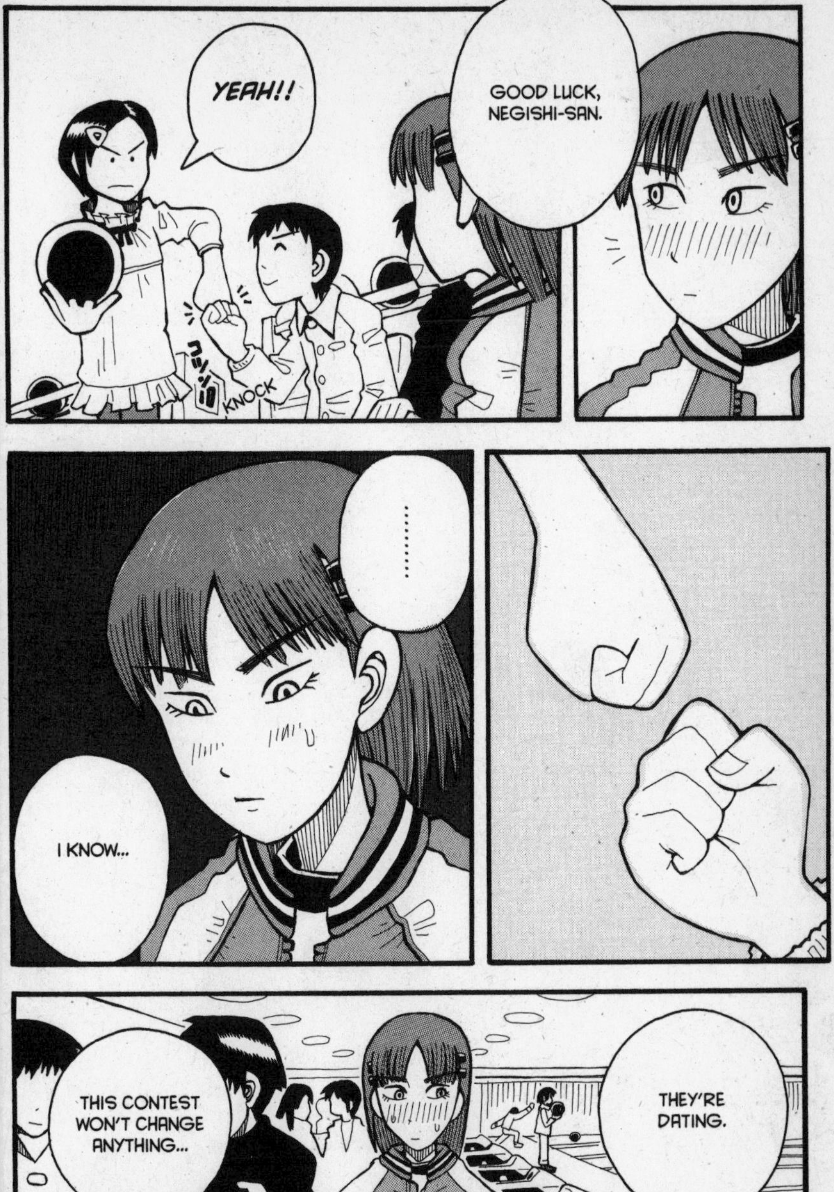
GOOD LUCK, NEGISHI-SAN.
YEAH!!
KNOCK
....
I KNOW...
THEY'RE DATING.
THIS CONTEST WON'T CHANGE ANYTHING...

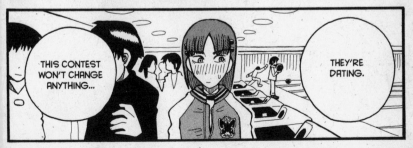

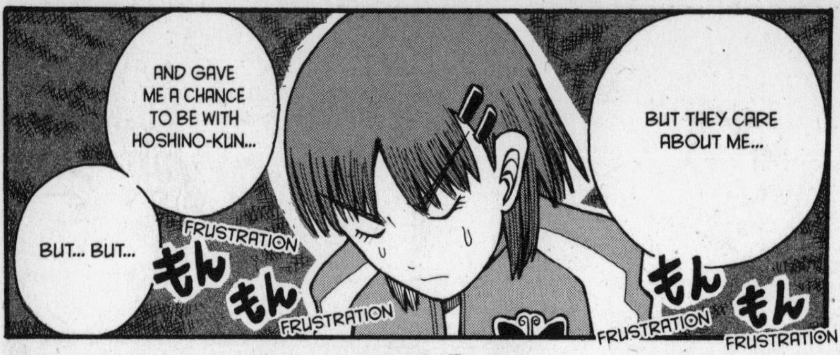
BUT THEY CARE ABOUT ME...
もん FRUSTRATION
もん FRUSTRATION
AND GAVE ME A CHANCE TO BE WITH HOSHINO-KUN...
もん FRUSTRATION
もん FRUSTRATION
BUT... BUT...
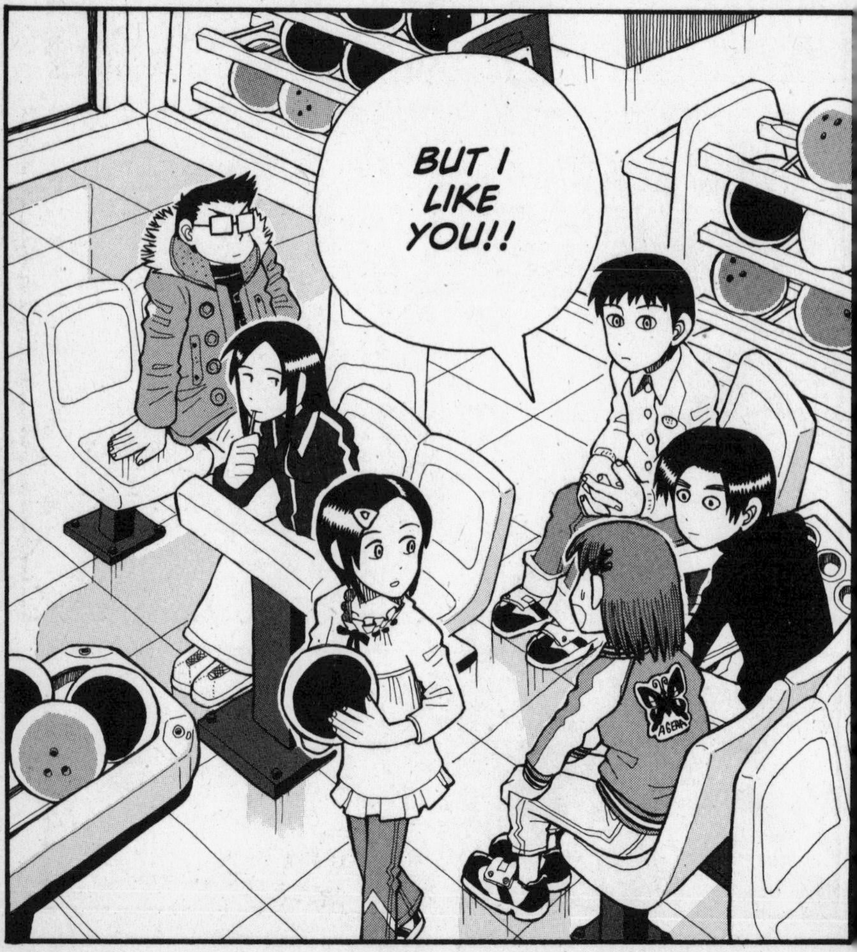
BUT I LIKE YOU!!
AGEHA

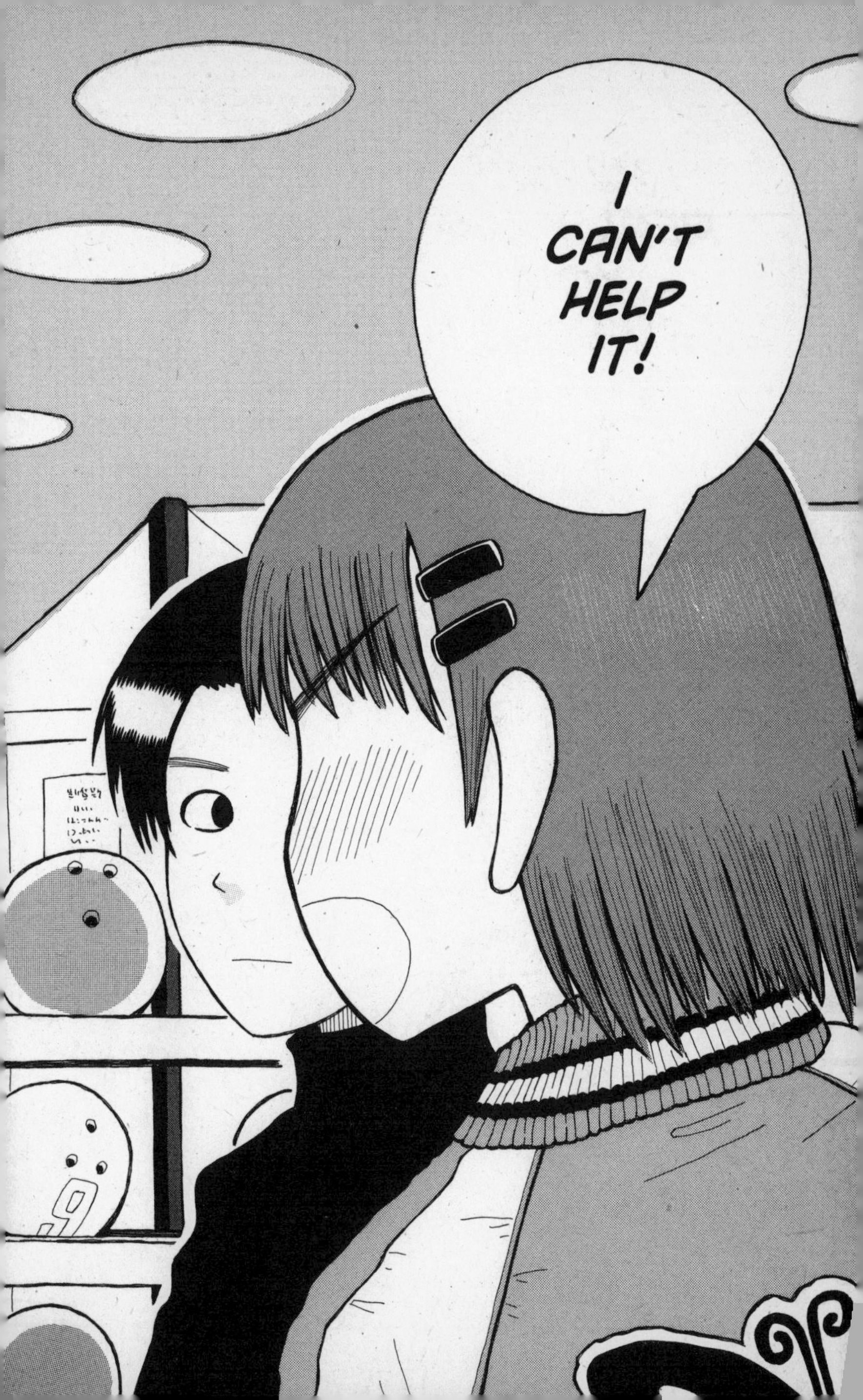
I CAN'T HELP IT!

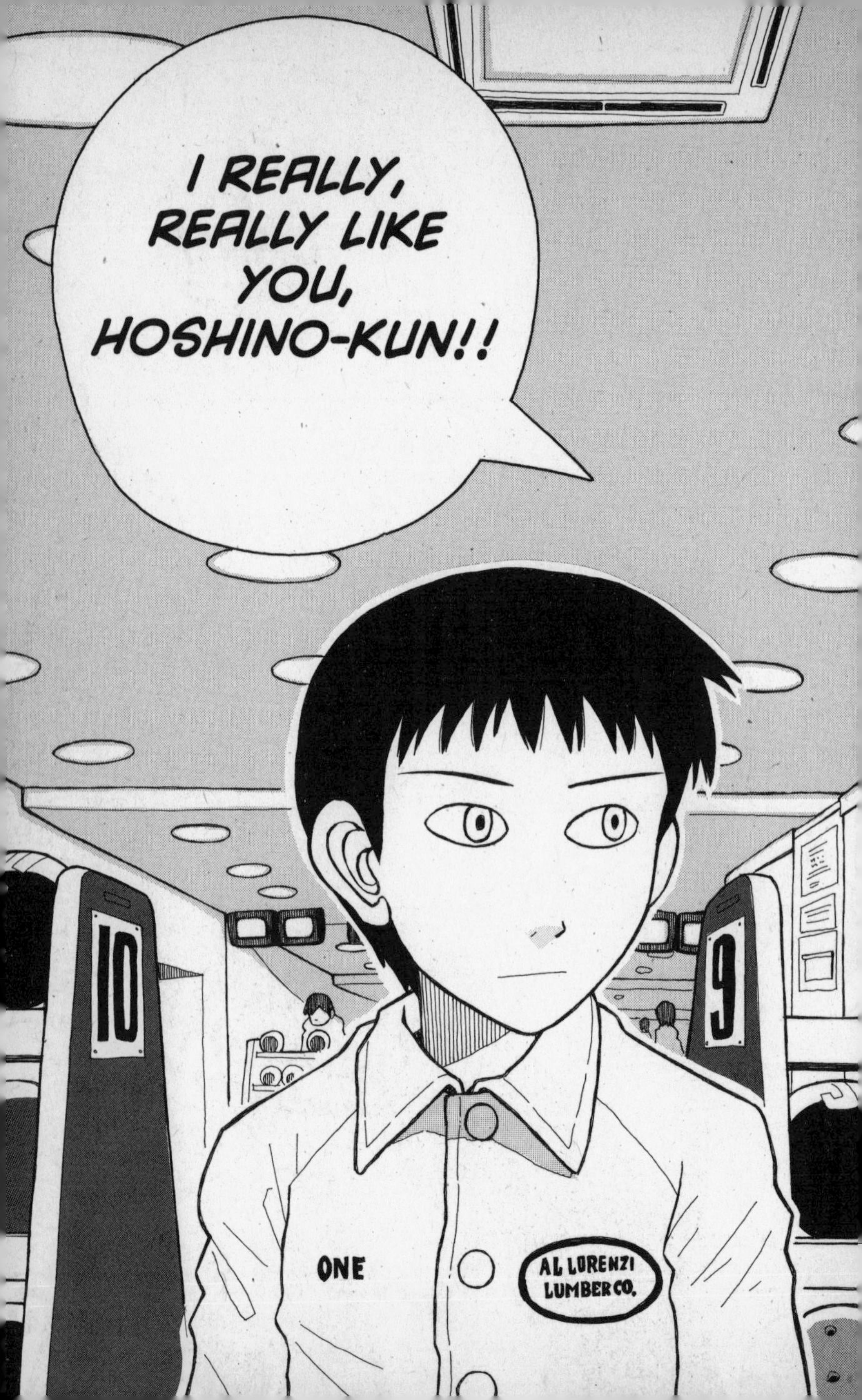
I REALLY, REALLY LIKE YOU, HOSHINO-KUN!!
10
9
ONE
AL LORENZI LUMBER CO.

BUT I LIKE NEGISHI-SAN.

I CAN'T HELP IT EITHER.

OKAY...

I'M REALLY
SORRY.

CRACK

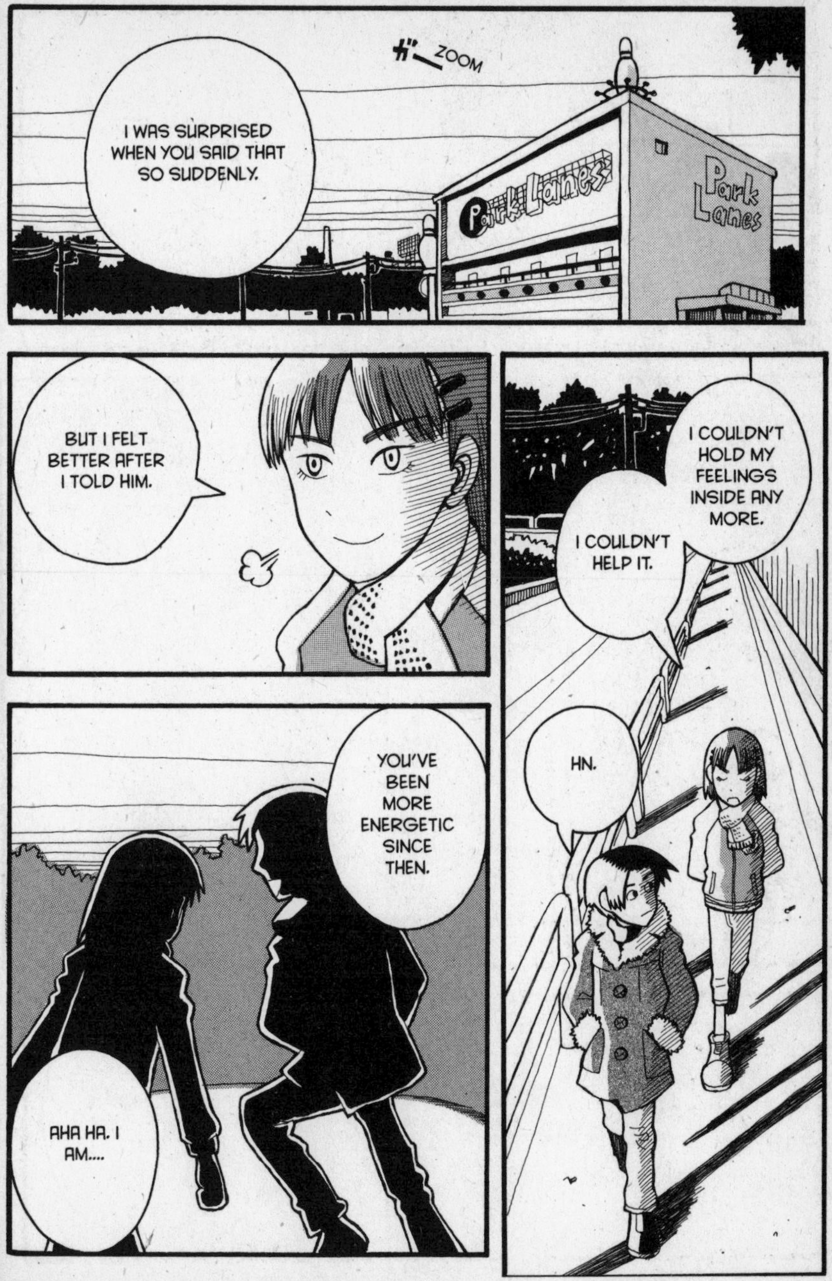

ガー ZOOM
I WAS SURPRISED WHEN YOU SAID THAT SO SUDDENLY.
I COULDN'T HOLD MY FEELINGS INSIDE ANY MORE.
I COULDN'T HELP IT.
HN.
BUT I FELT BETTER AFTER I TOLD HIM.
YOU'VE BEEN MORE ENERGETIC SINCE THEN.
AHA HA. I AM....

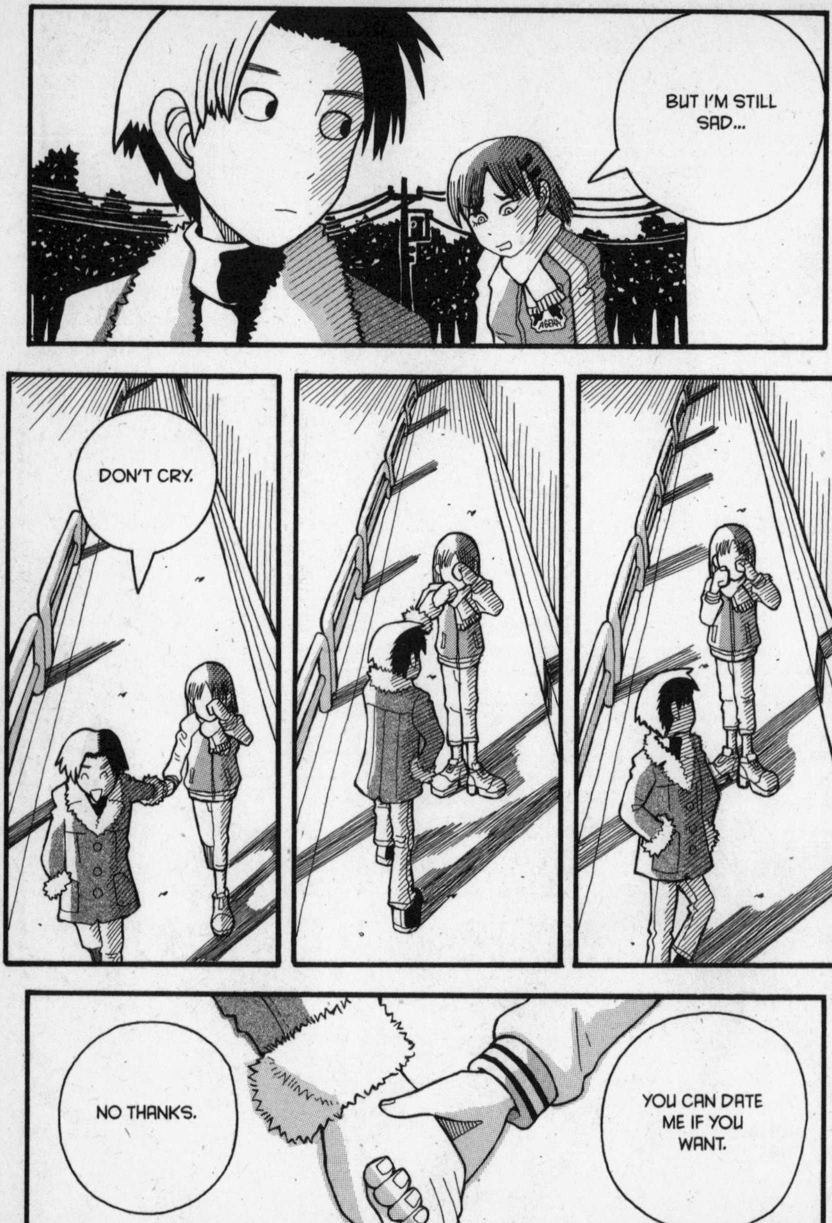
BUT I'M STILL SAD...
DON'T CRY.
YOU CAN DATE ME IF YOU WANT.
NO THANKS.

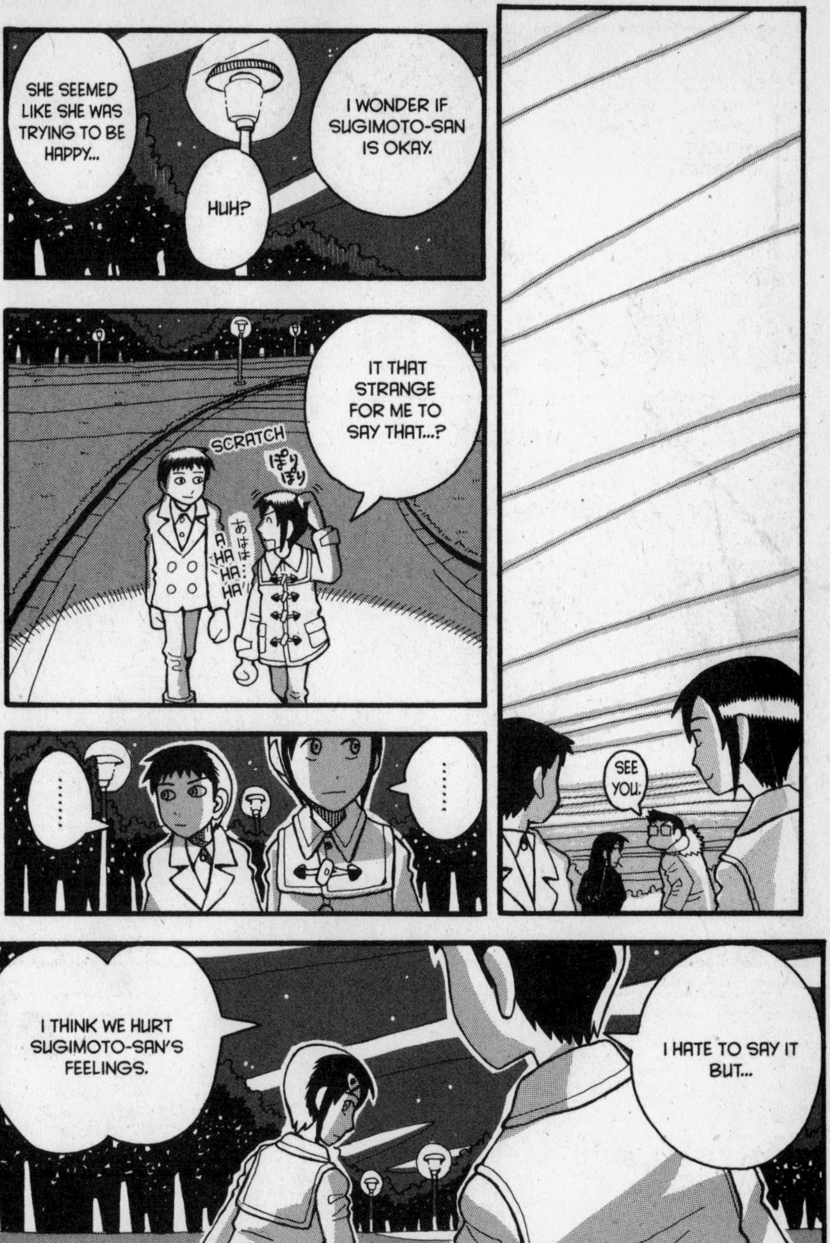

SEE YOU.
I WONDER IF SUGIMOTO-SAN IS OKAY.
HUH?
SHE SEEMED LIKE SHE WAS TRYING TO BE HAPPY...
IT THAT STRANGE FOR ME TO SAY THAT...?
SCRATCH
ぽりぽり
あはは…
A HA HA HA
......
......
I HATE TO SAY IT BUT...
I THINK WE HURT SUGIMOTO-SAN'S FEELINGS.

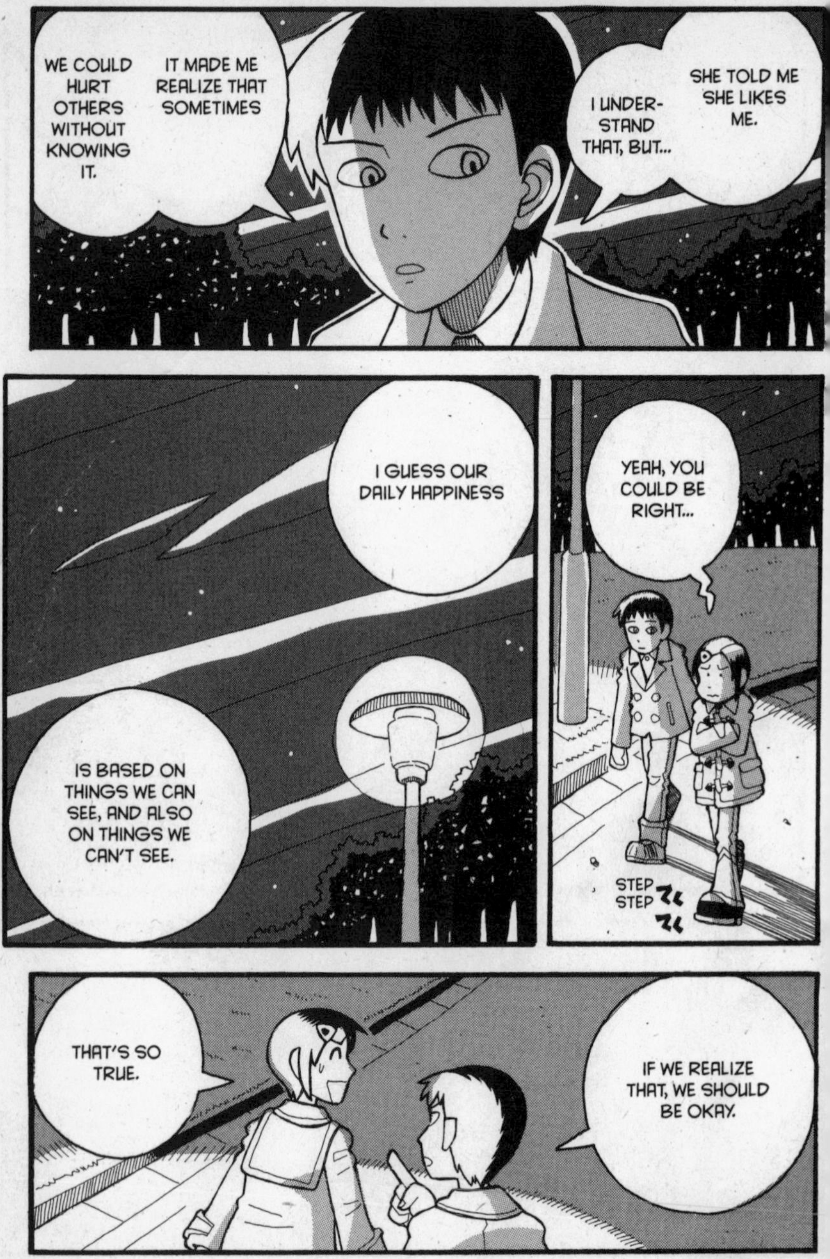
SHE TOLD ME SHE LIKES ME.
I UNDER-STAND THAT, BUT...
IT MADE ME REALIZE THAT SOMETIMES
WE COULD HURT OTHERS WITHOUT KNOWING IT.
YEAH, YOU COULD BE RIGHT...
STEP STEP
I GUESS OUR DAILY HAPPINESS
IS BASED ON THINGS WE CAN SEE, AND ALSO ON THINGS WE CAN'T SEE.
IF WE REALIZE THAT, WE SHOULD BE OKAY.
THAT'S SO TRUE.

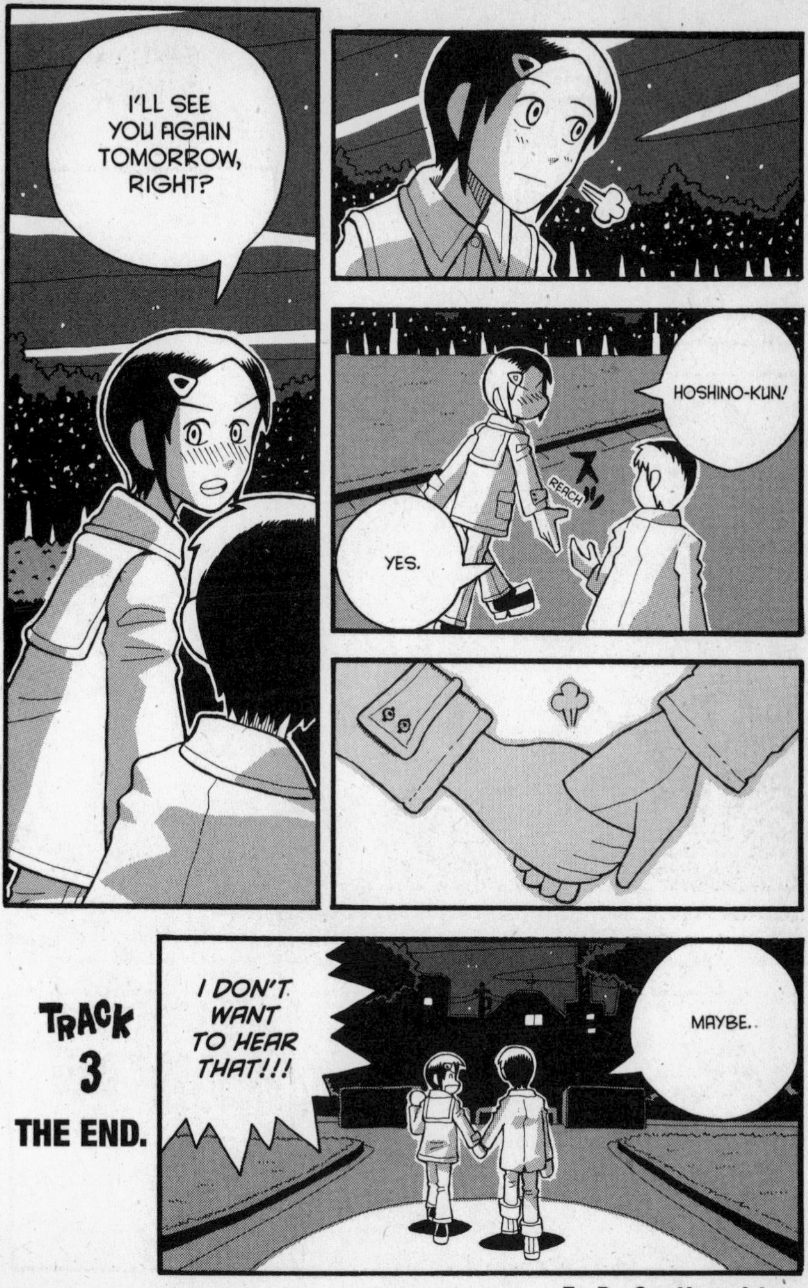
HOSHINO-KUN!
REACH
YES.
I'LL SEE YOU AGAIN TOMORROW, RIGHT?
MAYBE..
I DON'T WANT TO HEAR THAT!!!

TRACK 3 THE END.

To Be Continued to...

BONUS TRACK

EXTRA

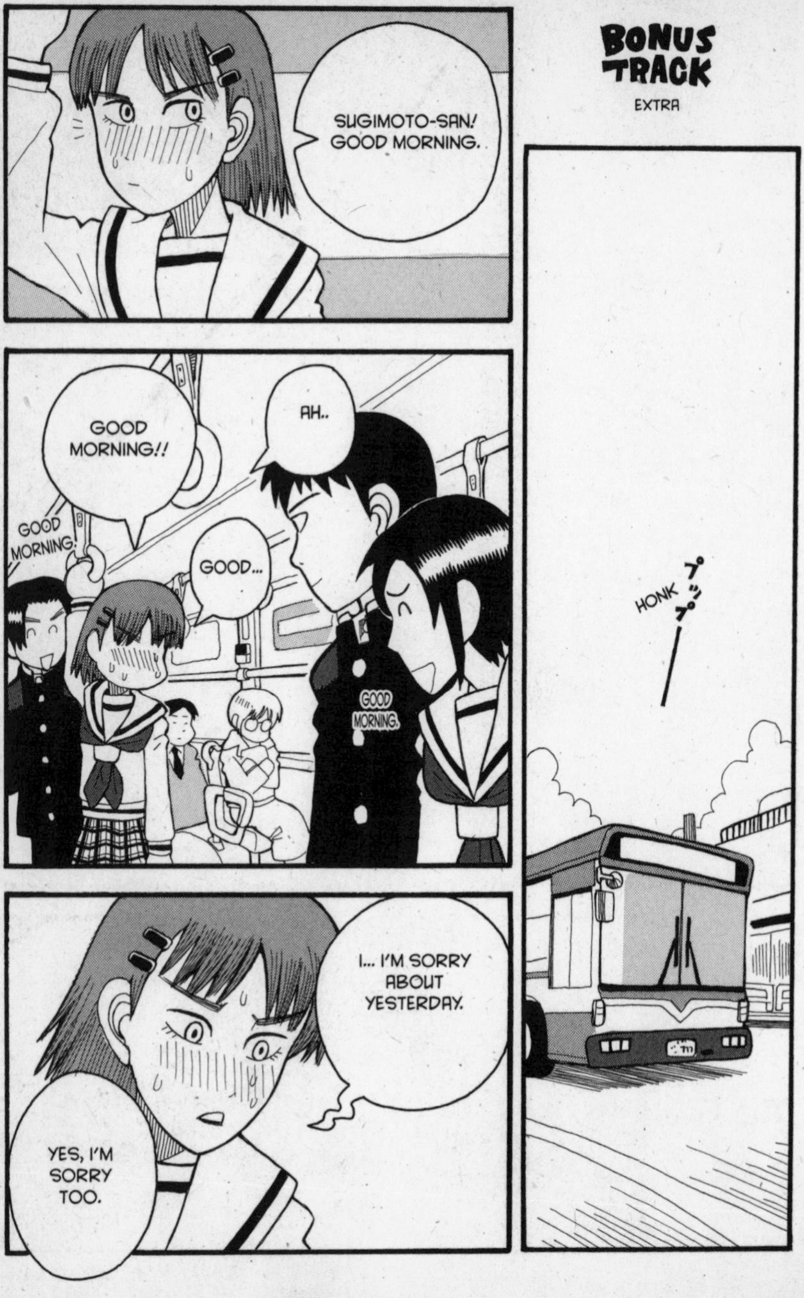
HONK
プップー
SUGIMOTO-SAN! GOOD MORNING.
AH..
GOOD MORNING!!
GOOD...
GOOD MORNING.
GOOD MORNING!
I... I'M SORRY ABOUT YESTERDAY.
YES, I'M SORRY TOO.

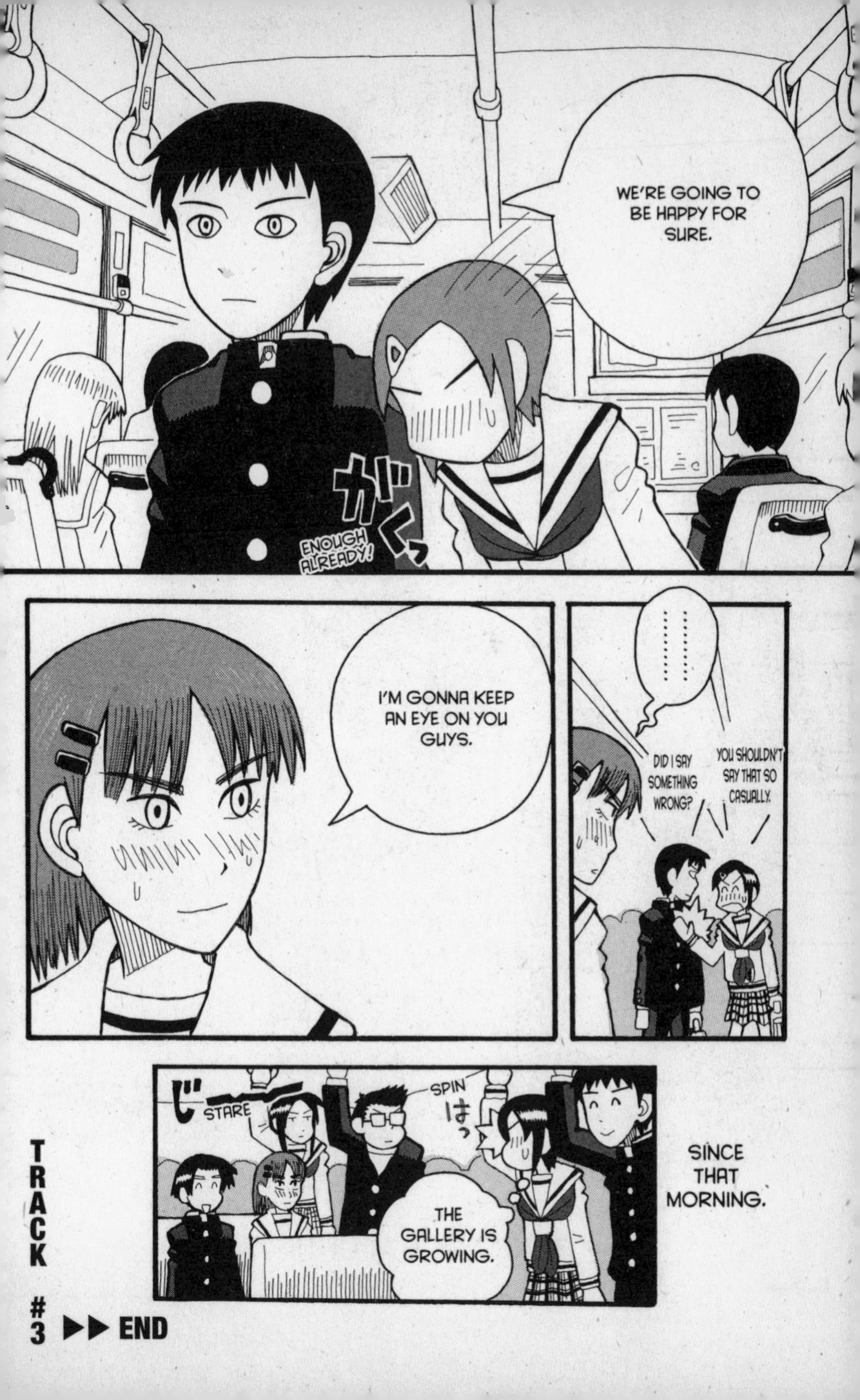
WE'RE GOING TO BE HAPPY FOR SURE.
がくっ
ENOUGH ALREADY!
......
YOU SHOULDN'T SAY THAT SO CASUALLY.
DID I SAY SOMETHING WRONG?
I'M GONNA KEEP AN EYE ON YOU GUYS.
SINCE THAT MORNING.
はっ
SPIN
じー
STARE
THE GALLERY IS GROWING.
TRACK #3 ▶▶ END

TRACK #4

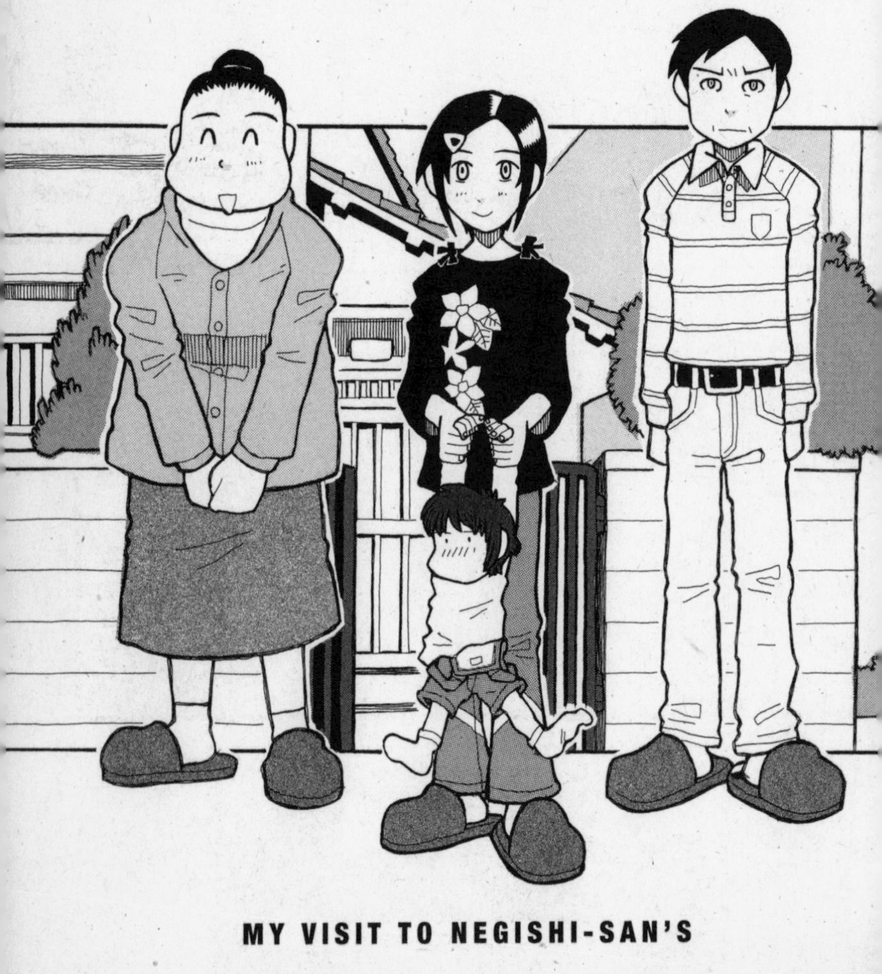

MY VISIT TO NEGISHI-SAN'S

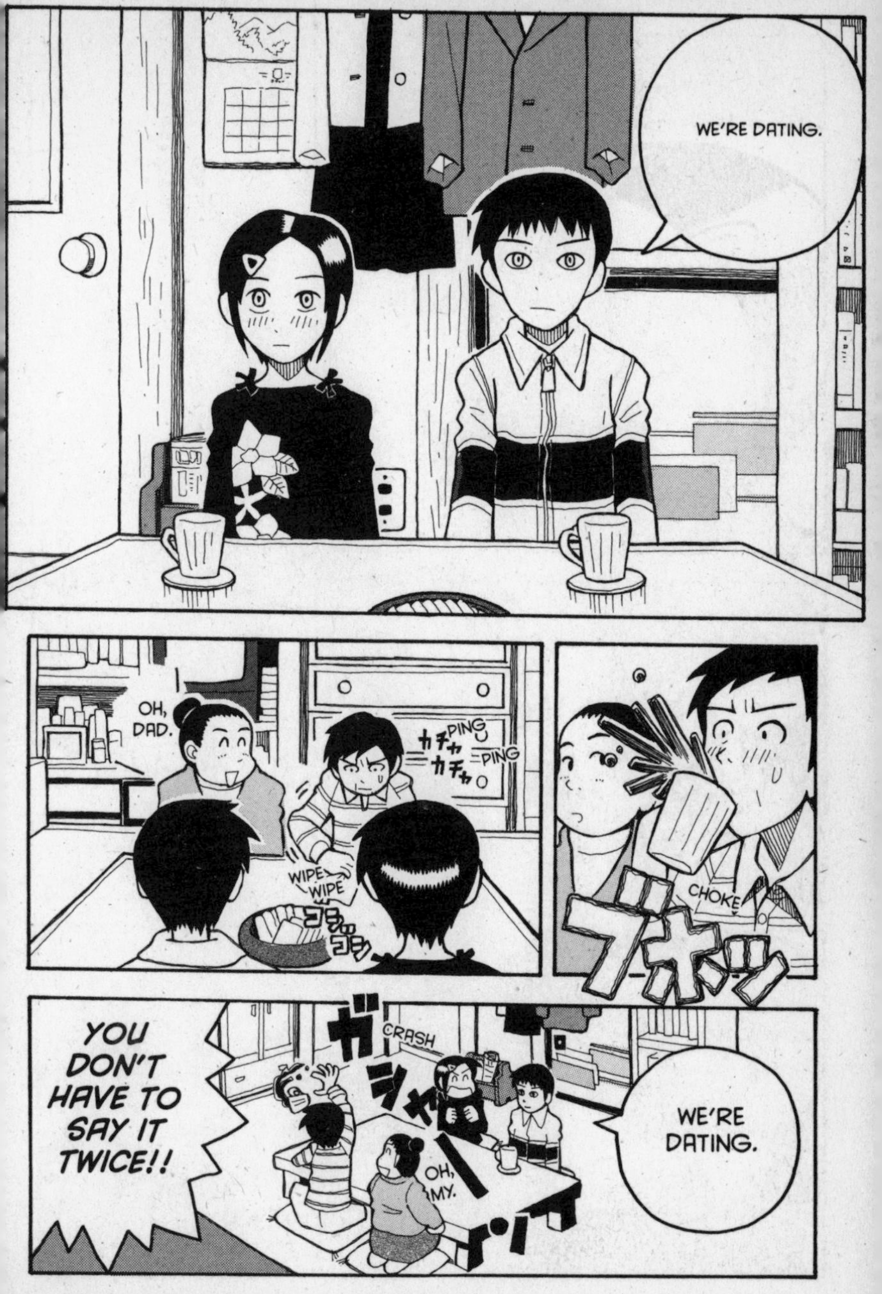
WE'RE DATING.
ブホッ
CHOKE
OH, DAD.
カチャ カチャ
PING PING
WIPE WIPE
ゴシゴシ
WE'RE DATING.
ガシャ
CRASH
OH, MY.
YOU DON'T HAVE TO SAY IT TWICE!!

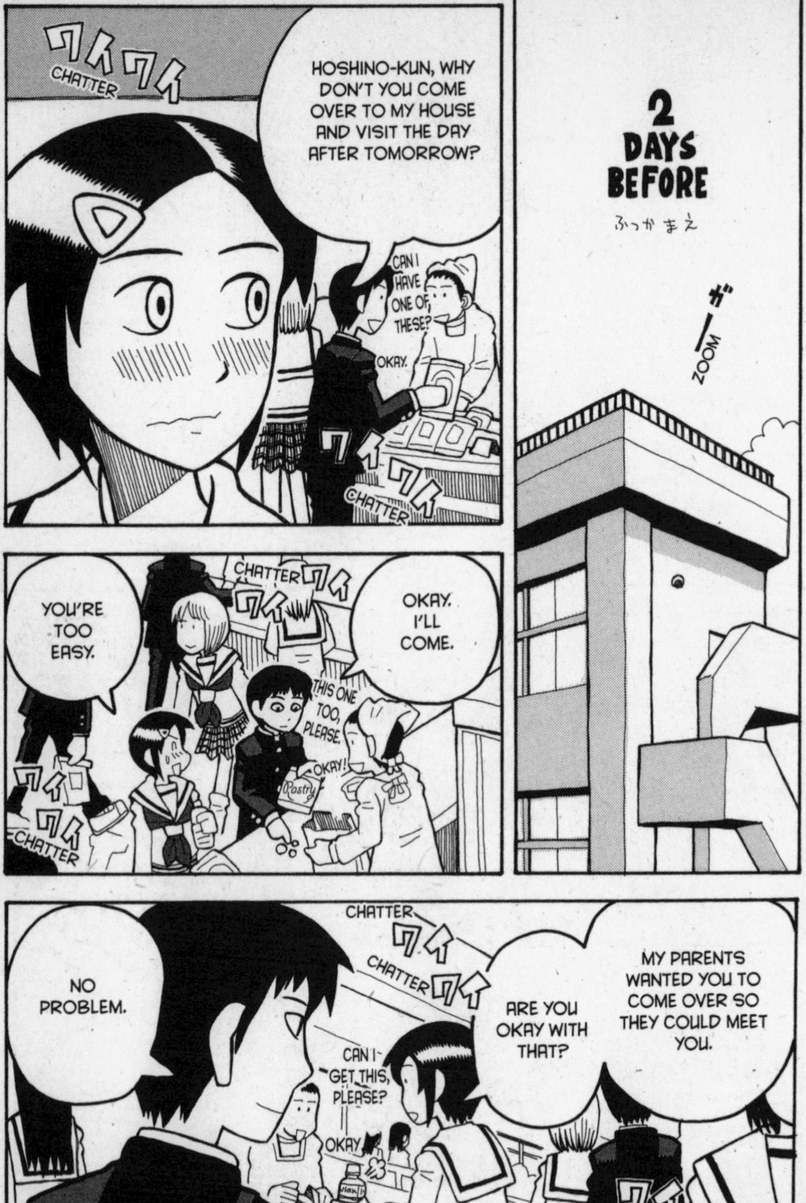
2 DAYS BEFORE
ふつかまえ
ガー
ZOOM
HOSHINO-KUN, WHY DON'T YOU COME OVER TO MY HOUSE AND VISIT THE DAY AFTER TOMORROW?
ワイワイ
CHATTER
CAN I HAVE ONE OF THESE?
OKAY.
ワイワイ
CHATTER
OKAY. I'LL COME.
CHATTER
ワイワイ
YOU'RE TOO EASY.
THIS ONE TOO, PLEASE.
OKAY!
Pastry
ワイワイ
CHATTER
MY PARENTS WANTED YOU TO COME OVER SO THEY COULD MEET YOU.
ARE YOU OKAY WITH THAT?
CHATTER
ワイ
CHATTER
ワイ
CAN I GET THIS, PLEASE?
OKAY
NO PROBLEM.
ワイワイ

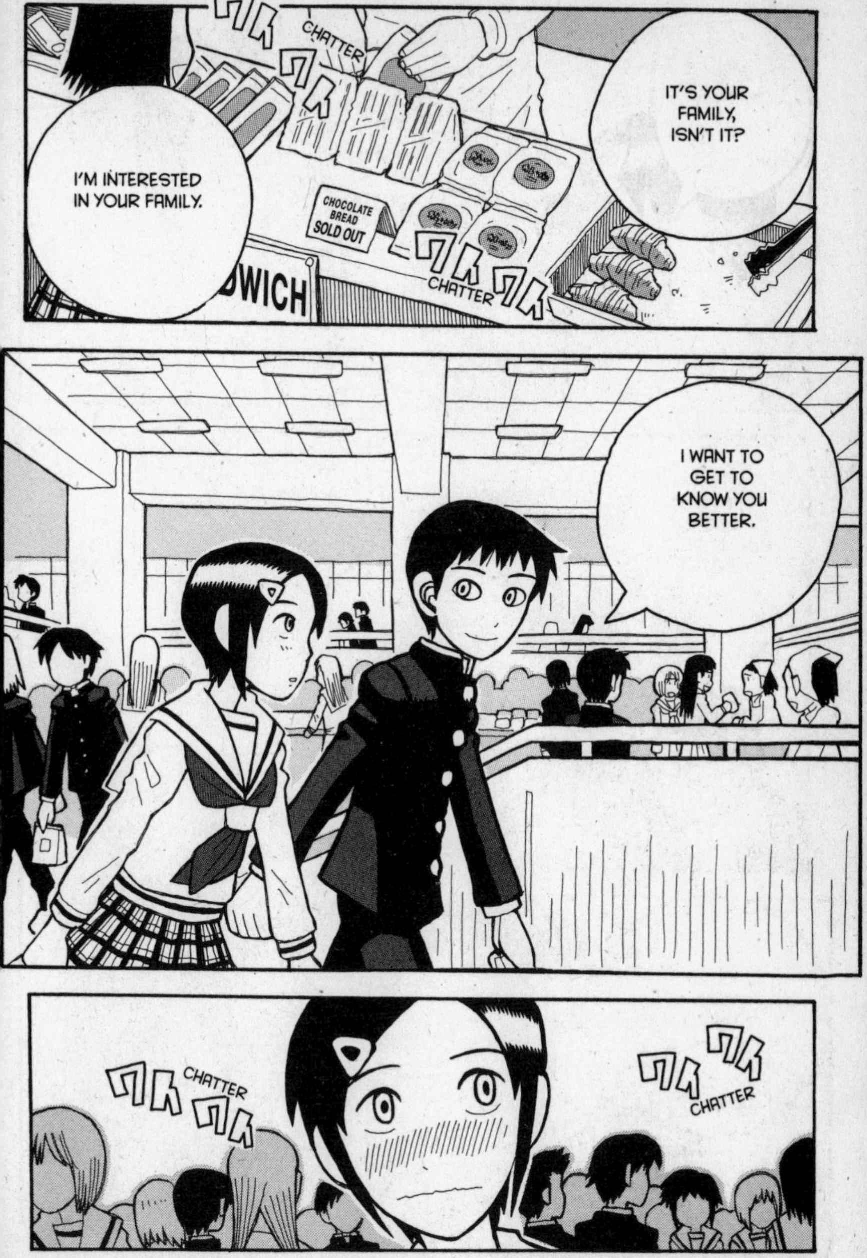
IT'S YOUR FAMILY, ISN'T IT?
CHATTER
I'M INTERESTED IN YOUR FAMILY.
CHOCOLATE BREAD SOLD OUT
CHATTER
DWICH
I WANT TO GET TO KNOW YOU BETTER.
CHATTER
CHATTER

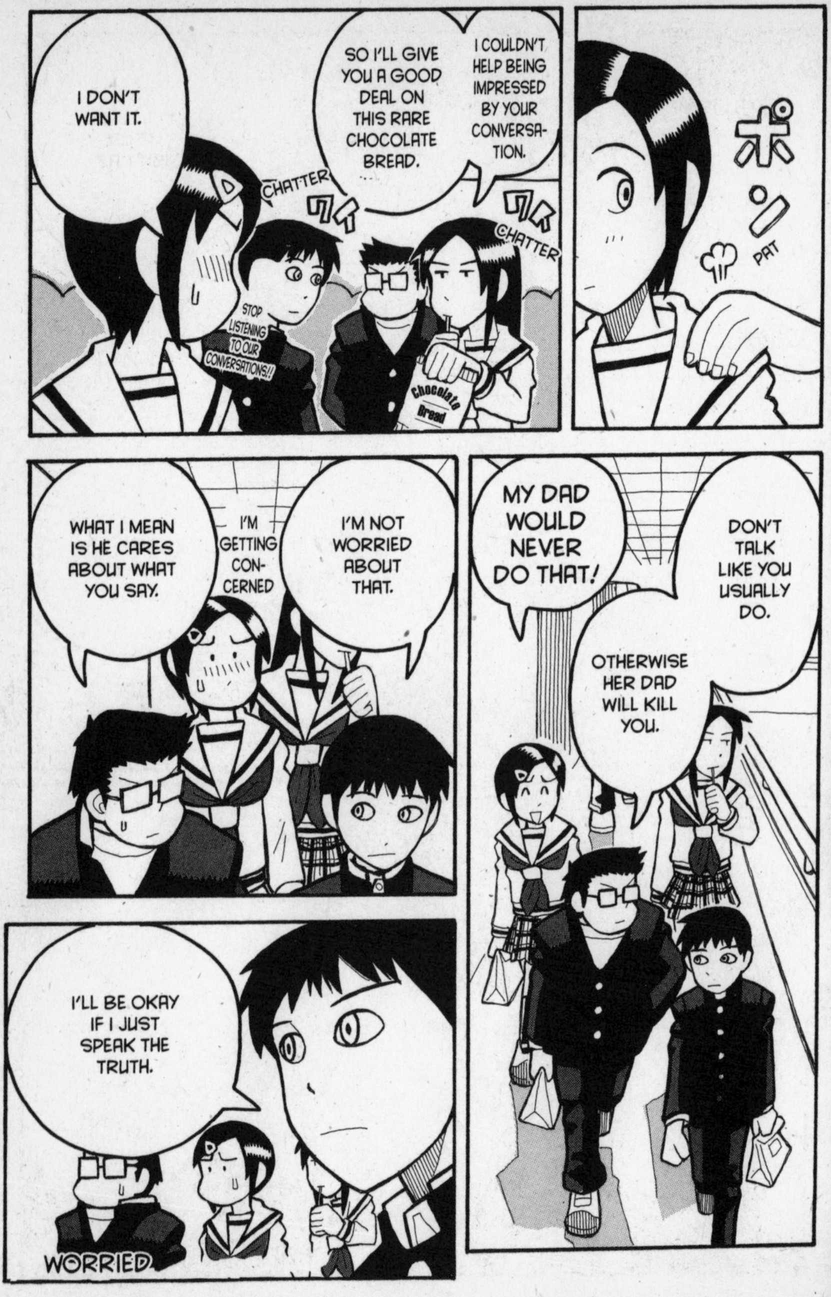
ポン
PAT
I COULDN'T HELP BEING IMPRESSED BY YOUR CONVERSATION.
SO I'LL GIVE YOU A GOOD DEAL ON THIS RARE CHOCOLATE BREAD.
CHATTER
CHATTER
ワイ
I DON'T WANT IT.
STOP LISTENING TO OUR CONVERSATIONS!!
Chocolate Bread
DON'T TALK LIKE YOU USUALLY DO.
MY DAD WOULD NEVER DO THAT!
OTHERWISE HER DAD WILL KILL YOU.
I'M NOT WORRIED ABOUT THAT.
I'M GETTING CONCERNED
WHAT I MEAN IS HE CARES ABOUT WHAT YOU SAY.
I'LL BE OKAY IF I JUST SPEAK THE TRUTH.
WORRIED

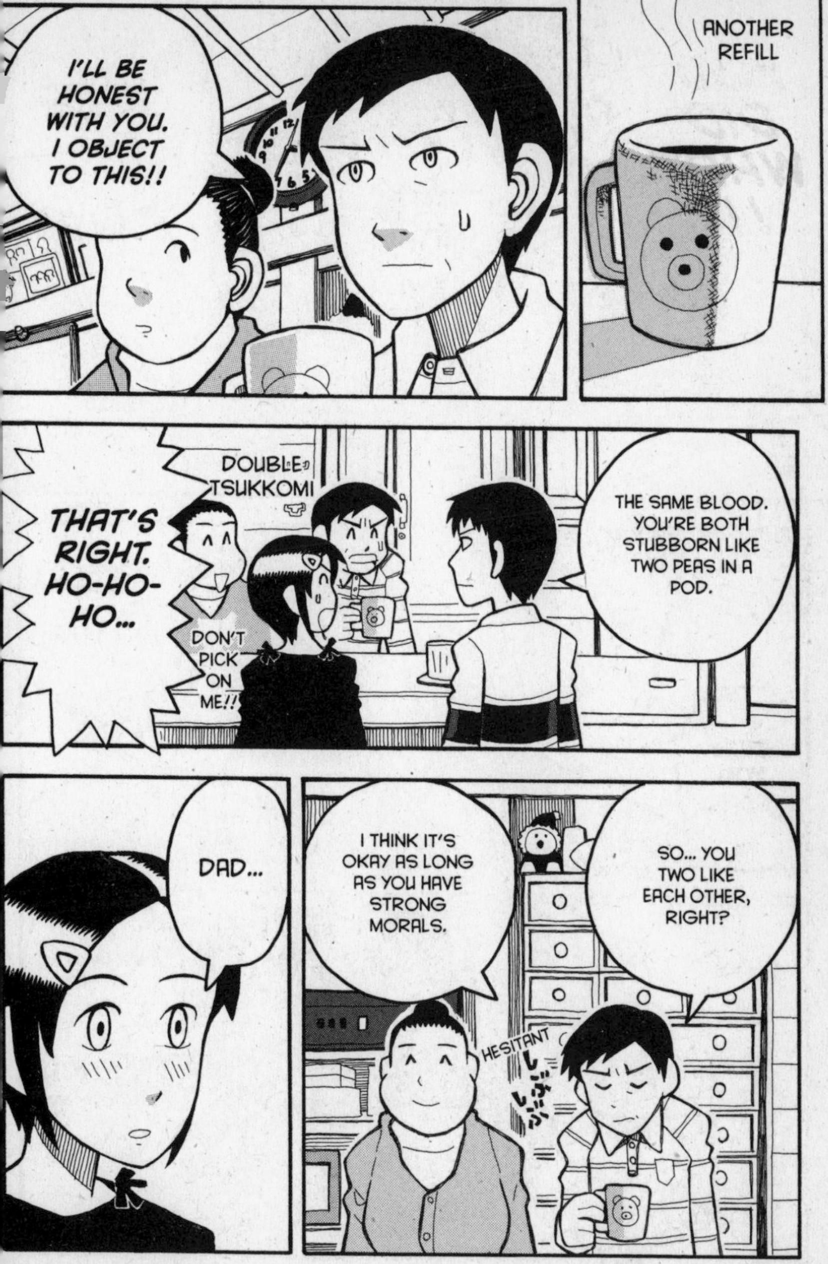
ANOTHER REFILL
I'LL BE HONEST WITH YOU. I OBJECT TO THIS!!
THE SAME BLOOD. YOU'RE BOTH STUBBORN LIKE TWO PEAS IN A POD.
DOUBLE TSUKKOMI
THAT'S RIGHT. HO-HO-HO...
DON'T PICK ON ME!!
SO... YOU TWO LIKE EACH OTHER, RIGHT?
I THINK IT'S OKAY AS LONG AS YOU HAVE STRONG MORALS.
HESITANT
しぶしぶ
DAD...

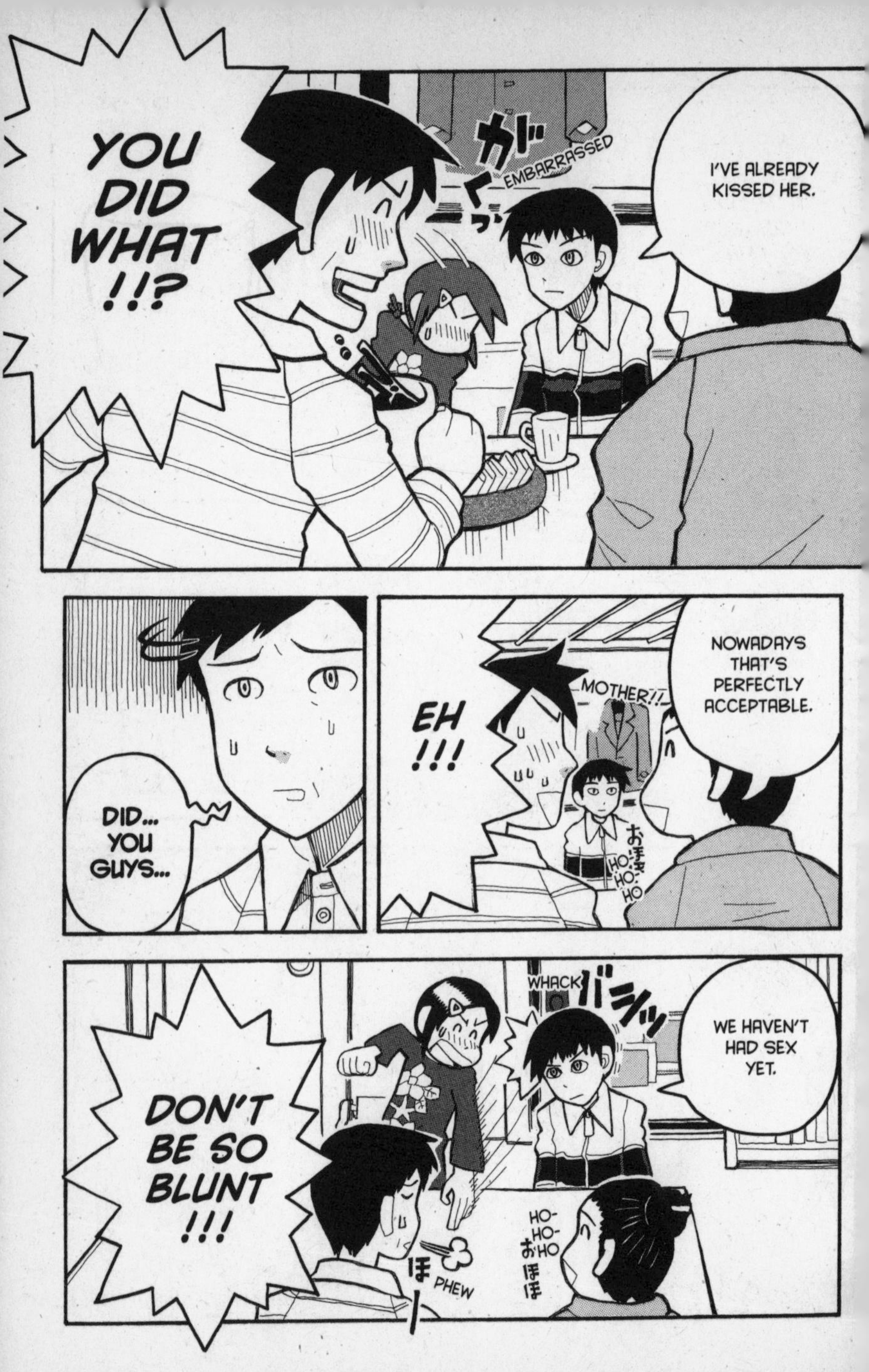
I'VE ALREADY KISSED HER.
EMBARRASSED
YOU DID WHAT!!?
NOWADAYS THAT'S PERFECTLY ACCEPTABLE.
MOTHER!!
EH!!!
HO-HO-HO
DID... YOU GUYS...
WE HAVEN'T HAD SEX YET.
WHACK
HO-HO-HO
DON'T BE SO BLUNT!!!
PHEW

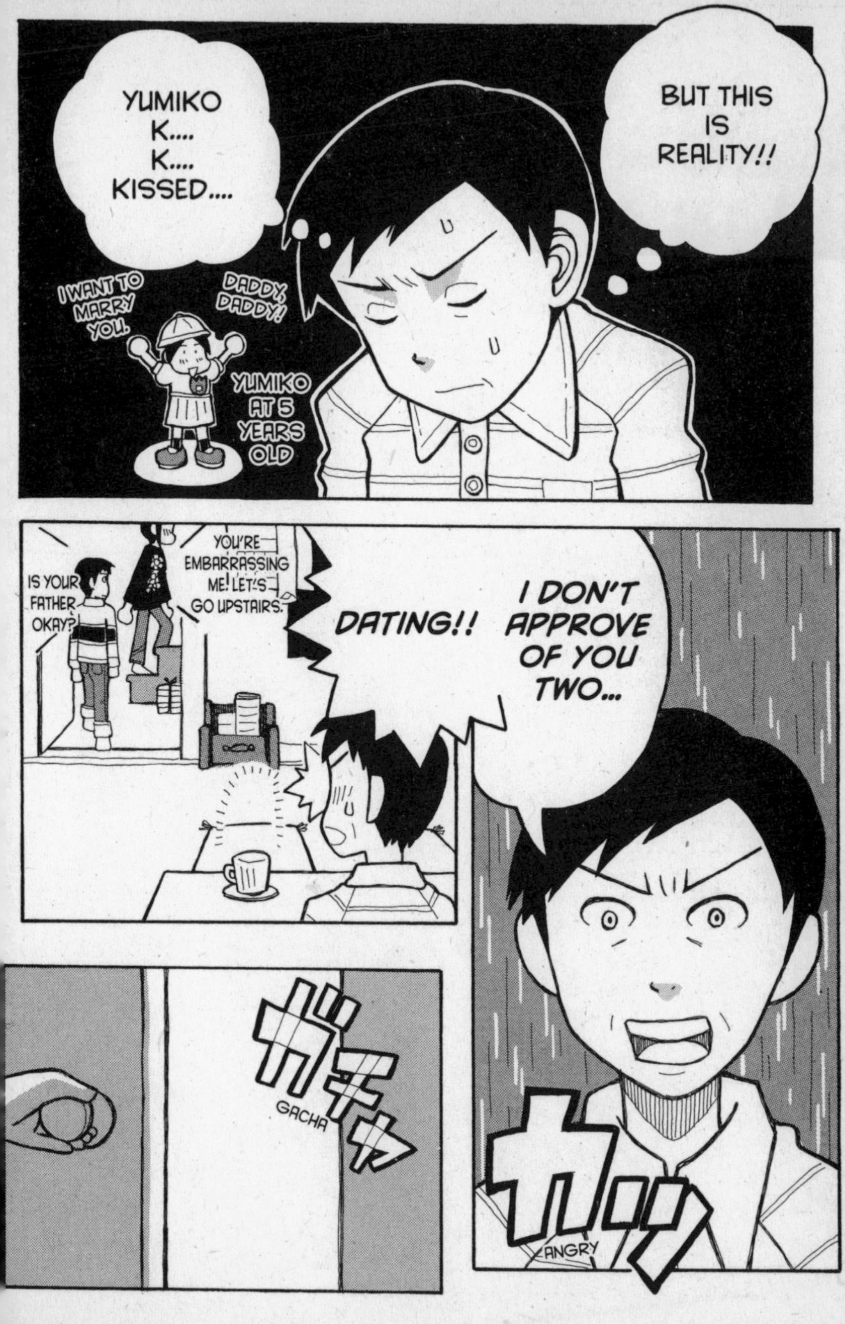
BUT THIS IS REALITY!!
YUMIKO K.... K.... KISSED....
DADDY, DADDY!
I WANT TO MARRY YOU.
YUMIKO AT 5 YEARS OLD
I DON'T APPROVE OF YOU TWO...
DATING!!
ANGRY
YOU'RE EMBARRASSING ME! LET'S GO UPSTAIRS.
IS YOUR FATHER OKAY?
GACHA

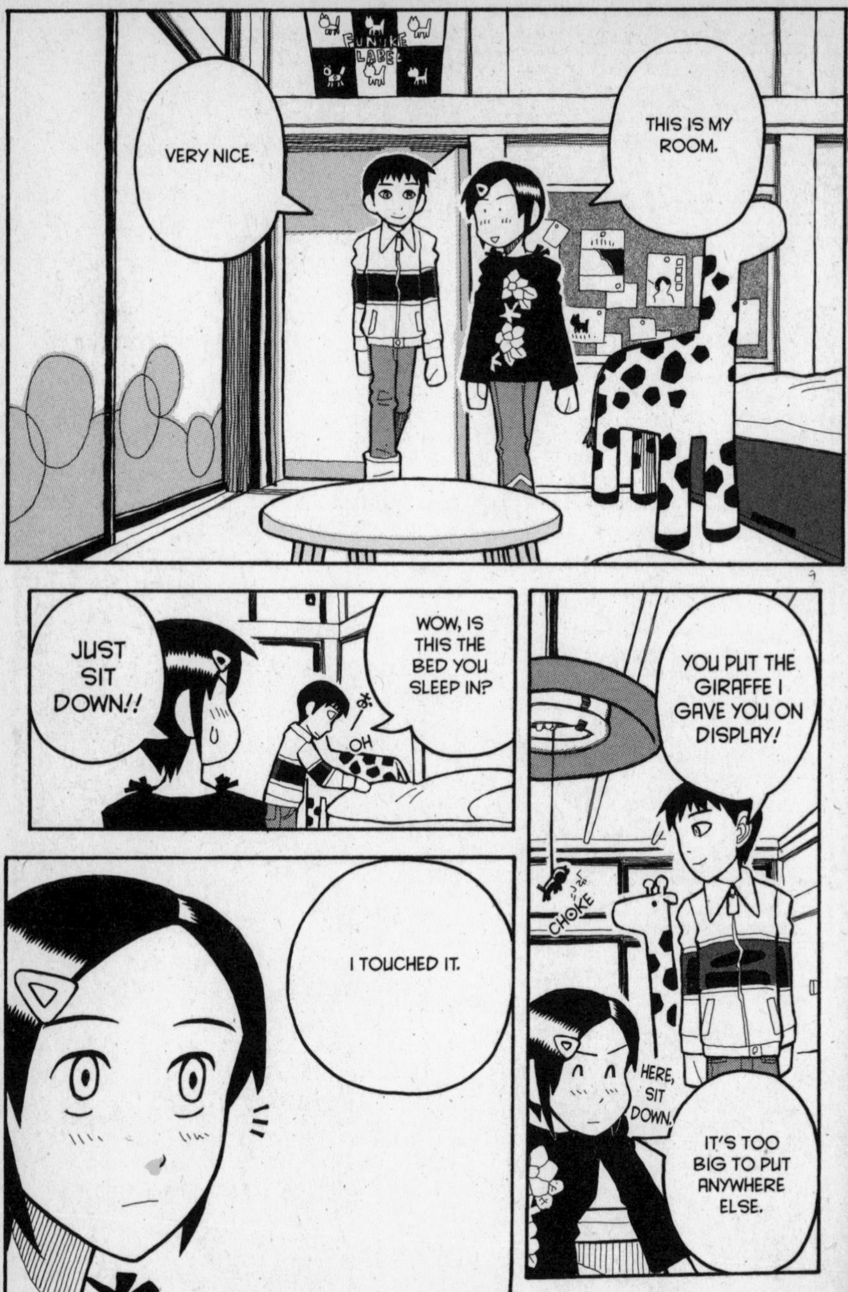
FUNIKE LABEL
THIS IS MY ROOM.
VERY NICE.
YOU PUT THE GIRAFFE I GAVE YOU ON DISPLAY!
CHOKE
HERE, SIT DOWN.
IT'S TOO BIG TO PUT ANYWHERE ELSE.
WOW, IS THIS THE BED YOU SLEEP IN?
OH
JUST SIT DOWN!!
I TOUCHED IT.

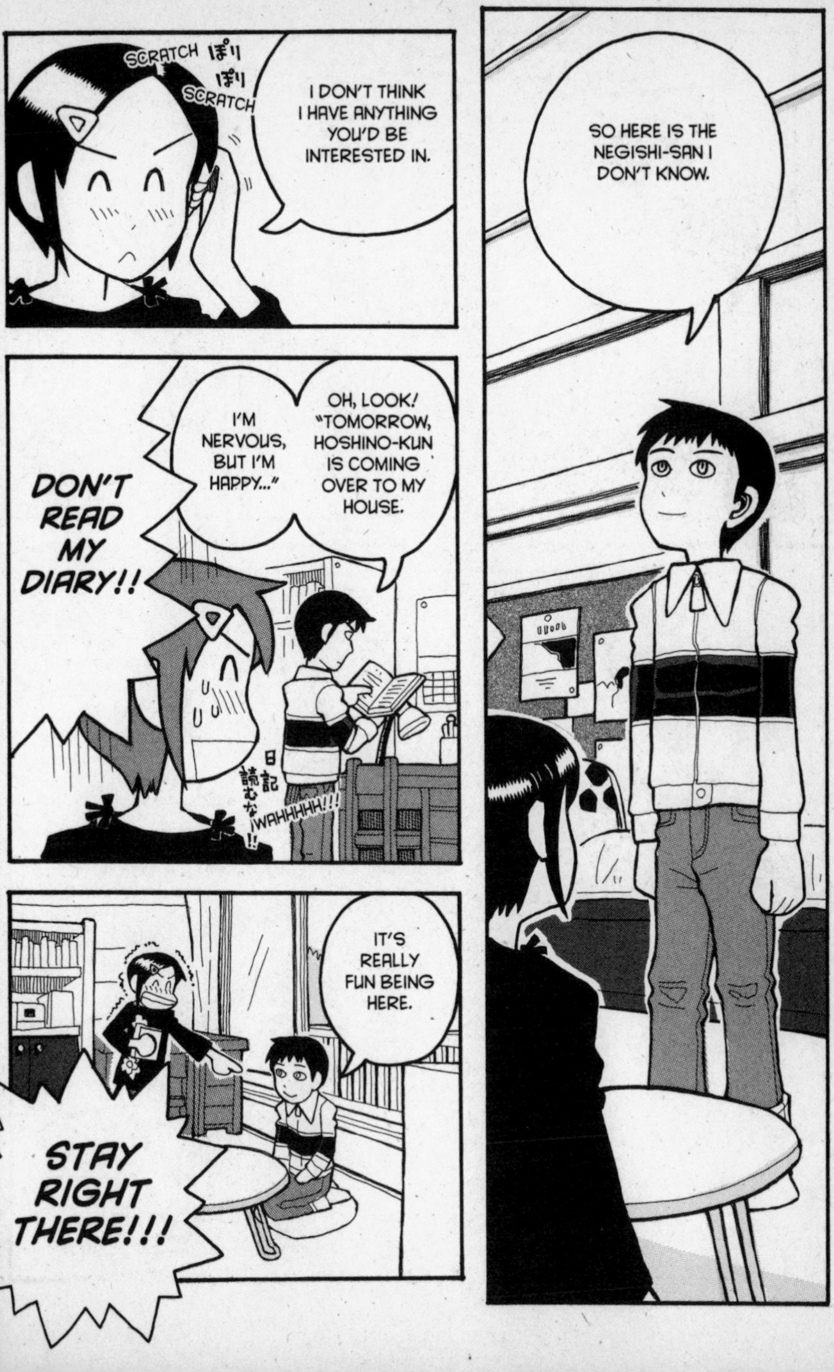
SO HERE IS THE NEGISHI-SAN I DON'T KNOW.
I DON'T THINK I HAVE ANYTHING YOU'D BE INTERESTED IN.
SCRATCH ぽり ぽり SCRATCH
OH, LOOK! "TOMORROW, HOSHINO-KUN IS COMING OVER TO MY HOUSE.
I'M NERVOUS, BUT I'M HAPPY..."
DON'T READ MY DIARY!!
日記読むな!! WAHHHHH!!!
IT'S REALLY FUN BEING HERE.
STAY RIGHT THERE!!!

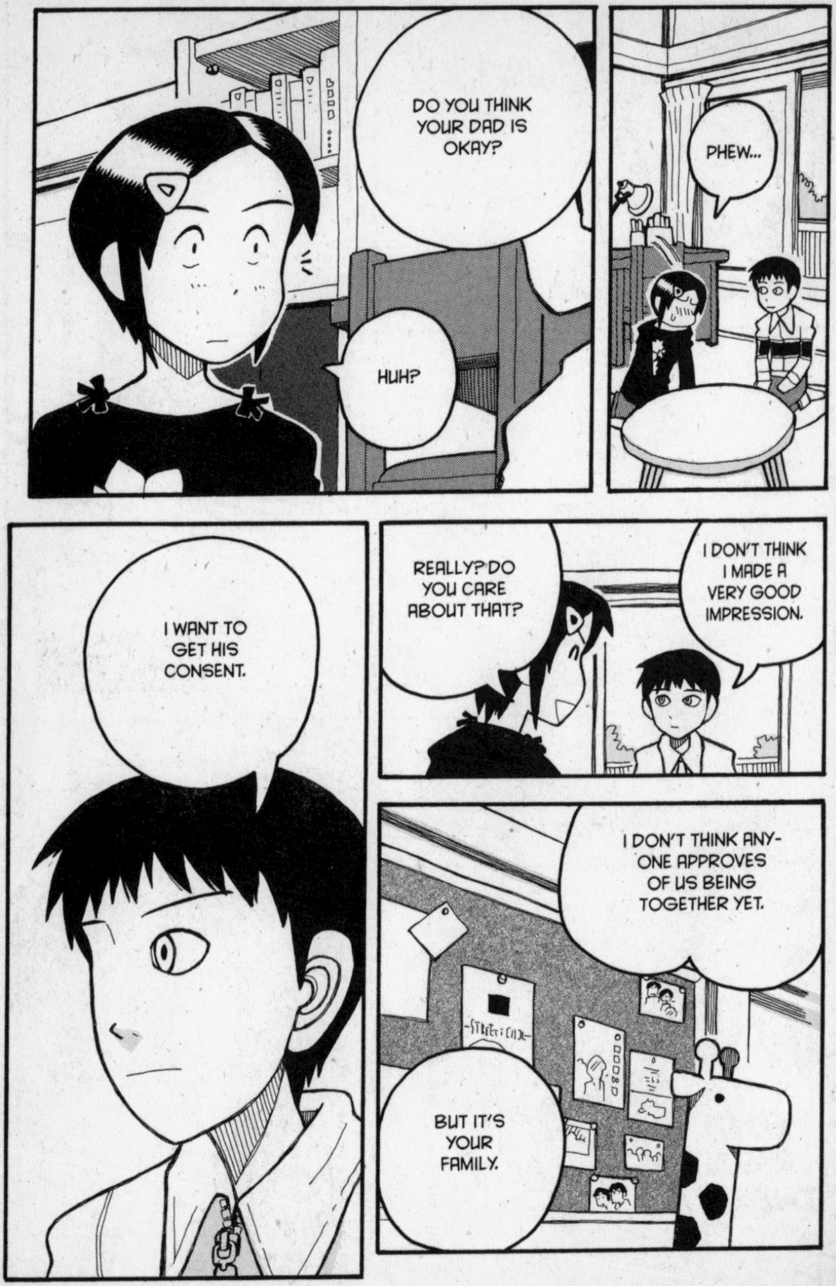
PHEW...
DO YOU THINK YOUR DAD IS OKAY?
HUH?
I DON'T THINK I MADE A VERY GOOD IMPRESSION.
REALLY? DO YOU CARE ABOUT THAT?
I DON'T THINK ANY-ONE APPROVES OF US BEING TOGETHER YET.
BUT IT'S YOUR FAMILY.
I WANT TO GET HIS CONSENT.

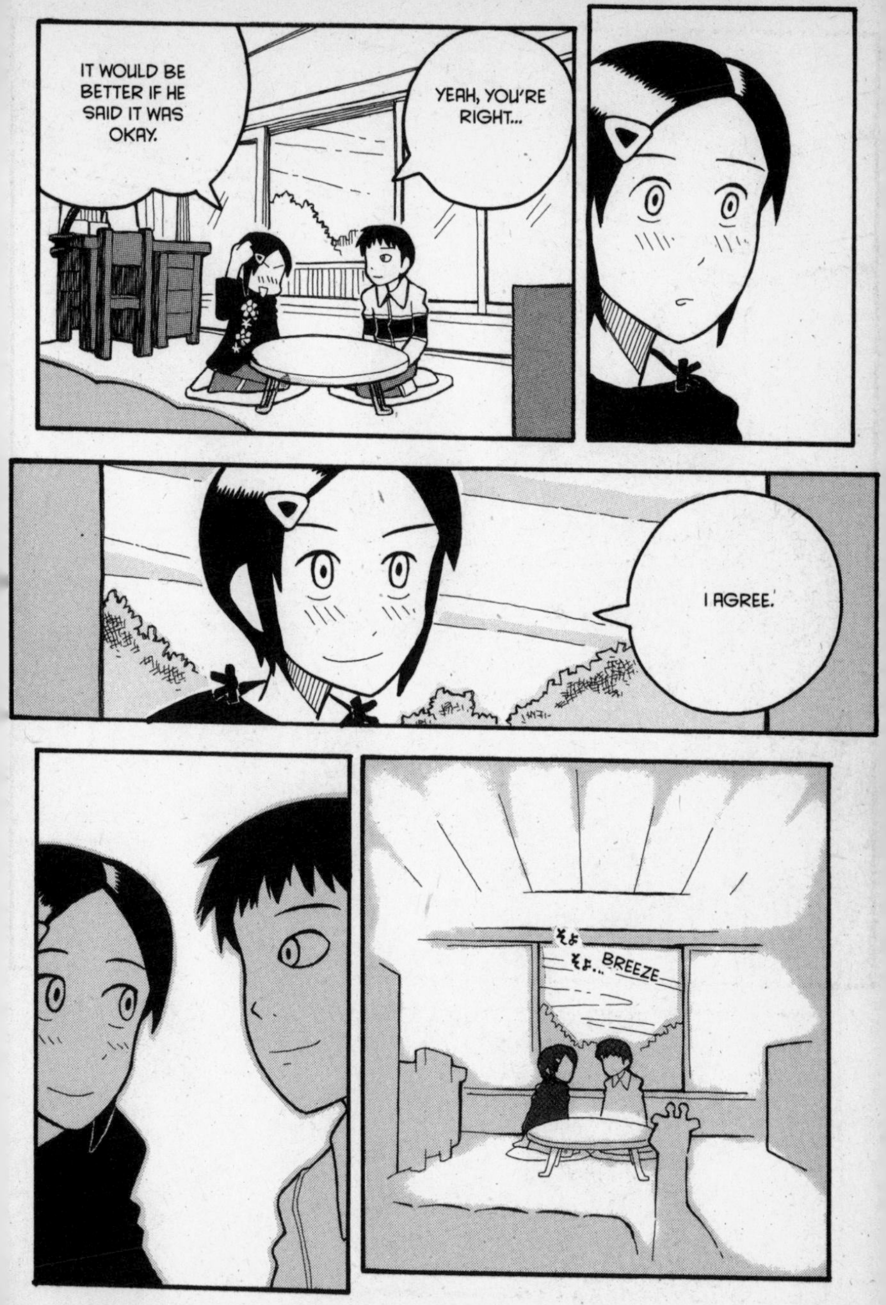
YEAH, YOU'RE RIGHT...
IT WOULD BE BETTER IF HE SAID IT WAS OKAY.
I AGREE.
そよ
そよ...
BREEZE

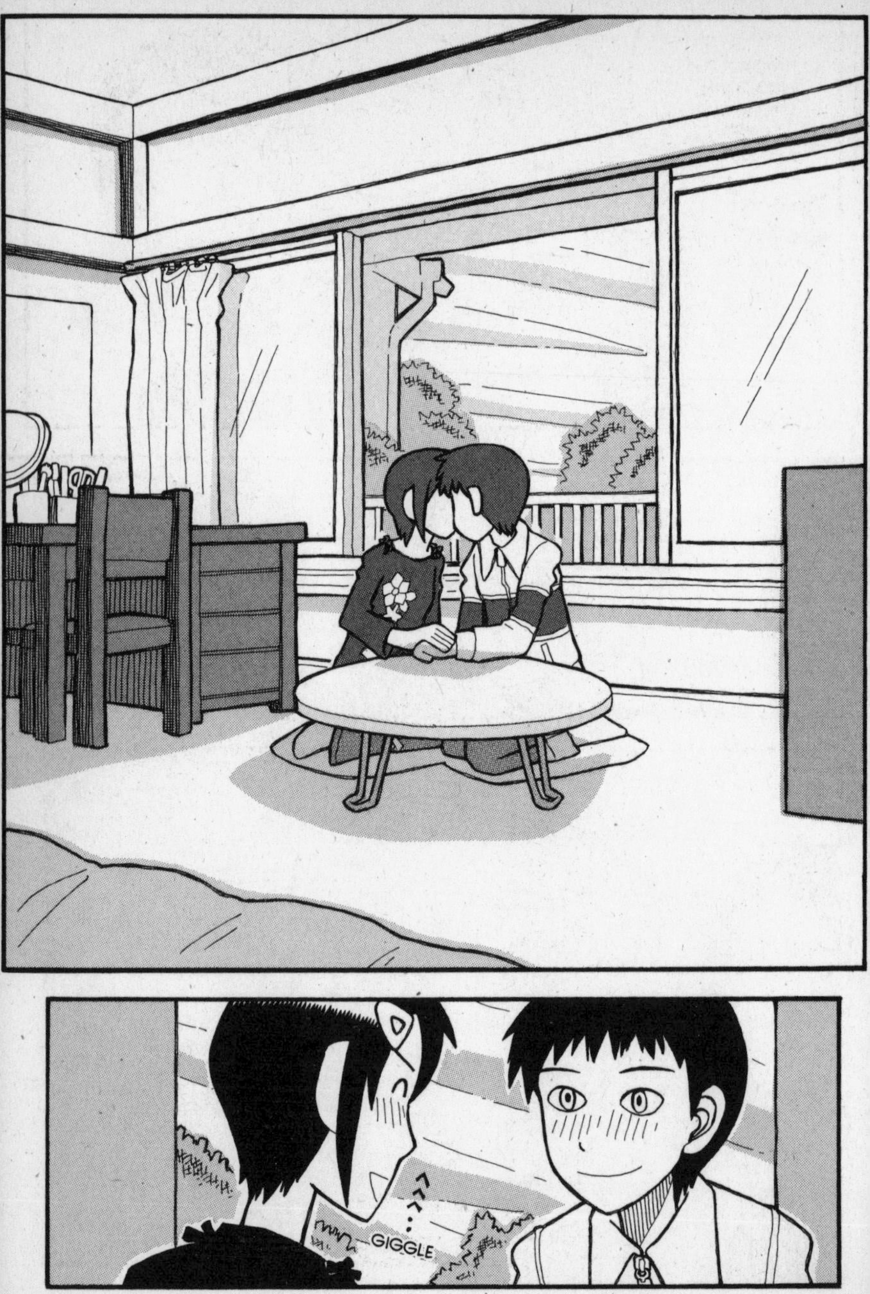
へへへ..
GIGGLE

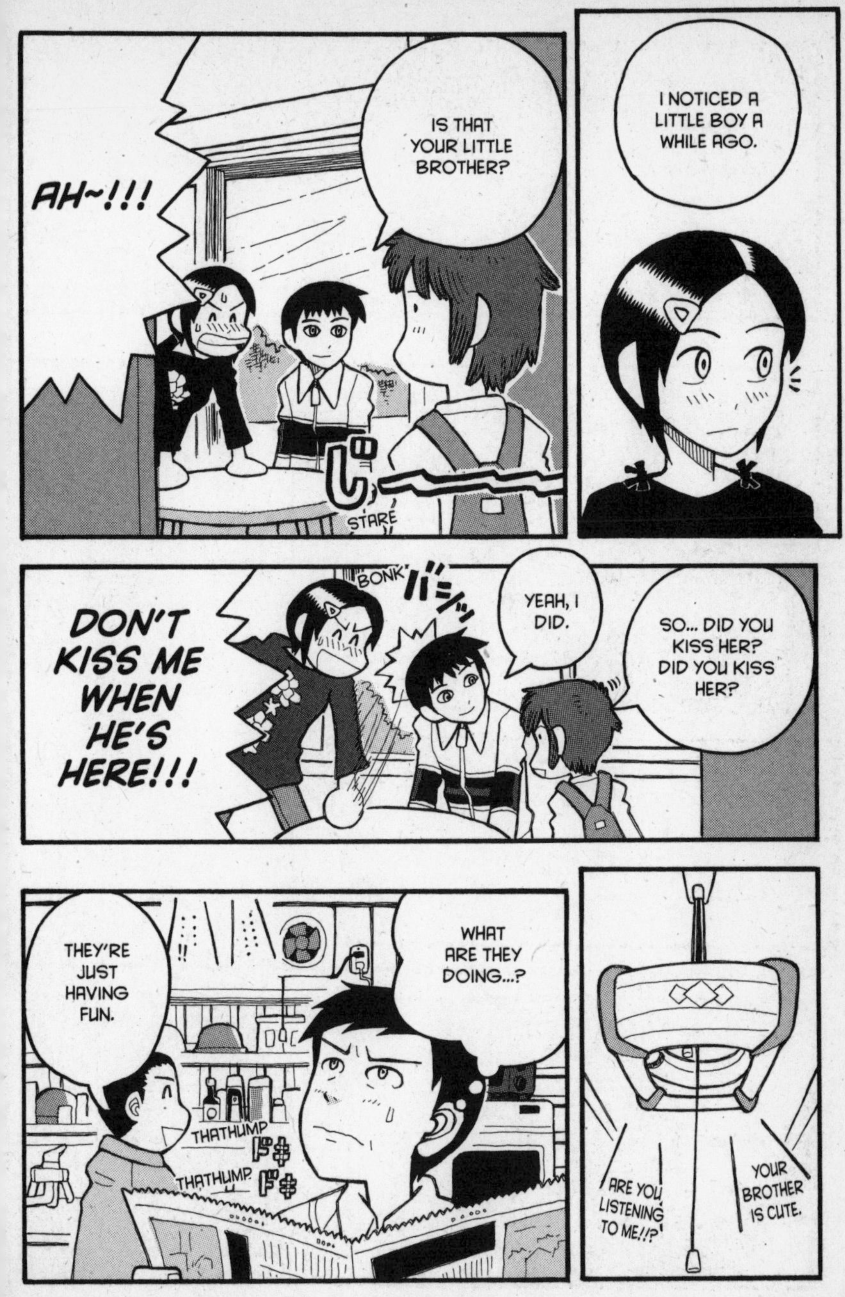
I NOTICED A LITTLE BOY A WHILE AGO.
IS THAT YOUR LITTLE BROTHER?
AH~!!!
STARE
SO... DID YOU KISS HER? DID YOU KISS HER?
YEAH, I DID.
BONK
DON'T KISS ME WHEN HE'S HERE!!!
YOUR BROTHER IS CUTE.
ARE YOU LISTENING TO ME!!?
WHAT ARE THEY DOING...?
!!
THEY'RE JUST HAVING FUN.
THATHUMP
THATHUMP

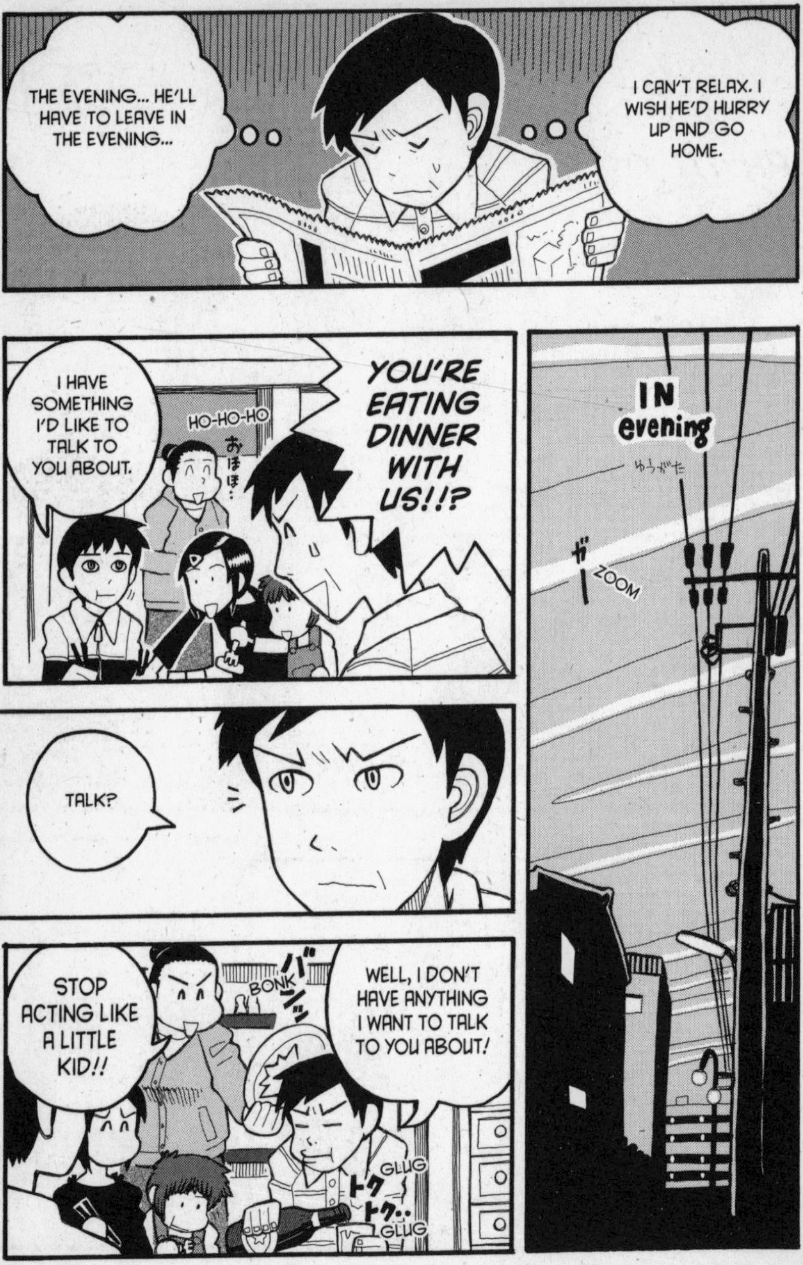
I CAN'T RELAX. I WISH HE'D HURRY UP AND GO HOME.
THE EVENING... HE'LL HAVE TO LEAVE IN THE EVENING...
IN evening
ゆうがた
ガー
ZOOM
YOU'RE EATING DINNER WITH US!!?
HO-HO-HO
おほほ…
I HAVE SOMETHING I'D LIKE TO TALK TO YOU ABOUT.
TALK?
WELL, I DON'T HAVE ANYTHING I WANT TO TALK TO YOU ABOUT!
バン
BONK
STOP ACTING LIKE A LITTLE KID!!
GLUG
トク
トク…
GLUG

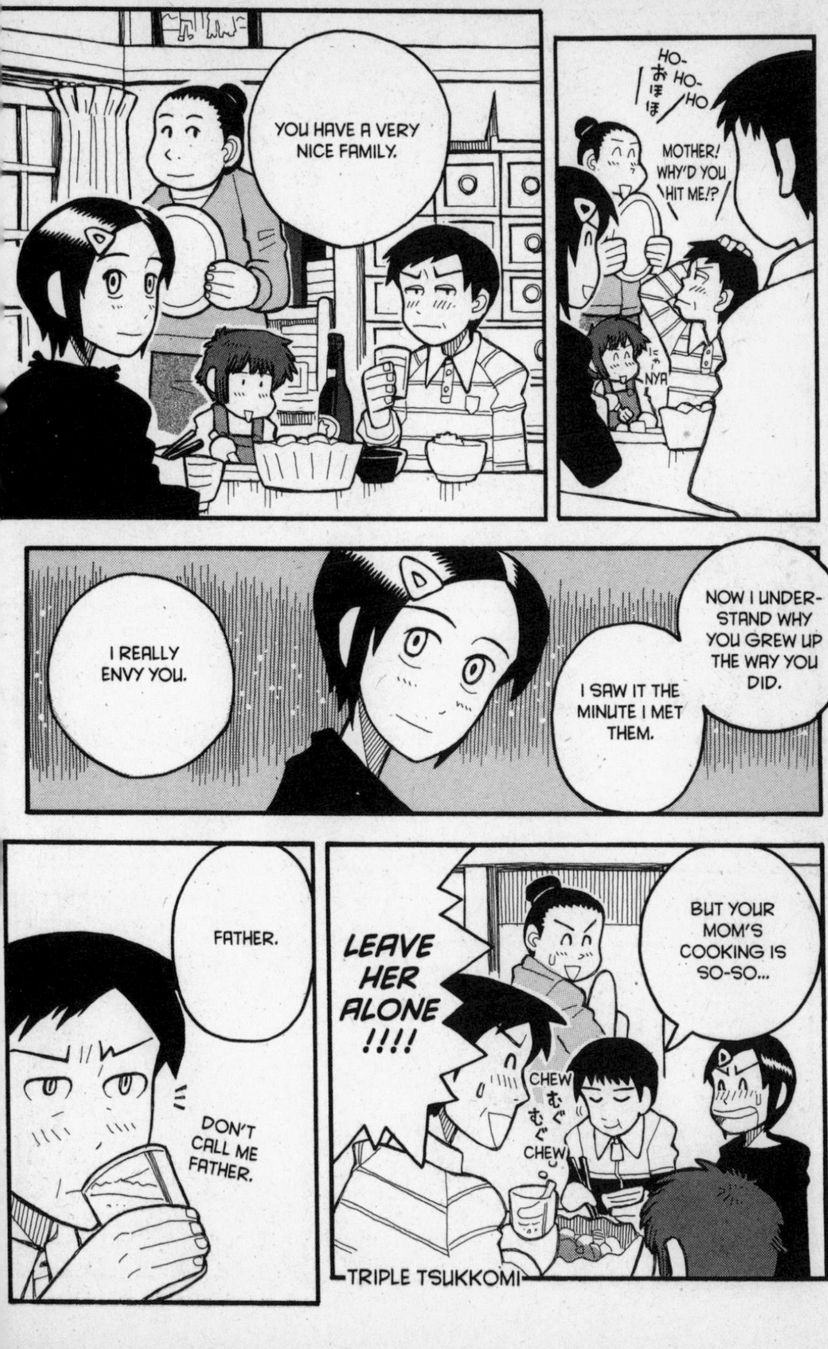
HO- HO- HO
おほほ
MOTHER! WHY'D YOU HIT ME!?
にゃ NYA
YOU HAVE A VERY NICE FAMILY.
NOW I UNDER-STAND WHY YOU GREW UP THE WAY YOU DID.
I SAW IT THE MINUTE I MET THEM.
I REALLY ENVY YOU.
BUT YOUR MOM'S COOKING IS SO-SO...
LEAVE HER ALONE !!!!
CHEW むぐ むぐ CHEW
TRIPLE TSUKKOMI
FATHER.
DON'T CALL ME FATHER.

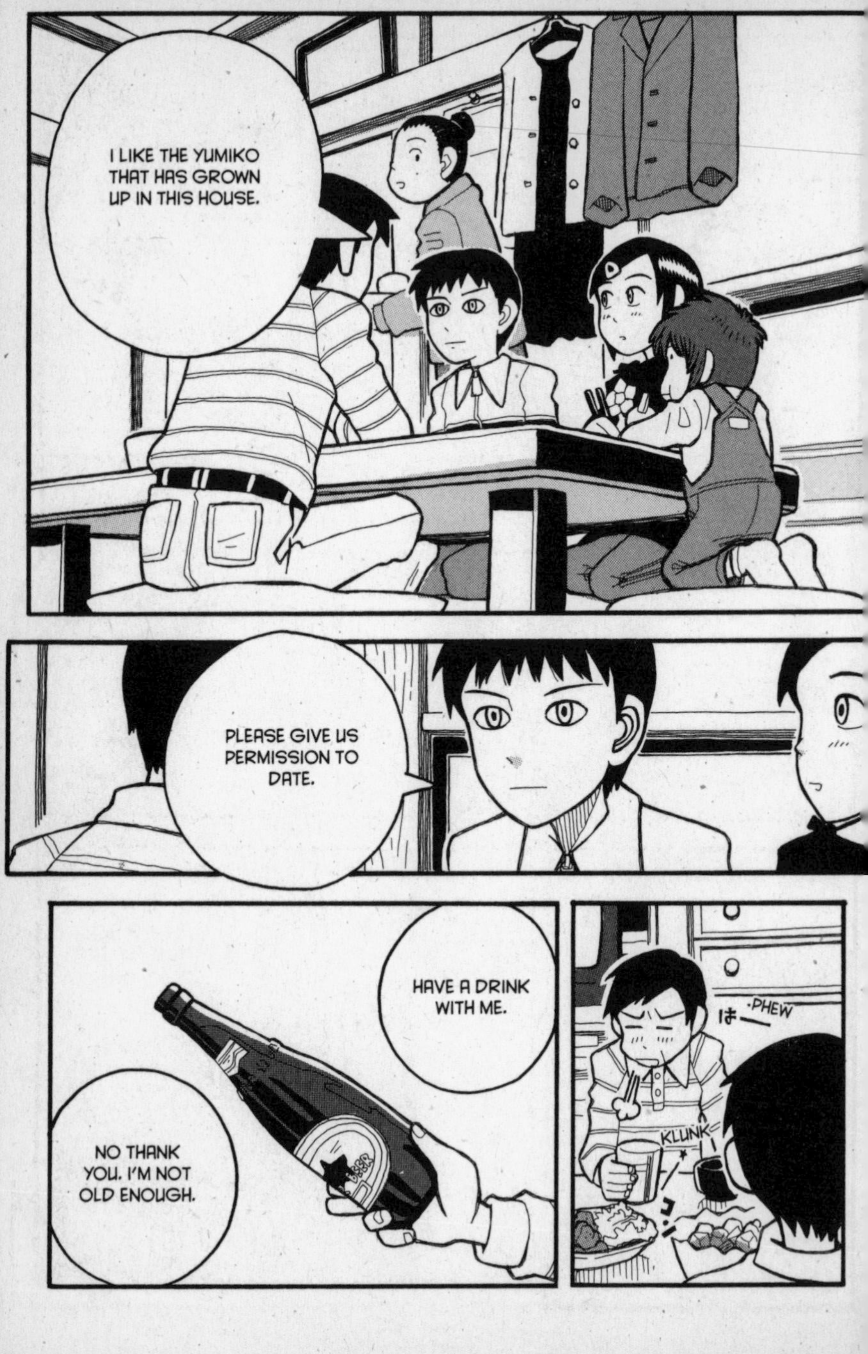
I LIKE THE YUMIKO THAT HAS GROWN UP IN THIS HOUSE.
PLEASE GIVE US PERMISSION TO DATE.
は—
PHEW
KLUNK
コ
HAVE A DRINK WITH ME.
NO THANK YOU. I'M NOT OLD ENOUGH.

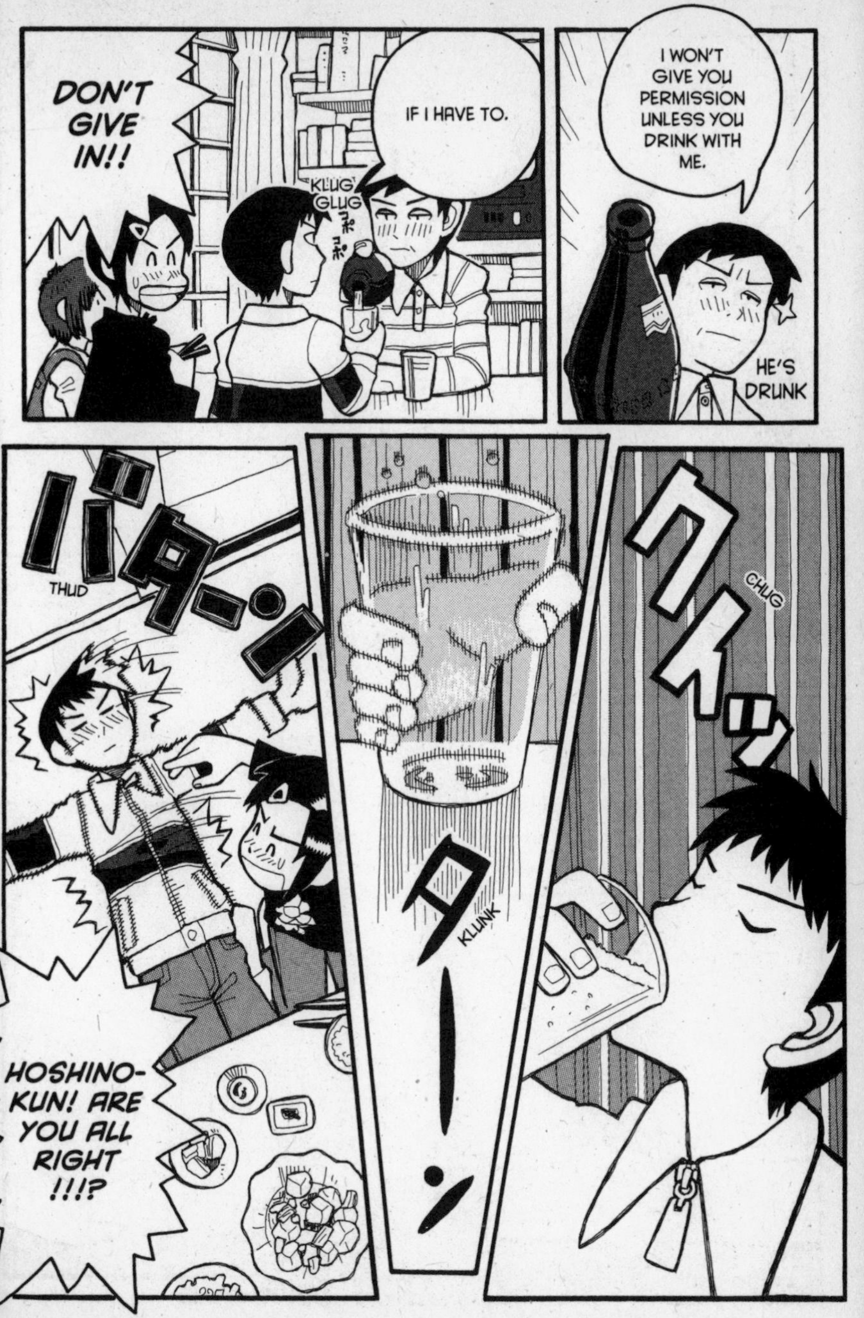
I WON'T GIVE YOU PERMISSION UNLESS YOU DRINK WITH ME.
HE'S DRUNK
IF I HAVE TO.
KLUG GLUG
DON'T GIVE IN!!
CHUG
KLUNK
THUD
HOSHINO-KUN! ARE YOU ALL RIGHT!!!?

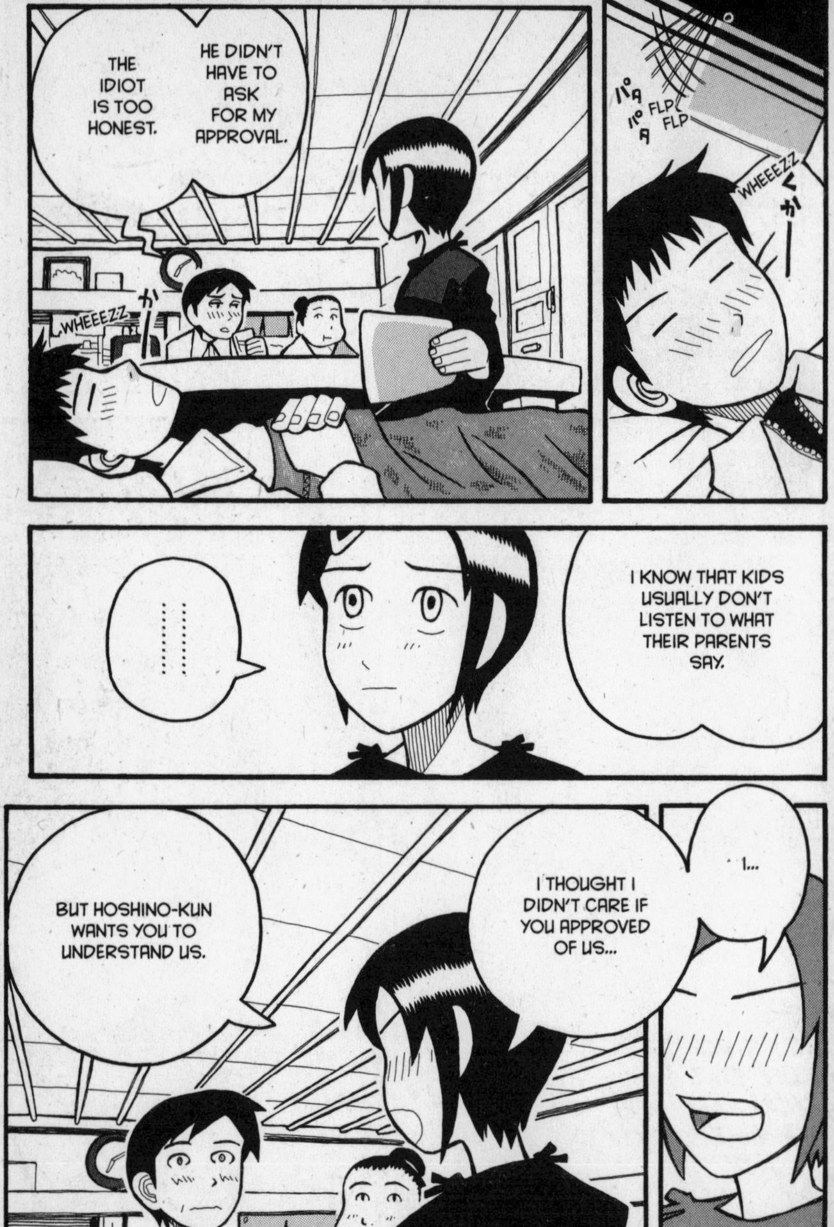

パタ パタ FLP FLP
WHEEEZZ
HE DIDN'T HAVE TO ASK FOR MY APPROVAL.
THE IDIOT IS TOO HONEST.
WHEEEZZ
I KNOW THAT KIDS USUALLY DON'T LISTEN TO WHAT THEIR PARENTS SAY.
......
I...
I THOUGHT I DIDN'T CARE IF YOU APPROVED OF US...
BUT HOSHINO-KUN WANTS YOU TO UNDERSTAND US.

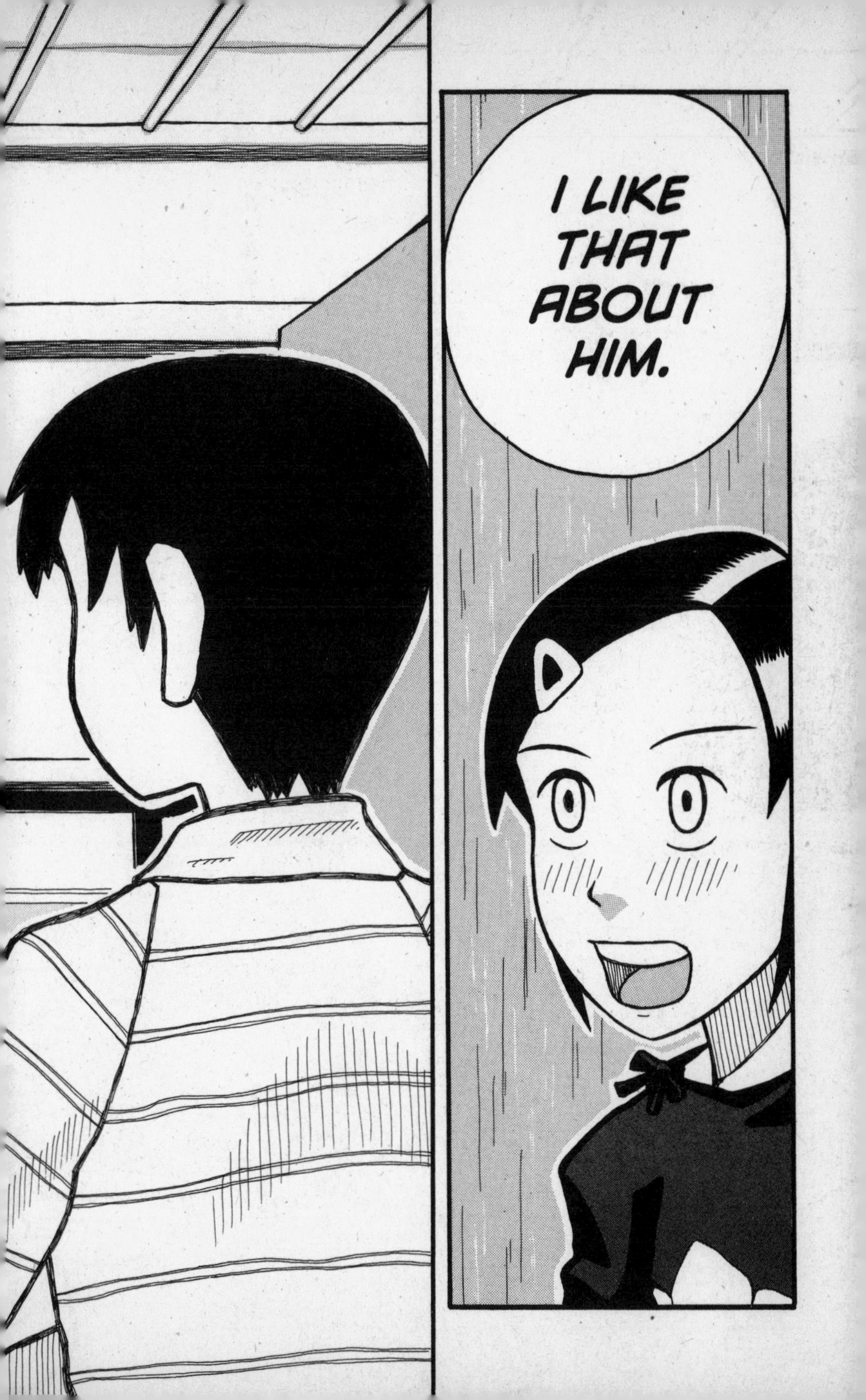
I LIKE THAT ABOUT HIM.

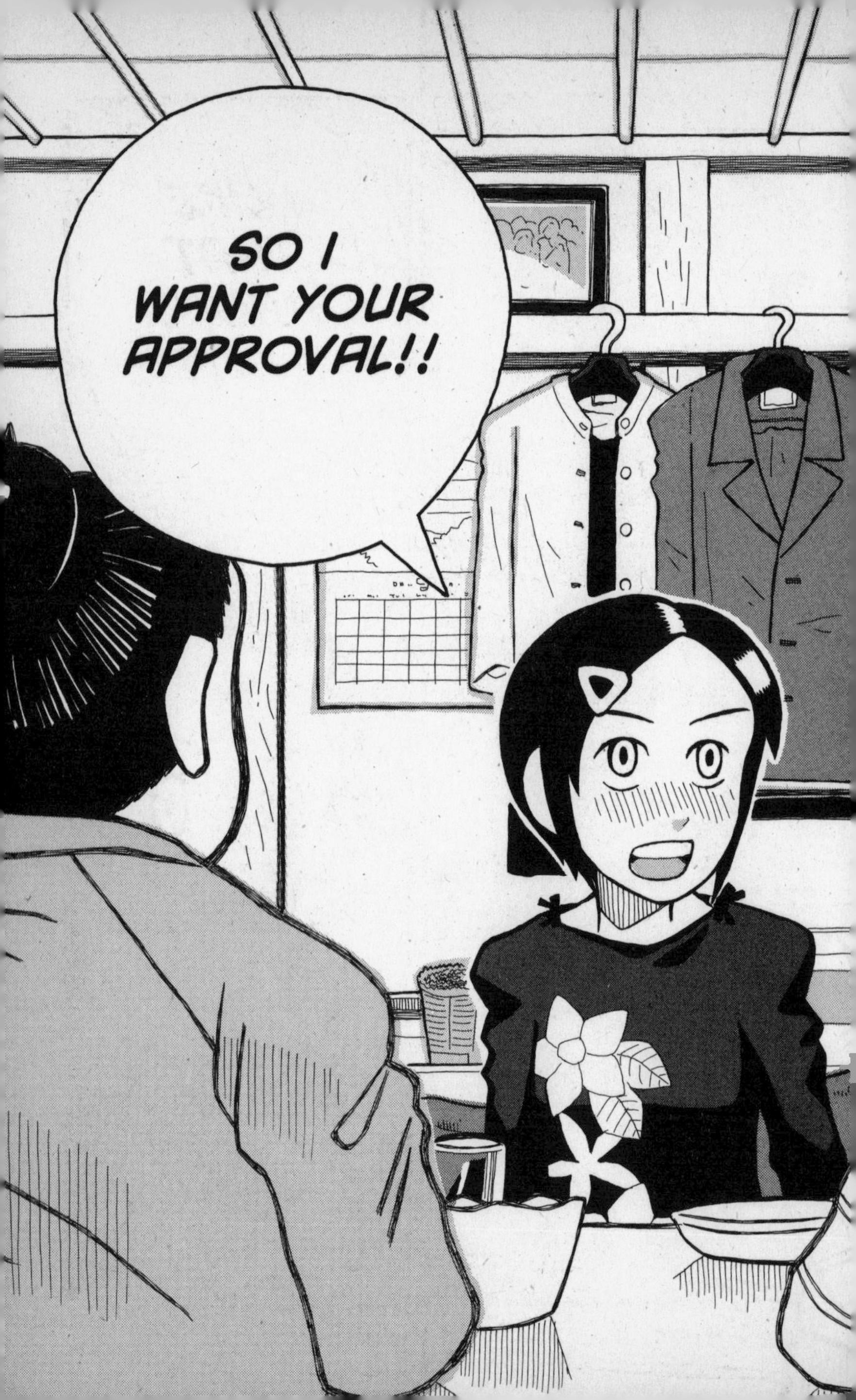
SO I WANT YOUR APPROVAL!!

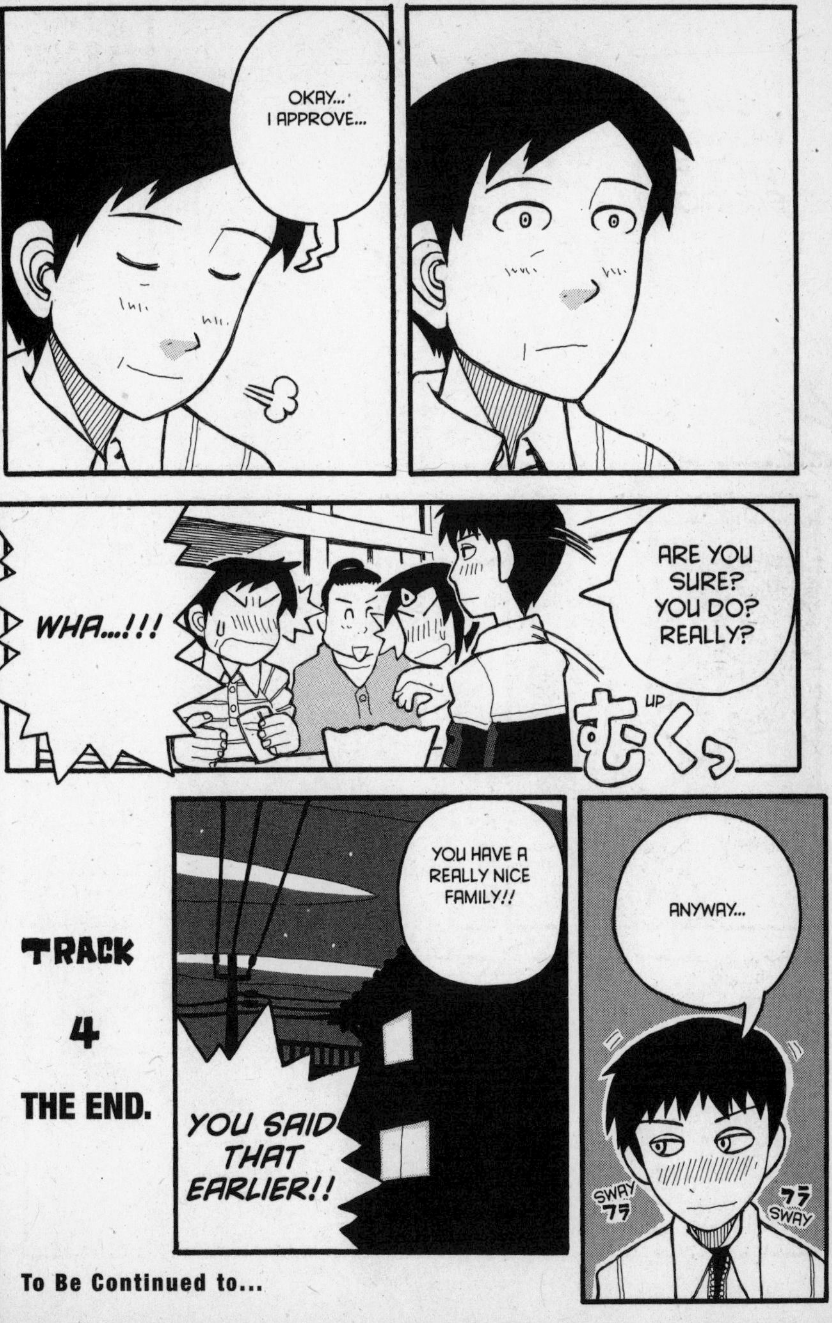
OKAY... I APPROVE...
ARE YOU SURE? YOU DO? REALLY?
むくっ
UP
WHA...!!!
ANYWAY...
フラ SWAY
フラ SWAY
YOU HAVE A REALLY NICE FAMILY!!
YOU SAID THAT EARLIER!!
TRACK 4 THE END.
To Be Continued to...

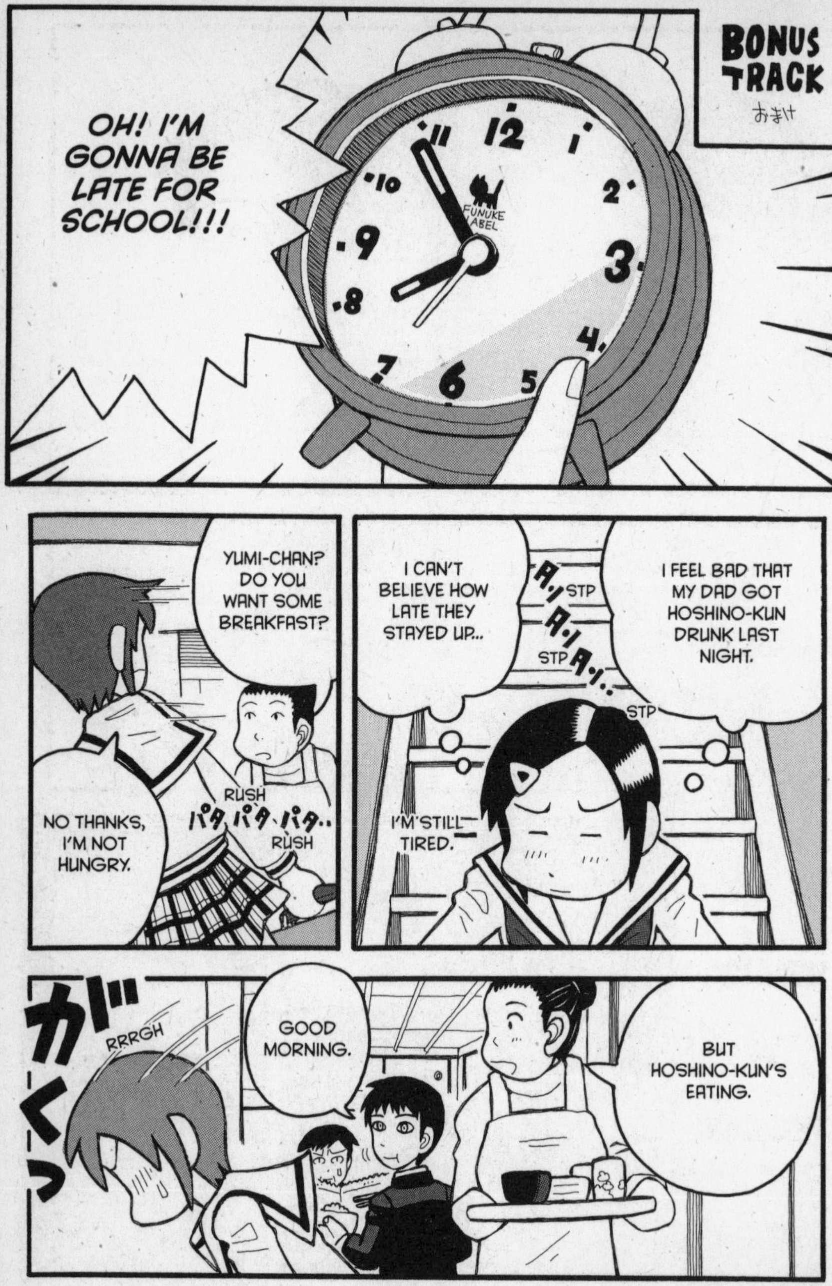
BONUS TRACK
おまけ
OH! I'M GONNA BE LATE FOR SCHOOL!!!
FUNUKE LABEL
I FEEL BAD THAT MY DAD GOT HOSHINO-KUN DRUNK LAST NIGHT.
I CAN'T BELIEVE HOW LATE THEY STAYED UP...
STP
STP
STP
I'M STILL TIRED.
YUMI-CHAN? DO YOU WANT SOME BREAKFAST?
RUSH
パタ パタ パタ..
RUSH
NO THANKS, I'M NOT HUNGRY.
BUT HOSHINO-KUN'S EATING.
GOOD MORNING.
RRRGH
がくっ

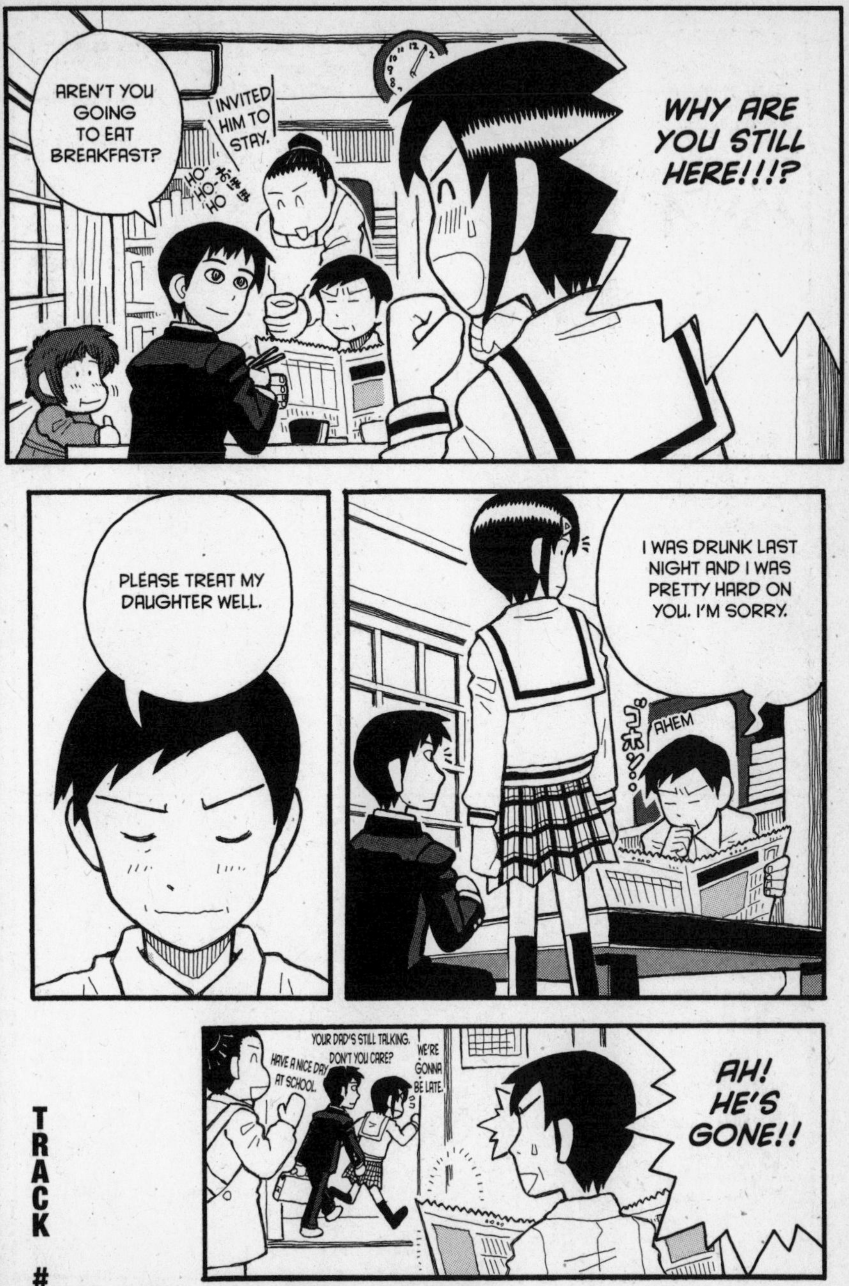
WHY ARE YOU STILL HERE!!!?
I INVITED HIM TO STAY.
HO-HO-HO
AREN'T YOU GOING TO EAT BREAKFAST?
I WAS DRUNK LAST NIGHT AND I WAS PRETTY HARD ON YOU. I'M SORRY.
AHEM
PLEASE TREAT MY DAUGHTER WELL.
AH! HE'S GONE!!
WE'RE GONNA BE LATE.
YOUR DAD'S STILL TALKING. DON'T YOU CARE?
HAVE A NICE DAY AT SCHOOL.

TRACK #4 ▶▶ END   LOVE ROMA 1 ▶▶ END

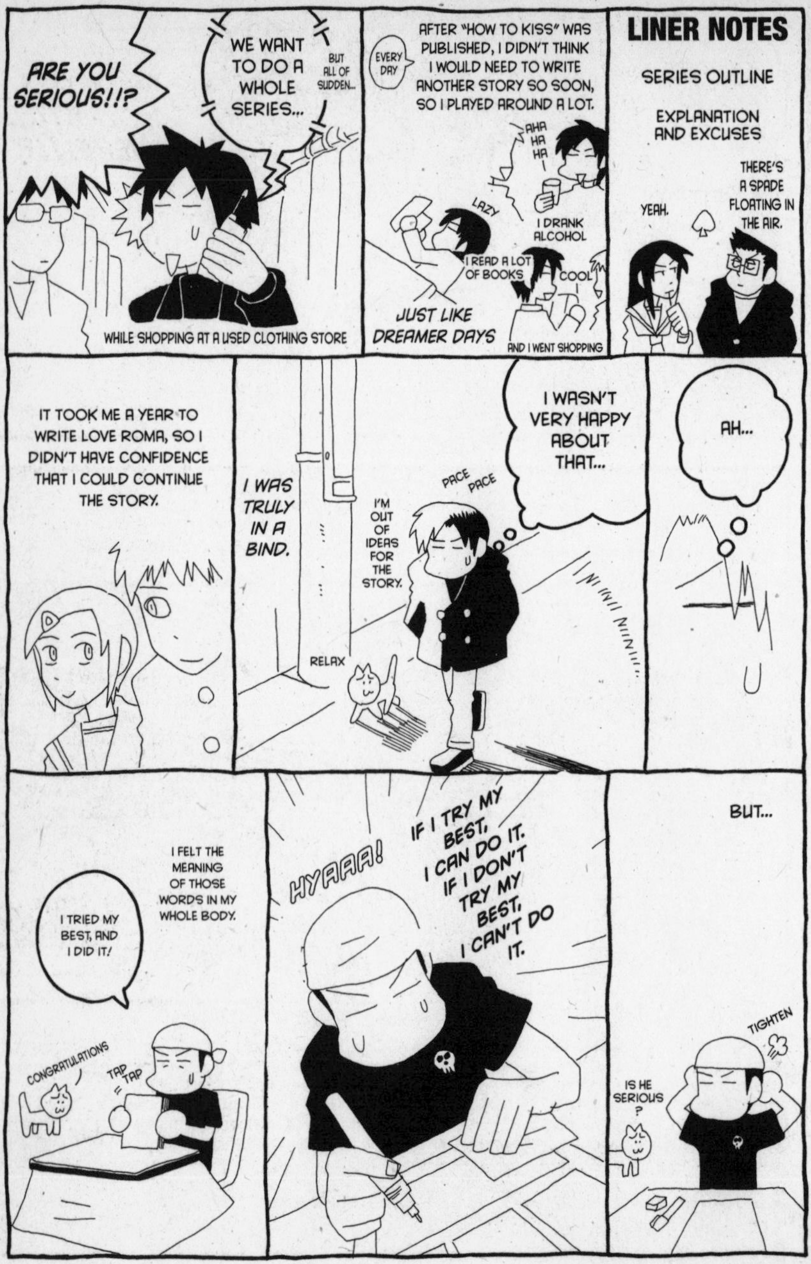
LINER NOTES
SERIES OUTLINE
EXPLANATION AND EXCUSES
THERE'S A SPADE FLOATING IN THE AIR.
YEAH.
AFTER "HOW TO KISS" WAS PUBLISHED, I DIDN'T THINK I WOULD NEED TO WRITE ANOTHER STORY SO SOON, SO I PLAYED AROUND A LOT.
EVERY DAY
AHA HA HA
I DRANK ALCOHOL
LAZY
I READ A LOT OF BOOKS
COOL
AND I WENT SHOPPING
JUST LIKE DREAMER DAYS
BUT ALL OF SUDDEN...
WE WANT TO DO A WHOLE SERIES...
ARE YOU SERIOUS!!?
WHILE SHOPPING AT A USED CLOTHING STORE
AH...
I WASN'T VERY HAPPY ABOUT THAT...
PACE PACE
I'M OUT OF IDEAS FOR THE STORY.
I WAS TRULY IN A BIND.
RELAX
IT TOOK ME A YEAR TO WRITE LOVE ROMA, SO I DIDN'T HAVE CONFIDENCE THAT I COULD CONTINUE THE STORY.
BUT...
TIGHTEN
IS HE SERIOUS?
IF I TRY MY BEST, I CAN DO IT. IF I DON'T TRY MY BEST, I CAN'T DO IT.
HYAAAA!
I FELT THE MEANING OF THOSE WORDS IN MY WHOLE BODY.
I TRIED MY BEST, AND I DID IT!
TAP TAP
CONGRATULATIONS

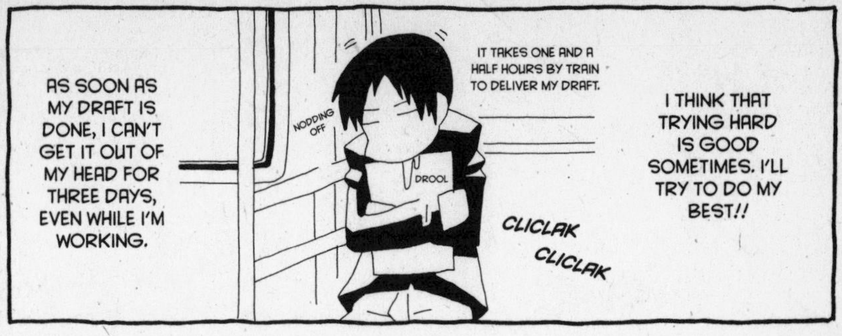
IT TAKES ONE AND A HALF HOURS BY TRAIN TO DELIVER MY DRAFT.
I THINK THAT TRYING HARD IS GOOD SOMETIMES. I'LL TRY TO DO MY BEST!!
AS SOON AS MY DRAFT IS DONE, I CAN'T GET IT OUT OF MY HEAD FOR THREE DAYS, EVEN WHILE I'M WORKING.
NODDING OFF
DROOL
CLICLAK
CLICLAK

STORY OUTLINES

DEMO TRACK

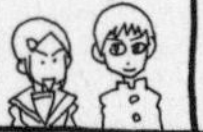

THIS IS MY MEMORIAL PIECE... THE FIRST TIME I WAS EVER PUBLISHED IN A MAGAZINE. UNTIL NOW I HAD ONLY WRITTEN SF AND FANTASY. WHEN I STARTED WRITING LOVE COMEDY, I CONSIDERED IT A JOKE. BUT THEN I STARTED ENJOYING IT. OF ALL THE MANGA I'VE WRITTEN, I'VE ENJOYED THIS ONE THE MOST. I THOUGHT I COULD WRITE MORE AND MORE OF THESE, BUT IT IS HARDER THAN I THOUGHT.

TRACK 0

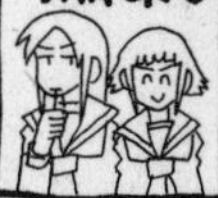

SEVEN MONTHS AFTER I GOT THE AWARD FOR "DEMO TRACK," "TRACK #0" WAS PUBLISHED. I THINK THE WHOLE STORY HAS A LOT HAPPENING AND IT'S REALLY FUN TO READ IT. COMPARED TO THE FIRST STORY, THIS ONE IS MUCH SILLIER AND I WAS VERY WORRIED THAT IF I USED CERTAIN WORDS MY EDITOR WOULD BE ANGRY AT ME. I WAS VERY CONCERNED. THE OCCULT RESEARCH CLUB AND WADA-SAN SHOWED UP FOR THE FIRST TIME IN THIS EPISODE.

TRACK 1

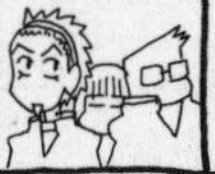

THE FIRST PART TO THE SERIES, "DEMO TRACK," "TRACK #0," AND "FIRST EPISODE," ALL HAD TO BE REWRITTEN THREE TIMES SO THEY WOULD FLOW MORE NATURALLY. THAT WAS THE HARDEST PART. I KEPT ASKING MYSELF, HOW MANY TIMES AM I GOING TO HAVE TO REWRITE THIS EPISODE, DAMN IT! I WAS MAD AT MYSELF. I WANTED TO CREATE AN EXCITING STORY, BUT NOW I FEEL LIKE THERE'S TOO MUCH IN IT. THE MUSIC CLUB, YOSHITSUNE AND HASHIBA ALL SHOWED UP FOR THE FIRST TIME IN THIS EPISODE.

TRACK 2

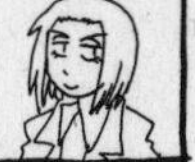

THIS IS A STORY ABOUT LUNCH. IT'S A SILLY STORY, THE SAME AS "HOW TO KISS." I WAS RELAXED AT THE TIME AND ENJOYED WRITING IT. I GOT A RECIPE BOOK FOR HOSHINO-KUN AND NEGISHI-SAN'S LUNCHBOXES FROM MY SISTER FOR MY RESEARCH. I LIKE COOKING, BUT ONLY A LITTLE BIT. BEAUTIFUL HAYASHI-SENSEI SHOWED UP FOR THE FIRST TIME IN THIS EPISODE.

TRACK 3

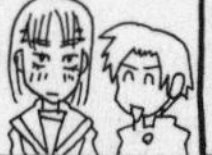

BOYFRIEND-STEALING EPISODE. I PERSONALLY LIKE THIS EPISODE, BUT ACCORDING TO LETTERS I GOT FROM READERS, THE REACTION WAS MIXED. THE BOWLING ALLEY I USED IN THE END WAS A REAL PLACE I USED TO GO TO WHEN I WAS IN HIGH SCHOOL, BUT IT ISN'T THERE ANY MORE. AND I HOPE SUGIMOTO-SAN LIVES HAPPILY EVER AFTER. GOOD LUCK TO MAKI, TOO.

TRACK 4

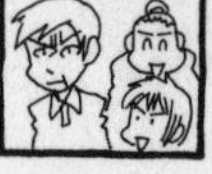

I TRIED TO THINK HOW I WOULD FEEL IF I HAD A DAUGHTER AND SHE BROUGHT HER BOYFRIEND HOME TO MEET ME. BUT IT WAS HARD FOR ME TO DO. THIS EPISODE WAS A TOUGH ONE. WHEN I WAS TRYING TO DECIDE WHAT TO WRITE IT ABOUT, I WAS WALKING IN A BANK AND WONDERING IF I SHOULD QUIT WRITING MANGA. BUT I'M GLAD I DIDN'T QUIT. NEGISHI'S FAMILY SHOWED UP IN THIS EPISODE FOR THE FIRST TIME. HER BROTHER'S NAME IS KATSUYA.

I'M REALLY APPRECIATIVE TO EVERYBODY THAT BOUGHT AND READ THIS BOOK. LOVE.

HTTP://MEMBERS.EDOGAWA.HOME.NE.JP/POO1007/
(IN JAPANESE)

FUNUKE LABEL

AUTHOR PROFILE

MINORU TOYODA

MANGA DEBUT

The first episode of Love Roma in Kodansha's Afternoon magazine.

AWARDS

Minoru won a prize for Reonizumu in 2000, but he won first place for Love Roma in 2002. The award was the "Afternoon Shiki Prize," which is awarded to new cartoonists.

DATE OF BIRTH

Oct. 7, 1971

STATUS

Living with his parents.

FAVORITE THING

Nothing but comics.

LEAST FAVORITE THING

The occult.

ASPIRATIONS

Minoru hopes that his comics will overcome differences in language or culture and will be enjoyed by a large number of people.

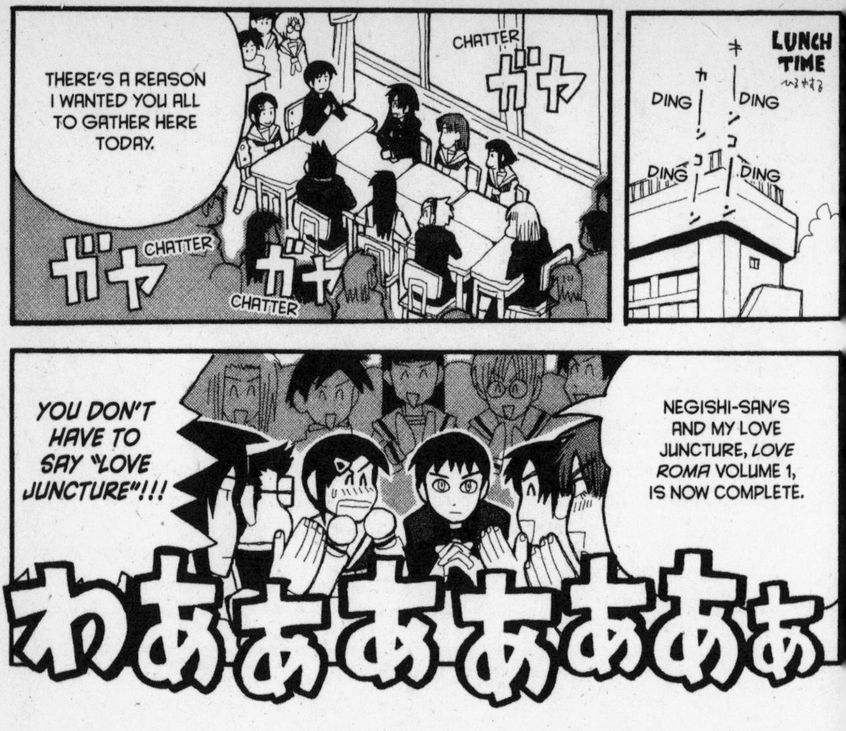
LUNCH TIME
DING DING DING DING
キーンコーン
カーンコーン
CHATTER
ガヤ
THERE'S A REASON I WANTED YOU ALL TO GATHER HERE TODAY.
ガヤ
CHATTER
ガヤ
CHATTER
NEGISHI-SAN'S AND MY LOVE JUNCTURE, *LOVE ROMA* VOLUME 1, IS NOW COMPLETE.
YOU DON'T HAVE TO SAY "LOVE JUNCTURE"!!!
わあああああああぁ

LOVE ROMA **HIDDEN TRACK** **EVERYBODY GET ALONG**

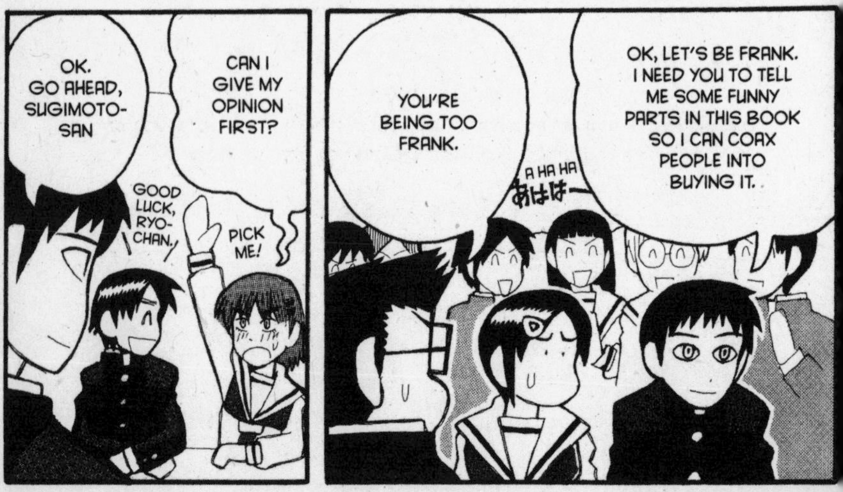
OK, LET'S BE FRANK. I NEED YOU TO TELL ME SOME FUNNY PARTS IN THIS BOOK SO I CAN COAX PEOPLE INTO BUYING IT.
YOU'RE BEING TOO FRANK.
A HA HA
あははー
CAN I GIVE MY OPINION FIRST?
OK. GO AHEAD, SUGIMOTO-SAN
PICK ME!
GOOD LUCK, RYO-CHAN.

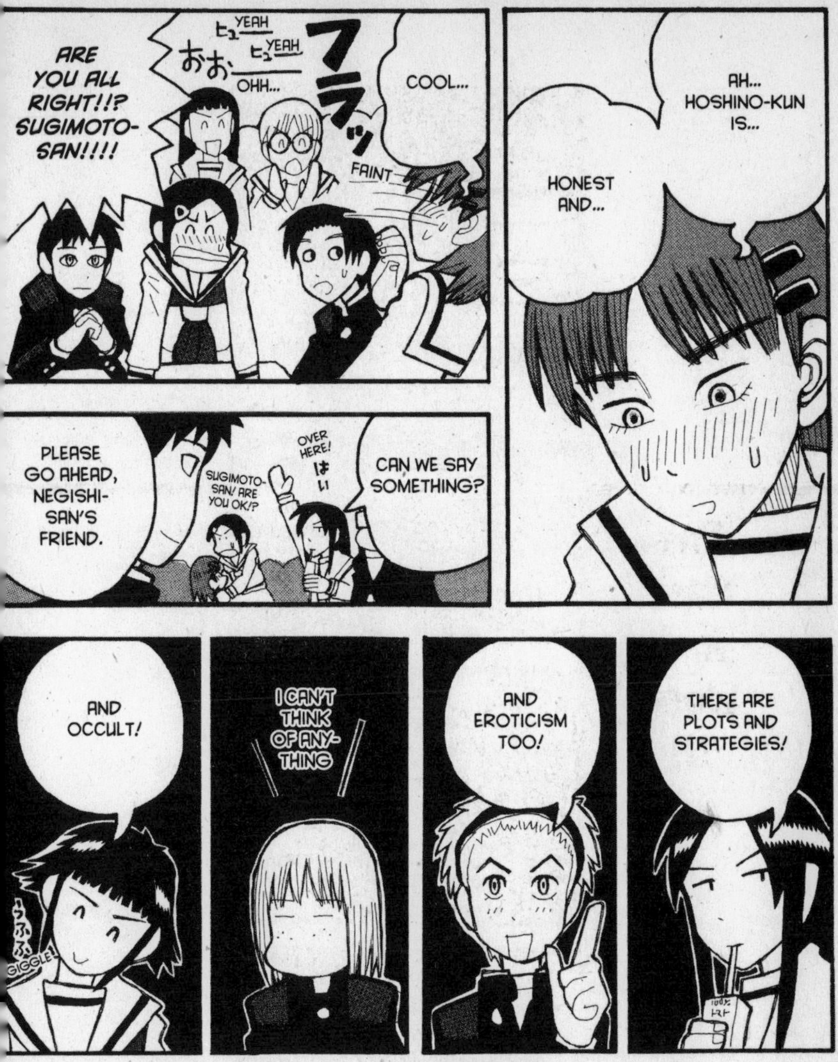
AH... HOSHINO-KUN IS...
HONEST AND...
COOL...
FAINT
フラッ
ヒュ YEAH
ヒュ YEAH
おお— OHH...
ARE YOU ALL RIGHT!!? SUGIMOTO-SAN!!!!
CAN WE SAY SOMETHING?
OVER HERE! はい
SUGIMOTO-SAN! ARE YOU OK!?
PLEASE GO AHEAD, NEGISHI-SAN'S FRIEND.
THERE ARE PLOTS AND STRATEGIES!
AND EROTICISM TOO!
I CAN'T THINK OF ANYTHING
AND OCCULT!
うふふ GIGGLE

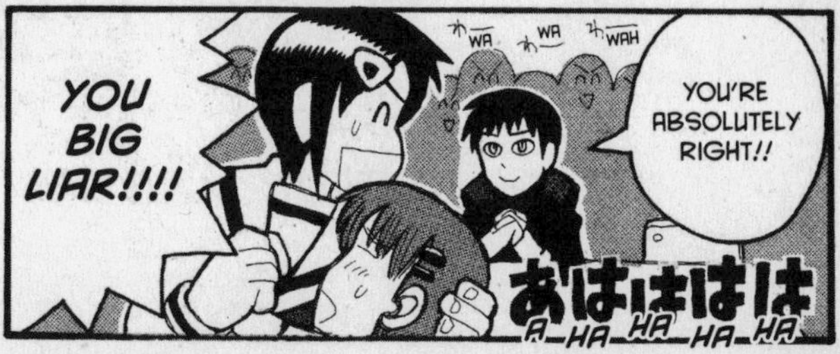
YOU'RE ABSOLUTELY RIGHT!!
わ WA
わ WA
わ WAH
YOU BIG LIAR!!!!
あはははは A-HA HA HA-HA

THE TRUTH IS, THIS IS A FASTBALL LOVE COMEDY.

LOVE ROMA,

THE COMPLETE FIRST VOLUME!!

The Cast in a Word !!!

HONEST
COOL
SCHEMING
Mm-hmm.
TSUKKOMI
WHAT DOES THIS WORD MEAN ?!?!
She's doing it right now.

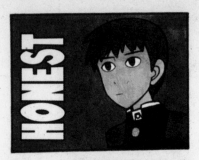

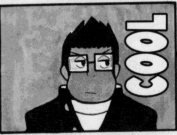

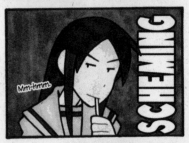

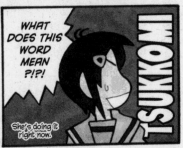

Translation Notes

Japanese is a tricky language for most Westerners, and translation is often more art than science. For your edification and reading pleasure, here are notes on some of the places where we could have gone in a different direction in our translation of the work, or where a Japanese cultural reference is used.

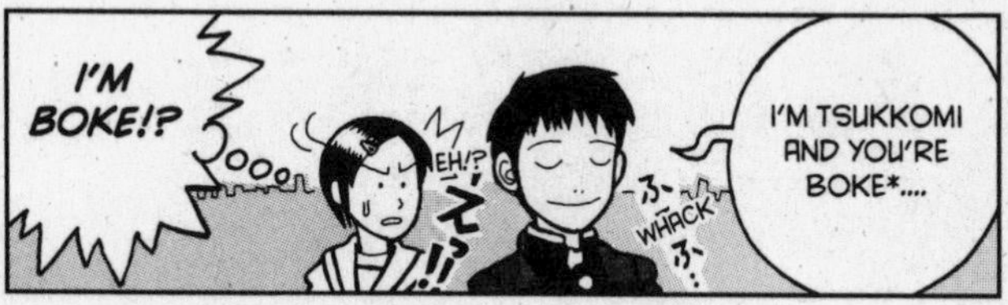
I'M TSUKKOMI AND YOU'RE BOKE*....
WHACK
EH!?
I'M BOKE!?

Page 38, Tsukkomi and Boke

In this Japanese comedic style, one person plays the role of the *tsukkomi* and the other is the *boke*. The *boke* will say something stupid or make a silly mistake, then the *tsukkomi* will correct him, usually accompanied by a smack on the head. This exchange is so common in Japan that people are often referred to as being one or the other. In this example, Negishi takes offense to being considered the *boke* in the relationship. People are thought to be good matches in life if they are naturally like a *tsukkomi* and *boke* pair.

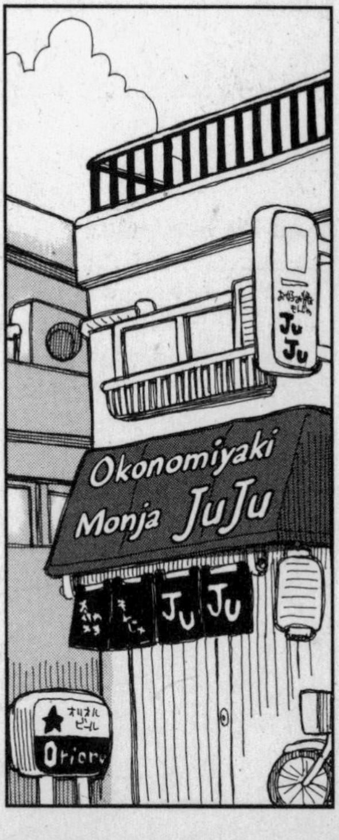
Okonomiyaki
Monja JuJu
JuJu

Page 47, Okonomiyaki

They call it Japanese pancakes or Japanese pizza, but the only thing similar between those and *okonomiyaki* is that all are round and flat. *Okonomiyaki* is made of flour, water, cabbage (mixed with other veggies), egg, seasonings, some kind of meat (seafood is common), and a delicious *okonomiyaki* sauce (similar to steak sauce). The *konomi* means "like" or "love," and it indicates that you can put the veggies or meat you like most in it. The *yaki* means fried (the same as with *teriyaki* or *sukiyaki*).

Page 73, Ouija Board

What is a Ouija board? It's a playing board with the alphabet and the words "yes," "no," and "goodbye" printed on the top. You ask it a question, and by putting two or more people's fingertips on a sliding heart-shaped disc, it will slide to spell out an answer or move to "yes" or "no." You may speak to spirits or delve into the unconscious mind. Wada tries to use one with Negishi and Yoko, but Negishi fights Yoko from moving the pointer to prevent her from spelling the answer she wants.

BONUS TRACK EXTRA
WE CALL THIS A OUIJA BOARD.
CLAIRVOYANTS USE IT TO COMMUNICATE WITH SOMEONE'S SPIRIT.

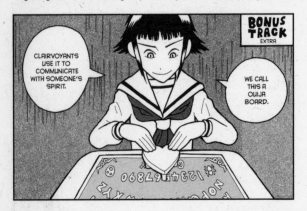

Page 79, Senbazuru

In Japan, the custom of *senbazuru* (1000 cranes) is used as a means of wishing good health or good fortune for those you care about. *Senbazuru* is a string of one thousand origami-folded paper cranes and is often assembled by a group of friends for a wedding or a get-well wish. Health and safety are the most common wishes, but it can be used for anything the giver wishes to express. Hoshino gave one to Negishi after she was absent from school for one day with the flu. She is embarrassed because he is making such a big deal about it.

PLAN 2
SENBAZURU. WAS REFUSED.
YOU TWO ARE A GOOD COUPLE.

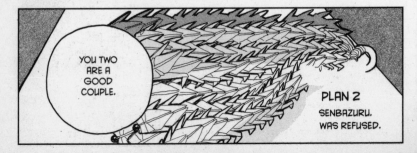

Page 94, Amida

Amida is a game played to help make a decision, usually to determine who will do a certain task. It is much like a coin toss, but can be played by multiple people at once. A series of vertical lines are drawn on a piece of paper, then each player will initial a line and draw horizontal lines connecting the verticals. Then each player will follow a path from top to bottom, making a horizontal move at each line encountered, then continuing downward at the next vertical line. Only one player will end up at the designated "loser" bottom and will be the victim of the contest, thus the one elected to do the dirty work. Tsukahara lost both times in the story: once to help Hoshino in the radio broadcast room, and then again to help him write the message on the school lawn.

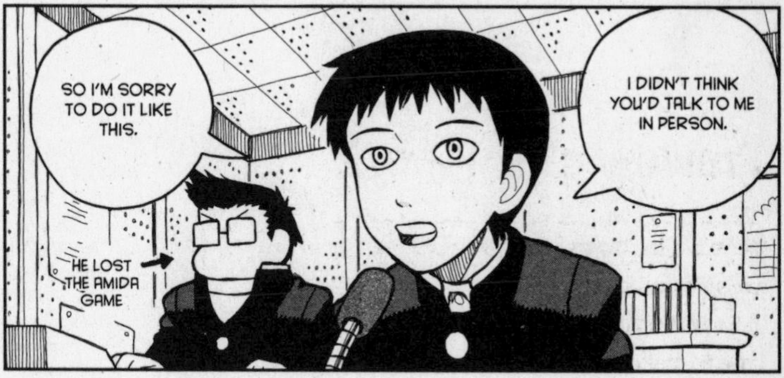
I DIDN'T THINK YOU'D TALK TO ME IN PERSON.
SO I'M SORRY TO DO IT LIKE THIS.
HE LOST THE AMIDA GAME

Page 119, Kaiseki- and Kyoto-style cooking

Kaiseki-ryori is a traditional Japanese seasonal cuisine. In fact, it can be said that *kaiseki-ryori* is the ultimate Japanese cuisine. In Japanese, *ryori* means dishes, but *kaiseki* is a little more complicated and is rooted in Buddhist culture, in which there is a story that says Buddhist priests in strict Zen training used to keep a hot stone *(seki)* in their kimono pocket *(kai)* in order to make their fasting more bearable. The *kaiseki-ryori* was originally served during traditional tea ceremonies and is also called *cha* (tea) *kaiseki*. It was thought that the tea would taste better if the people weren't starved. So the word *kaiseki* is used for the light meal served during the tea ceremony.

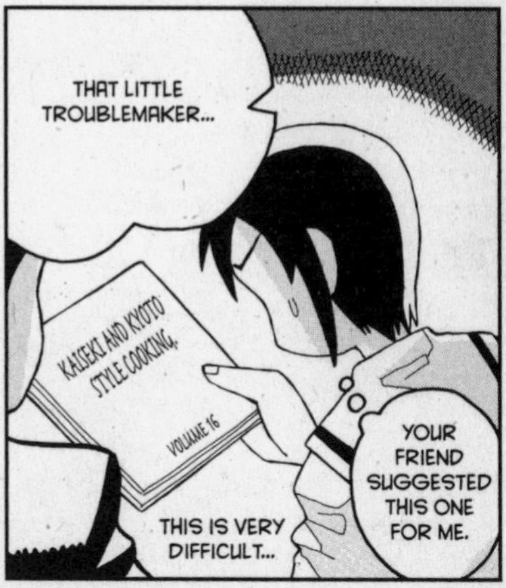
THAT LITTLE TROUBLEMAKER...
YOUR FRIEND SUGGESTED THIS ONE FOR ME.
KAISEKI AND KYOTO STYLE COOKING
VOLUME 16
THIS IS VERY DIFFICULT...

Preview of Volume 2

We're pleased to present you a preview from
Love Roma Volume 2. This volume will be available
in English on January 31, 2006, but for now you'll
have to make do with Japanese!

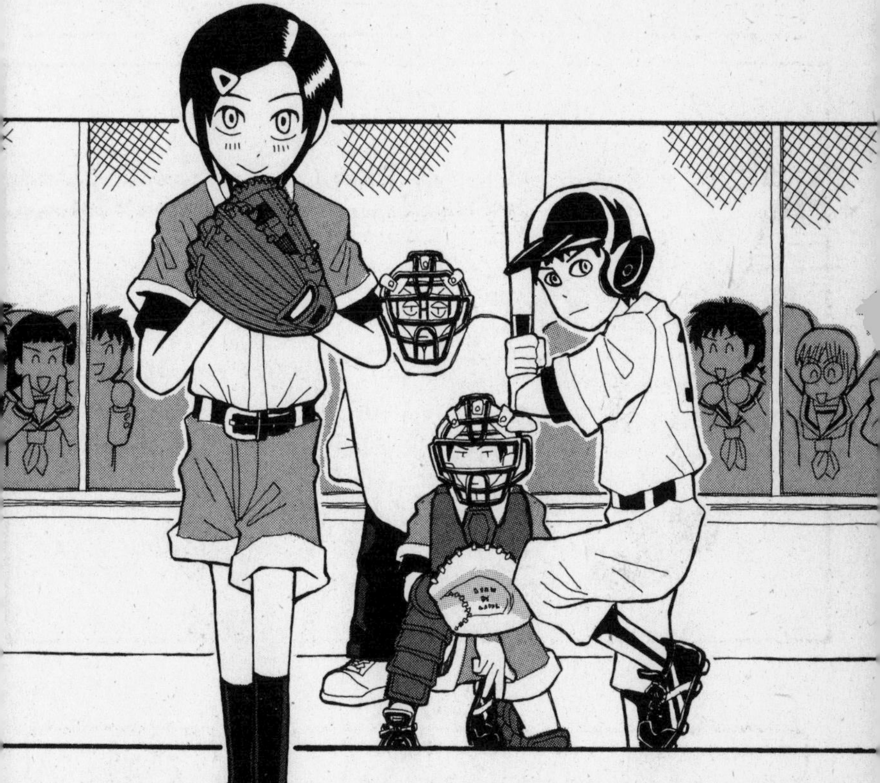

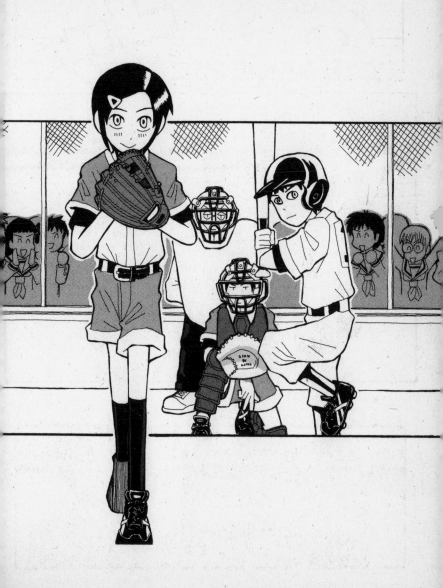

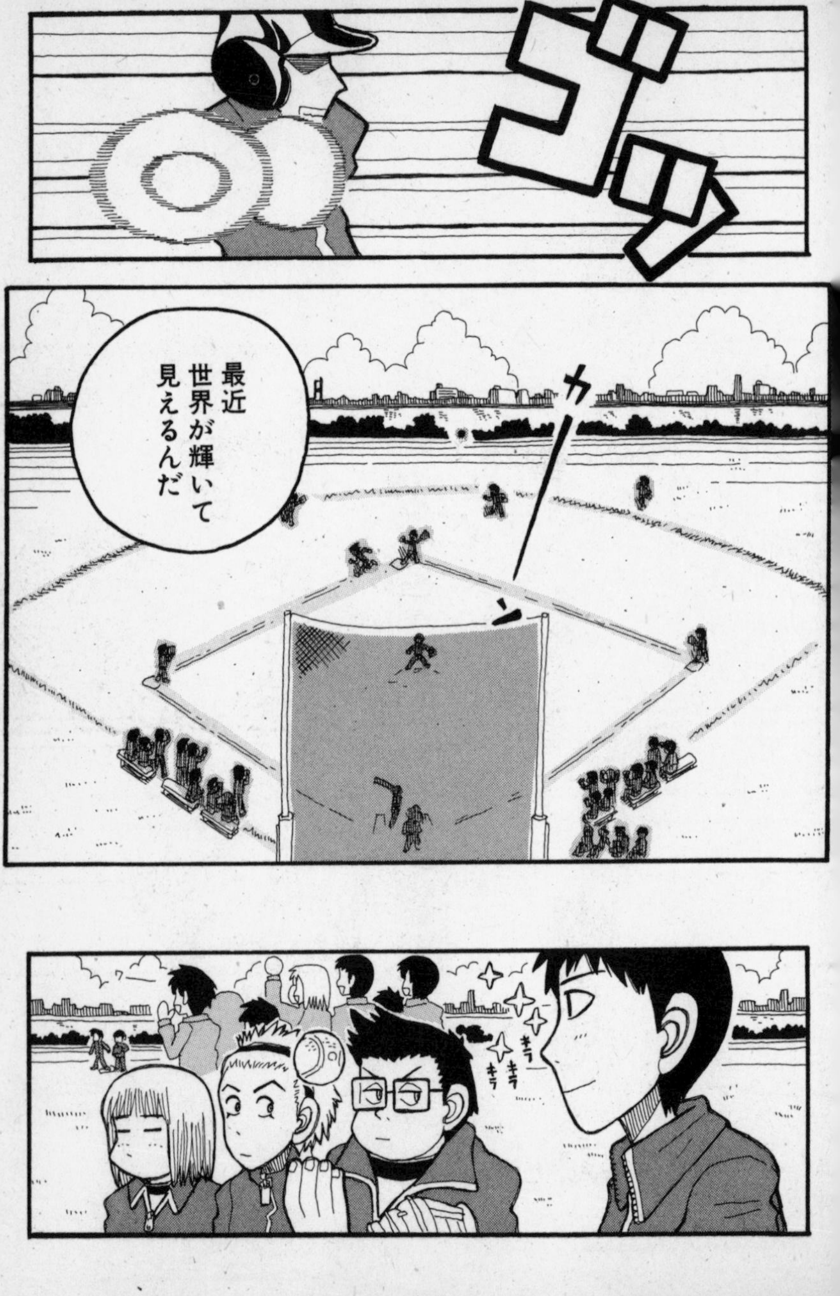
ゴッ
カーン
最近世界が輝いて見えるんだ
キラ
キラ
キラ
ワー

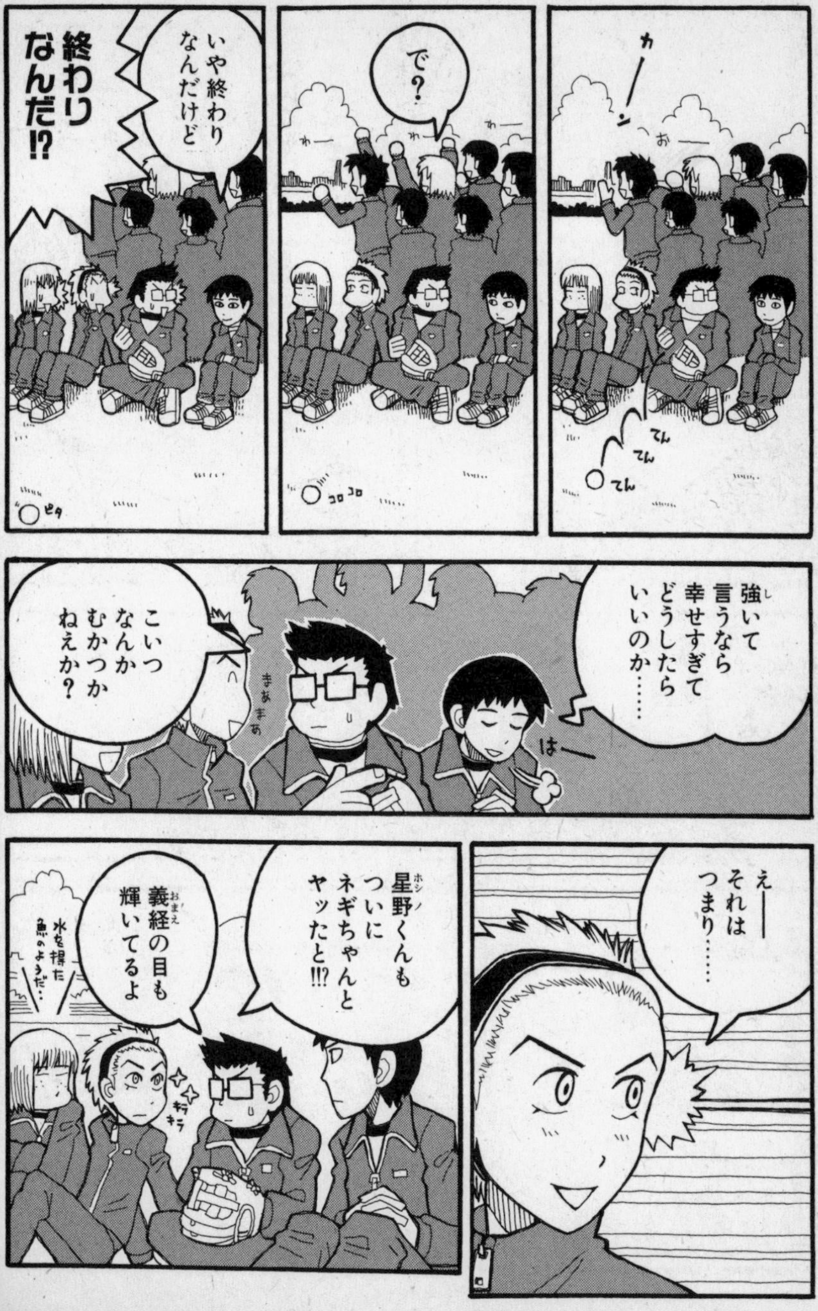
カーーン
おーー
てん
てん
てん
で？
わー
わー
わー
コロコロ
いや終わりなんだけど
終わりなんだ!?
ピタ
強いて言うなら幸せすぎてどうしたらいいのか……
はー
まあまあ
こいつなんかむかつかねえか？
えーそれはつまり……
星野くんもついにネギちゃんとヤッたと!!?
義経の目も輝いてるよ
水を得た魚のようだ…
キラキラ

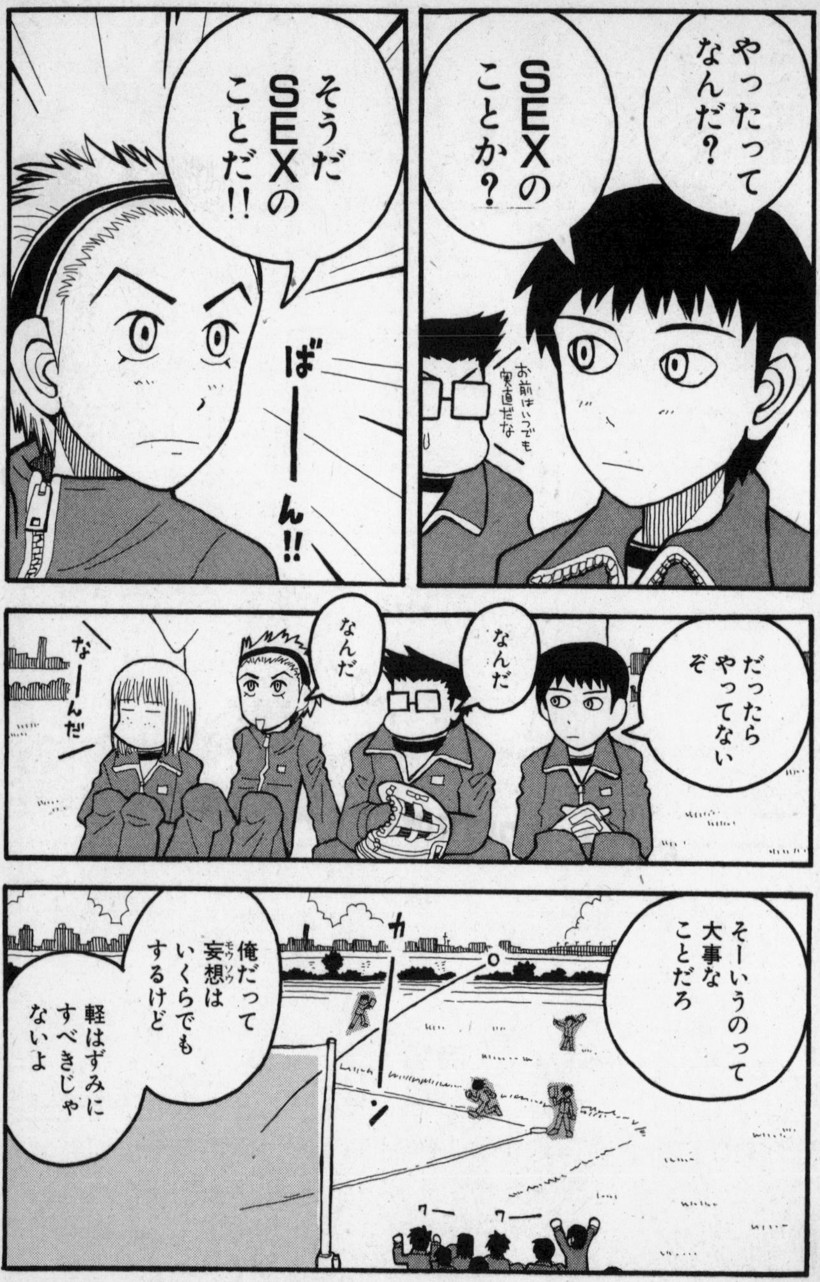
やったってなんだ？
SEXのことか？
お前はいつでも実直だな
そうだSEXのことだ!!
ばーーーん!!
だったらやってないぞ
なんだ
なんだ
なーーんだ
そーいうのって大事なことだろ
カーン
俺だって妄想(モウソウ)はいくらでもするけど
軽はずみにすべきじゃないよ
ワー
ワー

STOP!

YOU'RE GOING THE WRONG WAY!

MANGA IS A COMPLETELY DIFFERENT TYPE
OF READING EXPERIENCE.

TO START AT THE BEGINNING, GO TO THE END!

THAT'S RIGHT!

AUTHENTIC MANGA IS READ THE TRADITIONAL
JAPANESE WAY—FROM RIGHT TO LEFT. EXACTLY THE OPPOSITE
OF HOW AMERICAN BOOKS ARE READ. IT'S EASY TO FOLLOW:
JUST GO TO THE OTHER END OF THE BOOK, AND READ EACH PAGE
—AND EACH PANEL—FROM RIGHT SIDE TO LEFT SIDE,
STARTING AT THE TOP RIGHT. NOW YOU'RE EXPERIENCING
MANGA AS IT WAS MEANT TO BE.